10/25/12
#49.95

SPEAKING OF DEATH

Recent Titles in
Psychology, Religion, and Spirituality
J. Harold Ellens, Series Editor

Married to an Opposite: Making Personality Differences Work for You
Ron Shackelford

Sin against the Innocents: Sexual Abuse by Priests and the Role of the
Catholic Church
Thomas G. Plante, editor

Seeking the Compassionate Life: The Moral Crisis for Psychotherapy
and Society
Carl Goldberg and Virginia Crespo

Psychology and the Bible: A New Way to Read the Scriptures, 4 volumes
J. Harold Ellens and Wayne G. Rollins, editors

Sex in the Bible: A New Consideration
J. Harold Ellens

Where God and Science Meet: How Brain and Evolutionary Studies
Alter Our Understanding of Religion, 3 volumes
Patrick McNamara

Sexual Liberation: The Scandal of Christendom
Raymond J. Lawrence

The Destructive Power of Religion: Violence in Christianity, Judaism and
Islam, Condensed and Updated Edition
J. Harold Ellens, editor

The Serpent and the Dove: Celibacy in Literature and Life
A.W. Richard Sipe

Radical Grace: How Belief in a Benevolent God Benefits Our Health
J. Harold Ellens

Understanding Religious Experiences: What the Bible Says about
Spirituality
J. Harold Ellens

Miracles: God, Science, and Psychology in the Paranormal, 3 volumes
J. Harold Ellens

SPEAKING OF DEATH

America's New Sense of Mortality

Edited by Michael K. Bartalos, M.D.

Foreword by Robert Belknap, Ph.D.

Psychology, Religion, and Spirituality
J. Harold Ellens, Series Editor

Westport, Connecticut
London

Library of Congress Cataloging-in-Publication Data

Speaking of death : America's new sense of mortality / edited by
Michael K. Bartalos ; foreword by Robert Belknap.
      p. cm. — (Psychology, religion, and spirituality, ISSN 1546–8070)
  Includes index.
  ISBN 978–0–313–36426–6 (alk. paper)
  1. Death—United States.   I. Bartalos, Michael K.
  BD444.S68 2009
    306.90973—dc22   2008029551

British Library Cataloguing in Publication Data is available.

Library of Congress Catalog Card Number: 2008029551
ISBN: 978–0–313–36426–6
ISSN: 1546–8070

First published in 2009

Praeger Publishers, 88 Post Road West, Westport, CT 06881
An imprint of Greenwood Publishing Group, Inc.
www.praeger.com

Printed in the United States of America

It is less important that we all believe alike than that we all inquire freely and put at the disposal of one another such glimpses as we may obtain of the truth for which we are in search.

—John Dewey, *Experience, Knowledge and Value*

Contents

PART II
FROM AWARENESS TO ACCEPTANCE

PART III
SOCIETAL ASPECTS OF THE ACCEPTANCE OF DYING

FOREWORD

This book emerged at Columbia University from many meetings of the University Seminar on Death. The Seminar on Death was founded in 1970 by Dr. Austin H. Kutscher and is one of about 80 university seminars that link New York professors and others across the boundaries of institutions and departments. Each of the seminars manages its own program of monthly meetings. Some solve practical or intellectual problems, and others bring experts together to discuss other people's solutions. The Seminar on Death has been concentrating on a subject that demands both practical and intellectual attention, coping with death.

Few institutions have thanatology departments, but many have experts in medicine, psychiatry, journalism, religion, anthropology, art, literature, or other fields who encounter the intellectual and practical meanings of death in ways that vary enormously. The Columbia university seminars are designed to turn such experts, who might otherwise never meet, into a community devoted to enquiry.

Some subjects demand a narrow, focused monograph. This subject is so loaded emotionally that it demands a book like this. The authors, and the University Seminars, hope that readers of diverse persuasions as well as philosophers, psychologists, social scientists, practitioners, and advocates will mine this book for the variety of experience, expertise, and outlook that it brings together on a subject that helps to shape our virtues and vices.

This diversity enriches the text of the book. For some, the denial of death generates all religion and almost all culture. For others it leads to outlandish behavior, or to the kind of scene that needs a doctor or a dramatist to describe it, as in this example from the book:

> Several years ago, this writer made a home visit to an elderly gentleman who was dying of kidney failure. Prior to my visit, his wife instructed me not to talk about the progression of his disease because her husband was focused on maintaining hope and did not believe he was dying. During the first ten minutes of the home visit, while his wife answered an incoming phone call, the patient whispered to me: "Do you know I'm dying? My wife can't talk to me about it—it's too painful and she has to believe that there'll be a miracle and that I won't die."

The beauty of this denial resides in its symmetry but also in its exploration of the utility of truth—Sir Philip Sydney said poesy could not lie because it did not claim to be true. The couple who thought they were deceiving one another in their last days together were not lying about death either; they did not mention it at all. Both recognized it but tried lovingly to exclude it from their relationship. This book studies our civilization's long denial of death, debates whether it is ending, and considers whether its end would be a good or a bad thing. The truth is noble, but sad and painful truths demand the kind of response that this book offers, the disputatious interaction of good minds.

Robert Belknap, Ph.D.
Director, Columbia University Seminars

PREFACE: FACING OUR MORTALITY

We live in cataclysmic times. The schisms between groups of humans are deep, the stakes are high, antagonisms fierce, and emotions at their highest pitch. Our interconnectedness and advanced technology have brought us closer, not closer to embracing but closer to annihilating each other. The falsehood that was the stuff of our life is exploding in our faces. Our relationship to our environment has brought us to the brink of an ecological disaster (Wilson 2006). Our relationships to others are still governed by outdated concepts (Dennett 2006) of mythical figures with imagined precepts, super-human powers, and demands that reflect the tribal views of the people who lived in early historic times (Hitchens 2007). Our relationship to ourselves is likewise in need of revision.

OUR RELATIONSHIP TO THE ENVIRONMENT

Our time—it seems to me—is a time of encounter, a time when we finally become aware of our shortcomings and recognize that we have a genuine crisis on our hands, not unlike the legendary dragon with several heads each exuding deadly fire, and that unless we act decisively and wisely, intelligent life on earth could come to an end.

OUR RELATIONSHIP TO OTHERS

We are forced to face the falsehood that has shrouded our existence until now. We cannot survive and maintain human proximity unless we become guardians of our planet (Wilson 2006). We cannot have peace while maintaining our illogical belief systems that continue to breed hatred, pain, and suffering (Dawkins 2006). Instead we need to establish a global society where mutual respect, concern for each other, and cooperation are the moral imperatives (Bartalos 1990).

The attitude of too many toward others is exploitive and abusive. Legions of humanity's exploiters inflict unquantifiable human suffering under such diverse guises as leading politicians and captains of industry who are spreading global capitalism (Soros 1997). Religious leaders and leaders of terrorists are encouraging the faithful in self-demolition and in massacre of the innocents (Ellens 2007), and individuals with selfish motives are helping to maintain social, political, and economic systems that are unjust and in violation of human rights, dignity, and health. We have an aversion toward people who look or act or speak or think differently than we do. We also have little tolerance for individuals with unconventional sexual orientations and/or sexual identities.

OUR VIEW OF OURSELVES

Why is it that we do not see ourselves as reasonable human beings in charge of our destiny, using our intellect for the betterment of all mankind? Why are we quick to attack and slow to cooperate? Why do we consider ourselves lowly creatures who are unable to handle our own affairs? Why do we assume that prayer is superior to reasoned action, to goodwill, and to cooperation in solving our problems? We indeed behave in a lowly fashion that reinforces our negative self-image. I hold that the doctrine of original sin is the culprit for such self-defeating behavior.

As children we are told by our religious teachers that mortality is a punishment for the sins of our archaic forebears Adam and Eve, who disobeyed God's order. Individuals who were told at a young age that they are doomed to die as the result of a wrong that they never committed carry a deep, often unarticulated, resentment against such a colossal miscarriage of justice. If you add to this a lifetime spent trying to live up to the precepts of a religion whose rules were drawn up in complete disregard of the biological dictates of the human organism and therefore are impossible to follow in every details, at life's end you have a guilt-ridden individual who is terrified of dying, terrified of the final judgment, and terrified of what will follow thereafter. In broad outlines this scheme is discernible in Christianity, Judaism, and Islam, the three major monotheistic religions. It is taught in all three religions that the only way out of this dilemma is the unconditional acceptance of the precepts and diligence in following the prescripts of each respective religion. The demands, in each case, are such that no individual can achieve all that is required of her. Further, since all three religions claim that only their respective doctrine is true, the embrace of the teachings of any one of these religions sets one automatically in conflict with all others. Indeed, it is an utterly unfair and manipulative arrangement that, if adhered to, makes global cooperation impossible. And indeed, we do demonstrate lowly behavior as we, through the practice of religion, spread antagonism and cause misery both among the faithful and the "others." We cannot dream of world peace as long as religions compete. To achieve a lasting global peace, the religions need to form a true brotherhood or sisterhood devoted to helping every human being or for a new, truly humanistic mentality to arise that could absorb and accommodate the now fragmented, mutually suspicious, but equally betrayed populations.

Now that the ailment has been diagnosed, what, then, is the treatment plan? I feel that we should attempt to remove the negative emotions that are attached to dying. Contrary to religious doctrine, there is no basis to assume that one is born a sinner (or a saint, for that matter; we are born with the potential for both). No one should be held responsible for a crime they did not committed. A rational judge or god could not disagree with that. Thus instead of horror, fear, and indignation, the knowledge of our mortality should remind us of the limited time we have on earth to develop our talents and to contribute to the common good. The knowledge of our mortality should serve as an impetus for benevolent actions, for good will towards others, and not to become the source of despair and self-incrimination.

We need to reform our view of ourselves. We need to stop our irrational selfishness and callous indifference toward others. While we may despise dying, we can still formulate a worthwhile agenda for living. In nearly all areas of human endeavor, change is called for and change is slowly forthcoming. This volume deals with a small but important segment of the human problem complex, namely, our attitude toward dying. It represents an attempt to rise above the divisive influence of religious doctrines and to appeal to what is common to us all: our humanity. The Age of Encounter.

We Americans as a group, nudged on by the September 11, 2001, terrorist attack on the World Trade Center and the wars in Iraq and Afghanistan, along with the looming global ecological disaster, gathered our composure, metaphorically speaking, took a deep breath, and with a giant leap became conscious of our ephemeral nature. This realization gives cause for celebration. Through this step in our collective consciousness, we reached an important milestone toward maturity. We finally dared to look into the mirror and come face to face with our mortality. The concept of mortality, both ours and that of others, has entered our conscious thinking. We now consciously recognize our temporariness and have begun to deal with it. The mental state of awareness demands action, and action is taking place. Ours is the Age of Encounter, the age when we are acting on our newly recognized problems. This represents a new era, an era of pragmatic activism, in Western thought.

In the area of mortality awareness, our current state of encounter will likely prove to be a way station on the road leading from the denial of our mortality toward its acceptance. We cannot yet speak of an acceptance of our mortality. That stage will be reached when the awareness of our temporariness becomes fully integrated into our self-image, into our thinking, and into our actions. This book is an attempt to define the current era of mortality awareness and to help society on the road toward maturity, that is, toward the acceptance of our mortality as individuals and toward our survival as a species.

REFERENCES

Bartalos, M. K. "Human Survival from the Viewpoint of Contextual Individualism: Discussion Paper." *Journal of the Royal Society of Medicine* (London) 83 (September 1990): 573–75.

Dawkins, Richard. *The God Delusion.* Boston: Houghton-Mifflin, 2006.

Dennett, Daniel C. *Breaking the Spell: Religion as a Natural Phenomenon.* New York: Penguin Books, 2006.

Ellens, J. Harold, ed. *The Destructive Power of Religion: Violence in Judaism, Christianity, and Islam.* Condensed and updated. Westport, Conn.: Praeger, 2007.

Hitchens, Christopher. *God Is Not Great: How Religion Poisons Everything.* New York: Twelve, 2007.

Soros, George, "The Capitalist Threat." *Atlantic Monthly,* February 1997, 45–58.

Wilson, Edward O. *The Creation: An Appeal to Save Life on Earth.* New York: W. W. Norton. 2–6.

Introduction: The Age of Encounter—The New Reality

As the twenty-first century made its debut, two propositions were current regarding the attitude of the American people and American culture toward death and dying. The older view, still shared by many, held that denial of death is a characteristic of our culture, while others were beginning to claim that awareness of death is the new reality. Following the 9/11 terrorist attack in 2001 on the World Trade Center in New York City and the Pentagon in Washington, DC, attendees of the University Seminar on Death at Columbia University in New York—a faculty-level study and debating group that has been in existence since 1970—decided to examine the validity of the conflicting opinions stated above. Their findings and their reflections are described in this book. In brief, they concluded that death, indeed, is no longer in the tabooed territory. An awareness of death has developed along with an awareness of such contemporary problems as the population crisis, the dwindling natural resources, the global energy shortage, the health care crisis, the gross inequality in the distribution of wealth, and the rise of violence-prone extremists in the dominant religions of the world.

OVERVIEW

In the foreword, Michael Bartalos argues that the recent change in our attitude toward death is not an isolated phenomenon. Rather, it is part of a larger transformation whereby we grudgingly face the problems created by our irresponsible use of the earth's natural resources and the social ills fostered by our exploitive social and economic policies. A new awareness is rising in the human psyche, prompting us to face and deal with issues of human existence and finitude, just as we face and deal with our other broad societal issues.

Part I of this book deals with selected areas that reflect on our current attitude toward living and dying. Christina Staudt reviews the road traveled from denial to our current awareness of our mortality as it is reflected in the thanatology literature. Sherry Schachter describes her experiences with dying cancer patients and makes us sensitive to the observation that what at times might appear to be denial is in fact a coping device. The patients in question are well aware of their predicament, but with an overburdened agenda they have to limit the number of problems that they can deal with at a given time. While they are alive they have to deal with other matters, too, and coping demands that they do not dwell uninterruptedly on their mortality. As Alan Segal analyzed Americans' belief in an afterlife, he observed that a surprisingly large number believed in some form of existence after death. One explanation of this phenomenon is that as circumstances force people to accept their finitude, in the absence of other emotionally acceptable alternatives they turn toward mythical explanations.

Increased preoccupation with improving the length and the quality of life can be regarded as an indirect indication of the increasing societal acceptance of mortality. In the face of death, life assumes an increasing importance. Kevin Keith provides an analysis of the current phenomenon that is referred to as the life extension movement. The final chapter in this section deals with the news media. Because of its influence, Christina Staudt chose *Time* magazine and examined how the momentous event of 9/11 was covered in print and in photographs by the publishers of this influential U.S. weekly.

In Part II, we contemplate issues that we must deal with on the next segment of our journey, that is, on the road from awareness to acceptance. For starters, Bartalos contrasts the states of mortality denial and mortality acceptance and the collateral meanings that each condition entails. Jerry Piven provides an overview of the psychoanalytic theories as they apply to mortality awareness, coping and its reverse, violence. Thomas Caffrey offers the cogent observation that in the life of many of us there comes a time when the trajectory of one's existence suddenly changes, when dying suddenly appears not far off. "Caffrey's warp" signals the time when the business of living transmutates into the business of dying. It is a time when one's outlook changes and when life strategies need to change too. It demarcates a period of human existence with unique characteristics and meaning.

Finally, Michael Bartalos, in chapter 9, proposes a method of cultivated acceptance of our mortality. by contrasting his views with those of Ernest Becker, In this process he attempts to stay at an all-human level, that is, at a level above religious differences. While he does not endorse the teachings of any religion, he strives to offer a way that is compatible with and is augmentable by a humanistic religious belief. Bartalos recommends his brand of philosophy, called contextual individualism, combined with his brand of psychological approach (adaptive or tensamatic psychology) and a cognitive-like methodology, as a way of lending meaning to living and to dying. Along the way he offers new definitions of illness and health and living and dying. One part of the chapter offers practical advice on conscious preparation for and acceptance of dying. In Bartalos's vision, the individual human being needs to be an active participant in shaping his/her future.

Part III is a look into the near and very distant future. Both chapters here are written by Bartalos. In the first, he expresses his aversion to and disapproval of the ancient and current use of religious sentiments as a recruiting tool for deadly political missions. In the final chapter, using commonly understandable language, he reviews some recent proposals by cosmologists and physicists regarding the fate of our universe eons from now. The reviewed material points toward a way whereby humankind's achievement might survive indefinitely. Ways are envisioned by scientists by which humanity's intellectual heritage might be stored, packaged, and transported from one universe into another and reconstructed after such transfer—all this without violating the known laws of physics. This insight represents a momentous event in human intellectual development that went totally unnoticed by the general public. It is extremely significant because it is the first time that we can visualize a physically feasible afterlife. It is the first time that we can see a credible alternative to the immensely negative apocalyptic view. This insight provides the first glimmer of hope that human achievements might not be doomed to oblivion.

The authors of this book are in general agreement that today the biological facts of living and dying are better integrated into our personal life and into our societal manifestations than they were at any time in the recent past. Throughout the book, an effort was made to refrain from the endorsement or promotion of any particular religious or political belief. The views expressed here are solely those of the individual authors. Readers may wish to consult the Web site of the Columbia University Seminar on Death: http://www.columbia.edu/cu/seminars/death/deathseminarindex.html.

PART I

MANIFESTATIONS OF MORTALITY AWARENESS

CHAPTER 1

From Concealment to Recognition: The Discourse on Death, Dying, and Grief

Christina Staudt

Concealment and disregard, forms of implicit denial, were the prevailing attitudes to death in Western societies for most of the twentieth century, reaching a culmination in mid-century.[1] In his introduction to *The Meaning of Death* (1959)—a groundbreaking attempt to document contemporary thinking, practices, and attitudes related to death—Herman Feifel identified denial as one of the central themes characterizing death in the twentieth century. Half a century later, denial is a much less notable aspect of the American "death system."[2] We have gone from ignoring and hiding mortal matters to, increasingly, recognizing and exploring the final stage of life. Instead of looking away, we are now trying to figure out techniques for observing death safely and with some level of comfort. Our aim is, if not to control death itself, then at least to supervise the process leading up to the ultimate outcome, and then to manage the remains and the aftermath.

Twenty-first century manifestations of mortality awareness do not hark back to the Victorian style of acceptance when death and dying centered on family and church. The growing recognition of the rights and needs of the dying in the early twenty-first century germinated in paradigmatic cultural, social, and scientific changes during the second half of the previous century. Advances in medical research, the information revolution, and the environmental movement, have all helped usher in the new approach to death and dying in this millennium. How we traveled through the last half century to arrive at the current, increasingly more widespread urge to understand and manage the vagaries of death can be traced through the public discourse of death and dying. To place the more recent developments in context, this chapter begins with a short review of death systems in the Western world over the last several centuries. This is followed by a review of the emergence of the literature on death in the last 50 years and the mention of critical events that precipitated the documents. More detailed discussions, with salient examples from contemporary discourse, are offered of the areas where the development towards a climate of greater acknowledgment is particularly apparent: the visual media, the hospice movement, legislation related to self-determination, and funerary practices. In my final observations and reflections I point to works that show a lingering attitude of denial and ambivalence but conclude that the overarching characteristic of our death system in the early twenty-first century is the impetus to manage and supervise our *finale* on earth: The pendulum between concealment and recognition has swung in favor of recognition. A postscript about death and diversity offers a *caveat* to the generalizations in the chapter and to the conclusion.

WESTERN APPROACHES TO DEATH AND DYING—A BRIEF HISTORY

Social norms and conventions on death and dying differ among the people of the world and are always amorphous and in flux. Practices and attitudes overlap from one era to the next, undergo change, and migrate among connected societies.

Philippe Ariès's *The Hour of Our Death* is currently the most accessible, broad historical survey of the attitude to death in Western civilization over time. Claiming Vladimir Jankélévitch and Edgar Morin as his inspiration (see especially Jankélévitch and Morin), Ariès presents literary, liturgical, testamentary, epigraphic, and iconographic documentation to categorize Western death cultures over the past two millennia as "tame death," "death of the self," "death of the other," and "invisible death." Writing in the beginning of the last quarter of the twentieth century, Ariès identifies death denial as a phenomenon of modern industrial times and the paramount attitude to death in modern Western civilization. Widely cited by scholars of all disciplines since its publication in France in 1977 (and in English translation in 1981), Ariès's work is accepted as a major contribution to the field, even among detractors who fault it for oversimplification. His categories are useful in setting the stage for our investigation of the defining features of the attitude to death in the post-modern Western world.[3]

According to Ariès, "tame death," characterized by tacit acceptance, covers approximately the first millennium of the Common Era, a time when prescribed, ritualized roles controlled the conduct of the dying and their surrounding community. Belief in an afterlife connected earthly life with a mystical universe in one cosmology.

The "death of the self," signified by the individual's desire to play an active role in the course of his own death, unfolded first among the rich, educated, and powerful around the turn of the first millennium and became widespread by the eighteenth century. Popularized with the introduction of the printing press in the fifteenth century, *artes moriendi*, treatises and illustrations describing the art of dying well, placed the burden of an appropriate ending of life on the individual person. The practice of creating written wills spread from a small powerful elite in the Middle Ages to the growing merchant class that would become Europe's bourgeoisie in the eighteenth century. The designated beneficiary of the inheritance shifted over time from the Church to the family of the deceased, but the principle of self-determination in regard to death and wealth remained intact. The idea of the "death of the self" was visually depicted in macabre *transi* figures—popular in the fourteenth to sixteenth centuries. Such two-tier tomb sculptures illustrated how the "self" divided into its two natures on the deathbed, the immortal, idealized person bound for heaven shown on top of the casket and the disintegrating body depicted below.

In the nineteenth century, Romantic currents and the emergence of the nuclear family as the heart of society placed close family members and loved ones at the center of the encounter with death, introducing the approach that Ariès calls the "death of the other."[4] This focus gave rise to affectionate, cult-like practices such as displays of photographs and memorabilia of the dead, personalized graves, and visits to the cemetery on All Saints' Day and other holidays. *Artes moriendi* changed character, with an eye to making death a beautiful experience for the family as well as the dying person. The afterlife became popularly reconstructed as a place where loved ones would be united.

As described by Ariès, denial of death was negligible during the periods when "tame death," the "death of the self," and the "death of the other" were the dominant attitudes to the end of life. The dying and the dead were present among the living; religious and social rituals imparted meaning to the end-of-life experience and helped the dying and the bereaved manage the passage; and belief in an afterlife and the immortality of the soul softened the cruelty of death and the suffering that accompanied it. In contrast, denial is a central characteristic of Ariès's model of death in the twentieth century; he labels the approach alternatively "invisible death" and "death denied."

Characterized by advanced, impersonally applied medical technology, the end of life began to retreat from view in the 1920s. In this model, the dead are hidden from the public while physicians marshal their resources to prolong life at whatever cost to the dying person and his family. The inability to overcome death is seen as a failure, making repression, isolation, and denial normative responses. A contributing factor to denial of death, in Ariès's estimation, is the separation in most people's mind of death from evil. The

ancient connection to evil gave death a place in the Judeo-Christian worldview and helped explain its role in the universe. In Christianity, the cruci-
fixion of Christ delivers sinners from evil and promises eternal salvation to
the faithful upon their own death. Without such spiritual justification, death
becomes an incomprehensible, savage force without redemptive value, and
denial emerges as a plausible defense.

THE WANING OF DEATH DENIAL

In the 1950s and 1960s, the concealment of death, which marked the entire
twentieth century in the West, was at its most evident. A handful of notable
scholars in different disciplines expressed their concerns about society's lack
of attention to issues of death in contemporary Western society but their
work had minimal impact on practices in ordinary life. The political historian and commentator Franz Borkenau, writing in the mid-1950s, looked
into the future and perceived an increasingly secular society living under
the threat of the atomic bomb. He feared the emergence of a culture that
might reject immortality and embrace death. Employing a comprehensive
historical perspective, he classified different civilizations as predominantly
"death denying," "death defying," "death accepting," or "death transcending."
He considered death denial "the most deeply rooted of the archetypes" and
believed that a balanced synthesis of death denial and death acceptance indicates the highest forms of civilization, while a deepening of denial is a sign
of societal disintegration. Concerned that modern Western society might
increasingly turn to death denial as its primary coping mechanism, he placed
his hope in psychoanalysis and science, believing that these disciplines might
succeed in making the immortal "personality" more intelligible and restore
the balance between death denial and death acceptance in the West (Borkenau 1955; Fulton 1965, 42–56).

The social anthropologist Geoffrey Gorer observed in his essay "The Pornography of Death" (1955), that death and its representations had become
taboo in the Western world. He posited that death and dying were denied in
the mid-twentieth century with the same vehemence as sex in the Victorian
era; neither had a place in polite society. Gorer originally commented on the
state of affairs in mid-twentieth-century Britain, but he found his observations equally applicable to the United States a decade later as he noted in the
introduction to the U.S. edition of *Death, Grief and Mourning* (1967).

The American psychologist and death study pioneer, Herman Feifel,
sounded an alarm about society's and individuals' ingrained tendency to
avert their eyes from matters of mortality in *The Meaning of Death*, published in 1959. In his introduction he noted that that "denial and avoidance
of the countenance of death" constituted one of the three leitmotifs among
the range of approaches to death presented by the "philosophers, religionists

and scientists" writing for his volume, and that "this has implications not only for the individual but for society as well." His anthology was a concerted attempt to break the prevailing taboo. By gathering reflections and information about death from experts representing different disciplines, Feifel sought to stimulate fresh insights on eschatological matters. He believed that "our science-conscious culture...does not furnish us with all the necessary parameters for investigating and understanding death" and saw "a pressing need for more reliable and systematic, controlled study in the field" (1959, xv–xvi). While Feifel's work was noted in academic circles, its message did not penetrate into society as a whole and did not lead to change among the general public.

Even in academia death was slow to emerge as a subject for monographs in the 1960s. The field was meager also in anthropology and art history, disciplines that could point to long traditions of works related to burial and death prior to the era of the so-called invisible death (e.g., *The Golden Bough* [1890] by a founder of the field of anthropology, James George Frazer, arguing that the handling and perception of corpses in different civilizations are central to their respective mythologies; and the seminal study of tomb sculpture [1924] by the so-called father of art history, Erwin Panofsky). While articles related to mortuary practices and funeral monuments appeared with some frequency in academic journals, and especially on archeological topics, the list of books published by academic presses on death-related subjects remained sparse throughout the decade. Among the noteworthy publishing events are *Death and Western Thought* (1963) by Jacques Choron, which establishes a close interconnection between philosophical traditions and the traditions surrounding death and dying; *Man's Concern with Death* (1968), with British historian Arnold Joseph Toynbee as the editor and principal contributor, a major attempt to cover every aspect of death from its definition to philosophical and cultural matters; and Geoffrey Gorer's *Death, Grief and Mourning*, published in slightly different versions in Britain and the United States in 1965. When Robert Blauner, a psychiatrist, reviewed the U.S. edition of Gorer's book he sounded an optimistic note: "this book is one of a half-dozen or more social science investigations of mortality that have appeared in the past two years—a welcome indication that the cover of repression on this taboo topic is being increasingly lifted" (Blauner, 1968, 521).

In fact, it was not the productions of the academic world that began to lift the veil concealing the matters of death and dying for the American public but two books by two very different European women who were passionately engaged in their work in the United States. The first glimpse came in 1963, when the British-born, some-time communist activist Jessica Mitford, who worked as an investigative reporter of the America Civil Rights' movement, was persuaded by her husband to look into the U.S. funeral industry. The result was *The American Way of Death*, a scathing account of the

exploitive pursuits of funeral directors. Congressional hearings on the practices of the industry ensued as a result of the attention this book engendered.
It turned out that placing a taboo on the matters of death had a financial as
well as an emotional cost and the public began to sit up and take notice.

The second book that caught the imagination and attention of the public
was *On Death and Dying* (1969) by Elisabeth Kübler-Ross. Reprinted several
times since then, this book is frequently considered groundbreaking and its
publication is generally considered the starting point of the death awareness
movement in the United States. During the 1960s, the Cold War and the
superpowers' buildup of a nuclear arsenal placed America in peril of annihilation and created a public atmosphere of dread. The Vietnam War brought
the reality of death and dying into America's living rooms via television.
The atmosphere of fear and frustration was compounded as the threat of
being drafted into combat hung over many American families, and others
were mourning or feared for those who actually served. The assassinations,
first of President Kennedy in 1964 and then of Robert Kennedy and Martin
Luther King Jr. in 1968, were repeatedly shown on television and reported
in pictorial form, as were the shooting of Kent University students by agents
of the state and the riots in Watts and other inner cities. The societal sense
of unrest mounted, and the presence of violent death in the world became
more difficult to ignore. Untimely death, outside the control of the individual, seemed a real possibility for many. Yet the deaths of relatives and friends
that occurred as a matter of course, due to aging or illness, continued to
remain largely invisible and unaddressed in mainstream American communities. The publication of Elisabeth Kübler-Ross's *On Death and Dying* in 1969
began to change the status quo and moved the subject of ordinary death and
dying into the public arena.

PRACTICAL AND THEORETICAL CONCERNS
ABOUT DEATH—PARALLEL DISCOURSES
IN THE PUBLIC AND ACADEMIC SPHERES

Dr. Kübler-Ross, a Swiss-born psychiatrist had worked with the terminally ill since her arrival in the United States in 1958 and had attempted to
educate medical students on the special needs of the dying. In *On Death and
Dying* (1969), she posited a model of five steps that people follow after receiving a terminal diagnosis. The idea that the dying person necessarily follows
the stages set forth by Kübler-Ross—denial, anger, bargaining, depression,
and acceptance—has since been refuted and refined. Nevertheless, this, her
first book—she later published several more—became an international bestseller and is arguably both the turning point in bringing the needs of the
dying back into public discourse and the beginning of the postmodern phenomenon we now refer to as the death awareness movement.

But the road was long and hard for those who sought to wrest dying and death from the medical establishment and back under the control of the individual and her family.[5] An apparently critical step toward recognition was Kübler-Ross's testimony in 1972 at the first national hearings on the subject of death with dignity, conducted by the U.S. Senate Special Committee on Aging. Kübler-Ross stated, "We live in a very particular death-denying society. We isolate both the dying and the old, and it serves a purpose—they are reminders of our own mortality" (National Hospice and Palliative Care, "History of Hospice Care"). In spite of the prominence of the forum, her words took a long time to penetrate the general consciousness to any substantial degree.

When Feifel, two decades after publishing his first volume, laid out the issues that focused the debate on death in the 1970s, in *New Meanings of Death* (1977, 4), he noticed that "surface considerations of death...have become more lively," although "Americans still approach dying and death warily and gingerly" (1977, 4). Feifel remained concerned that a waning of belief in personal immortality might complicate the public's ability to cope. He wrote of death as having changed from traditionally being "a door" to "becoming a wall" (1977, 4). Feifel's concern about the problems that may loom for a science-focused society that is trying to understand death was shared by the social scientist and philosopher Erich Fromm. Fromm postulated that since at least the Renaissance the haughty ambition of Western civilization has been to conquer and dominate nature and that death is irrefutable evidence that we have failed in our task, contributing to our urge to deny death (Funk 2003, 103).

Denial as a defense against death emerged as a central issue in the discourse on death and dying in the last quarter of the twentieth century. This was largely due to the publication in 1973 of *The Denial of Death* by cultural anthropologist Ernest Becker, who came to deeply influence the debate on death among psychologists and psychoanalysts as well as among the broader public. The crux of Becker's thesis is that the fear of death ultimately determines all our actions and experiences as individual beings and as communal societies. His argument starts with the premise that awareness of our own mortality gives our lives unique meaning and drives the human spirit. According to Becker, denial is human beings' natural, instinctive, and universal way to cope with the fear produced by an awareness of death. From this he infers that all our physical, cultural, and symbolic systems and productions are founded in the fear of death. Referring to Kierkegaard and Otto Rank, he posits that our need for religious rituals and communal ceremonies, as well as our construction of heroes and monuments, grows out of our death anxiety.

Among those who countered Becker and saw life-affirming solutions to the problem of denial was Erich Fromm. He did not see the denial of death as intrinsic to the human being but rather as her inability to love life well. Fromm argued for the cultivation of the joy of life, productivity, creativity, self-expression, and humanistic religiousness as the means of transforming a person. He saw denial as a consequence of the individual's focus on "having" rather than "being." "There is only one way—taught by the Buddha, by Jesus, by the Stoics, by Master Eckart—to truly overcome the fear of dying, and that way is by *not hanging onto life, not experiencing life as a possession....* The fear is not of dying but of *losing what I have:* the fear of losing my body, my ego, my possessions, and my identity; the fear of facing the abyss of nonidentity, of 'being lost.'... The more we rid ourselves of the craving for possession in all its forms, particularly our ego-boundness, the less strong the fear of dying, since there is nothing to lose" (1976, 126, 127).

In *The Broken Connection* (1979), Robert Jay Lifton, a post-Freudian psychiatrist who has treated the topic of death from several historic and psychological vantage points, also argues from a more life-affirming perspective than Becker that "while the denial of death is universal, the inner life-experience of a sense of immortality, rather than reflecting such denial, may well be the most authentic psychological alternative to that denial" (13). Lifton sees a sense of immortality as "an appropriate symbolization of our biological and historical connectedness" (17). To Lifton, it is the awareness of the end of life—not the denial of death as for Becker—that underlies "whatever additional constructs or gaps we call forth in our symbolizing activity" (47). Lifton does not see death denial as central to humankind's attitudes and approaches to life but as one component of our psychological makeup that drives us to seek meaning in our impending death.

Edelstein, Nathanson, and Stone, documenting a symposium among psychoanalysts, considered the nuances of purpose for which the denial of death is employed to process human experiences in *Denial—A Clarification of Concepts and Research* (1989). Some presenters at the symposium entertained the idea that denial is not invariably an inappropriate response to death, that it can be a skill as much as a defense and should not necessarily be a negative description of actions taken or avoided (see Schachter, Chapter 2 in this volume).

During the last two decades of the twentieth century, the threat of a nuclear attack by a foreign superpower was eliminated. While it came to be replaced by the threat of terrorism by groups of fanatics and "rogue" states, the American psyche seemed to begin to accommodate the idea that death and dying were integral parts of life and that they needed attention. A major factor in this development was the outbreak of the AIDS epidemic. Recognized by the U.S. Centers for Disease Control and Prevention in 1981, AIDS had a devastating impact on American society and notably on homosexual communities. Finding a cure, or at least life-prolonging treatment, for AIDS became a *cause célèbre*, and AIDS education came to feature in school curricula as well as public service announcements. The depiction of victims and writings about the disease and its deadly consequences became commonplace, not just in medical journals and the mainstream press; AIDS and its victims also became the central characters in plays, novels, stories, and musicals (see Vaucher 1993; E. White 1997).

The 1990s began to see the fruits of the work of those who had been members of the hospice movement and had advocated for medical self-determination at the end of life. The baby boomers were caring for their aging and dying parents and did not like the options available. Knowing that 20 or 30 years hence they would be in their parents' place, they marshaled their energy to remedy what they saw. Many were particularly appalled by the advances in medical technology that made it possible and common to extend the life span when there was little apparent quality of life.

The need to know and understand all aspects of death became critical. Respondents included Sherwin Nuland with *How We Die—Reflections of Life's Last Chapters* (1994) and Cedric Mims with *When We Die—The Science, Culture, and Rituals of Death* (1998). A physician and a microbiologist respectively, Nuland and Mims describe scientifically what happens to the body as it goes through the four most common ways of dying and what happens to the body in its state as a corpse. Writing for the general public, they avoid a textbook format and include a great deal of cultural and sociological information, together with personal comments and illustrative narratives from their clinical experience, bringing the dying process and its aftermath into the cultural realm and within reach for the lay person.

Issues of increasing concern in the latter part of the twentieth century were related to individuals with a terminal diagnosis and their place in the health care system. Long and debilitating illnesses frequently preceded death as the tools of medical technology made it possible to prolong life but not always with the desired quality. Doctors and nursing staff encountered situations on a daily basis that required decisions on withholding or withdrawing treatment. To help resolve these ethical dilemmas, which had not existed in eras prior to life-sustaining machines, bioethics teams were set up in hospitals. Bioethics in its contemporary guise is a discipline founded in the 1960s. One of its pioneers was Robert Fulton, the editor of *Death and Identity* (1965), who became the first Director of the Center for Death Education and Bioethics (CDEB), located at the University of Minnesota when it was founded in 1969 and later relocated to the University of Wisconsin—La Crosse). Another notable person in the field is the philosopher and ethicist Daniel Callahan who, in 1969, co-founded The Hastings Center, an independent, nonpartisan, and nonprofit bioethics research institute located in Garrison, New York. The purpose of the CDEB and the Hastings Center is to explore fundamental and emerging questions in medicine, health care, and biotechnology. Much of their research has centered on the care and decision making at the end of life. Daniel Callahan's, *The Tyranny of Survival and Other Pathologies of Civilized Life* (1973) was seminal in bringing attention to the unrestricted use of all-out technologies to keep a person alive arguing that this may not always be morally defensible, either for the community or the patient and her family "if the price of survival is human degradation, then there is no moral reason why an effort should be made to ensure that survival" (93). This delicate point has continued to be debated for the last 35 years. The National Reference Center of Bioethics (NRCB) of the Kennedy Institute of Ethics at Georgetown University publishes an annual *Bibliography of Bioethics* of the mounting volume of books, journal articles, government reports, and Web documents on this and other related issues in the field of bioethics. The 2008 volume contained almost 6,000 citations covering the "ethical, legal, and public policy aspects of health care and biomedical research" (National Reference Center of Bioethics, 2008).

Simultaneous with the private and public debates among clinicians, patients, and families to achieve fair and comfortable treatment for individuals at the end of life, academia became increasingly engaged in the phenomenon of death. The scholarly work on death in the 1970s and early 1980s mostly employed traditional methods of data collection and research of its respective fields. It addressed matters of mortality at considerable geographic or temporal distance—possibly to allow the scholar (and his reading public) a "safe" entry into the field of death without treading too close, at a time when the taboo of death was only beginning to be lifted. Examples from different disciplines of books that are frequently cited might include: in archeology, J.M.C. Toynbee *Death and Burial in the Roman World* (1971); in American studies, David Stannard, *The Puritan Way of Death—A Study in Religion, Culture and Social change* (1975); in anthropology, Richard Huntington and Peter Metcalf, eds. *Celebrations of Death: The Anthropology of Mortuary Ritual* (1979); and in social history, Joachim Whaley, ed. *Mirrors of Mortality: Studies in the Social History of Death* (1981).

During the 1980s and into the 1990s, academic studies of death became increasingly highly theorized with scholars of English, linguistics, and cultural studies drawing on French poststructuralists such as Michel Foucault, Roland Barthes, Georges Bataille, and Jean Baudillard. (A summary of some of the most influential works of poststructuralism is available on The Science Encyclopedia, History of Ideas Web site.) Scholarly writers also turned to, and expanded on, theories of Marxism, Feminism, Psychoanalysis, and Semiotics (including Deconstruction) for their Cultural and Literary Criticism. And the 1990s also saw a plethora of books with focus on identity politics (race, gender, ethnicity, and sexual orientation). A representative list of studies on death, which employ one or more of these tools, would likely include Maurice Bloch and Jonathan Parry, *Death and the Regeneration of Life* (1982); Garrett Stewart, *Death Sentences: Styles of Dying in British Fiction* (1984); Ronald Schleifer's *Rhetoric of Death: The Language of Modernism and Postmodern Discourse Theory* (1990); Regina Barreca's anthology *Sexuality and Death in*

Victorian Literature (1990); Elizabeth Bronfen's *Over Her Dead Body: Death, Femininity and the Aesthetic* (1992); and Sarah Webster Goodwin's and Elisabeth Bronfen's anthology *Death and Representation* (1993).

The serious literary and historical discourse on death exemplified above is firmly rooted in contemporary, more or less fleeting, popular theories and moves convincingly and sure-footedly among the representations and historical evidence under analysis. It expands the horizon and allows for new ways of thinking about old problems—and it is also of limited consequence beyond the walls of academia. In contrast, the themes surrounding death in the public and private sphere over the last five decades in the scientific, ethical, and clinical debate battle the problems of daily life in hospitals, nursing homes, and clinics and are marked by ambiguity and uncertainty. They exhibit an underlying current of concern about overcoming taboos and the fears of death and about balancing the needs of the dying and their families with the resources and obligations of the health care system.

Looking back on the twentieth century, Mervyn F. Bendle (2001) argues that the shift in the culture of death from the nineteenth to the twentieth century is so monumental that it marks the arrival of a new episteme of death.[6] The change from one episteme to another is characterized not by a gradual, linear development but by a seismic shift, usually occurring during intellectually fertile periods or historical upheavals. According to Bendle, the twentieth-century episteme of death flows "from the cumulative effects of vast institutional and discursive systems based on rationalism, scientism, technological rationality, bureaucratic calculation, utilitarianism, economic rationalism, and neo-liberalism" and has "displaced traditional epistemes derived predominantly from religious philosophical, mythological and traditional sources" (2001, 353). Bendle sees the twentieth-century experience of death as dominated by two institution-based processes: the "medicalization" and the "militarization" of death, with militarization being the main factor in the first part of the century and medicalization overshadowing militarization in the second half. In the health care sector, death has generally been so medicalized that it is managed with relatively little concern for the value of the individual person and the needs of families and their communities (2001, 362). Death, of course, continued to be inevitable, but the dying and everything to do with their management were removed as far as possible from the living and the normalcy of quotidian life. Aspects of Ariès' and Bendle's historic models of concealed death remain with us in the twenty-first century, but the movements pushing back against it have become so forceful that we can justifiably say that the twenty-first century is well on its way to giving birth to yet a new episteme of death. The tendency toward denial lingers when the issues get too complex, but "death denied" and the "invisible death" are no longer signature marks of the American death system.

Before looking further into what we are calling the "American death system" of the twenty-first century, an important question needs to be asked and
a note inserted. Endnote 2 explains what is here meant by "death system."
But what (and whom?) is referenced in the word "American?" The answer
is "A general, mainstream notion of something (or someone) that is present
within the geographical boundaries of the United States." Given the ethni-
cal, religious, and cultural diversity of the United States, such a definition
becomes less meaningful, as psychologists, social workers, ethicists, and clinicians discovered when, in the late 1980s and the 1990s, they began to pay
attention to the variations in attitudes and approaches to matters of death
among different ethnic groups. The differences are critical in meeting individual needs at the end of life. Because of the many variables, statements
on death and personal identity risk being specious as well as underscoring
or creating stereotypes; and they have therefore been avoided in the general text of this chapter. As a postscript to this chapter, I have included an
overview of some of the diversity-related issues that need consideration in a
discussion of death in "America." The postscript serves as a notice that much
of what is being said in this chapter about the public may not be applicable to
large swathes of the population.

THE EMERGING TWENTY-FIRST-CENTURY
DEATH EPISTEME: AWARENESS, MANAGEMENT,
AND SUPERVISION

It is a joke among baby boomers that they are accustomed to rebelling
against authority and having their way, controlling their environment, creating their own style, and getting what they want. And that this won't change
just because they happen to be dealing with death. As the members of the
post–World War II generation now moves into the sunset years of their lives,
they plan to do it their own way. The demographic bulge that they represent
has a force that has been felt in the past.

Whether or not we credit the baby boomers with fertilizing the seeds of
change toward recognition sown in the twentieth century, the evidence of
a new attitude toward death is discernible, especially in the growth of the
hospice and palliative care movement; in changes in legislation related to
medical self-determination; and in contemporary tendencies to prepare final
arrangements. Since the death system at any given time is an integrated set of
discourses and practices, causes cannot be cleanly separated from effects; it is
better to think of these areas as concentrations of activity, with an impact on
the system as a whole. But for organizational purposes these areas of noticeable change will be surveyed separately below.

The growth and nature of new practices strongly suggest that the emerging episteme of death centers on management and control. The findings of

a survey on issues related to death and dying conducted among mature residents in Massachusetts (conducted in March/April 2005 and published in September 2005) offer supporting evidence.[7] The survey (Massachusetts Commission on End of Life Care Survey Project 2005) showed that death should no longer be viewed as a taboo subject; 8 in 10 respondents indicated that they are very or somewhat comfortable talking about death. In all, 85 percent of the respondents considered it very important to get honest answers from doctors and to understand their treatment options. A concern about quality of life at the end of life emerged as a consistent theme. People expressed their desire for "communication, connection, comfort and control" (9).

To the list of new spaces of discourse density we need to add the fact that we have moved into the information age and that this has allowed images of the dead and dying to enter our homes via television and the Internet in unprecedented numbers and forms. The whole electronic communication revolution, especially the Internet, also acts as connective tissue among disciplines and peoples around the world and serves to magnify and expedite ideas. Although it is difficult to determine what is demand driven and what is supply driven when it comes to visually explicit reporting of wars and catastrophe and blood-soaked entertainment, there is no arguing that the dead and dying have been brought into our living rooms to a saturation point that would make them difficult to ignore. How can we not be aware?

The Visual Ubiquity of Death

Arguably, Ariès' descriptive labels for the Western death system, "death denied" and "invisible death," definitively expired on September 11, 2001. Although no corpses resulting from the terrorist attack were shown on television that day, all the news media were filled with reminders and memorials of this new "day of infamy" in American history for weeks and months afterward. A force seems to have been set in motion that brought us across an imaginary line, and in short order we were flooded with images of war, famine, and pestilence. Only a few years earlier, similar events were sparsely presented, or censored altogether.

The Internet and 24-hour media outlets have brought unprecedented access to disastrous and threatening events and have also introduced us to cultures and social practices around the world that would only recently have appeared alien. The relatively predictable news on the shifting, but mostly stable, balance of power between the Cold War superpowers has been replaced by reports of the threats of rogue nuclear powers and terrorist attacks. The death toll of devastating natural disasters and genocidal ethnic conflicts reach us along with vivid pictures of those who have died or are dying. The news media, with a long history of unrelenting fascination with murder and violence but also an acknowledged role in reporting on war, disaster, and current affairs, are offering death imagery in vivid techno-color in real time, around the clock. The Twin Towers collapsing in fire and ash (2001). A journalist pleading for his life at gunpoint (2002). Muslim women in Iraq bent in mourning over their husbands' dead bodies (2002–). Starving children in Darfur (2003–). Long swathes of beach in Banda Aceh with remnants of homes and their former residents (2004). Terri Schiavo's vacant smile (2005). A corpse floating in the Mississippi River after the ravages of Hurricane Katrina (2005). Virginia Tech students morning their dead classmates (2007). Firefighters battling deadly California wildfires (2007). Cyclone victims starving in Burma (2008). Schoolchildren crushed under buildings after a Chinese earthquake (2008).

Not to mention the less visually harrowing reports on insidious threats to our well-being by pandemics—SARS (2002–3), avian influenza (2003–), E. coli infestations of fresh spinach and at Taco Bell (2006–); life-threatening toys and pharmaceuticals from China; and childhood obesity, which according to the American Academy of Pediatrics may result in the current generation of young people being the first in national history to die younger than their parents (Daniels 2006, 47–67). Living, indeed, seems more mortally dangerous than ever.

It appears there is only a limited demand to curtail the flow of information, except to protect underage children from exposure to excessively violent material. Americans have become used to having access to information in all areas of life, and this has also translated into matters related to death and dying. While there is still respect for the idea that for reasons of propriety certain personal pictures may be withheld, the American public does not appreciate having its information censored. There has been a burst of outrage over the fact that the coffins of Americans who died in Iraq and Afghanistan have been hidden from public view and that the funerals have been poorly and rarely covered by the press. What may once have been a sign of respect for the dead and their families is now frequently interpreted as being a sinister concealment of the reality of war by the Bush administration. The public in this case wants to be aware of the bodies that come home and wants to participate in the grieving process.

Coming in from around the globe, images and their accompanying commentary give definition to our time and help construct who we are and the values we embrace. The media messages bring us together in common causes (9/11 and the tsunami) but also widen the ideological rift among factional groups (as, for example, with the Terri Schiavo video and reports of American soldiers killing Muslim civilians). While death denial has not been erased, either in individual psyches or in overall cultural attitudes, death-related matters can at times be seen to be obsessively embraced.

Death imagery appears everywhere, seemingly integral to the American imagination. Morbid references and explicit images of the dead and dying saturate segments of popular culture, with television shows focusing on the lives of undertakers and violent crimes and the goriest of violent videos accessible with a couple of clicks on our Internet-connected computer screens. Even though the average life-expectancy at birth in America in 2005 was 78, as compared with 49 in 1905 (National Center for Health Statistics 2004, 34; 2008, 26), the world—as presented in the barrage of media imagery—seems like a more dangerous place than the one we envision existed a century ago.

But we are not only exposed to gore and shocking images that assault our senses; we are also beginning to be instructed via the media how to better manage the ordinary deaths of our friends and family members. In a pioneering move for a mainstream magazine, *Time* magazine published a feature story titled "A Kinder, Gentler Death," in September 2000, and billed on the cover as "Dying on Our Own Terms," with photographs of contemporary dying Americans and interviews with them and their families. Examples from public television include Bill Moyers's series *On Your Own Terms*, promoting acceptance of the natural course of death and openness among professional caregivers, families, and dying persons (Moyers 2004); and "A Lion in the House," a two-part documentary following the lives and deaths of children diagnosed with terminal cancer, and the lives of their families (Bognar and Reichert 2006). These media events are part and parcel of the new ubiquity of images, but they are also illustrations of the death awareness movement, whose most visible manifestations are the hospice and palliative care movement and the call for self-determination at the end of life.

The Growth of the Hospice and Palliative Care Movement

"Enough lies, we all know that I am dying! Stop lying to me, at least." Like so many others, Philippe Ariès quotes from Leo Tolstoy's *The Death of Ivan Ilyich* to exemplify the horrors of dying (1981, 567). Ilyich's experience stands at one end of the spectrum, a death in pain and without dignity. At the other end of the spectrum is Art Buchwald, who in his last months delivered a book-long eulogy to hospice,[8] in *Too Soon to Say Goodbye* (2006). Fully aware of his impending demise, he speaks openly about what is coming and praises hospice for the way it allows him to live out the end of his days. "Dying isn't hard," he jokes, "Getting paid by Medicare is" (9).

Hospice, a system of care for those with an estimated prognosis of six months or less to live, was officially recognized by the U.S. Congress in 1987 as a Medicare/Medicaid–reimbursable treatment option. Because as Ariès notes, we are not just dealing with fear of death when we look at the dying, "the physical aspects—nausea, unbearable pain—may also 'turn our stomach'" (1981, 568). With an interdisciplinary team consisting of physician, nurse, social worker, chaplain, and volunteer, hospice is designed to relieve physical as well as emotional and spiritual suffering and to give support to the family surrounding the dying. As part of her testimony to Congress in 1972, Kübler-Ross outlined the case for hospice: "We should not institutionalize people.—We can give families more help with home care and visiting nurses, giving the families and the patients the spiritual, emotional, and financial help in order to facilitate the final care at home"(quoted from National Hospice and Palliative Care Web site, History of Hospice care). In spite of the fact that the number of people served by hospice grew from 25,000 in 1982 to 800,000 in 2002, it appeared that the hospice idea was still struggling to gain traction. According to a study published by the National Hospice and Palliative Care Organization (NHPCO) in 2007, only one-third of the people eligible and appropriate for hospice care received such services in 2002.[9] Judging from a series of articles in NHPCO publications, among the substantial barriers were the state of denial among family members, the fear of physicians to openly discuss the cessation of treatments—even when these could no longer provide a cure and diminished the patient's quality of life—and the difficulty of open communication among those involved. Other reasons of a regulatory manner also contributed to the low rate of hospice enrollment. Yet the momentum was such in 2002 that spokespersons for the death awareness movement, a loosely defined collection of people and organizations advocating a more open attitude toward death, predicted in panel discussions at the Rallying Points 2nd National Conference *one community at a time* in November 2003 that America had reached the "tipping point," where those concerned with the improvement of the end-of-life experience would meet little societal resistance to their cause. And less than two years later, the 2005 Massachusetts Commission study showed that of the more than 90 percent of respondents who had heard at least something about hospice, more than three-quarters would consider using hospice services (2005).

A major step toward the advancement and acceptance of palliative care was achieved in 2006, when the American Academy of Hospice and Palliative Medicine and the American Board of Hospice and Palliative Medicine working together achieved recognition for the subspecialty of hospice and palliative medicine within the American Board of Medical Specialties (ABMS) and the Accreditation Council for Graduate Medical Education (ACGME). It appears, indeed, that the tipping point may have been passed.

The NHPCO has evolved over the years as a membership and educational organization and has as one of its primary aim to promote patient-and-family-centered care. Patient-and family-centered care is an approach to the planning, delivery and evaluation of healthcare that is grounded in mutually beneficial partnerships among patients, families, and healthcare practitioners. It is founded on the understanding that the family plays a vital role in ensuring the health and well being of patients. The ultimate goal of "patient-and family-centered care is to create partnerships among health care practitioners, patients and families that will lead to the best outcomes and enhance the quality and safety of health care" (quoted from NHPCO Web site, Patient and Family Centered Care). Such an approach to healthcare delivery is a far cry from the physician-as-supreme-authority based medical care that was the norm during the twentieth century. In the new model of care, the family and the patient are asked to participate in the treatment decisions and are often assumed to do their own research on the condition and keep their own records (a useful tool in complicated cases when communications among several specialists are not always up-to-date). Many physicians welcome the exchange with an informed patient. Others, perhaps concerned with the litigious nature of American society, appreciate that some responsibility for the care and its outcome has moved from their shoulders to the patient's. But the patient-managed case also has its problems. Many patients are more comfortable following authority rather than taking charge. (For ethnic differences in this regard, see the postscript.) And information that is available on the Internet—the most common research tool for laymen—is not always accurate or complete.

In spite of these issues, a family/patient–centered and family/patient–involved approach to end-of-life care is the trend in the industry, and it is increasingly the aim among professional caregivers and patient care advocates as reflected in recent literature: see for example, Joanne Lynn's *Sick to Death and Not Going to Take It Anymore* (2004) and Sharon R. Kaufman's … *And a Time to Die—How American Hospitals Shape the End of Life* (2005).

The ethical issues involved in hospice and palliative care have grown in complexity with laws that allow for patients' self-determination and with advances in life-sustaining medical technology. The issues surrounding the cessation or continuation of treatment have never been more complex.

The Dying Process and Medical Self-Determination

The bombardment of reports and alerts has awakened us to the futility of avoiding an encounter with death in some form. But between looking and controlling is a long road. The idea that death can be controlled has roots in the scientific revolution of the seventeenth century and the rationalist thinking of the Enlightenment, both of which suggested to humans that God's creation might not be immutable. In the eighteenth and nineteenth centuries, the modern class system and the urban family unit developed in tandem with industrialization and modern capitalism. Contemporary studies noted that the poor died younger than the rich, and the idea of death as the great equalizer was called into question. Humans considered the idea that they might control their own destiny, "that most of the contingencies which affect human activity are humanly created, rather than merely given by God or nature" (Giddens 1990, 32). Nineteenth-century news magazines provide evidence that people had faith in the power of scientific progress and supported technical developments that appeared to hold death at bay, if only temporarily (Staudt 2001, 94–95). For those who are skeptical about humanity's potential to permanently overcome death or even substantially prolong life through bionics or similar measures, the issue of control is still relevant. But the focus is turned to controlling the path toward death, allowing the individual, rather than the medical establishment, to take charge of the journey.[10]

The legislative development of medical self-determination has a complicated history brought about by specific, challenging cases. The journey is briefly outlined in *A Palliative Ethic of Care—Clinical Wisdom at Life's End* by Joseph J. Fins, a guidebook primarily addressing medical students and residents (2006, 19–61). The 1914 court case *Schloendorff v. Society of New York Hospital* appears to grant the adult individual of sound mind the right "to determine what shall be done with his own body" (*Schloendorff*, quoted in Fins 2006, 19). A survey of physicians in the 1960s showed, however, that the patient's decision-making capacity was undermined by the fact that 90 percent of physicians at that time did not share the truth of a sensitive diagnosis with the patient (Oken, cited in Fins 2006, 21). A complete reversal had taken place by 1979, when a similar physician survey showed that 97 percent of physicians "indicated a preference for telling a cancer patient his diagnosis" (Novack, quoted in Fins, 22).

In 1976, the case of Karen Quinlan, whose parents were granted the right to remove her life support, signaled the beginning of the right to die legislation. After the Quinlan case, in the 1980s, reports by the Hastings Center and other bioethical authorities argued for the right to forego excessive treatments. In the 1990s, the Joint Commission on Accreditation of Healthcare Organizations (JCAHO) laid down rules for "the establishment of a mechanism for the consideration of ethical issues arising in the care of patients" (quoted in Fins 2006, 34). The Nancy Cruzan case, involving another young woman in a coma, hinged on the lack of evidence of Cruzan's wishes and became the impetus for legislation to promote and authorize advance directives. The Patient Self-Determination Act, passed in 1991.

Today all 50 states have some form of self-determination act that enables an individual to designate someone to make medical decisions for him or her, should s/he become unable to do so, using so-called durable powers of attorney for health care or health care proxies. Yet the case of Terri Schiavo in 2005 brought renewed attention to the importance of having a designated health care agent and renewed efforts to promote the signing of documents that clarify who is in control of the decision-making process in case of a person's inability to make such decisions.

In the 2005 Massachusetts Commission survey, more than 8 in 10 respondents indicated that they were "very" much or "somewhat" afraid of dying painfully, lending support to the notion that it is not *being* dead that people fear so much as the process of dying. More than two-thirds of the respondents to each of the surveys indicated that they considered living with great pain to be worse than death. While this suggests that people would be eager to take necessary measures to maintain control of their destiny, the survey reveals a gap between the personal preferences people express about death and dying and the actions they take—or, more accurately, do not take—to make those preferences known and honored. Likewise, 7 in 10 respondents said it is very important to be off machines that extend life when they think about dying and over 89 percent said it is at least somewhat important. Yet only 37 percent of the general population of respondents had appointed a health care proxy to act for them if they became unable to speak for themselves (Massachusetts Commission 2005).

In a similar study of Minnesota residents 18 years or older in 2003, it was found that 27 percent had filled out some form of advance directive and that the reasons for not having done so were that they didn't think they needed such a document (32 percent), they had not gotten around to it (31 percent), and they felt it would take too much time (24 percent). Twenty-three percent didn't know where to get the documents, and 18 percent had never heard of the document before (Silberman 2004, 4). These results suggest that there is a lingering tendency among the general public to avert the eyes from matters (that could be) related to death and dying.

Kastenbaum suggested at the turn of the millennium that the incongruities between the public's avowed preference for medical self-determination and the effective implementation of the Self-Determination Act (i.e. people signing advance directives) may in part be attributed to the unease that many physicians still feel with the idea that patients should be allowed to determine their own course of medical treatment (2000, 190–91). While the increase is the signing of advance directives has only increased moderately over the last decade.

The movement that promotes the right to physician-assisted death, a right that in the United States currently exists only in Oregon law, is seen by its proponents as an extension of the rights set forth in the Self-Determination Act. The movement—in an earlier manifestation represented by the American Hemlock Society—gained publicity during Dr. Jack Kevorkian's several trials for murder in the latter part of the twentieth century. Much of the publicity surrounding the so-called Dr. Death was negative but it brought about a national discourse about matters of death and people's right to self-determinations that may otherwise not have taken place. Among noteworthy books generated by proponents of physician-assisted death are: Charles F. McKahn's *A Time to Die—The Place for Physician Assistance* (1999) and Derek Humphry's and Mary Clement's *Freedom to Die—People, Politics and the Right-to-Die Movement* (2000). In *Easeful Death—Is There a Case for Assisted Dying?* (2008) Mary Warnock and Elisabeth Macdonald review both sides of the debate and specifically argue for compassion. They suggests that

the question is not whether or not individuals should have the right to manage their own lives and treatment preceding death but rather to what degree
public and private interests can be balanced.

A position statement approved by the Board of Directors of the American Academy of Hospice and Palliative Medicine (AAHPM) acknowledged
in 2007 the validity of a persistently suffering terminal patient's request for
help to die, showing that the movement is being taken seriously by the medical profession.[11]

Final Arrangements

In the twentieth century, the nineteenth-century public "cult of the tomb"
was replaced by the "cult of memory," which requires no association with the
distaste inspired by thoughts of the dead body (Ariès 1981, 577). When and
if a corpse appeared in public, it had undergone an elaborate embalming process so as to appear as lifelike as possible. At funeral services the presence of
a casket, the concrete material reminder of death, became increasingly rare.
A "positive, upbeat, and hopeful funeral liturgy" became the norm (Bregman
1999, 121). The funeral, especially among protestant Christians, was often
replaced by a memorial service, subtitled "A Celebration of the Life of..."
The person's accomplishments and personal relationships were remembered
amid laughter and tears. This manner of accommodating death was intended
to be, and often was, psychologically helpful to the survivors. Nevertheless,
the practice may suggest a culture of death avoidance and contrasts sharply
with premodern ways that focused on the deceased's departure into the afterlife, the rituals by the graveside, and the loss felt by those left behind.

Many of the new traditions of the twentieth century remain entrenched
in the new millennium. A change that can be discerned, however, is an ever-
increasing personalization of the funeral and memorial services, as well as
of the manner and form of disposing of the corpse. It is not uncommon
today for thoughtful people to plan all the details of their own services,
whether to spare the survivors the trouble or to maintain control beyond
the grave is a question that probably needs to be answered on a case-by-
case basis. Lisa Takeushi Cullen's *Remember Me—A Lively Tour of the New
American Way of Death* (2006) is a collection of new American funerals and
rituals, Cullen notes the "booming" cremation industry, idiosyncratic personalized caskets, and immigrant groups that do their best to maintain their
traditional practices in a new land. Granted, Cullen is highlighting unusual
cases, but the overwhelming impression of her tales is that people search
for personalized meaning in their end-of-life rituals and hence often have to
create and supervise them in advance, for themselves or for their loved ones
whom they honor after their death. The movement toward "green" burial is
not surprising, given the permeation of the environmental movement in all

of American society in the twenty-first century. Mark Harris, who describes himself as an environmental journalist, presents in *Grave Matters* (2007) a range of "green" personalized burial solutions for those who do not want to go the route of traditional embalming, and heavy, slow-to-break-down oak caskets. He describes, for example, the spreading of ashes at sea, the creation of artificial coral reefs, and how to achieve environmentally friendly earth burials.

The enormous interest in Randy Pausch's *The Last Lecture*, presented in front of 400 people in an auditorium at Carnegie-Mellon on September 18, 2007, and subsequently viewed by millions on YouTube, demonstrates that death is no longer hidden. Pausch had pancreatic cancer and his physicians had given him a terminal diagnosis of a few months. His lecture, which urged the audience to achieve their childhood dreams, was videotaped for the future benefit of his young children. His message was inspirational but, in all likelihood, it was Pausch's willingness to acknowledge his situation and speak about it that was the primary attraction to his audience. Pausch showed that it was possible to plan for what was inevitable, prepare a legacy, and simultaneously enjoy the days that are left. And he showed that the choices he made were his and his family's. He was dying but he was supervising the process. His action resonated with the young YouTube viewers. The video recording of the lecture spread like wildfire across cyberspace and eventually returned to earth in the form of a printed bestseller, co-written by Jeffrey Zaslow.

Tuesdays with Morrie—An Old Man, a Young Man and Life's Greatest Lesson by Mitch Albom (1997), a story in which a terminally ill professor imparts lessons in dying well—and living well—to his former student, is another runaway success with over 10 years on the bestseller list. The enormous popularity of this nonfiction work—made into a television film in 1999—has surely contributed to a societal climate where it is more comfortable to speak about death and how to manage than it was before we shared in the experiences of Morrie and Mitch.

In the twentieth-century America, public grief had almost been eliminated. The bereaved no longer carry the traditional signs of mourning—black clothing, armbands, and lapel bands—that once sent explicit messages of loss and vulnerability and were reminders that death is always in our midst. When death touches someone in contemporary America, neighbors and friends tend to offer awkward condolences, quickly change the subject or, all to often, avoid encounters with the grieving person altogether. The bereaved are given little time and space to grieve openly. Society generally expects mourners to "move on" quickly. Those who have difficulty doing so are often left to suffer in silence. But changes are discernable in several areas. Public grief seems to be creeping back in the form of memorial tattoos commemorating the deceased and on interactive Web sites that offer opportunities for individualized expressions of grief in a virtual, public space.[12] A change in this arena is also discernible in Sandra Gilbert's *Death's Door—Modern Dying and the Ways We Grieve* (2006). This collection of essays on death-and grief-related matters by a literature professor is simultaneously a history book, an instruction book, and a book of comfort. While it covers a much broader spectrum of manners and practices of funerals, memorials, and grief, it has kinship with Joan Didion's *The Year of Magical Thinking* (2005). Both are rooted in the authors' experience as recent widows searching for meaning.

REFLECTIONS AND OBSERVATIONS

If as Vovelle suggests, "death in all its manifestations is the best meta-phoric guide to the problems of life" (1990, 80), then the guide is sending an ambiguous message about our problems in the first decade of twenty-first-century America. Ample evidence still abounds to show that we try to deny what we cannot comfortably control and manage and that we distance ourselves from those who remind us of our weakness. Lacking in power and productivity—and evoking discomfiting feelings—the dying population re-ceives scant attention from society at large for economic as well as psycho-logical reasons. Stoicism and privacy are prized values in many groups, in which the dying are praised for not focusing on the subject of death. Imper-sonal hospital routines prescribed for the body have been developed over the course of the last century and remain more common than new versions of soothing and meaningful rituals that serve the whole human being. But there is also evidence that many institutions—hospitals, nursing homes, and medical schools—are boosting their training to better treat patients at the end of life. They work actively to give patients a sense of autonomy and indi-viduality as well as to provide and train chaplains, social workers, and others who can support terminally ill patients and act as their advocates. Those who desire to speak openly about the end-of-life experience in contemporary America are more likely to find resonance and less likely to encounter resis-tance in contacts with professionals in the health care field as well as with close family and friends than just a few years ago.

Robert J. Kastenbaum, the author of the commonly assigned textbook *Death, Society, and Human Experience*, published the ninth edition of this book in 2007. The changes from the 2004 edition reflect changes in our "death system" during the last several years. Perhaps most importantly, the preface describes in the past tense how "society featured the strategy of ignoring death and practically everything connected with it." The problems it created for health care professionals and the dying and grieving—"little comfort...little coun-seling...[i]nadequate communication...burdensome defenses...anxieties"—are described as if they are problems we have left behind. "There was at first a lot of resistance to what has now become known as death education. By now, however, many people recognize that *thanatology*—the study of life, with death left in—can be one of the most valuable projects for a students of any age" (xvii). This view may reflect an exaggerated optimism about society's attitude to death and typify a select group of professionals who are pleased to finally see their field of study recognized by a broader segment of the population. Kastenbaum's life-embracing definition of thanatology as "the study of life, with death left in" (xvii) is not a lingering avoidance to face up to death but rather a manifestation of a new and more palatable way to manage death. (Another popular college-level textbook in thanatology is *The Last Dance—Encountering Death and Dying* by DeSpelder and Strickland (2005), currently in its seventh edition.)

When Kastenbaum (2007) writes that "[n]ot thinking about death has been a failed experiment. Listening and communicating are far more help-ful approaches" (27), or "The new social and medical climate for end-of-life decisions favors strengthened participation, communication, and patients' rights" (190), he echoes the message of Ira Byock, one of the gurus of the death awareness and hospice movements. Byock's prescriptive writings on how best to manage the difficulties surrounding death, dying, and grief are used in professional settings as well as private homes to figure out "how to be and what to do" around death. Byock's best-known works are *Dying Well—Peace and Possibility at the End of Life* (1997) and *The Four Things That Matter Most—A Book about Living* (2004).

The growing demand for the right to medical self-determination func-tions as a counterforce to the impersonal end-of-life care of medical institu-tions. The death awareness movement has spawned an array of handbooks and guides designed to help us handle the last chapter of life. The publication and wide distribution of the many handbooks constitute, *per se*, a refutation of the culture of denial. Notably, recommendations to ignore the impend-ing death and focus on other matters are practically nonexistent in these guides. Since 2001, Amazon.com has annually offered 12–14,000 nonfiction publications with the word "death" in the title. Popular manuals include Ste-phen Levine, *A Year to Live* (1997) and David Kessler, *The Needs of the Dying* (2000). Kessler's book in an earlier (1997) edition was entitled *The Rights of the Dying*, but Kessler came to realize that it was not so much the "rights" of the dying that was the concern of loved ones as their needs (2000, xiv). What the dying need are "a little psychology, a little medicine, and a little spirituality, mixed with a whole lot of love" (xiv). In Joanne Lynn, et al., *Handbook for Mortals: Guidance for People Facing Serious Illness* (1999), two physicians offer a holistic model of care and also offer advice on the practical aspects of managing life before death. In *Peaceful Dying—The Step-by-Step Guide to Preserving Your Dignity, Your Choice, and Your Inner Peace at the End of Life* (1999) Daniel R. Tobin describes a personalized "FairCare program," which he developed at a Veterans Hospital he directed. Many small-press, personalized stories such as *Death without Denial; Grief without Apology: A Guide for Facing Death and Loss* (2002) by Barbara Roberts, former governor of Oregon's story of the cancer death of her husband Frank, invite the reader into a community of compassion and caring.

Guy Brown's *The Living End—The Future of Death, Aging and Immortality* (2008) is a light-hearted self-help volume, ending with nine suggestions as to what we should do "before we die." In contrast to Ira Byock's four suggestions, which deal with interpersonal relationships, Brown takes a broader view, for example: "Rage, rage against the dying of the light"; "Accept that death is an analog process rather than a digital event. Death is part of life"; "Face the fact that we are going to die and prepare for it" (259–260). Many of these suggestions share the idea that there is something you can DO, if not to prevent death, at least to make it more attractive.

More unorthodox works have emerged as by-products of the New Age movement, e.g. Starhawk et al., *The Pagan Book of Living and Dying. Practical Rituals, Prayers, Blessings and Meditations on Crossing Over* (1997) and Mary Anne Saunders's *Nearing Death Awareness—A Guide to the Language, Visions, and Dreams of the Dying* (2008). Starhawk, according to the back cover of her book, is "a witch, eco-feminist, peace activist and the author of several books—co-founder of The Reclaiming Collective, a group of men and women working to unify spirit and politics in the San Francisco Bay Area." Saunders has a profession that until recently was unheard of. She is a spiritual guidance mentor. In her work on "transpersonal studies," she has discovered that people who are nearing death have a recognizable pattern of behavior. She has coined the phrase "nearing death awareness" (NDA) and discusses how those that face impending death, their families, friends, and caregivers can use this as a vehicle for spiritual growth (15). Hundreds of similar books have been produced, many self-published, in the decade between the appearance of the two works cited here. The New Age movement is dismissed by many professional caregivers and counselors, but the movement has undoubtedly opened up new venues for looking at death among its adherents and has contributed to the recent rising awareness of death and dying as an integral part of life.

As important as it is for members of the general public to navigate the healthcare system, understand their treatment choices and be in control of their lives, it is also of fundamental importance that all medical staff and other professional caregivers are properly trained to take care of those at the end of life. That the medical profession is more inclined in this direction is evidenced by expansions of such sections in medical text books (cf. Kastenbaum 2007) and by the publication of books such as Joseph Fins' *A Palliative Ethic of Care* (2006) that seeks to advice young physicians. Guidance for healthcare professional who are caring for the dying and their families in available from the work of the Institute of Medicine's Committee on the Care at the End of Life in Field's and Cassel's (eds) *Approaching Death: Improving Care at the End of Life*.

To account for the diversity of approaches and attitudes to death, Tony Walter's *The Revival of Death* (1993), an outline of three different, simultaneously present attitudes toward death—the *traditional*, the *modern* and the *neomodern*—is useful. Walter traces the traditional model to a time when death was quick and ubiquitous. The familiar village or town provided the social context and religious texts and the prevailing authorities provided the leaders. Those who die embracing traditional practices can accept their fate with equanimity and die assured that their soul will have a place in eternity and their families will find comfort in established rituals and congregational life. In the modern model, currently pervasive but waning, described above, death is hidden and the medical establishment is the voice of authority.

Walter's neomodern model is based on the ideals of the death awareness movement. The movement promotes a culture that is willing to confront the reality of death and that places a high value on the individual's right to self-determination and personal control. Employing an activist strategy, the adherents of this approach argue for the dying and their families to take charge of the course of death. The dying person is seen as the primary authority. With counselors as guides in a home or hospice setting, meaning is found in interpersonal relations. An inner spirituality replaces a given (traditional-model) or chosen (modern-model) religion. To cope with his situation, the dying person following the neomodern model resorts to personal expression, not to ritual or silence, as in the traditional and modern models, respectively. The worst sin among those who adopt the neomodern model is neither unbelief (traditional) nor intrusion (modern) but isolation and denial.

Walter emphasizes that the traditional, modern, and neomodern models should not be seen as discrete or oppositional but as theoretical constructs that in practice overlap and crisscross each other. While one approach may be dominant in a particular context, blended models are discernible in the environment of many dying persons. Conflicts between the traditional and the modern approach often occur in immigrant families, with the older generation holding on to known practices and the younger family members embracing the power of modern medicine and technology. Walter's research is primarily in a British context, but his estimation that the conflict between the modern and neomodern approach to death occurs mostly within middle-class white families would presumably hold true in the United States as well (1993, 47–60).

If, in the early years of the new millennium, we are seeing that "the American relationship to death and dying is changing [and a]voidance and denial seem to coexist with a newly fashioned thrust towards openness," this begs the question: "[does] the thanatology movement, with its focus on dignity and openly acknowledging death as a vital part of the human experience, represent a transformation of attitudes or is [it] a recasting of the American framework of denial into a new form?" (Moller 2000, 75) According to Robert A. Burt, a professor of law with an interest in issues of the Bible, the Holocaust and apartheid, the focus on denial as the culprit in death-related manners is misplaced. La Rochefoucauld's proposition "that death like the sun should not be stared at" (Burt's version of the maxim) is not meant to convey "that death cannot be observed, that human psychology is somehow grounded on denying the existence of death. The maxim suggests that death can be directly faced just as the sun can be stared at—but that in both cases the prolonged effort will induce a kind of dazzled blindness" (Burt 2002, 4).

Robert Burt proposes that the dichotomy between acceptance and denial is inherent in the individual and deeply embedded in Western culture. "Death is not viewed simply as a fearful event; there is an aura of wrongfulness, of intrinsic immorality, attached to the idea of death" (2002, 12). Burt sees the discussions of self-determination at the time of death as insufficiently separating "whether death-related matters can be rationally discussed and whether these matters are amenable to purposeful rational control" (4). In his view, our perception of death as wrongful is persistent, and society will never "embrace" death. He believes that society is well served by ambivalence toward death, which promotes attempts to preserve and prolong life with a realist's awareness of what is in store for all who have been born.

As has been demonstrated, the seeds of the new episteme of death were planted in the mid-twentieth century, germinated slowly, and have finally taken root and begun to sprout. An example of how the twenty-first century episteme of death can manifest itself in an historical study is Drew Gilpin Faust's *This Republic of Suffering—Death and the American Civil War* (2008). She demonstrates how the experience of death during the Civil War "created the modern American union—not just by ensuring national survival, but by shaping national structures and commitments" (xiv). The scholars of the 1990s analyzed death through the theoretical prisms of poststructuralism and identity politics. In contrast, to Faust, death is not the object of observation but the prism she uses to investigates the transformation of the American nation. In her analysis death achieves the role of generator (of the future American nation) rather than its destroyer. She picks up a term that Civil War Americans used: "the work of death" and explains how "'work' incorporate[s] both effort and impact—and the important connection between the two" (xiv). Faust shows how death was the agent of change in the Civil War and also notes the connection to contemporary times. "We still seek to use our deaths to create meaning when we are not sure any exists. The Civil War generation glimpsed the fear that still defines us—the sense that death is the only end. We still work to live with the riddle that they—the Civil War dead and their survivors alike—had to solve so long ago" (271). In her examination, she employs, wittingly or not, the possibilities presented by the new episteme of death, "death recognized" or "death managed," as Ariès might have expressed it were he to label the attitude and approach to death in the early twenty-first century.

POSTSCRIPT: DEATH, DYING AND GROUP IDENTITY

The phrase "the American death system" requires that we pay attention to certain questions—even if no answers are available. What is implied in the word "American" beyond belonging within the territorial limits of the 50 states? How do the differences among population groups affect their approach to death and death denial? How are members of different racial and cultural groups portrayed and discussed by the dominant media? In an example of the acute need for sensitivity, the *New York Times* did not publish photographs of the mangled bodies that resulted from the terrorist attack on September 11, 2001. It did, however, print pictures of bloated corpses floating in the Mississippi River after Hurricane Katrina four years later. Had so much death and destruction in the intervening years inured the public to such pictures? Did the origin of the calamity play a role? Or did mainstream America view those who were hit worst by Katrina, largely poor African Americans, as "other" and therefore more permissible motifs? Was the suffering population of New Orleans' Ninth Ward seen with the compassionate but distancing eyes that mainstream America trains on ideologically alien Iraqis and culturally remote tsunami victims?

The discussion below does not aspire to provide exhaustive coverage but is intended to offer examples that point to the kinds of issues that need to be taken into account. Much research remains to be done in this area.

Seventy-five percent of Americans describe themselves as "white" when asked to self-identify their race (Grieco 2001, 3). In broad—but often simplistic—terms, this group may be seen as constituting the dominant group in America. Color alone does not, however, include a person in the mainstream or exclude a person from the mainstream, whether one is talking about death and dying practices and needs, or other cultural manifestations. Race is but one of many variables that *may* influence a person's, family's or larger group's attitude and approach to death and dying. Religious and ethnic belonging play a role, as do age and gender (Braun, Pietsch, and Blanchette 2000; Johnson and McGee 1998; Nebraska Coalition for Compassionate Care 2004). An individual's attitude, values, beliefs, and behaviors in relation to the end of life are also affected by additional "cultures" to which the person belongs or feels affinity with, such as geographic region or place, professional affiliation, socioeconomic class, interest group, and extended family, especially that of a spouse or life-partner (Braun, Pietsch, and Blanchette 2000). Factors that go beyond a person's group identity also participate in determining the approach to death and dying. The way in which a person is socialized regarding death from childhood and subsequent experiences with and exposure to death will affect the attitude to death, as will the person's self-image as an individual and as a participant in a given group or relationship (Lopata 1999). To these considerations need to be added the person's medical diagnosis and the legal, ethical, and health care environment that is experienced by a particular patient.

Taking all these factors into account in an attempt to understand a dying patient and his or her family is a daunting but worthwhile endeavor for professional caregivers who as a result can better help alleviate emotional, spiritual, and even physical suffering. However, practitioners and scholars who venture into this arena rightly warn of the risk of stereotyping. The differences within a group may be as great as between one group and another. There is also the potential risk of underestimating the dynamic nature of a group's or individual's approach to the end of life. The wise course, it is generally agreed, is to be sensitive to the existence of cultural differences and perspectives while staying focused and open to individuals and family groups, and honoring their needs (e.g., Braun, Pietsch, and Blanchette 2000; Fry 1999; Lipson, Dibble, and Minarik 1996).

With these weighty caveats in mind, the following findings from research on selected minorities exemplify the kinds of differences that may be found among Americans. The most detailed survey to date about the end-of-life attitudes and preferences of a segment of African Americans was conducted among AARP members in North Carolina in 2003 (Nebraska Coalition 2004). African Americans, who may be recent immigrants or have roots in colonial times, represent 12.3 percent of the population in the United States, or approximately 35 million people according to the 2000 Census. Cummins found in a report prepared for the AAARP that African American AARP members (by definition, all over the age of 50) in North Carolina are marginally more likely than non–African American AARP members to have talked often or occasionally about death and dying during their childhood, 47 percent as compared to 42 percent among the non–African Americans. Over 52 percent of the non–African American respondents were "very much or "somewhat" afraid of dying in an institution such as a nursing home, whereas the comparable percentage among the African Americans was 30 percent. While 71 percent of African American AARP members in North Carolina attended religious or spiritual services regularly, only 5 percent of non–African Americans did so. Among other things, the survey also determined that the African American respondents were less likely to view certain limiting conditions as "worse than death" as compared with their non–African American counterparts: for example, 90 percent of the non–African American population thought that "total physical dependency on others, such as being in a coma" would be worse than death, while only 72 percent of the African Americans held this view. When dealing with their own dying, 88 percent of the non–African American respondents thought it important to be able to stay in their own home, while 78 percent of the African Americans fell in the same category. When asked, "if you were terminally ill and could choose where to die, where would you MOST want to die?" 24 percent of African Americans had no preference and 46 percent chose "at home." In comparison, 14 percent of the non–African Americans had no preference and 61 percent chose "at home." Comfort through religious/spiritual services or persons were important to 91 percent of the African Americans and to 83 percent of the non–African Americans. Similar results are apparent in smaller earlier surveys of African Americans in other regions or sharing medical diagnoses (see Mouton 2000).

The fastest-growing minority group in America is the population describing itself as Hispanic. Reported in the 2000 Census as comprising 12.5 percent of Americans, Hispanics—not a "race"—may be of European, Asian, or African descent. Studies of Hispanics at the end of life suggest that "Hispanic Americans are less likely than Europeans Americans to appreciate autonomous decision making, complete advance directives, endorse the withholding or withdrawal of life-prolonging treatments in seemingly futile conditions, support physician-assisted death, use hospice services, or embrace organ donation and autopsy" (Talamantes, Gomez, and Braun 2000, 92–93). While acknowledging the great diversity among Hispanics, five traits have been identified as commonly found among Hispanics and likely affecting their decisions regarding end-of-life issues. *Familismo*, "emphasis on the welfare of the family over the individual and strong family," may explain why patient autonomy is less important to Hispanics than to European Americans and also why issues of death and dying need to be discussed among a circle of relatives. *Jerarquismo*, "respect for hierarchy," means not only that the head of the family needs to be consulted regarding important issues but also that patients who view doctors as figures of authority will not be comfortable questioning them. A lack of *personalismo*, "trust building over time based on the display of mutual respect," may result in poor communication between health care attendants and patients and their families. *Espiritismo*, "belief in good and evil spirits that can affect health and well-being," may make some Hispanics less reluctant than European Americans to look to the medical establishment for answers. *Presentismo*, "emphasis on the present, not the past or future," may hinder Hispanics from filling out advance directives. (Talamantes, Gomez, and Braun 2000, 85, 93–94.)

Asians and Pacific Islanders (APIAs) make up 3.4 percent (or 10 million) of the population in the United States (2000 Census). Within this statistical category are people who have immigrated from over 30 countries, representing dozens of religions and hundreds of ethnic groups. Such a diverse population category brings to the foreground concerns about stereotyping. The following are examples of conflicts some APIA populations might encounter with American mainstream medical practices. The family plays a more important role in the decision-making process than the individual among most APIA families. Many, perhaps especially among Japanese Americans, value filial duty and obligation and stoicism over personal needs. Such an attitude may impede open discussions of pain management. In several Asian countries, many people believe that patients need to be protected from knowing about a terminal condition, since such information may hasten death. This attitude is particularly strong among Chinese Americans, who consider it "bad luck" to mention death at any time, and hinders their signing of advance directives. Many Japanese American and Asian Indian Americans hide a terminal prognosis from patients, for fear that the patients' ability to cope with the condition will weaken if they are told of their impending death. In an American health care setting, a patient's wish not to know about a terminal diagnosis can make informed consent to treatment difficult. A belief in the possibility of miracles among some Asian Americans may encourage a family to ask for life-extending treatments regardless of the quality of life they would bring the patient and the futility of the measures. Practices vary widely among Asians as to the treatment of the body at the time of death and right afterward. For many, autopsies and organ donations may be precluded (Yeo and Hikoyeda 2000).

The results of studies that specifically address death and dying among people of a specific cultural group, such as Fry's 1999 study of elderly, dying, Indian-born Hindus in Canada, highlight the common desire of reconnecting with traditional practices but also point to the difficulty of drawing conclusions even about a relatively homogeneous group.

While acknowledging the differences among and between the different tribes of American Indians and Alaska Natives—just under 1 percent or 2.5 million (2000 Census)—researchers have attributed to these groups certain frequently identifiable characteristics regarding death beliefs. Among most tribes, the dominant traditional perception is that life and death are interdependent rather than dualistic in nature and the life/death course is cyclical rather than linear in chronology. If death is viewed as an integral and natural part of all existence, issues of denial are moot, since living beings, the dying, and the corpses that are returned to the earth to nourish it are all part of an endless circle of creation and re-creation. Anthropological studies of the Navajo from the 1940s and 1960s found that the tribe avoided discussions of death and the names of dead persons. With modern acculturation, this view may be breaking down. Substantial variations exist among and within tribes on whether death should be openly confronted (Westlake Van Winkle 2000).

Religious dogma outlines the meaning of death for its adherents and colors the expectations of the dying (Johnson and McGee 1998). Our spirituality—or lack thereof—plays a role in how we approach death. Most major religions and sects practicing in the United States subscribe to some concept of an afterlife. (Unitarian Universalists are exceptions to this norm.) A survey of Nebraska residents indicates that 91 percent of the respondents, (more than 97 percent of whom are non–African American), believe it important to get comfort from religious services and persons at the end of life (Nebraska Coalition 2004). The way in which the answers may change with the removal of the issues of death and dying is indicated by the AARP North Carolina survey. Among those respondents, 55 percent of the non–African Americans surveyed stated they never found strength in their religion or spirituality; only 3 percent of the African American respondents gave the same answers.

Many religious persons would consider their belief in an afterlife to be a reason not to fear death and would argue that they do not need to deny death; they will be ready when the time comes to accept biological death and move on to an eternal life. They see death as a threshold to more life, not as a final ending. Such a belief in an afterlife may per se be construed as a form of death denial as argued by Ernest Becker and as one of the tools we use to help define ourselves and what is important in our lives.

Herman Feifel's concern about the waning belief in personal immortality proved to be a miscalculation. According to a Gallup poll published in 1982, 71 percent of the American public (only 1 percent less than among the respondents in 1952) agreed that there is a heaven where people who have led good lives are eternally rewarded (McDannell and Lang 1988, 307). In 2004, Gallup reported that 81 percent of Americans believed in heaven (Gallup, May 2004). Erich Fromm's reference to nontraditional religious leaders as offering answers to our fear of death appear prescient with regard to the New Age spirituality that has practically become mainstream in the twenty-first century.

Claims of causality are untenable, but a correlation may exist between levels of spiritual/religious activities and openness to death. The growing secularization of America from the 1920s through the 1960s was contemporaneous with an intensified repression of death as a public subject. And simultaneous with an increase in attention to end-of-life issues at the end of the twentieth century, America experienced a surge of interest in religious matters, albeit in a broadly defined "spirituality." Many sects among the monotheistic religions are growing their congregations by calling for a return to fundamentalism, while, at the other end of the spectrum, Eastern-style meditation and other nonsectarian spiritual practices have spread among the general population.

In addition to ethnicity, race, and religion, variables such as age, class, and gender influence attitudes to the end of life. It has, for example, been determined that advance directives about terminal care are more likely to be filled out by well-educated, middle-class Caucasians than by members of minority groups and people with lower education levels (Braun and Kayashima 1999;

Talamantes, Gomez, and Braun 2000). From this we cannot draw the conclusion that less well-educated people and minorities are more death denying. It
is likely, however, that people who are comfortable with and used to reading
and filling out forms are more likely to respond to the presentation of printed
material.

Expectations for men and women at the time of a death differ. According
to some studies, women are given more opportunity to process grief than
men (see White, D. 1999). Since this is considered healthy behavior, one may
conclude—quite possibly simplistically—that women who have grieved properly are subsequently more likely to accept and confront death with reduced
anxiety. Extrapolating from Lopata's findings in "Grief and the Self-Concept"
one may also surmise that widowhood that leads to a reduced appreciation
of self may lead to a desire to seek (rather than deny) death. This could be
especially true in traditional Hindu settings, where widowed women have no
assigned place in the culture.

Most of the above-mentioned studies do not directly address denial, and
drawing conclusions about death denial from them is complicated by the fact
that denial and acceptance may need to be defined in different ways for different groups and in different circumstances. Mouton describes trust and
communication as the primary issues for many African Americans making
end-of-life decisions in a predominantly Caucasian health care system. Studies
of disease-specific patients have shown that African Americans are substantially more likely than Caucasians to prefer a treatment approach that focuses
on extending life and life-sustaining treatments as opposed to relieving pain
(Mouton 2000, 77). Historically, African Americans have had inferior health
care, compared to the Caucasian population, and the demand for all-out treatment and the newest technologies may reflect a concern that services are
being withheld rather than a refusal to accept that death is impending. Similar
factors may also be present among other ethnic or racial groups that have
experienced discrimination.

What may appear as death denial, or lack thereof, when encountered in
one group of Americans may be a manifestation of religious belief or traditional rituals among others. Is the label of denial appropriately applied to a
family that refuses to articulate that a family member is dying, if its profound
belief is that such an acknowledgment will hasten death? Studies have found
that Christian and Buddhist Americans with Japanese ancestry are "death accepting" as compared with what one study described as the overall American
"death-denying" culture (Yeo and Hikoyeda 2000, 132). Because of the many
variables that need to be considered, however, such cross-cultural conclusions may never be entirely valid.

Among some social groups, accepted norms and peer pressure may result in actions that appear to the outside world as reckless forms of death
denial, for example, the risky behavior exhibited by (often young) persons

who engage in unprotected sex, fast driving, and extreme sports. Traumatic events may also color a person's propensity to deny death. Daily confrontation with the dying may either "burn out" a clinician or make him/her more comfortable with death. On the one hand, most hospices have found a need for professional support groups to help their team members. On the other hand, hospice nurses who have close and frequent contact with the dying have been shown to have a more positive attitude to death and less fear than nurses with less contact with terminal patients (Servaty and Hayslip 1999, 230). When confronted with sudden violence in a fatal accident, a murder, or a terror attack, temporary denial may be a necessary shield. Age and disease prognosis may also create variances in what we define as denial. Those who avoid preparing for the death that looms for everyone when the body has worn itself out are probably differently motivated than the young person who ardently refuses to accept a terminal prognosis.

NOTES

1. While the attitude and approach to death, dying and bereavement are often similar in Europe and the United States and I have drawn on relevant European writers as well as American, this chapter primarily surveys the situation in the United States.

2. "Death system," a commonly used term, is defined by John Morgan as "the sum total of the persons, places, ideas, traditions, acts, omissions, emotions, and statements that we make or think about death" (12) and by Kastenbaum (2007) as "the interpersonal, sociophysical, and symbolic network through which an individual's relationship to mortality is mediated by society" (104).

3. *Postmodern* here is used in its most literal sense (i.e. "of, relating to, or being an era after a modern one.") Merriam Webster online dictionary, available at http://www.merriam-webster.com/dictionary/post-modern.

4. "The other" in Ariès' account is intimately connected to the speaking "self" and wholly different from "the Other," a postmodern way of designating a group that is alien to the dominant group in society.

5. By the "episteme of death" Bendle means the embedded meanings of death as they function and are used in discourse and practice in a particular culture or civilization (355). Bendle employs the word episteme, not in the traditional Greek sense but in the vein of Michel Foucault in his analysis of historical changes in society (e.g., *The Order of Things*, 1970), referring to the totality of relations among all disciplines and epistemologies that inform a concept in a particular society. Sensitive to an ever-changing environment, foucaultian epistemes are inherently unstable.

6. An indication that historians were paying attention—while as a caring community we were not—was the emergence of an abundance of historical treatises on death, beginning with the British classical historian Jocelyn M. C. Toynbee's now classic *Death and Burial and the Roman World* in 1971.

7. Working on behalf of the Massachusetts Commission on End of Life Care, Life's End Institute, *The Missoula Demonstration Project* sent one survey to a random sample of 3,000 Massachusetts residents age 35 and over. AARP sent one survey to a random sample of 3,000 AARP members in Massachusetts age 50 and older. The general population random sample yielded a response from 755 people

(a 25% response rate). The AARP random Massachusetts member sample yielded 1,448 responses (a 48% response rate).

8. The term "hospice" (from the same linguistic root as "hospitality") can be traced back to medieval times when it referred to a place of shelter and rest for weary or ill travelers on a long journey. The name was first applied to specialized care for dying patients in 1967 by physician Dame Cicely Saunders, who founded the first modern hospice—St. Christopher's Hospice—in a residential suburb of London.

9. The National Hospice and Palliative Care Organization (NHPCO) is the umbrella organization for organizations that advocate for and promote hospice and palliative care.

10.The increasingly common use of the word "journey" serves to indicate that the last period of one's time on earth is a continuation of a life that has been ongoing. It also signals that terms like victory or failure are not part of the equation. In a battle there is a victor and a vanquished, so this would be an unfortunate metaphor for the management of a terminal illness. In the end, the patient will always "lose the battle" against death and hospice workers and other thoughtful individuals are staying away from such combat vocabulary when they deal with someone with a terminal diagnosis. Death should be seen neither as a personal nor a medical failure when the best possible care has been given.

11. While the attitude and approach to death, dying and bereavement are often similar in Europe and the United States and I have drawn on relevant European writers as well as American, this chapter primarily surveys the situation in the United States.

12. "Death system," a commonly used term, is defined by John Morgan as "the sum total of the persons, places, ideas, traditions, acts, omissions, emotions, and statements that we make or think about death" (12) and by Kastenbaum (2007) as "the interpersonal, sociophysical, and symbolic network through which an individual's relationship to mortality is mediated by society" (104).

REFERENCES

Albom, Mitch. *Tuesdays with Morrie—An Old Man a Young Man and Life's Greatest Lesson.* New York: Doubleday, 1997.

American Academy of Hospice and Palliative Medicine. Position (AAHPM) Statement: Physician-Assisted Death. Approved by Board of Directors February 14, 2007. http://www.aahpm.org/positions/suicide.html.

Ariès, Philippe. *The Hour of Our Death.* Trans. Helen Weaver. Oxford: Oxford University Press, 1981. Orig. L'homme devant la mort. Paris: Editions du Seuil, 1977.

Barreca, Regina, ed. *Sexuality and Death in Victorian Literature.* Bloomington: Indiana University Press, 1990.

Becker, Ernest. *The Denial of Death.* New York: Simon and Schuster, 1973.

Bendle, Mervyn. "The Contemporary Episteme of Death." *Cultural Values* 5, no. 13 (July 2001): 349–67.

Blauner, Robert. "Review of *Death, Grief, and Mourning.* Geoffrey Gorer. London: The Cresset Press, 1965." *Psychoanalytical Review.* 1968, 55:521–522.

Bloch, Maurice, and Jonathan Parry. *Death and the Regeneration of Life.* Cambridge: Cambridge University Press, 1982.

Bognar, Steven and Julia Reichert. *A Lion in the House.* An independent film premiered on PBS, June 21 and 22, 2006.

Borkenau, Franz. "The Concept of Death." Orig. in *The Twentieth Century*, April 1955. Reprinted in Robert Lester Fulton, ed., *Death and Identity*. New York: John Whiley & Co, 1965, 42–56.

Braun, Kathryn L., James H. Pietsch and Patricia L. Blanchette (eds.). *Cultural Issues in End-of-Life Decision Making*. Thousand Oaks, CA: Sage, 2000.

Braun, Kathryn L., and Reiko Kayashima. "Death Education in Churches and Temples: Engaging Religious Leaders in the Development of Educational Strategies." In Brian de Vries, ed., *End of Life Issues—Interdisciplinary and Multidimensional Perspectives*. (Springer Series on Death and Suicide.) New York: Springer, 1999.

Bregman, Lucy. *Beyond Silence and Denial: Death and Dying Reconsidered*. Louisville, Ky.: Westminster John Knox Press, 1999.

Bronfen, Elisabeth. *Over Her Dead Body—Death, Femininity and the Aesthetic*. New York: Routledge, 1992.

Brown, Guy. *The Living End—The Future of Death, Aging and Immortality*. New York: MacMillan, 2008.

Buchwald, Art. *Too Soon to Say Goodbye*. New York: Random House, 2006.

Burt, Robert A. *Death Is That Man Taking Names: Intersections of American Medicine, Law, and Culture*. Berkeley: University of California Press, 2002.

Byock, Ira. *Dying Well—Peace and Possibility at the End of Life*. New York: Riverhead Books, 1997.

Byock, Ira. *The Four Things That Matter Most—A Book about Living*. New York: Free Press, 2004.

Callahan, Daniel. *The Tyranny of Survival and Other Pathologies of Civilized Life*. New York: MacMillan, 1973.

Choron, Jacques. *Death and Western Thought*. New York: Macmillan, 1963.

Cloud, John. "A Kinder, Gentler Death." *Time*. Time Inc. September 18, 2000.

Cullen, Lisa Takeuchi. *Remember Me—A Lively Tour of the New American Way of Death*. New York: HarperCollins, 2006.

Cummins, Rachelle. *End of Life Care Survey: African American Members*. AARP North Carolina. Washington, D.C.: AARP Knowledge Management, 2003.

Daniels, Stephen R. "The Consequences of Childhood Overweight and Obesity." Special issue, *The Future of Children, Childhood Obesity* 16, no. 1 (Spring 2006): 47–67.

DeSpelder, Lynne Ann and Albert Lee Strickland *The Last Dance—Encountering Death and Dying*. New York: McGraw-Hill, 2005.

Didion, Joan. *The Year of Magical Thinking*. New York: Alfred. A. Knopf, 2005.

Edelstein, E. L., Donald L. Nathanson, and Andrew M. Stone. Denial—A Clarification of Concepts and Research. New York: Plenum Press, 1989.

Faust, Drew Gilpin. *This Republic of Suffering—Death and the American Civil War*. New York: Alfred A. Knopf, 2008.

Feifel, Herman, ed. *The Meaning of Death*. New York: McGraw-Hill, 1959.

Feifel, Herman, ed. *New Meanings of Death*. New York: McGraw-Hill, 1977.

Field, Marilyn J. and Christine Cassel, (eds). *Approaching Death: Improving Care at the End of Life*. Washington: Institute of Medicine's Committee on the Care at the End of Life, 1997.

Fins, Joseph J. *A Palliative Ethic of Care—Clinical Wisdom at Life's End*. Sudbury, Mass.: Jones and Bartlett, 2006.

Foucault, Michel. *Les mots et les choses*, Paris: Gallimard, 1966 (The Order of Things, New York: Vintage, 1973).

Fromm, Erich. *To Have or to Be?* New York: Harper & Row, 1976.

Fry, Prem S. "The Sociocultural Meaning of Dying with Dignity: An Exploratory Study of the Perceptions of a Group of Asian Elderly Persons." In Brian de Vries, ed., *End of Life Issues—Interdisciplinary and Multidimensional Perspectives.* (Springer Series on Death and Suicide.) New York: Springer, 1999.

Fulton, Robert Lester, ed. *Death and Identity.* New York: John Whiley & Co, 1965.

Funk, Raine. *The Essential Fromm, Life between Having and Being.* New York: Continuum, 1995.

Stewart, Garrett. *Death Sentences: Styles of Dying in British Fiction.* Cambridge: Harvard University Press, 1984.

Gallup. "External Destinations: Americans Believe in Heaven and Hell. *GPNS Commentary.* http://www.gallup.com/poll/11770/Eternal-Destinations-Americans-Believe-Heaven-Hell.aspx.

Giddens, Anthony. *The Consequences of Modernity.* Stanford, Calif.: Stanford University Press, 1990.

Gilbert, Sandra M. *Death's Door—Modern Dying and the Ways We Grieve.* New York: W. W. Norton, 2006.

Goodwin, Sarah Webster, and Elisabeth Bronfen, eds. *Death and Representation.* Baltimore: Johns Hopkins University Press, 1993.

Gorer, Geoffrey. "Introduction to the American Edition." *Death, Grief and Mourning.* Paperback Edition. Garden City, N.Y.: Doubleday-Anchor, 1967, ix–xiv.

Gorer, Geoffrey. "The Pornography of Death." 1955. Reprinted in *Death, Grief, and Mourning in Contemporary Britain.* Geoffrey Gorer, ed. London: The Cresset Press, 1965. U.S. edition: *Death, Grief, and Mourning.* Garden City, N.Y.: Doubleday, 1965. Paperback Edition. Garden City, N.Y.: Doubleday-Anchor, 1967, 192–199.

Grieco, Elizabeth M. and Rachel Cassidy. Overview of Race and Hispanic Origin. Census 2000 Brief. C2KBR/01-1. Issued March 2001.

Harris, Mark. *Grave Matters: A Journey through the Modern Funeral Industry to a Natural Way of Burial.* New York: Scribner, 2007.

Humphry, Derek and Mary Clement. *Freedom to Die—People, Politics and the Right-to-Die Movement.* New York: St. Martin's Press, 2000.

Huntington, Richard, and Peter Metcalf. *Celebrations of Death: The Anthropology of Mortuary Ritual.* Cambridge: Cambridge University Press, 1979.

Jankélévitch, Vladimir. *La Mort.* Paris: Flammarion, 1966.

Johnson, Christopher Jay, and Marsha G. McGee, eds. *How Different Religions View Death and the Afterlife.* 2nd ed. Philadelphia: Charles Press, 1998.

Kastenbaum, Robert J. *Death, Society, and Human Experience.* Boston: Pearson, 2007 and 2004.

Kastenbaum, Robert J. *The Psychology of Death.* 3rd ed. New York: Springer, 2000.

Kaufman, Sharon R. . . . *And a Time to Die—How American Hospitals Shape the End of Life.* New York: Scribner, 2005.

Kessler, David. *The Needs of the Dying—A Guide for Bringing Hope, Comfort, and Love to Life's Final Chapter [sic].* New York: HarperCollins, 2000; earlier edition: The Rights of the Dying. New York: HarperCollins, 1997.

Kübler-Ross, Elisabeth. *On Death and Dying.* New York: Macmillan, 1969.

La Rochefoucauld. *Maximes 26, Oeuvres.* Paris: Pléiade, 1957.

Levine, Stephen. *A Year to Live. How to Live This Year as if It Were Your Last.* New York: Bell Tower, 1997.

Lifton, Robert Jay. *The Broken Connection—On Death and the Continuity of Life.* New York: Simon and Schuster, 1979.

Lipson, J. G., S. L. Dibble, and P. A. Minarik. *Culture and Nursing Care: A Pocket Guide. San Francisco.* San Francisco: University of California Press, 1996.

Lopata, Helena Znaniecka. "Grief and the Self-Concept." In Brian de Vries, ed., *End of Life Issues—Interdisciplinary and Multidimensional Perspectives.* (Springer Series on Death and Suicide.) New York: Springer, 1999.

Lynn, Joanne. *Sick to Death and Not Going to Take It Anymore.* Berkeley: University of California Press, 2004.

Lynn, Joanne, Joan Harrold and The Center to Improve Care of the Dying. *Handbook for Mortals: Guidance for People Facing Serious Illness.* New York: Oxford University Press, 1999.

Massachusetts Commission on End of Life Care Survey Project. Executive Summary. September 2005, http://www.endoflifecommission.org/download/Executive_Summary_Key_Findings_2005.pdf.

McDannell, Colleen, and Bernhard Lang. *Heaven—A History.* New Haven, Conn.: Yale University Press, 1988.

McKhann, Charles F. *A Time to Die—The Place for Physician Assistance.* New Haven, Conn.: Yale University Press, 1999.

McManners, John. *Death and the Enlightenment.* Oxford: Oxford University Press, 1981.

Merriam Webster's Online Dictionary. "Postmodern." Available at http://www.merriam-webster.com/dictionary/postmodern.

Mims, Cedric. *When We Die—The Science, Culture, and Rituals of Death.* New York: St Martin's Press, 2000; first published in the UK as When We Die: What Becomes of the Body. London: Robinson, 1998.

Mitford, Jessica. *The American Way of Death.* New York: Simon and Schuster, 1963.

Moller, David Wendell. Life's End: Technocratic Dying in an Age of Spiritual Yearning. Amityville, N.Y.: Baywood, 2000.

Morgan, John. "Living Our Dying and Our Grieving: Historical and Cultural Attitudes." In J. D. Morgan, ed., *Readings in Thanatology.* Amityville, N.Y.: Baywood, 1997.

Morin, Edgar. *L'homme et la mort.* Paris: Seuil, 1951.

Mouton, Charles P. "Cultural and Religious Issues for African Americans." In Kathryn L. Braun, James H. Pietsch, and Patricia L. Blanchette, eds., *Cultural Issues in End-of-Life Decision Making.* Thousand Oaks, Calif.: Sage, 2000.

Moyers, Bill. *On Our Own Terms: Moyers on Dying.* Produced by Public Affairs Television, Inc. and presented on PBS by Thirteen/WNET New York. Broadcast September 10–13, 2004.

National Center for Health Statistics. U.S. Department of Health and Human Services. *National Vital Statistics Reports,* Vol. 52, No. 14, February 18, 2004.

National Center for Health Statistics. U.S. Department of Health and Human Services. *National Vital Statistics Reports,* Vol. 56, No. 10, April 24, 2008.

National Hospice and Palliative Care Organization. "History of Hospice Care." http://www.nhpco.org/i4a/pages/index.cfm?pageid=3285&openpage=3285. National Hospice and Palliative Care Organization, Patient and Family Centered Care. http://www.nhpco.org/i4a/pages/index.cfm?pageid=4894.

National Reference Center for Bioethics Literature. Georgetown University. *Bibliography of Bioethics*. Vol. 34, Washington, D.C.: Kennedy Institute of Ethics, 2008, http://bioethics.georgetown.edu/publications/biobib/.

Nebraska Coalition for Compassionate Care. Nebraska End of Life Survey Report. 2004. Available at http//www.nebrccc.org/end_of_life_survey_report.htm.

Nuland, Sherwin. *How We Die—Reflections of Life's Last Chapters.* New York: Alfred A. Knopf, 1993.

Oken D. "What to Tell Cancer Patients." *Journal of American Medical Association.* 175 (1961): 1120–1128.

One community at a time. Rallying Points 2nd National Conference. Boston Park Plaza Hotel. Boston, Mass., November 16–18, 2003.

Panofsky, Erwin. *Tomb Sculpture: Four Lectures on Its Changing Aspect from Ancient Egypt to Bernini.* New York: Harry N. Abrams [1924].

Pausch, Randy and Jeffrey Zaslow. *The Last Lecture.* New York: Hyperion, 2008.

Roberts, Barbara K. *Death without Denial; Grief without Apology: A Guide for Facing Death and Loss.* Troutdale, OR: NewSage Press, 2002.

Saunders, Mary Anne. *Nearing Death Awareness—A Guide to the Language, Visions, and Dreams of the Dying.* London: Jessica Kingsley, 2008.

Schleifer, Ronald. *Rhetoric of Death: The Language of Modernism and Postmodern Discourse Theory.* Urbana: University of Illinois Press, 1990.

Science Encyclopedia. History of Ideas. Structuralism–Poststructuralism. http://science.jrank.org/pages/11349/Structuralism-Poststructuralism-Poststructuralism.html.

Servaty, Herbert L, and Bert Hayslip Jr. "The Communication Apprehension Regarding the Dying Scale: A Factor Analytical Study. In Brian de Vries, ed., *End of Life Issues—Interdisciplinary and Multidimensional Perspectives.* (Springer Series on Death and Suicide.) New York: Springer, 1999.

Silberman, Susan L., collector of data. 2003 Minnesota Advance Directives Survey. Data Collected by Minnesota Center for Survey Research. Washington, D.C.: AARP. Knowledge Management, 2004.

Stannard, David E. *The Puritan Way of Death: A Study in Religion, Culture and Social Change.* Philadelphia: University of Pennsylvania Press, 1975.

Starhawk, M. Macha Nightmare and The Reclaiming Collective. *The Pagan Book of Living and Dying. Practical Rituals, Prayers, Blessings and Meditations on Crossing Over.* San Francisco: Harper, 1997.

Staudt, Christina. *Picturing the Dead and Dying in Nineteenth-Century* "L'Illustration." Ann Arbor, Mich.: Bell & Howell, 2001.

Stein, Arnold. *The House of Death: Messages from the English Renaissance.* Baltimore: Johns Hopkins University Press, 1986.

Talamantes, Melissa A., Celina Gomez, and Kathryn L. Braun. "Advance Directives and End-of-Life Care: The Hispanic Perspective." In Kathryn L. Braun, James H. Pietsch, and Patricia L. Blanchette, eds., *Cultural Issues in End-of-Life Decision Making.* Thousand Oaks, Calif.: Sage, 2000.

Tobin, Daniel R. with Karen Lindsey. *Peaceful Dying—The Step-by-Step Guide to Preserving Your Dignity, Your Choice, and Your Inner Peace at the End of Life.* Reading, MA: Perseus Books, 1999.

Toynbee, Arnold J. *Man's Concern with Death.* London: Hodder & Stoughton, 1968.

Toynbee, Jocelyn M. C. *Death and Burial in the Roman World.* Baltimore: Johns Hopkins University Press, 1971.

Van Winkle, Nancy Westlake. "End-of-Life Decision Making in American Indian and Alaska Native Cultures." In Kathryn L. Braun, James H. Pietsch, and Patricia L. Blanchette, eds., *Cultural Issues in End-of-Life Decision Making.* Thousand Oaks, Calif.: Sage, 2000.

Vaucher, Andrea R. *Muses from Chaos and Ash: Aids, Artists, and Art.* New York: Grove Press, 1993.

Vovelle, Michel. *Ideologies and Mentalities.* Trans. Eamon O'Flaherty. Chicago: University of Chicago Press, 1990.

Walter, Tony. *The Revival of Death.* London: Routledge, 1993.

Warnock, Mary, and Elisabeth Macdonald. *Easeful Death—Is There a Case for Assisted Dying?* Oxford: Oxford University Press, 2008.

Whaley, Joachim, ed. *Mirrors of Mortality: Studies in the Social History of Death.* New York: St. Martin's Press, 1981.

White, Diana, L. "Grandparents' Participation in Bereavement." In Brian de Vries, ed., *End of Life Issues—Interdisciplinary and Multidimensional Perspectives.* (Springer Series on Death and Suicide.) New York: Springer, 1999.

White, Edmund. "Journals of the Plague Years." *The Nation,* May 12, 1997, 13–18.

Yeo, Gwen, and Nancy Hikoyeda. "Cultural Issues in End-of-Life Decision Making among Asians and Pacific Islanders in the United States." In Kathryn L. Braun, James H. Pietsch, and Patricia L. Blanchette eds., *Cultural Issues in End-of-Life Decision Making.* Thousand Oaks, Calif.: Sage, 2000.

CHAPTER 2

Cancer Patients Facing Death: Is the Patient Who Focuses on Living in Denial of His/Her Death?

Sherry R. Schachter

A diagnosis of cancer affects the entire family structure, not just the patient, and no family emerges from the experience unchanged (Beck-Friis & Strang, 1993; Davies, Cherkryn, Brown, & Martens, 1995; Fitch, 1994; Kristjanson & Ashcroft, 1994). In order to determine how the dying process affects patients and their family caregivers and contributes to bereavement outcomes, one must identify the patients' and the family caregivers' coping styles. The coping mechanisms that are utilized by the patient and family during this time of crisis will ultimately affect the bereavement process after the death. How individuals with end-stage cancer, as well as other chronic debilitating illnesses, view and incorporate their impending death is an important factor in helping clinicians design therapeutic models of care for both the patient and the family. It is pivotal that health professionals seek an understanding of the concerns of the patient and the family caregiver and that s/he deal honestly with them (Schachter & Coyle, 1998).

Cancer has been called a family illness because it devastates the entire family, often disrupting familial relationships and cohesion (Alexander, 1993). A review of the literature reveals conflicting findings (Schachter, 1999) with contradictory views as to whether the diagnosis of cancer actually brings families closer together, or, conversely, that the numerous acknowledged stressors can be so great that the diagnosis of cancer actually contributes to the distancing of family members (Kristjanson & Ashcroft, 1994; Rait & Lederberg, 1990). The dynamic, fluid relationship between the cancer patient and his or her family contributes to the stresses imposed on the family structure (Fitch, 1994; Kristjanson & Ashcroft, 1994; Schachter & Holland,

1995). Typically, family caregivers prioritize the patient's needs as more important than their own (Kristjanson, 1989). Therefore, it is important for clinicians to know and understand exactly how the family is coping. Reinforcement of the knowledge that there is no "one right way" and no "one right place" to die begins the discussion around end-of-life palliative care (Schachter & Coyle, 1998), wherever that care is delivered (e.g., home, hospital, hospice, nursing home, or other facility). Clear, concise, and open communication is a potent tool in initiating and later maintaining effective interventions for end-of-life care (Schachter and Coyle, 1998). At times these interventions can, for some individuals, facilitate spiritual and emotional growth. However, problems often arise when the dying patient or family caregivers fail to appreciate the significance of having a poor prognosis, are thought to be in denial, and insist on maintaining unrealistic hopes for a cure. For physicians and other health care professionals this can be a frustrating and problematic period, since the dialogue between patients, family caregivers, and themselves is challenging. However, one questions whether this is an attempt on the part of the patient and/or family to maintain a hopeful attitude or whether it is truly denial.

As an oncology clinician with over 26 years of experience working at Memorial Sloan-Kettering Cancer Center and Calvary Hospital, both in New York City I have been taken aback by the responses of bereaved family members, who often report that they never realized their loved one was dying. A common theme in many of my bereavement groups tends to focus around the perception that the patient and or the family did not realize that death was imminent. From the perspective of the bereaved family member, maintaining hope was so important to them as well as for their dying loved one that they would not allow themselves to think about preparing for death (i.e. saying goodbye, talking about things that were important, completing unfinished business, etc.). Afterwards, when they reflected back they would often wish they had taken time to have meaningful end-of-life discussions and do what was important for them. These situations often impacted and limited the way in which family members communicated with one another or with the physician. The mere fact that patients suspect (or have even been told) that they have a life-threatening illness or that their disease has progressed doesn't mean that patients or families give up hope and "accept" the impending death. There is often a disconnect between what people have (or have not) been told, what they believe, and how they incorporate that information. What individuals hope for and how they express that hope constitute a unique and multifaceted process (Dean, 2002). This chapter addresses this complex phenomenon, by reviewing the literature on hope and denial, and by utilizing relevant quotes from patients, their families, and the professional staff (physicians and nurses) caring for them to illustrate the points that are made.

DOCTORS THINK

"I've told him he is dying and he doesn't want to talk about it. Either he doesn't understand or he must be in denial."

"Why can't she [this patient] accept that there is nothing more we can do for her?—she must be in denial."

"We had a family meeting to discuss DNR [Do Not Resuscitate] and end-of-life care orders—but the family is still talking about getting blood transfusions and undergoing more chemotherapy. Don't they understand/accept that their father is dying?"

"This patient is so frustrating for me and the staff. It's gotten to the point where we don't want to enter his hospital room. We keep trying to get him to face his death, which will probably be in four to six months, and he keeps talking about taking a trip to Europe. Doesn't he understand what we're telling him? Why won't he face the fact that he is going to die and needs to get his affairs in order?"

"I really like this patient. She is so young—young enough to be my wife or my sister. I don't want to discuss hospice or palliation with her because I don't want her to feel that I'm giving up on her. I can't destroy her hope."

"My residents think this patient has some dementia. She doesn't seem to understand what they keep telling her. Over and over they tell her that her husband is dying—he's not going to wake up from this coma. The patient's wife acts like we've never told her this. Every time we tell her it's as if she's hearing it for the first time."

PATIENTS SAY

Mary, 50 years old, couldn't bear the thought of not seeing the birth of her first grandchild. "Isn't there something else you can do? I'll try anything. Please don't give up on me. I have so much more to do and see."

Robert, 81 years old, couldn't understand his physician's reluctance to treat his liver cancer. "Why can't I go on that Phase I protocol I've heard about? I'm willing to try anything to give it a shot."

Bruce, a 64-year-old engineer dying of prostate cancer, kept insisting: "I'm not in denial. I know I'm dying but I have to remain hopeful. . . .

In order to go on, I need hope; either real hope or false hope. The doctor says it [the radiation treatment] has a good chance of working. I was feeling more positive after he said that."

Eileen, a 52-year-old housewife dying of lung cancer, insisted she wasn't in denial: "I'm not in denial. I just want to focus on my living, not my dying."

Penny was a 43-year-old woman dying of lung cancer. She would often stress the importance of maintaining hope. Penny believed that as long as she remained hopeful and positive she would continue to live. If she stopped any treatment (chemotherapy or radiation) that would indicate that she was quitting and giving up. Penny believed that the continuation of hope was not quitting: "It's doing all you can for as long as you can. It's taking control and deciding for oneself."

As a way of helping patients continue their fight and as a mechanism for maintaining hope, patients and family caregivers often pursue alternative therapies. As one patient explained, "Seeking alternative treatment is not quitting and doesn't mean I'm in denial. I know I'm dying. But it doesn't hurt to try." A 59-year-old man dying of pancreatic cancer was waiting and praying for a miracle; he was eager to try anything. When his physician refused to give him more chemotherapy, the patient sought out several alternative therapies. "I'll try herbal teas, special diets, vitamins; anything at all. I'm even going on the macrobiotic diet."

Ellen was a 32-year-old woman dying of gastric cancer. She was clearly deteriorating and her prognosis was grave. She cried with relief when her doctors informed her: "We can't promise you any miracles. But we'll try to drain off some of the fluid, which will hopefully give you a chance to take some more chemotherapy." Ellen was overcome with relief and cried, saying: "Thank you. Thank you for at least trying."

After visiting his oncologist, Charles, a 68-year-old with prostate cancer, said: "I'm more hopeful today than last month. Being in limbo medically is very hard for me. I can't stand it. If something is being done I'm more in control of it. Since I've started palliative radiation I feel better. Oh I know the effects of radiation won't be seen for three months, but emotionally I feel better 'cause I'm doing something. Longevity runs in my family and I should have 20 more good years before I die."

FAMILIES BELIEVE

Reflecting back on the death of his young 36-year-old wife, Lenny said: "I'm angry with her doctors. What was the sense of telling my wife she was dying? She couldn't do anything about it anyway. She couldn't get up out of the hospital or even out of her bed and do things; she couldn't enjoy herself. It's not as if she could get to the movies or go out to dinner."

"There was no way I could entertain the thought of my wife dying. She was my war bride; we were together for 68 years. We did everything together. Since I came back from the war we've never been apart. We all had to maintain hope and never talked about her dying."

Maria reflected on the death of her partner: "I was always so enthusiastic about hope and the future. And I was there for him, but I knew in my heart that he was going to die. But my feeling at that point was that I had to be hopeful for him until he died, because I didn't understand that you could be hopeful even when you decide to die. All I knew at that point was that he had to be hopeful and for as long as possible he had to keep his spirits high to have a fine quality of life. I equated that with hope."

Thomas felt the need to remain hopeful for his wife of 62 years. "I had to remain hopeful for her and for our children and grandchildren. I couldn't allow myself to think that she was not going to make it. It was too painful for me to think about her not being here for me after all these years."

Two adult daughters, whose father had died from leukemia, reflected on his last hospitalization: "Our hope was taken away when the doctors were talking down to my father; demoralizing him." The daughters described their difficulty in trying to discuss discharge plans in their father's hospital room. They felt his nurses and physicians were insensitive, talking about diapers; managing their father's incontinence was painful to them as they tried to maintain hope, not only for the sake of their dying father but for their elderly mother as well.

George, 61 years old, now describes his feelings of guilt for not doing enough for his wife of 28 years: "I was always the protector. That was my role in our family. My wife kept looking at me, asking if she were going to make it. How could I tell her otherwise? 'Of course you will,' I told her repeatedly from the time she was diagnosed with stomach cancer until the day before she died. It was important for me to maintain hope for her. I knew she was afraid to die."

WHAT IS HOPE?

There is no universal definition of hope (Farran, Kerth, & Popovick, 1995). Hegarty (2001) notes that hope is a process rather than a specific state to be attained (p. 42); it's a mysterious, intangible (Weisman, 1979), and elusive concept (Farran et al., 1995). Hope can be seen when individuals remain optimistic about the future; with the expectation that the object of one's hope can be achieved if one is motivated (Morgante, 2000). The concept of hope is intertwined with and inseparable from faith (Fromm, 1968) and can be viewed as the positive expectation for meaning attached to life events (Parker-Oliver, 2002).

Good coping skills, regardless of the patient's prognosis, are dependent on past successful experiences. Resourceful people are not restricted in their choices and have ample strategies upon which to draw. Coping requires that the individual should recognize a problem and find appropriate methods to deal with that problem. Good coping skills mean that the individual has good solutions for current problems and the resources for addressing unexpected future problems (Weisman, 1979).

A small study of dying cancer patients noted that hope could be influenced by several factors including the progression of the disease and its treatment, and the influence of friends, family members, and health care professionals (Flemming, 1997). There are several characteristics associated with maintaining a hopeful attitude, including fostering one's self-esteem (Morgante, 2000), encouraging one's feelings of self-competence, and believing that one can maintain some control of one's life (Flemming, 1997; Hegarty, 2001; Post-White et al., 1996; Winterling, Wasteson, Glimelius, Sjoden, & Nordin, 2004).

Individuals' ability to project themselves into the future and be hopeful about their situation can be interpreted by some as wishing or "magical thinking." Irion (2002) describes the differences between magical thinking and maintaining hope: "Hope…may be seen as different from wishing. To wish for something to be different is a passive emotion and tends to lead toward wanting someone to effect a magical solution. Hope, on the other hand, is a goal-directed vision that enables one to live effectively in the present and move trustingly toward future possibilities" (quoted by Dobihal & Stewart, 1984, p. 984).

One could argue that since the emphasis on hope is directed toward the future, it may be of limited usefulness with terminally ill patients (Nekolaichuk & Bruera, 1998; Rousseau, 2000) and perhaps even of no use at all. Cassell (1976) has written of the notion that for the dying person time stands still, while it continues to march forward for everyone else. Cassell (1991) notes that we all perceive ourselves as having a future and describes hope as one of the necessary traits for the achievement of a successful life. In order to understand the complexity of maintaining hope, clinicians need to acknowledge the dynamic and fluid manner in which hope changes over time, especially during the dying process. While the dying patient may no longer be able to hope for a cure, their focus can change to hoping for better symptom and pain control or the preservation of the quality of their remaining life (Winterling et al., 2004). Hope can be attached to the meaning that the dying person ascribes to his or her life, as well as to the various ways the person wishes to be remembered.

SYMBOLIC IMMORTALITY

When people are dying they often find comfort by maintaining hope and focusing on their living. According to Lifton (1974, 1979), faced with the inevitability of death, healthy individuals seek a sense of life continuity or immortality by finding symbolic ways to continue that which was valuable in their lives. Lifton's construct of symbolic immortality was initially developed as an attempt to provide a deeper psychological understanding of the ways in which survivors of the Holocaust, Hiroshima, and Vietnam confronted the

terror of death. Symbolic immortality encompasses several modes linking us
to those who have died before us and those who will live on and remember us
after we have died (Lifton, 1979). Several modes or spheres have been identified by Lifton.

Biological immortality is the belief that one lives on in one's children and
grandchildren, always preserving our connection to others. Dick, a young
38-year-old dying of sarcoma, lamented: "You know that's why God never
had me marry or have children. He knew it would end like this. I don't think
I'm being punished—but I think God knew. Could you imagine if I were
dying and leaving a wife and young children? That would be even sadder.
But since I have no siblings there is no one to carry on our family's name. It
all ends with me."

Communal immortality exists when one lives on in his/her community.
As long as stories of the deceased are told and shared within the family
or the greater community, (e.g., one's church, synagogue, workplace, or
social club) the deceased will live on in the memory of that community.
Before Isabella died, she often talked about the importance of rituals and
leaving stories that her children and grandchildren would remember. The
summer before her death she said: "the family is coming over this weekend to make ice cream. I got a machine and my oldest son has a machine
so we can do two ice creams at once. My youngest son was saying he's
not going to get an ice cream machine 'cause how many times do you do
it—once a year? But I said some things you do because you have wonderful memories...and it doesn't matter if it's once a year, or more than once
a year. You remember licking the dasher from childhood and it gives you
pleasure now; what difference does it make how often you did it? I'm hoping that they will be telling this story for years to come." Just weeks before
Isabella's death she recalled: "You know, all you leave behind when you die
is an imprint in people's minds that they can recall when something evokes
it. I would like my granddaughter to have memories of grandma playing
with her and of course, making homemade ice cream."

Creative immortality is the belief that individuals live on, albeit symbolically, in their creative skills (e.g., a published book or one's handiwork). A
handmade quilt can be passed down from generation to generation. Another
form of creative immortality, one that is often not recognized, is the deep
interpersonal relationships that are fostered with others, for example, the
relationship between mother and child or between teacher and student. Gary
was a professor and author. Before his death from multiple myeloma, he reflected on his life as a teacher and his hope that he would be remembered.
Just days before his death, Gary was able to arrange for the making of a
home video in which he described his experiences as a patient and focused
on his first-hand observations of the problematic communication skills of
the medical team caring for him. Gary made this video specifically to be used

as a teaching tool for young medical students. At his funeral, several of his colleagues described his love of teaching, and his former students talked about the difference he had made in their careers and lives.

Medical immortality exists when the deceased has made provisions for his/her organs to be donated and transplanted into others. One's life may have ended but the heart, lungs, cornea, and other organs can live on in someone else.

Another mode of symbolic immortality is the expression of *theological or religious* imagery. Practically every religion contains the concept of life after death (Husebo, 1997). The quest to get beyond the inevitability of one's death through belief in a heaven and an afterlife contributes to one's sense of spiritual immorality. Although hope in an afterlife may become a source of peace and serenity (Wren, Levinson, & Papadatou, 1996) for some, others, who are nonbelievers, may not find the concept of an afterlife comforting. Instead, perhaps, these individuals have a need to deny their impending death and continue to focus on remaining hopeful.

The concepts encompassed by symbolic immortality can provide individuals with a mechanism through which they can achieve a sense of control and, in some way, mastery over death. Loss of control or a sense of helplessness can be tied in with feelings of uselessness and hopelessness. At times, patients communicate that they are not able to cope with the fact that they are about to die. Husebo (1997) suggests that alternative strategies are needed in order to be able to preserve individuals' dignity.

Clinicians need to listen to their patients; not only to what they are verbally saying but also to what they're not saying. Weisman (1979) notes that individual growth and openness develop according to the individual's timetable, not that of the clinicians. Recognizing and respecting the individual's values and beliefs, as well as past history, can help provide clinicians with further assistance and understanding and thus facilitate the support that the patient needs and desires. The importance of hope can not be understated at the end of life, and since hope is linked with meaning, the provision of a sense of meaning and continuation for patients is something clinicians can and should offer. Physicians and other health care professionals can acknowledge the specialness of their dying patient, suggesting that the patient is extraordinary and will be remembered. This provision of a lasting legacy can provide hope for the dying patient that she will be remembered by others.

THE CHANGING FACE OF HOPE

Although hopefulness remains, what people wish for often changes over time (Dean, 2002; Winterling et al., 2004). For example, people can hope that their financial affairs are put in order or that they can enjoy a specific event or celebration. Conversely, a small longitudinal study of dying cancer patients (Herth, 1990) found that as individuals neared death, their descriptions of what they hoped for did not change and their level of hope remained stable (Post-White et al., 1996).

In a phenomenological study of 19 dying patients and their family care-givers, Schachter (1999) described the importance for dying patients and families who viewed not quitting as an important component of maintaining hope. One patient said: "Maintaining hope is very important. Sometimes you have to take control and tell the doctor what YOU want to do—not just what he wants you to do. You have to be in control" (Schachter, 1999 personal correspondence). As a way of helping individuals continue their fight, and as a mechanism for maintaining hope, patients and family caregivers often pursued alternative therapies. As one patient put it, "seeking out and exploring alternative treatment does not mean that I'm quitting and it doesn't mean I'm in denial. I know I'm dying but it doesn't hurt to try. "I don't have a lot of energy so I need to focus on my living not my dying." (Schachter, 1999, p. 194).

It's easier to remain hopeful when things are going well, but periods of hopelessness can accelerate when individuals are faced with cumulative losses (Irion, 2002). One 49 year old woman with a 13 year old daughter was willing to do anything to stay alive no matter what the cost of her quality of life: "My first priority is to be alive no matter how I do it. Even if I have to live in a wheel chair for the rest of my life I want it...I would do anything to live. (Schachter, 1999, p 125). This patient believed that her positive mental attitude contributed towards fighting her disease and hoped it would ultimately save her. "The news is not good. My MRI shows more lesions...I'm more hopeful today than last week. Being in limbo medically is very hard for me. I can't stand it. If something is being done I'm more in control of it. Since I've started [palliative] radiation I feel better. Oh I know the effects of radiation won't be seen for three months but emotionally I feel better. I know I'm doing something." (Schachter, 1999, p 191).

However we define it, hope is essential for life itself" (Christopher, 1999, p. 5) and is a critical element for coping with illness and maintaining quality of life (Herth, 1990; Owen, 1989; Skevington, Macarthur, & Somerset, 1997; Stoner & Keampfer, 1985). Several disciplines, including philosophy, nursing, theology, and psychology as well as medicine, agree that hope, in some form, is vital for both the individual's mental health and his/her general well-being (Christopher, 1999).

FRANKL: FINDING MEANING

In *Man's Search for Meaning*, Viktor Frankl (1946/1984), the Austrian psychiatrist who survived several Nazi concentration camps, has greatly contributed to our current understanding of suffering and survival. His journals and numerous books (totaling 32) have formulated the basis of logotherapy—the therapy of meaning. Frankl described his experiences as a survivor of Auschwitz and maintained that those prisoners who were unable to create meaning, psychologically gave up hope, and became apathetic and lost faith, did not survive the concentration camps. Prisoners who survived did so because they maintained hope or wanted an opportunity to complete their life's work (Christopher, 1999). Prisoners who survived defined hope as a spiritual freedom, one that could not be taken away. Frankl maintained that physical discomfort (e.g., pain) and deprivation alone, no matter how extreme or severe, does not cause suffering. The true cause of human suffering, Frankl says, stems from the loss of meaning in one's life. Meaning, Frankl believed, is irrespective of one's age, sex, educational background, intelligence, or religion. Frankl used his early experiences to illustrate the importance of meaning as a basic drive in human psychology (Breitbart, 2002) as human beings seek for a sense of meaning or purpose in their life as well as in their death. We don't have the freedom to prevent death, but we do have the freedom to choose our attitude. Meaning can be found not only in hopes for the future but also in the joys of the past as well as the present. Life has meaning, Frankl believed, and never ceases to have meaning.

HOPE EQUALS CURE

Studies of hope indicate that health care professionals often equate hope with the notion of a "cure" or the "absence of disease" (Carter, McKenna, MacLeod, & Green, 1998; Rousseau, 2000), thereby contributing to their hesitancy in giving bad news for fear of taking hope away from a patient. There is a belief, widely shared by physicians, patients, and family members, that telling the truth about a chronic or terminal illness will "rob" them of hope (Christopher, 1999; MacLeod & Carter, 1999; Wenrich et al., 2001).

Carter and colleagues (1998) analyzed the responses of 317 New Zealand health professionals working in hospitals, hospice programs, and the community. They found that health care professionals frequently had difficulty conveying hope to patients with severe disabling disorders (e.g., those with motor neuron disease), and that conveying a sense of hope to patients suffering from diseases with no chance of remission was even more difficult.

Another study, conducted in Boston at Brigham and Women's Hospital and the Dana Farber Cancer Institute (Lee, Fairclough, Antin, & Woods, 2001), looked at discrepancies between 313 stem cell transplant patients and their physicians. This longitudinal study recorded predictions about cures with and without transplantation. Patients were asked two questions: "What do you think is your chance of being cured with a stem cell transplant?" and "What do you think is your chance of cure without a stem cell transplant?"

A third question, about treatment-related mortality within the first year, was also asked ("What percentage of people do you think die during the transplant hospitalization or from complications within the first year?"). Researchers found that both physicians and patients had accurate expectations when the outcome of stem cell transplantation was likely to be favorable (i.e., when actual mortality was < 30%). However, patients having more advanced disease (i.e., needing allogeneic transplantation for intermediate or advanced disease, where mortality was > 30%) often didn't fully appreciate their poor clinical situation and the higher risk for them. The expectations of physicians were considerably lower than the expectations of patients, who tended to remain hopeful and optimistic. Similarly, physicians provided lower estimates of disease-free survival in cases of intermediate or advanced disease, while patient expectations remained high and constant regardless of disease stage.

An article by Daniel Goleman in the *New York Times* (Goleman, 1985) reported on a study at London's King's College Hospital. Researchers looked at 57 postoperative women diagnosed with early-stage breast cancer and found that those women who remained hopeful and believed they could conquer their illness had the best results, with 7 out of 10 women still alive 10 years later. Women who had denied their life-threatening illness showed the next best results, with 5 out of 10 women alive 10 years later. Those women who stoically accepted their disease and those who felt hopeless and helpless did the poorest, with most having already died at the time of follow-up.

Lee and her colleagues (2001) acknowledged that when a patient's condition deteriorated and the prognosis worsened, both patients and physicians avoided discussions about end-of-life care and discouraging statistics. Instead, the focus of their discussions/conversations centered on the curative potential of a procedure. Fearing that patients would become distressed and lose hope (Miyaji, 1993; Weeks et al., 1998), physicians tended to withhold or minimize some pertinent information, changing the language they used when communicating with their patients. Does the physician who believes that reporting favorable, but inaccurate, prognoses can improve cancer patients' lives through optimism and hope, and does he or she also believe that reporting unfavorable, albeit accurate, prognoses can compromise the lives of patients (Lamont & Christakis, 1999)? This belief is at least implied by Miyaji's findings (1993) that two-thirds of physicians modify the information given to patients when they think that the truth "will have a seriously bad outcome." Similar studies found that the concept of preserving hope was a central component used in softening the impact when giving patients bad news, even if it meant that the physician withheld information in order to help the patient maintain a positive attitude (Friedrichsen & Strang, 2003).

SOURCES OF HOPE

Herth (1990) described three potential obstacles that hinder or obstruct hope for patients: (1) if the patient feels abandoned and isolated; (2) if the patient's pain is not appropriately managed and remains uncontrolled; and (3) if the patient feels devalued as a person. Along with spiritual beliefs, specific individuals have been identified as being sources for providing hope; these include supportive families, friends, and health care professionals (Rousseau, 2000). Koopmeiners, Post-White, and Gutnecht (1997) described a study of 32 cancer patients, concluding that the communication styles of nurses and physicians could influence not only how the patient received information but also how hope was maintained. Hope was reduced when physicians and nurses were insensitive or disrespectful, while caring-like behavior (e.g., being very friendly and addressing the patient by name) was perceived by patients as enhancing their feelings of hope. Similarly, a small phenomenological study by Flemming (1997) described the positive influence of both physicians and nurses whom cancer patients identified as "being there" and showing an interest in them. Studies have shown that supportive relationships are significant in fostering and maintaining hope, while conversely the withdrawal of these supportive relationships is detrimental to maintaining hope. Supportive relationships are not forged just between patients, family members, and friends. It is not unusual for patients to develop strong positive partnerships with members of their medical team.

Charlotte was a likable single woman in her early 40s when she was diagnosed with colon cancer. Towards the end of her life, she relied on friends to do her shopping and take her to and from treatments. During the two-year course of her treatment she was befriended by her visiting nurse, who would frequently call to "check in" with Charlotte. Unable to eat, Charlotte was receiving nutrition via a feeding tube. The nurse frequently stopped by at the end of her working day to help out either with Charlotte's personal needs or with her medical care. As Charlotte was living alone, one of her fears was that she might fall in her apartment. Frequently the visiting nurse would take the extra time and sit in the apartment so that Charlotte could take a shower. This incredible act of kindness was pivotal in maintaining Charlotte's independence and self-esteem.

The interventions described as engendering hope include, among others, managing symptoms; developing interpersonal connectedness and relationships; having assistance in attaining practical goals; exploring spiritual beliefs; and recalling uplifting memories by participating in a life review (Rousseau, 2000). Ann Marie was a young, single woman dying of lung cancer. Two months before her death, when she was feeling "really down," three of her girlfriends came over her house to "dress her up." It was the middle of a cold winter, but her girlfriends came to her apartment door with their bathing suits under their coats. They put a chair in the shower for Ann Marie to sit on and all climbed in and proceeded to shampoo and set her hair. Ann Marie could barely breathe and was on oxygen at the time, but she told me afterward that having her friends come over and do that for her was like "old times" when they would all joke around and hang out together. She felt very special. It had been a long time since anyone had washed and set her hair or put bright red nail polish on her toes.

LIFE REVIEW

In many cases the most significant challenge for dying persons is the struggle to achieve a sense of meaning. What good have I achieved in this world? What is my legacy? Who will remember me? What will they remember about me? These and other questions of meaning can be addressed by initiating a life review. We live in stories—they are the historical context of our lives, since human beings are fundamentally storytellers (Romanoff & Thompson, 2006). Life review is the process of recalling the events of one's life and evaluating goals, failures, accomplishments, and achievements. The concept was developed by Dr. Robert Butler, who used these counseling techniques as he was working with the elderly. The process encourages people to self-examine and review their life as death approaches. For families and dying patients, this review can facilitate a sense of control as it fosters opportunities to communicate with one another and perhaps even complete unfinished business, depending of course on the patient's physical or cognitive abilities.

There are different formats or styles for initiating a life review. These can include making audio or video tapes (my experience has been that for many dying patients their preference tends to be for audio rather than video); conducting an oral history; journaling; telling family stories; and preparing written or oral ethical wills.

FALSE OPTIMISM

Researchers (The, Hak, Goeter, & van der Wal, 2000) explored factors resulting in "false optimism" with 35 lung cancer patients treated both in an outpatient clinic and at a hospital in the Netherlands. They found that patients who were afraid of receiving a poor prognosis or "bad news" did not ask questions or want precise information. And even if the physician gave them the information, the patients often didn't "hear" the news.

Carol was a 49-year-old married woman with a 13-year-old daughter. After her diagnosis of inoperable lung cancer, she underwent radiation and chemotherapy. Although she was compliant with her medical regime, she asked no questions; she was not ready to die and was willing to do anything to stay alive no matter the cost to her quality of life. "My first priority is to be alive, no matter how I do it. Even if I have to live in a wheelchair for the rest of my life I want it. Yeah, it would be nice if I could be dancing and running around...." (Schachter, 1999, p. 125). Later on she noted: "I keep my appointments and do what I have to, but I never ask my doctor about anything. He continually asks me if I have questions, or if I want to talk about something, but I never do. I need to focus on being positive and maintaining hope" (Schachter, 1999, personal correspondence).

UNREALISTIC HOPE

Maintaining or fostering a sense of false hope can lead individuals to persistent denial of reality, which often promotes poor judgment. "It causes (1) persistent goal oriented behavior toward an unobtainable goal; (2) distraction from necessary activities; and (3) a delay in resolving emotional issues" (Buchholz, 1990, p. 2358). Weisman (1979) also cautioned clinicians not to offer false hope, which contributed to the patient's "chasing rainbows" (p. 26), adding that more problems are solved by awareness and acceptance than by disavowal, avoidance, and denial (p. 43). Michelle was a single mother dying of ovarian cancer. She had three children, all under the age of 10 years. Michelle had a supportive mother who lived out of state, and two single brothers who lived nearby. As her disease progressed, family members, as well as the hospital social workers, tried to get Michelle to appoint a guardian to care for her children. Michelle's religious beliefs were so strong she believed that she wouldn't die and that she herself would be able to raise her children to adulthood. Numerous attempts to convince Michelle of the necessity of appointing a guardian were unsuccessful, and she died without saying goodbye to her children or making long-term provision for them.

Although denial might be seen as reducing immediate distress, it often has a detrimental long-term effect if patients delay seeking medical help from their physicians. Seizing opportunities to improve pain, manage symptoms, respond to fears and concerns, explore unfinished personal business, and deepen the patient-physician relationship (Back, Arnold, and Quill, 2003) is crucial for appropriate and humane end-of-life care.

Harold, aged 77, had been aware of "something being wrong" for over a year, saying that every time he urinated he saw blood. However, he denied the importance of this symptom and never sought medical care. By the time he was diagnosed with bladder cancer, the tumor was inoperable. His denial not only contributed to his inability to receive curative treatment but also left his family angry and with numerous questions to deal with after his death.

Maintaining unrealistic hope can also be counterproductive because it doesn't foster an atmosphere of open communication in which the dying patient and his/her family can openly speak to and support one another. Such denial can obstruct open communications and the completion of life's tasks (Wein, 1996). When the dying patient focuses on unrealistic hope and isn't able to acknowledge the prognosis or impending death, family members may not have sufficient opportunity to prepare for the death. Bereaved survivors are left to deal with their anxieties on their own (Husebo, 1997).

Gabrielle struggled with feelings of guilt after her mother's death. She would frequently focus on the difficulties of living at home with her father and brother, since neither one was able to talk about her mom's illness. Because Gabrielle and her family believed that her mother would survive her cancer, they were never able to face the reality of her worsening condition. Despite the fact that each chemotherapy treatment made her mother very ill and debilitated, they continued "to push" for further treatment. Afterward the family members remained isolated from one another, unable to talk about their shared experiences. In her grief, as an attempt to try and make contact with her deceased mother to talk about unresolved issues, Gabrielle contacted a medium. After several unsuccessful attempts, she aborted this plan and began intensive psychotherapy.

Also problematic for patients maintaining unrealistic hopes for a cure may be their delay in exploring hospice options. If patients cannot accept the terminal nature of their illness, they will not be able to shift their goals from a curative mode to a palliative mode in which they are able to consider hospice as a viable, positive option. Ultimately, they are therefore compromising their own quality of life (Frank, 1995), since they often won't have adequate time to utilize hospice services (Christakis & Escarce, 1996). Studies continue to show the underutilization of hospice services, with 43.5% of hospice patients dying within 14 days of admission (Christakis, 1994; Christakis & Escarce, 1996). Not only is admission into a hospice program delayed, but so too is all end-of-life planning and decision making, since the patient's judgment of his or her life expectancy is distorted (Steinhauser, Christakis, & Clipp, 2000).

Yet Irion argues that "It is a great cruelty to deprive a person of hope" (2002, 97), since we as a culture are heavily invested and energized in maintaining hope. Physicians struggle to maintain hope for patients and families, while at the same time they try to facilitate realistic opportunities to discuss end-of-life concerns (Back et al., 2003). The key question for health care professionals is how do we emotionally support dying patients and their families while at the same time trying to maintain their hope?

TRUTH TELLING

Throughout medical literature, references to hope are most frequently linked with truth telling and giving "bad news" (Christopher, 1999). A 1993 study (Miyaji) looked at the perceptions of 32 American physicians regarding their practice of truth telling when caring for dying patients. She found that although physicians tried to adhere to the principles of truth telling and patient autonomy, they still recognized that they held the power to control information. This control is probably linked to the physicians' emotional coping styles, institutional and legal constraints, and other factors including physicians' desires to hold out and maintain hope for their patients. Miyaji found that two-thirds of physicians gave optimistic information to their patients, even when the patient's clinical course was uncertain. In addition, the information given to patients was frequently modified. Another study of doctor/patient communication and collusion (The et al., 2000) noted that patients' false optimism about recovery wasn't only the result of physicians' withholding of information from their patients. There was also a tendency for physicians to focus on action activities (i.e., treatment planning and tests being offered), thus refocusing the patient and presenting opportunities for the patient to "forget" the future and remain focused on the present.

Billings and Block (1997), in their study of deficiencies in medical education, reported that 41% of medical students never witnessed an attending physician talking about death with either patients or family members, and 35% never discussed the care of a dying patient with an attending teacher. Almost 50% of oncologists felt that their communication skills regarding breaking bad news to patients was poor to fair (Baile, Glober, Lenzi, Beale, & Kudelka, 1999), and nearly a quarter of the patients studied indicated that the information they received about their cancer diagnosis was unclear and not communicated to them in a caring way (Chan & Woodruff, 1997). What does this say about the way we are educating professionals entering the field? How do we, as professionals, model acceptable and appropriate behaviors?

An article in the Journal of the American Medical Association (JAMA) (Epstein, Alper, and Quill, 2004) focused on joint decision making and "collaborative partnerships" between physicians and patients. The article noted that physicians generally spent less than a minute out of a 20-minute visit discussing treatment and planning options with their patients (Waitzkin, 1984). The article further stated that only 9% of outpatient visits made provisions for informed decision making, with only a small fraction of physicians even asking if the patient had any questions (Braddock, Edwards, Hasenberg, Laidley, & Levinson, 1999; Braddock, Fihn, Levinson, Jonsen, & Pearlman, 1997).

Yet information can be given in such a way "that it is not unduly negative or falsely reassuring" (Penson, 2000, p. 96). Palliative care clinicians frequently describe how the process of hope can change (albeit sometimes slowly) over time as what one wishes for changes. For example, the hope for a cure can change to the hope to be pain free or the hope that one will not suffer or isn't alone. The importance of listening to patients and eliciting their comments, by either open-ended questions or direct questions, cannot be overstated.

Helping the patient and/or family to focus on what exactly they are hoping for now can be useful therapeutic techniques. Questions such as "What are you hoping for when you leave the hospital?" "At this stage of your illness, what are you hoping for?" and "What are you hoping for when you meet with the hospice team?" can help prompt this discussion with regard to end-of-life decisions.

Some health care professionals (and others) believe that truth telling can have serious negative outcomes, which may impact the patient's ability to maintain hope (Lamont & Christakis, 1999).

Woods, Beaver, & Luker (2000) remind clinicians that the patient and his or her health care providers may have very different goals that will influence how information is given and perceived. This points to the need to encourage patient and family meetings that occur over time. These family meetings are sometimes considered the gold standard in palliative care. They allow for the goals of care to be addressed and readdressed throughout the trajectory of the illness. One study surveyed cancer patients, oncologists, and oncology nurses, asking them what percentage benefit *they* would need in order to accept chemotherapy as a treatment for cancer (Selvin, Stubbs, & Plant, 1990). Cancer patients reported needing a 1% chance of a cure to make intensive chemotherapy acceptable to them, compared with the 10% cure rate demanded by oncologists and the 50% cure rate demanded by oncology nurses. Tensions often escalate when the expectations of the patient differ from those of the health care professionals. Nurses, for example, may focus on quality of life, whereas many patients might be more focused on the quantity of their life (Penson, 2000). The father and health care proxy of a 25-year-old woman insisted that "everything be done" for her as she was actively dying. His belief was that there would be a miracle, and he wanted his daughter kept alive "no matter what," so that she would be able to be saved by this miracle. The stress and anguish felt by the patient's oncologist and the treatment team were palpable. The father's goals of care were not in line with the team's goals of care, and the futility of her situation was devastating to the medical team as her father continued to maintain his hope for a miracle.

Cancer patients (or their health care proxies) often make decisions regarding their care and treatment in the midst of overwhelming fear. They may be willing to try anything in the hope of either delaying the progression of their disease or preventing death. Most cancer patients and health care providers seem to exist in intersecting and at the same time parallel worlds (Rayson, 2003). "The unafflicted discuss treatment options. The afflicted catch and cling to treatment lifelines" (p. 47s).

SELF-CENSORSHIP

A small study of 17 cancer patients in a London outpatient clinic (Leydon et al., 2000) found that patients wanted basic information about their diagnosis and treatment options. However, the times when they wanted and sought this information occurred at different stages in their illness. Patients, in order to remain hopeful and continue to maintain a normal life-style, censored the amount and type of information they wanted to receive. In essence, they often set up emotional screens to filter out distressing and overwhelming information that they deemed to be unpleasant and unsafe. These periods of self-censorship functioned to preserve patients' sense of hope by helping them to avoid receiving negative information about their illness or their prognosis.

Linda was a 41-year-old nurse who had never married and had no children. Although Linda lived alone, she had many supportive friends and family members surrounding her. She struggled with her diagnosis of lung cancer but remained hopeful because of her close relationship with her medical oncologist, whom she viewed as caring and supportive. One month before her death, during a home visit, Linda reflected: "When the doctor sees me tomorrow he's gonna have a heart attack [referring to her deteriorating physical condition]. He likes me. He keeps telling me he likes me and says, 'I don't understand what's with your tumor. I don't know what to do for you.' I'm worried that he'll take me off the protocol. I know that I'm not gonna die yet. I have years ahead of me. I keep telling my doc that I'd rather talk about your twins than talk about my illness. I want to hear nice things about the boys."

One of the challenges facing health care professionals is finding appropriate ways of providing and sharing information with those patients, struggling with their terminal illness, who may not want to know all this information.

PREDICTING SURVIVAL

Another problematic area is that of acknowledging physicians' role in predicting the patient's prognosis, that is, length of life, and the timeliness with which this is communicated to the patient and his/her family. Studies looking at the prognostic success of physicians indicate that generally physicians tend to be incorrect and overly optimistic (Lamont & Christakis, 1999). Several factors have been identified, including the method of prediction used and forecaster bias, that can reduce a physician's accuracy in predicting the survival of advanced cancer patients. Questions regarding the physician's capabilities of prognostication tend to focus on two different elements: foreseeing and foretelling. "Foreseeing" is described as the physician's silent cognitive estimate about a patient's illness, and "foretelling" is described as the physician's communication of that prediction to the patient or family. Lamont & Christakis (1999) have noted that physicians tend to be optimistic in both foreseeing and foretelling the patient's prognoses.

A study by Mackillop and Quirt (1997) asked oncologists to do the following: (1) predict the likelihood of a cure for cancer patients receiving ambulatory treatment; and (2) to estimate the survival rates for those cancer patients they identified as having no possible likelihood of achieving a cure. Although it was determined that the oncologists were accurate in predicting the likelihood of a cure, they were successful in predicting survival rates for only one-third of the patients.

Another study, analyzing data from 349 advanced cancer patients participating in a Phase I study, found that the median survival was 6.5 months (Janisch et al., 1994). This was well above the two months identified as a necessary criterion for participants' enrollment in the study. This suggests that physicians recruiting and enrolling patients in Phase I studies are generally able to predict which patients may have more than two to three months to live. Palliative care research studies, however, indicate that in aggregate, physicians tend to be incorrect in their ability to predict survival.

Many of these studies report findings that are in contrast to the findings of the Study to Understand Prognoses and Preferences for Outcomes and Risks of Treatments (known as the SUPPORT study) (SUPPORT Principal Investigators, 1995). Although the well-known SUPPORT study did not ask physicians to estimate time of death ($n = 1,757$ patients with advanced cancer), the investigators did ask physicians to estimate each patient's likelihood of surviving two and six months. The authors reported that, overall, physicians were quite accurate, and when their estimates differed substantially from a statistical model, they were as likely to be optimistic as pessimistic (Knaus, Harrel et al., 1995; SUPPORT Principal Investigators, 1995). Lynn, one of the principal investigators in the SUPPORT study later analyzed the SUPPORT data of patients having advanced cancer (Zhong & Lynn, 1999) and noted the same results.

One issue surrounding physicians' accurate assessments and estimates of patients' prognoses is crucial for many reasons, including the criteria for hospice admission. The Medicare hospice benefit specifies that admission into a hospice program is predicated on the patient's having a prognosis of six months or less, and that these patients must forgo therapy aimed at a cure (United States Department of Health and Human Services, 2000). The timeliness of referral of patients to a hospice program is crucial, since referrals coming too soon or too late can create organizational, financial, clinical, and emotional problems for both providers of health care and patients (Christakis, 1994). It frequently takes several weeks for a hospice team to build the much-needed trust and rapport at the end of life. The hospice team focuses on ameliorating the patient's distressing physical symptoms, as well as assisting the patient and family caregivers with emotional, psychological, and existential concerns. Of the 1.6 million people in the United States over 65 years of age, only 15% receive some hospice care prior to their death (Myers, 2002). As a thorough review of hospice benefits and the philosophy and concepts of hospice care is not feasible in this chapter, the reader is directed to the many articles and books devoted to this topic.

MISINFORMATION VS. NO INFORMATION

Patients and families often describe feeling as if they are at the mercy of the information provided by their health care professionals. Physicians sometimes withhold information that justifies what they say or don't say. Today in the United States, as in many countries, most individuals are informed of their cancer diagnosis. However, it remains unclear as to how many of these individuals are given information regarding their prognosis. In a study of 100 Canadian patients undergoing active treatment for cancer, 98 individuals recognized that they had cancer but only 87 of them were able to correctly identify their type of tumor; and 11 out of 33 patients with metastatic disease believed they had local or regional disease for which they were being aggressively treated for a cure. Sixteen of the 48 patients who were receiving palliative treatment believed that the physicians' aim was to cure them, and 5 out of 52 patients being treated for a cure thought that they were being treated palliatively (Mackillop, Stewart, Ginsburg, & Stewart, 1988). Other studies have indicated similar disparities between what patients believed and the actual facts (Eidinger & Schapira, 1984; Weeks et al., 1998). Five teaching hospitals throughout the United States were involved in a study of the relationship between patients' predictions of their prognosis and the treatment preferences they preferred (Weeks et al., 1998). Patients were substantially more optimistic about their prognoses than their physicians were. In 82% of physician-patient dyads, the patients' estimate of their chance of living six months was higher than the physicians' estimates. Those patients with non-small lung cancer (stage III or IV) or metastatic colon cancer who thought they were going to live for at least six months were more likely to favor aggressive, life-extending therapy over comfort care compared with patients who thought there was at least a 10% chance they wouldn't live for six months. Almost half (43%) of the patients who were estimated by their physicians to have less than a 10% chance of surviving six months believed that they had at least a 90% chance of living that long.

Studies have also reported that even though patients with advanced cancer claim they want to be given information relating to their illness and prognosis, the patients do little to take the initiative to initiate these discussions with their physicians (Borgers et al., 1993; Brandt, 1991; Buchanan et al., 1996). A report from the Institute of Medicine National Cancer Advisory Board concluded that there were barriers that contributed to and fostered ineffective communication between physicians and cancer patients. One such barrier or road block can occur with patients who have unrealistic expectations and may be too afraid to ask questions of their physicians (Smith, 2003).

Yet patients continue to describe their concerns about not having received *all* the information they need to help them make end-of-life decisions (Husebo, 1997). This may be due in part to the difficulties physicians have in confronting this distressing topic. Physicians may sometimes use their own denial as a way of shielding themselves from the painful reality of having to share bad news with their patients. It has been suggested that the physician's own anxiety affects the way his or her patient is informed of the cancer diagnosis and overall prognosis (Righetti & Giorgio, 1994).

The wife of a dying 51-year-old with non-Hodgkin's lymphoma felt abandoned by the medical community. "During my husband's last two hospitalizations, the doctors abandoned him. He was treated by different doctors, and each time his oncologist was not part of the treating team in the hospital. He was 'off service.' They [the oncologists] never told us that another round of chemotherapy was useless. If we had known that, we would never have agreed to more chemo. Just before we started hospice care, my husband was getting intravenous infusions at home. I was so afraid that I would kill him if any air got in the tubing like I'd seen in the movies. No one ever told me what to expect. Then when he started with home hospice, they [the hospice team] abandoned him as well. It was around the time of the holidays, and we never saw or spoke to the same person more than once. No one provided any information, support,or instruction on what he might need or what I could do to make him more comfortable. No one ever told us what we needed to know. It could have been so much easier if we knew what to expect."

It's not quite clear to me, however, whether patients misinterpret the information given to them by their physicians or whether some patients tend to deny the poor prognosis that is given to them by their physicians. Is it that the physician is not giving them the information they need/want? Or is it that the patients can't bear to hear and accept the information?

INFORMATION RECEIVED
FROM OTHER SOURCES

In today's changing world, in which access to the Internet is readily available to most people, and images on television and movies have replaced the auditory style of communication via radio, we are cognizant that physicians are *not* the sole source of provision of medical information. Our knowledge comes from our personal experiences (or those of friends and family members) (Kirk, Kirk, & Kristjanson, 2004) and from images in the media that strongly influence our beliefs. Diem, Lantos, and Tulsky (1996) examined the portrayal of cardiopulmonary resuscitation (CPR) in three popular medical television shows *(ER, Chicago Hope, and Rescue 911)*. During 97 television episodes, there were 60 occurrences of CPR, in which 75% of the patients (actors) survived the immediate arrest and 67% were discharged from the hospital. The survival rates on these three shows are 5 to 10 times higher than those observed in actual, real-life medical scenarios. Although 37 individuals (actors) died during the 97 episodes, in only eight of the situations was there a depiction of discussions about CPR or references to DNR (do not resuscitate) orders. One of the television shows, *Rescue 911*, used terminology related to hope and miraculous recoveries in 56% of its episodes. Researchers involved in the study indicate that the "misrepresentation of CPR" can undermine "trust in data and fosters trust in miracles" (Diem et al., 1996, p. 1581). In addition to perhaps maintaining unrealistic hope, these improbable portrayals of illness and death have the potential to strongly influence and mislead public beliefs about end-of-life issues, cardiopulmonary resuscitation, and DNR discussions.

DENIAL

Denial is defined and conceptualized in several ways, for example, as "a way of coping with unpleasant realities" (Kantz, 1999). It is a defense mechanism that provides protection to an individual as he or she avoids reality by negating a threat (e.g., cancer) and substituting another version of reality (e.g., "I have an infection"). Sometimes, however, attempts to break it down or negate its effects may be experienced as assaults and reinforce denial (Hegarty, 2001, p. 43). Although true denial can be harmful, it serves as a coping mechanism with three distinct aims: (1) keeping the individual's perception stable or according to the status quo; (2) simplifying a relationship; and (3) eliminating differences between what was and what will be (Weisman, 1979, p. 44).

Berta described her deceased husband Ricardo as a 72-year-old strong man, "an ox." He was a hard-working businessman who always managed to support his family. Berta could not understand how Ricardo could have developed the basal cell cancer that had invaded his entire chest wall. His fear of dying prohibited him from seeking medical help when he first noticed a lesion. As the lesion grew in size, he covered the area with a bandage. As he always wore a T-shirt, Berta never realized the extent of "this sore." It was only when the tumor began to smell that Berta realized just how sick he actually was. The time between his diagnosis and his eventual death was short—less than five months; however, the suffering he endured was great. Over time, Berta repeatedly tried to talk with him about his illness, their future, and what to do with the grandchildren they were raising, trying to make decisions regarding housing and other financial matters. Ricardo could not tolerate talking about these issues or his future, and he would actually turn his head to the wall. He became withdrawn, isolating himself from his family and loved ones. His death was difficult,and the family members were left to deal with their anger at his fear of doctors and his denial. Had he sought medical attention earlier, excision of his basal cell cancer could have given him the opportunity to live a long, long life. Berta was also left with intense feelings of guilt over the fact that she did not recognize the severity of his illness and "push" him to the doctor sooner.

Traditional views about denial are rooted deeply in Freudian theory, where denial is viewed as the most primitive of defense mechanisms used by the ego to keep individuals from being aware of painful stimuli that cause distress (Matt, Sementilli, & Burish, 1988). Denial is an individual's refusal to acknowledge the existence of a real situation (Freud, 1953); we defend against the stressful situation by unconsciously limiting our awareness. I first met Jacqueline when she was referred for evaluation and emotional support in helping her cope with her beloved 80-year-old husband who had been comatose for two months. Previous life events supported her belief in miracles, and she remained hopeful that her husband would "wake up" and their life would return to the active social pace they had enjoyed for the past 62 years. Her inability to face his grave condition made discussions about DNR impossible and frustrated the medical team.

Jacqueline's denial of her husband's impending death also influenced her decision-making with regard to notifying their daughter, from whom he had been estranged. How would the decisions Jacqueline makes about notifying her daughter (or not) impact on potential feelings of guilt? How strongly should the medical team be pushing Jacqueline to "give up unrealistic hope" and accept her husband's deteriorating situation? How should the medical staff protect the patient's interests while at the same time honoring the wishes of family caregivers? Whose interests should take precedence? The patient's? Jacqueline's? or those of the daughter who had no knowledge of her father's imminent death? Situations such as this present challenging decisions for health care professionals as they try to "do the right thing" by supporting the beliefs of the family while struggling with the moral/ethical dilemmas of autonomy.

In and of themselves, defense mechanisms are usually automatic and unconscious. They are neither good nor bad, as denial frequently acts as a barometer which can control one's level of stress (Wein, 1996). Recent research suggests that "severe denial" occurs in approximately 10% of cancer patients hospitalized with advanced cancer and moderate levels of denial occurs in 18% of hospitalized advanced cancer patients (Chochinov, Tataryn, Wilson, Enns, & Lander, 2000).

However, when denial contributes to maladaptive behaviors and interferes with either the initiation or the continuation of appropriate therapeutic options, it must be handled cautiously. When I first met Shari she was a 30-year-old woman suffering from panic attacks, obsessive compulsive disorder, and agoraphobia. Her mother called the psychiatry office requesting medical help for her daughter. For almost a year, Shari had ignored a lump in her breast that eventually broke through her chest wall and was now a huge fungating, foul-smelling, and bleeding tumor. Throughout that time, she had not left her parents' apartment. Shari was "treating her cancer" with antibiotic ointments and drinking huge quantities of herbal ginger tea. Because Shari's pain was so severe, her mother did not know what to do. Shari's mistrust of physicians and her fear of medical treatment did not allow her to seek help. Early attempts to break through her defense mechanisms resulted in an acute psychiatric event in the course of which Shari decompensated and became psychotic, rendering her family and the medical staff helpless. An emergency hospitalization resulted in a two-month stay prior to her death.

The dynamic process of denial may fluctuate from minute to minute, oscillating between situations and events; it's often not a once-only act. It is a complex, fluid process that takes on different meanings at different times. "Awareness and denying often run together, crossing over as one emotion or perception gains ascendance and blurs another" (Weisman, 1979, p. 45). In addition, denial is not bound to any one person. Sometimes a patient denies the situation or his or her feelings to a spouse or family members in order to preserve the relationship (Handron, 1993; Weisman, 1972) or to maintain self-esteem (Weisman, 1979) and a sense of control. Yet, at the same time, the patient may talk openly to a nurse or social worker, with whom he or she has an entirely different relationship (Weisman, 1972, 1979). Several years ago, the present writer made a home visit to an elderly gentleman who was dying of kidney failure. Prior to my visit, his wife instructed me not to talk about the progression of his disease, because her husband was focused on maintaining hope and did not believe he was dying. During the first 10 minutes of the home visit, while his wife answered an incoming telephone call, the patient whispered to me: "Do you know that I'm dying? My wife can't talk to me about it—it's too painful and she has to believe that they'll be a miracle and that I won't die."

True denial, in the psychoanalytic sense, is rare among people with cancer. Opposite to the Freudian view is the view of health psychologists who acknowledge that even people who are emotionally well balanced may occasionally use denial to help them cope with difficult situations like chronic illnesses (Davidhizar & Giger, 1998; Meyerowitz, Burish, & Wallston, 1986). Denial provides protection and can at times serve as an adaptive coping mechanism (Rousseau, 2002). I've had several patients over the years that could not tolerate discussions about end-of-life care or their eventual death. Because of their denial they could not entertain conversations with family and friends regarding their fears, wishes, or concerns. These patients focused on the present and on their future. Family members were left to face unanswered questions after the deaths, but for the patients, their deaths may have been appropriate and what they hoped for.

Regardless of one's theoretical concept, denial is no longer believed to be a mark of underlying psychopathology (Matt et al., 1988). Some (Rousseau, 2002) have described the dynamic nature of denial, which eventually allows dying patients to accept their terminal condition. However, maintaining unrealistic beliefs and denying one's situation can increase the patient's sense of isolation (Weisman, 1979) and abandonment. Others have suggested that in some situations, one of the most useful strategies for helping cancer patients to cope with their illness *can* be denial (Matt et al., 1988).

Weisman (1979) distinguished three degrees or levels of denial:

1. Repudiation (first order denial): The first level of denial is denial of the facts of an illness, whereby a person may ignore troublesome symptoms: "Everyone in this room has cancer except me," or "I have a lump but it's probably a stubborn infection, and I won't believe anything else."

2. Dissociation (second order denial): The second order of denial involves acceptance of the fact after a diagnosis has been made, but the individual denies the implications or seriousness. The individual recognizes he or she has cancer but refuses to acknowledge the severity of this life-threatening illness and the possibility of death. A woman, for example, with stomach cancer complains, "I know I have cancer, but why can't I eat?" or a man after undergoing a thoracotomy for lung cancer states: "I can't understand why I'm short of breath."

3. Renunciation (third order denial): This third category of denial occurs when the individual denies any possibility that the illness will result in his or her death. A dying woman who had received all the chemotherapy and palliative radiation she could tolerate expresses relief at the end of her treatment, saying, "Now that treatment is over, I think I'll take a trip around the world before I start up my new business venture." Matt et al. (1988, p. 128) note that "in the coping literature, a patient who remains exceedingly cheerful despite knowledge of his or her disease state is considered to be using the third category of denial."

Caregiver Tom was frustrated with his younger sibling, George, who was dying of bladder cancer. Although Tom lived out of state, he would visit every other week, trying to help his brother. While attempting to continue managing his own finances, George had made several major banking errors and bills had gone unpaid. One month before George's death, Tom attempted to set up a system whereby George's bills would come directly to Tom. "My brother and I are trying to figure out his insurance. We're sitting here with reams and reams of paper. I'm following up on bills. I found out that I could be the third party contact. That means if my brother screws up on his payments, instead of disconnecting his services or making him delinquent, they will contact me. I think that my brother has been resistant because he's afraid of losing control and he keeps telling me that he's not going to die. He's able to say that although he has no more medical options available to him, there's still no reason for me to take over his finances 'cause he's not gonna to die."

DENIAL: NOT ALL MALADAPTIVE

The traditional view of denial is considered maladaptive because it is said to create a distortion of reality (Lazarus & Folkman, 1984). However, denial can also be viewed as a potentially healthy coping response protecting an individual from the immediate shock of reality (Davidhizar & Giger, 1998; Forchuk & Westwell, 1987). There are some cases in which denial can be constructive, as studies suggest that people with life-threatening illnesses may use healthy denial, allowing them to keep going and eventually "the denial usually diminishe, and the person begins to face and accept the harsh reality of what has been blocked out" (Davidhizar, Poole, Giger, & Henderson, 1998, p. 10). The key for clinicians is recognizing when denial becomes problematic so that appropriate therapeutic interventions can be initiated (Davidhizar & Giger, 1998).

Denial may be viewed as having both adaptive and maladaptive tendencies. Some argue that if denial is an adaptive process then it should reduce the patient's stress, anxiety, and depression and at the same time improve functioning for the patient (Wein, 1996). The adaptive function of denial serves to protect individuals against grief that may be just too overwhelming for them, thereby keeping the individuals functional (Kaufman, 2001). Evelyn was a middle-aged woman dying of lung cancer. She could not tolerate talking about her disease or her prognosis. Although having a prior history of panic attacks, she remained on medication to control these attacks, and in fact it had been years since she was disabled by these attacks. Throughout her illness, Evelyn continued active treatment, never allowing herself to talk about death. At first Evelyn's adult children wanted the opportunity to talk with her about her death but eventually resigned themselves to the fact that this was not going to happen. Evelyn's use of denial was the only way she could function, and in fact she died peacefully while undergoing experimental chemotherapy.

For denial to be considered as bad, it should contribute to maladaptive behaviors (i.e., anxiety, mania, depression, or inappropriate refusal of treatment). Wein (1996) suggests that health care professionals need to assess the patient's anxiety. which is provoking the denial. If, as in Evelyn's case, denial is not interfering with the patient's care or causing psychiatric symptoms, then there may be no need for clinicians to interfere. Each situation must be assessed individually, not only when first meeting the patient but throughout the trajectory of the illness.

Investigators have long suggested an association between denial and longer recurrence-free survival time (Dean & Surtees, 1989). More recently, it's been suggested that denial may be associated with prolonged survival for some cancer patients (Greer, 1992). In contrast, anxiety has been associated with poorer survival for leukemia patients after undergoing bone marrow transplantation (Andrykowski, Bradly, & Henslee-Downey, 1994).

Watson, Greers, Blake, and Schrapnell (1984) studied 24 women with breast cancer who coped by using denial after undergoing a mastectomy. Researchers found that those patients who denied their diagnosis or prognosis had fewer mood disturbances than those patients who didn't use denial to cope. No negative consequences were found as a result of the patients' denial. Other studies indicate that a patient's "fighting spirit" and emotional expressiveness were associated with better adjustment (Classen, Koopman, Angell, & Spiegel, 1996; Greer, Morris, & Pettingale, 1990). Penson (2000) notes that even when goals shift from cure to palliation, some patients continue to pursue aggressive treatments in order to appease their family. Putting up a good fight is highly valued in our society, often making family members proud that the patient is refusing to give up active treatment.

Several factors have been seen as explaining the potential benefits of denial in cancer patients (Matt et al,. 1988). These include time frames in which patients frequently use denial during an adjustment period while they come to terms with painful and scary information. In these situations, denial can be a healthy coping mechanism because it allows people to buffer bad news and adjust accordingly using their own time frames.

Early studies of adolescents with leukemia (Zelter, 1980) and parents of terminally ill children (Chodoff, Friedman, & Hamburg, 1964) examined coping styles, noting that denial was found to be a healthy coping mechanism in that it allowed individuals to incorporate distressing information over a period of time. Parents who used denial to cope were less distressed both during the period of denial and then afterward when denial was replaced with the realization that their child was indeed dying.

Weisman (1979) contends that another potential positive function of denial includes allowing patients to maintain their self-esteem and remain in control of their environment. In a disease such as cancer, which is usually perceived as uncontrollable (Silberfarb & Greer, 1982), denial may be viewed as a helpful coping mechanism. Stan's 37-year-old wife Colleen was dying of melanoma. She had been diagnosed with melanoma early in her first trimester and had to abort the baby and initiate surgery followed by chemotherapy. Although devastated by the loss of their first child, Stan and his wife struggled with her illness, which numerous hospitalizations, trying to focus on the here and now and hopefully on future pregnancies. Colleen could not entertain the idea that she would die. Stan, although able to talk about his fears with his wife's medical team, remained strong in his belief that he should not "beat Colleen over the head" with the knowledge that she would die. He believed that Colleen needed to maintain some control over her environment—the hospital room, whom she would allow to visit her, her schedule, and her ability to focus on happy futuristic topics rather than on her disease. When she died, after a two-and-a-half-month hospitalization, Stan was at peace, knowing that they never had to have that "dreaded conversation."

Finally, denial may be an effective strategy in that it allows patients to maintain hope during difficult times. We each face our mortality in our own way. Some patients can't face their impending death and don't allow their family, friends, or health care providers the opportunity to have that discussion. This can be frustrating for those individuals wanting or needing to have end-of-life conversations. Robert felt cheated after his father's death, angry that he never had the opportunity to confront his father about past issues of abuse and abandonment. Throughout his father's short illness (cancer of the tongue), they never spoke about the "serious" parts of their relationship. His father could not tolerate talking about his death and did not want to review old hurts. When he died, his wife and Robert, his estranged son, were at the bedside. Ongoing bereavement therapy was needed to help facilitate Robert's healing and his coming to terms with challenging situations and feelings of abandonment and neglect.

PHYSICIANS WHO HAVE LIFE-THREATENING ILLNESSES

Even physicians themselves may have to cope with denial when faced with a life-threatening illness. Medical knowledge can be a mixed blessing for physicians when they themselves become patients with life-threatening illnesses. Physician-patients have greater access to medical information and professional literature and medical records than the average patient. What's more, they have greater access to the expertise of their colleagues. However, although they may have a greater grasp of their disease and the treatments they are undergoing, "their rational understanding does not necessarily translate into emotional comprehension or adjustment to the facts" (Fromme & Billings, 2003, p. 2049). In an attempt to protect themselves, some physicians try to distance themselves from their disease (von Eschenbach, 2001) and may in fact "hide" behind their expertise as physicians as a way of denying the reality that they have become patients (Kurland, 2002).

Physicians treating other physicians with life-threatening illnesses often face unique issues and problems related, in part, to their professional characteristics. It's not easy to be a doctor and a patient at the same time (Spiro & Mandell, 1998). It's shocking to realize that doctors get sick—they aren't supposed to be sick. Some health care professionals have made a conscious (or perhaps an unconscious) pact with God: I'll take care of the sick and you will grant me and my loved ones good health and long life.

Fromme and Billings (2003) describe a case study depicting unique issues for dying physicians and the therapies they undergo at the end of their lives.

The case presented is that of a physician with coronary disease, later diagnosed with polycythemia vera followed by myelofibrosis. The patient's son, also a physician, was very much involved in his father's care; which often took him away from his role as the patient's son. Despite the progression of his disease, the patient, Dr. B, continued to believe that his condition was going to improve. In fact, he was so sure of its reversal that he refused to establish a DNR order. The patient died six weeks later at the age of 70 years. When interviewed after the patient's death, his cardiologist noted: "I think he realized he was ill, but like most patients, every time he was ill, he always found a reason that was not an underlying severe illness. Again, this is not different from dealing with most patients but [it is] surprising that a physician could, in a sense, delude himself in the same way that other patients did" (Fromme & Billings, 2003, p. 2049). Additionally, physicians frequently downplay their anxiety, leading them to delay before seeking medical treatment. Denial of the meaning of their symptoms, self-diagnosing, and self-treatment are common, along with denial of the disease (Schneck, 1998).

CONCLUSION

My experience with dying patients has been that for most of them, maintaining a hopeful attitude is instrumental in the way they travel through their cancer experience. Patients and families frequently swing back and forth between remaining hopeful and tip-toeing around the notion of the reality of death. Often the full realization and knowledge of impending mortality is too much for one to bear. How can one really prepare for leaving one's loved ones and life behind? While I don't dispute the important role that hope plays at the end of life, I'm also aware of patients' need to be realistic and prepare not only themselves but their loved ones as well. When patients are able to realistically acknowledge their condition, they are better able to make their end-of-life wishes known and perhaps plan for their family's future.

One can ask, does remaining hopeful of obtaining a cure prevent a patient from being realistic and facing his or her own mortality? Hoping for a cure and simultaneously preparing for an impending death are not necessarily exclusive of one another (Back et al., 2003). Throughout this chapter, I've talked about the changing focus of hope, where hope can be refocused and redefined by the individual. "Accepting, affirming, and denying can and do coexist" (Weisman, 1979, p. 45). Do patients truly deny their impending death or do they prefer to concentrate what little energy they have left on the positive refocusing of their living? Denial may not necessarily be true denial in the historical sense, but rather a way for the dying person to focus on her living and not on the eventuality of his dying as she continues to make sound judgments in relationship to her medical care and treatment. When, for a few, true denial remains the core of their experience, these individuals are unable to tolerate their deteriorating condition; we cannot assume that denial is always a "bad" coping style. The medical staff needs sensitivity to help support the patient. When individuals die they frequently leave bereaved family members struggling to cope with unresolved issues of guilt and anger. Sensitive and well-trained therapists will be needed to help the bereaved cope with their often complicated grief reactions to their loved one's death.

Clinicians need to recognize the struggle between the two elements, hope and denial, and plan interventions accordingly. However, it is imperative for health care professionals also to achieve a deeper understanding of the complexity between hope and denial, as well as the ways in which their own actions and behaviors contribute to the actions and behaviors of their dying patients.

"Everything can be taken from a man but one thing: the last of the human freedoms—to choose one's attitude in any given set of circumstances, to choose one's own way" (Frankl, 1946/1984, p. 75).

NOTES

An oncology clinician and grief therapist, Schachter explores the coping mechanisms of terminal cancer patients and their families. She has been struck by the responses she has received from patients and family members when they are told of a terminal prognosis. She addresses this complex issue making reference to published clinical research and using quotes from patients, their families, and the professional staff caring for them.

REFERENCES

Alexander, D, (1993). Psychological/Social Research. In D. Doyle, G.W.C. Hanks & N. MacDonald (Eds.), *Textbook of Palliative Care*, pp. 92–96. New York: Oxford University Press.

Andrykowski, M. A., Bradly, M. J., & Henslee-Downey, P. J. (1994). Psychosocial Factors Predictive of Survival after Allogenic Bone Marrow Transplantation for Leukemia. *Psychosomatic Medicine*, 56: 432–439.

Back, A. L., Arnold, R. M., & Quill, T. E. (March 2003). Medical Writings: Words that Make a Difference: Hope for the Best, and Prepare for the Worst. *American College of Physicians—American Society of Internal Medicine*, 138(5): 439–442.

Baile, W. F., Glober, G. A., Lenzi, R., Beale, E. A., & Kudelka, A. P. (1999). Discussing Disease Progression and End-of-Life Decisions. *Oncology*, 13: 1021–1038.

Beck-Friis, V., & Strang, P. (1993). The Family in Hospital-Based Home Care with Special Reference to Terminally Ill Cancer Patients. *Journal of Palliative Care*, 9(1): 5–13.

Billings, J. A, & Block., S. (1997). Palliative Care in Undergraduate Medical Education: Status Report and Future Directions. *Journal of the American Medical Association*, 278: 733–738.

Borgers, R., Mullen, P. D., Meertens, R., Rijken, M., Meussen, G., Plagge, I., Visser, A. P., & Blijham, G. H. (1993). The Information-Seeking Behavior of Cancer Out-patients: A description of the Situation. *Patient Education Counseling*, 22: 35–46.

Braddock, C. H., Edwards, K. A., Hasenberg, N. M., Laidley, T. L., & Levinson, W. (1999). Informed Decision Making in Out-Patient Practice: Time to Get Back to Basics. *Journal of the American Medical Association*, 282: 2313–2320.

Braddock, C. H., Fihn, S. W., Levinson, W., Jonsen, A. R., & Pearlman, R. A. (1997). How Doctors and Patients Discuss Routine Clinical Decisions; Informed Decision Making in the Outpatient Setting. *Journal of General Internal Medicine*, 12: 339–345.

Brandt, B. (1991). Informational Needs and Selected Variables in Patients Receiving Brachytherapy. *Oncology Nursing Forum*, 18: 1221–1229.

Breitbart, W. (2002). Reframing Hope: Meaning-Centered Care for Patients near the End of Life: An Interview with William Breitbart, MD. *Innovations in End-of-Life Care* 4(6). Retrieved September 17, 2003, from www.edc.org/lastacts.

Buchanan, J., Borland, R., Cosolo, W., Millership, R., Haines, I., Zimet, A., & Zalc-berg, J. (1996). Patients' Beliefs about Cancer Management. *Support Care Cancer*, 4: 110–117.

Buchholz, W. M. (May 2, 1990). The Medical Uses of Hope. *Journal of the American Medical Association*, 263(17): 2357–2358.

Carter, H., McKenna, C., MacLeod, R. D., & Green, R. (1998). Health Professionals' Responses to Multiple Sclerosis and Motor Neuron Disease. *Palliative Medicine*, 12: 383–394.

Cassell, E., (1976). *The Healer's Art*. Cambridge, Mass.: MIT Press.

Cassell, E., (1991). *The Nature of Suffering and the Goals of Medicine*. Oxford: Oxford University Press.

Chan, A., & Woodruff, R. K. (Autumn 1997). Communicating with Patients with Advanced Cancer. *Journal of Palliative Care*, 13(3): 29–33.

Chochinov, H. M., Tataryn, D. J., Wilson, K. G., Enns, M., & Lander, S. (2000). Prognostic Awareness and the Terminally Ill. *Psychosomatics*, 41: 500–504.

Chodoff, P., Friedman, S. B., & Hamburg, D. A. (1964). Stress, Defenses and Coping Behavior: Observations in Parents of Children with Malignant Disease. *American Journal of Psychiatry*, 120: 743–749.

Christakis, N. A. (June 1994). Timing of Referral of Terminally Ill Patients to an Outpatient Hospice. *Journal of General Internal Medicine*, 9: 314–320.

Christakis, N. A., & Escarce, J. J. (1996). Survival of Medicare after Enrollment in Hospice Programs. *New England Journal of Medicine*, 335: 172–178.

Christopher, M. (Spring, 1999). My Mother's Gift—The Link between Honesty and Hope. *Bioethics Forum*, 15(1): 5–13.

Classen, C., Koopman, C., Angell, K., & Spiegel, D. (1996). Coping Styles Associated with Psychological Adjustment to Advanced Breast Cancer. *Health Psychology*, 15: 434–437.

Davidhizar, R., & Giger, J. N. (1998). Patients' Use of Denial: Coping with the Un-acceptable. *Nursing Standard*, 12: 43, 44–46.

Davidhizar, R., Poole, V., Giger, J. N., & Henderson, M. (1998). When Your Patient Uses Denial. *Journal of Practical Nursing*, 48: 10–14.

Davies, B., Cherkryn Reimer, J., Brown, P., & Martens, N. (1995). *Fading Away: The Experience of Transition in Families with Terminal Illness*. Amityville, N.Y.: Baywood.

Dean, A, (October 22, 2002). Palliative Care Nursing: Talking to Dying Patients of Their Hopes and Needs. *Nursing Times*, 98(43): 34–35.

Dean, C. & Surtees, P. G. (1989). Do Psychological Factors Predict Survival in Breast Cancer? *Journal of Psychosomatic Research*, 33: 561–569.

Diem, S. J., Lantos, J. D., & Tulsky, J. A. (1996). Cardiopulmonary Resuscitation on Television. Miracles and Misinformation. *New England Journal of Medicine*, 334: 1578–1582.

Dobihal, E. F., Jr., & Stewart, C. W. (1984). *When a Friend Is Dying.* Nashville, Tenn.: Abingdon Press.

Eidinger, R. N., & Schapira, D. V., (June 15, 1984). Cancer Patients' Insights into Their Treatment, Prognosis, and Unconventional Therapies. *Cancer*, 53: 2736–2740.

Epstein, R. M., Alper, B. S., & Quill, T. E. (May 19, 2004). Communicating Evidence for Participatory Decision Making. *Journal of the American Medical Association*, 291(19): 2359–2366.

Farran, C. J., Kerth, K. A., & Popovick, J. M. (1995). *Hope and Hopelessness: Critical Clinical Constructs.* Thousand Oaks, Calif.: Sage.

Fitch, M. I. (1994). How Much Should I Say to Whom? *Journal of Palliative Care*, 10(3), 90–100.

Flemming, K. (1997). The Imponderable: A Search for Meaning: The Meaning of Hope to Palliative Care Cancer Patients. *International Journal of Palliative Nursing*, 3(1): 14–18.

Forchuk, C. & Westwell, J. (1987). Denial. *Journal of Psychosocial Nursing and Mental Health Services*, 25(6): 9–13.

Frank, A. W. (1995) *The Wounded Storyteller.* Chicago: University of Chicago Press.

Frankl, V. E. (1946/1984). *Man's Search for Meaning.* New York: Simon & Schuster. First published in 1946 under the title *Ein Psycholog erlebt das Konzentrationslager.* This translation first published by Beacon Press in 1959.

Freud, S. (1953). *The Ego and the Id.* Standard Edition of the Complete Psychological Works of Freud. Vol. 19. London: Hogarth Press.

Friedrichsen, M. J., & Strang, P. M. (2003). Doctors' Strategies when Breaking Bad News to Terminally Ill Patients. *Journal of Palliative Medicine*, 6(4): 565–574.

Fromm, E. (1968). The Revolution of Hope: Toward a Humanized Technology. New York: Harper & Row.

Fromme, E., & Billings, J. A. (2003). Care of the Dying Doctor: On the Other End of the Stethoscope. *Journal of the American Medical Association*, 290(15): 2048–2055.

Goleman, D. (1985). Strong Emotional Response to Disease May Bolster Patient's Immune System. *New York Times*, October 22, 1985, C1 (ProQuest Historical Newspapers).

Greer, S. (1992). The Management of Denial in Cancer Patients. *Oncology*, 6(12): 33–40.

Greer, S., Morris, T., & Pettingale, K. W. (1990). Psychological Responses to Breast Cancer: Effect on Outcome. *Lancet*, 2: 785–787.

Handron, D. S. (January–March 1993). Denial and Serious Chronic Illness—A Personal Perspective. *Perspectives in Psychiatric Care*, 29(1): 29–33.

Hegarty, M. (2001). The Dynamic of Hope: Hoping in the Face of Death. *Progress in Palliative Care*, 9(2): 42–45.

Herth, K. A. (1990). Fostering Hope in Terminally-Ill People. *Journal of Advances in Nursing*, 15: 1250–1259.

Husebo, S. (1997). Communication, Autonomy, and Hope. *Annals of the New York Academy of Sciences*, 809: 440–459.

Irion, P. E. (2002). Living with Grief: Loss in Later Life. *Hospice Foundation of Americas Year 2002 Initiative*. Retrieved June 13, 2002, from http://www.hospicefoundation.org/laterlife/irion.htm.

Janisch, L., Mick, R., Schilsky, R. L., Vogelzang, N. J., O'Brien, S., & Kut, M. (1994). Prognostic Factors for Survival in Patients Treated in Phase I Clinical Trials. *Cancer*, 74:1965–1973

Kantz, H. (1999). *Getting On.* Retrieved June 17, 2003, from http://www.awa.com/w2/getting_on/go-3.9html.

Kaufman, J. (2001). Denial. In G. Howarth & O. Leaman (Eds.), *Encyclopedia of Death and Dying, 150–151*. London: Routledge.

Kirk, P., Kirk, I., & Kristjanson, L. J. (June 2004). What Do Patients Receiving Palliative Care for Cancer and Their Families Want to Be Told? A Canadian and Australian Qualitative Study. *British Medical Journal*, 328(7452): 1343. Retrieved June 7, 2004, from doi: 10.1136/bmj.328.7452.0-a.

Koopmeiners, L., Post-White, J., & Gutnecht, S. (1997). How Healthcare Professionals Contribute to Hope in Patients with Cancer. *Oncology Nursing Forum*, 24, 1507–1513.

Kristjanson, L. J. (1989). Quality of Terminal Care: Salient Indicators Identified by Families. *Journal of Palliative Care*, 5(1), 21–28.

Kristjanson, L. J., & Ashcroft, T. (1994). The Family's Cancer Journey: A Literature Review. *Cancer Nursing*, 17(1), 1–17.

Kurland, G. (2002). *My Own Medicine. A Doctor's Life as a Patient.* New York: Henry Holt.

Lamont, E. B., & Christakis, N. A.(August 1999). Some Elements of Prognosis in Terminal Cancer. Retrieved June 17, 2003, from http://www.cancernetwork.com/journals/oncology/09908e.htm.

Lazarus, R., & Folkman, S. (1984). *Stress Appraisal and Coping.* New York: Springer.

Lee, S. J., Fairclough, D., Antin, J. H., & Woods, J. C. (2001). Discrepancies between Patient and Physician Estimates for the Success of Stem Cell Transplantation. *Journal of the American Medical Association*, 285(5): 1034–1038.

Leydon, G. M., Boulton, M., Moynihan, C., Jones, A., Mossman, J., Boudioni, M., & McPherson, K. (April 2000). Cancer Patients' Information Needs and Information Seeking Behavior: In Depth Interview Study. *British Medical Journal*, 320(7239): 909–913.

Lifton, J. R. (Spring 1974). On Death and the Continuity of Life: A "New" Paradigm. *History of Childhood Quarterly*, 1(4): 681–696.

Lifton, J. R. (1979). The Broken Connection: On Death and the Continuity of Life. New York: Simon & Schuster.

Mackillop, W. J., & Quirt, C. F. (1997). Measuring the Accuracy of Prognostic Judgments in Oncology. *Journal of Clinical Epidemiology*, 50(1): 21–29.

Mackillop, W. J., Stewart, W. E., Ginsburg, A. D., & Stewart, S. S. (1988). Cancer Patients' Perceptions of Their Disease and Its Treatment. *British Journal of Cancer*, 50: 355–359.

MacLeod, R., & Carter, H. (1999). Health Professionals' Perception of Hope: Understanding Its Significance in the Care of People Who Are Dying. *Mortality* 4(3): 309–317.

Matt, D. A., Sementilli, M. E., & Burish, T. G. (April 1988). Denial as a Strategy for Coping with Cancer. *Journal of Mental Health Counseling*, 10(2): 136–144.

Meyerowitz, B. E., Burish, T. G., & Wallston, K. A. (1986). Health Psychology: A Tradition of Integration of Clinical and Social Psychology. *Journal of Social and Clinical Psychology*, 4: 375–392.

Miyaji, N. (1993). The Power of Compassion: Truth-Telling among American Doctors in the Care of Dying Patients. *Social Science and Medicine*, 36: 249–264.

Morgante, L. (June 2000). Hope in Multiple Sclerosis: A Nursing Perspective. *International Journal of MS Care* 2(2): 2000. Retrieved October 21, 2003, from http://www.mscare.com/a0006/page03.htm.

Myers, G. E. (September/October 2002). Can Illness Narratives Contribute to the Delay in Hospice Admission? *American Journal of Hospice and Palliative Care*, 19(5): 325–329.

Nekolaichuk, C. L., & Bruera, E. (1998). On the Nature of Hope in Palliative Care. *Journal of Palliative Care*, 14: 36–42.

Owen, D. C. (1989). Nurses' Perspectives on the Meaning of Hope with Cancer: A Qualitative Study. *Oncology Nursing Forum*, 16: 75–79.

Parker-Oliver, D. (March/April 2002). Redefining Hope for the Terminally Ill. *American Journal of Hospice and Palliative Care*, 19(2): 115–120.

Penson, J. (2000). A Hope Is Not a Promise: Fostering Hope within Palliative Care. *International Journal of Palliative Nursing*, 6(2): 94–98.

Post-White, J., Ceronsky, C., Kreitzer, M. J., Nickelson, K., Drew, D., Watrud Mackey, K., Koopmeiners, L., & Gutknecht, S. (1996). Hope, Spirituality, Sense of Coherence, and Quality of Life in Patients with Cancer. *Oncology Nursing Forum*, 23, 1571–1579.

Rait, D., & Lederberg, M. S. (1990). The Family of the Cancer Patient. In J. C. Holland & J. H. Rowland (Eds.), *Handbook of Psycho Oncology: Psychological Care of the Patient with Cancer*, 585–597. New York: Oxford University Press.

Rayson, D. (2003). Sweet Time Unafflicted. *Classic Papers, Supplement to Journal of Clinical Oncology*, 29(9): 46s–48s.

Righetti, A., & Giorgio, G. (1994). Factors Influencing the Communication of the Diagnosis to Patients who Have Cancer. *Journal of Cancer Education*, 9: 42–45.

Romanoff, B. D., & Thompson, B, E, (August/September 2006). Meaning Construction in Palliative Care: The Use of Narrative, Ritual, and the Expressive Arts. *American Journal of Hospice and Palliative Medicine*. 23(4): 309–316.

Rousseau, P. (2000). Hope in the Terminally Ill. *Western Journal of Medicine*, 173(2): 117–118.

Rousseau, P. (December 2002). The Art of Oncology: When The Tumor Is Not the Target: Death Denial. *Journal of Clinical Oncology*, 18(23) 3998–3999.

Schachter, S. R. (1999). *The Experience of Living with a Life-Threatening Illness: A Phenomenological Study of Dying Cancer Patients and Their Family Caregivers*. Unpublished dissertation, Union Institute University. Cincinnati, Ohio

Schachter, S. R., & Coyle, N. (1998). Palliative Home Care—Impact on Families. In J. C. Holland (Ed.), *Psycho-Oncology*, 1004–1015. New York: Oxford University Press.

Schachter, S. R., & Holland, J. C. (1995). Psychological, Social, and Ethical Issues in the Home Care of Terminally Ill Patients: The Impact of Technology. In J. C. Arras (Ed.), *Bringing the Hospital Home: Ethical and Social Implications of High-Tech Home Care*, 91–106. Baltimore: Johns Hopkins University Press.

Schneck, S. A. (1998). "Doctoring" Doctors and Their Families. *Journal of the American Medical Association*, 280(23): 2039–2042.

Selvin, M. L., Stubbs, L., & Plant, H. J. (1990). Attitudes to Chemotherapy: Comparing Views of Patients with Cancer with Those of Doctors, Nurses and General Public. *British Medical Journal*, 300(6737): 1458–1460.

Silberfarb, P. M., & Greer, S. (1982). Psychological Concomitants of Cancer: Clinical Aspects. *American Journal of Psychotherapy*, 36: 470–478.

Skevington, S. M., Macarthur, P., & Somerset, M. (1997). Developing Items for the WHO-QOL: An Investigation of Contemporary Beliefs about Quality of Life Related to Health in Britain. *British Journal of Health Psychology*, 2: 55–72.

Smith, T. J. (2003). Tell It Like It Is. *Classic Papers, Supplement to Journal of Clinical Oncology*, 21(9): 12s-16s.

Spiro, H. M., & Mandell, H. N. (January 1998). When Doctors Get Sick. *Annals of Internal Medicine*, 128(2): 152–154.

Steinhauser, K. E., Christakis, N. A., & Clipp, E. C. (2000). Factors Considered Important at the End of Life by Patients, Family, Physicians, and Other Care Providers. *Journal of the American Medical Association*, 284: 2476–2482.

Stoner, M. H., & Keampfer, S. H. (1985). Recalled Life Expectancy Information, Phase of Illness and Hope in Cancer Patients. *Research in Nursing and Health*, 8: 269–274.

SUPPORT Principal Investigators.(1995). A Controlled Trial to Improve Care for Seriously Ill Hospitalized Patients: The Study to Understand Prognoses and Preferences for Outcomes and Risks of Treatments (SUPPORT). *Journal of the American Medical Association*, 274: 1591–1598.

The, A. M., Hak, T., Goeter, G., & van der Wal, G. (December 2000). Collusion in Doctor-Patient Communication about Imminent Death: An Ethnographic Study. *BMJ*, 321: 1376–1381.

United States Department of Health and Human Services. *Social Security Medicare Publication No 02154*, revised April 2000. Retrieved September 26, 2008, from http://medicare.gov/Publications/Search/Results.asp?PubID=02154&Type=PubID.

von Eschenbach, A. C. (2001) *The Physician as Patient*, chapter 8. Retrieved January 20, 2004, from www.conversationsincare.com/web_book/printerfriendly/chapter8pf.html.

Waitzkin, H. (1984). Doctor-Patient Communication: Clinical Implications of Social Scientific Research. *Journal of the American Medical Association*, 252: 2441–2446.

Watson, M., Greer, S., Blake, S., & Schrapnell, K. (1984). Reaction to a Diagnosis of Breast Cancer: Relationship between Denial, Delay, and Rates of Psychological Morbidity. *Cancer*, 53: 2008–2012.

Weeks, J. C., Cook, E. F., O'Day, S. J., Peterson, L. M., Wenger, N., Reding, D., Harrell, F. E., Kussin, P., Dawson, N. V., Connors, A. F., Jr., Lynn, J., & Phillips, R. S. (1998). Relationship between Cancer Patients' Predictions of Prognosis and

Their Treatment Preferences. *Journal of the American Medical Association*, 279 (21): 1709–1714.

Wein, S. (October 1996). Evaluating Denial in Patients with Life-Threatening Illnesses. *Primary Care Cancer* 16 (9): 1–6.

Weisman, A. D. (1972). On Dying and Denying: A Psychiatric Study of Terminality. New York: Behavioral Publications.

Weisman, A. D. (1979). *Coping with Cancer.* New York: McGraw Hill.

Winterling, J., Wasteson, E., Glimelius, B., Sjoden, P. O., & Nordin, K. (2004). Substantial Changes in Life. *Cancer Nursing* 27(5): 381–388.

Woods, S., Beaver, K., & Luker, K. (2000). Users' Views of Palliative Care Services: Ethical Implications. *Nursing Ethics*, 7(4): 314–326.

Wren, L. R., Levinson, D., & Papadatou, D. (1996). *End of Life Decisions: Guidelines for the Health Care Provider.* Tucson: University of Arizona.

Zelter, L. K. (1980). The Adolescent with Cancer. In J. Kellerman (Ed.), *Psychological Aspects of Childhood Cancer*, 70–99. Springfield, Ill.: Thomas.

Zhong, Z., & Lynn, L. (August 1999). Reviewers' Comments: Some Elements on Prognosis in Terminal Care. Retrieved June 17, 2003, from http://www.cancernetwork.com/journals/oncology/09908e.htm.

CHAPTER 3

THE AFTERLIFE IN MODERN AMERICA

Alan F. Segal

AMERICAN AFTERLIVES: RESURRECTION VS. IMMORTALITY OF THE SOUL

The church father Tertullian, equated Christianity with a belief in resurrection: "By believing in resurrection, we are what we claim to be."[1] By "resurrection," he opined, "orthodox" Christians should believe in literal, fleshly resurrection, with its attendant end of time and judgment of sinners. Even though Tertullian was a churchman, his opinion did not go unchallenged. Many Christians of his day believed with the Platonists that the soul was immortal but the body perished forever. Tertullian's view of the phenomenon is itself governed by his personal dispositions and the historical context in which he lived. In the Christianity that Tertullian prescribed, bodily resurrection was something he devoutly wished for, nay, prayed for, preached, and held other Christians heretical because they did not believe it literally. Any other hereafter was seen as threatening and unchristian. Time and again, the afterlife is where the battles of this world are fought.

Today, most American Christians of all denominations continue to assent to a belief in resurrection. But closer scrutiny shows that many do not believe that the physical body will be resurrected, as Tertullian preached, but that the soul will dwell in heaven after death. What they call the *resurrection of the body* actually refers technically to the *immortality of the soul.*[2] There is a gradient in religious belief. But that distinct line three-quarters of the way toward the right of the religious spectrum is the big story in American religion at the beginning of the twenty-first century. Americans on the left of that line—let us call them the liberal, mainline religions for lack of a better term—have more in common with each other than they do with their coreligionists across the line. Liberal Jews, Protestants, Catholics, Muslims, and adherents of the great Asian faiths actually have more in common with each other, in terms of attitudes toward politics and economic and moral questions, than they do with their own coreligionists in the fundamentalist camp. Fundamentalists of all religions in the United States also have more in common with each other in terms of moral, political, and economic views than they do with their coreligionists in the liberal camp.[3]

The notion of resurrection is strongly characteristic only of a sizable minority of Americans—those on the right side of the line that separates the fundamentalist and evangelical churches from the liberal and mainline ones.[4] A traditional, strong, and literal view on the resurrection of the body is, in fact, a very strong indicator that the person is on the evangelical, fundamentalist, or Orthodox Jewish side of the line.

WHAT THE GALLUP POLL HAS FOUND

In their interesting and provocative book, George Gallup Jr. and James Castelli note that there is a fundamental difference between the liberal and mainline churches in the United States on the one hand and the fundamentalist and evangelical churches on the other. This distinction is more fundamental now for the envisioning of heaven than the split among Protestants, Catholics, and Jews. Asking people whether they believe in the immortality of the soul or the resurrection of the body (when the terms have been clarified) is probably the simplest way to discover that basic rift in American life.

We already know that religion is much more significant on average to Americans than it is to Europeans or even to Canadians, our closest neighbors. Since the time of De Tocqueville, Europeans have noted our special American interest in religion.[5] More recently, Gerhard Lenski showed that our religious choices are statistically as important for predicting our other attitudes as is anything else that can be measured or named in our lives.[6] We know a great deal about a what a person is likely to think politically or how she will spend money or vote or what kind of occupations she will seek, what kind of recipes he will bake or what kind of organizations she will join, or what kind of child-rearing practices a person will practice and advocate, and a myriad of other things, when we have some specificity about religious beliefs and community. The very notion of which pronouns are appropriate to each of these activities is governed as significantly by religious values as anything else.

Asking about the afterlife still defines a crucial and highly conflicted battlefield in American life, one that runs through our political as well as religious convictions. It separates liberal from conservative, Republican from Democrat, northerner from southerner, rich from poor, educated from uneducated, and pious from impious. But it is more fundamental than any of these. It cuts to the very quick of what we Americans think is important in life.

Americans still answer "yes" to the question, "Do you believe in God," far more often and more enthusiastically than the inhabitants of most other Western countries, up to a level of 94% in one poll,[7] on a level equal to Ireland and India and far higher than Scandinavia, England, France, Spain, Italy, or even our close neighbor Canada. Even more important for the discussion of religiosity, a conventionally religious person in the United States will attend religious services far more regularly, on average, than his European counterpart will. The reasons for this religious temperament and behavior are not well understood or even undisputed.[8]

Perhaps we are just being accommodating, just feeling we should answer those kinds of questions affirmatively, displaying our need for approval.[9] In fact, we Americans are misleading ourselves about our church attendance. In polls, we affirm that we attend church often, but studies of how we actually spend our time weekly, without religion being privileged in any way, show that we spend far less time in church than we report when asked directly about it. It is unlikely that we are simply lying. Probably we feel that spending time in church is so important that we mislead ourselves about how often and long we do it. The fact that we are willing to mislead ourselves demonstrates the importance that religion still has in our society, even if we do not live up to its responsibilities.[10]

COMPETITION IN THE RELIGIOUS MARKETPLACE

So why do we rely on claims of religion so much more frequently than other nationalities when we actually do not practice it as much as we think? Perhaps it is our ethnic history: Americans often came here to avoid religious persecution. More important is likely to be the way religion and government interact in our society. One interesting result of our history is enshrined in the First Amendment, absolutely forbidding the establishment of any state religion, and arguably guaranteeing the separation of church and state. Not only does every other country named above sponsor a religion as an instrument of the state, but by doing so, it also provides a protected market for one religion to live in. Our society, on the contrary, encourages competition among religions within the marketplace of ideas, though fundamentalist Christianity continues to lobby the government for more government support, even while criticizing Jews and Catholics for trying to subvert the government. Although we accuse ourselves of being unfair to religious organizations and superficial in our beliefs,[11] we have also inadvertently created a competitive environment for healthy religious life. Competition in the marketplace of religious ideas has produced a very important set of religious organizations in our society, even if our culture tends to transform religion into a weekend or after-hours affinity group. Like anything else that has been mass-marketed, our religion comes to us in sound bites and slogans, which make it seem trivial and superficial in comparison to religious discussions in the past.

Our religious vibrancy, then, is a double-edged sword. Whatever we think of religion, we must admit that religion is still an important part of our lives, in spite of the once-touted, enormous secularization of American society after the Vietnam War. By the 1970s, the opinion polls seemed to indicate that we were growing more secular. By the early 1990s, these numbers had decisively turned around. We forgot that when the baby boomers all entered young adulthood together, their numbers would skew our statistics toward the secular, unless we also controlled for age. Adolescents and young adults are very much less likely to take doctrines of religion or fear of mortality seriously in American life. Questions of career and family predominate in the early adult years. But, as we age, we Americans apparently still return to these more perennial and more ultimate human questions. This may well explain why we mistakenly thought we were about to enter a secular age.

The effect of age on interest in the afterlife is easy enough to see. I once had the experience of giving a series of classes on the Bible to a group made up exclusively of adolescents and retirees, a classic bimodal distribution. There were certain interesting characteristics to this hard-to-teach class, but none was more dramatic than the differing beliefs in the afterlife. When it came time to study the Bible's doctrines of the afterlife, I asked the class members if they believed in one. All the retirees in the audience answered affirmatively, no surprise given their age and the fact that the course was being held in front of children in a Conservative synagogue. (What they would have said more privately is anyone's guess.) But even in that context, none of the twenty or so teenagers would answer "yes" to the question. Age is an important factor in the articulation of and interest in beliefs in an afterlife. Older people characteristically show more recognition of mortality and at the same time, unexpectedly, lower anxiety about death. Church membership and high commitment also correlates with low death anxiety. Conventional religiosity—church membership with low commitment—has so far not shown any measurable effects on the fear of death.[12]

RELIGION RETURNS WHEN THE AFTERLIFE BECKONS

When the baby boomers began to return to religion and church membership in the 1980s, their return corresponded dramatically to an upswing in the political action of conservative religious groups. These religious groups were apparently taking a lesson from the activists of the 1960s and 1970s when they organized for political action. As a result, no one would today question the importance of religion as an indicator of political and economic values in American life. The correlation is much higher in international affairs, where Islam led the way into the political arena. After the Iranian revolution of 1979, we realized we had to factor religion into our international political policies and, after 9/11, we realized that we are no longer an island fortress. Being part of the globalization process means that we are deeply affected by extremist religious beliefs and movements brewing elsewhere in the world.

For all these reasons, our stated beliefs in the afterlife are increasing significantly, according to studies done by Andrew M. Greeley and Michael Hout.[13] A significantly larger fraction of American adults believed in life after death in the 1990s than in the 1970s. According to data from the General Social Survey (hereafter GSS, see note 8), there has been a marked change in some groups' beliefs in life after death. Although Protestants who say that they believe in life after death have stayed stable at about 85% (this percentage was very high to begin with, anyway), Catholics, Jews, and people of no religious affiliation have become more likely to report beliefs in the afterlife. For instance, the percentage of Catholics believing in an afterlife rose from 67% to 85% for those born between 1900 and 1970. When the various variables are analyzed, one important factor that the writers identified was contact with Irish clergy, who have communicated their commitment to the Catholic population in general.

Among Jews, the percentage was even more interesting but very puzzling. Jews who report important and stable notions of life after death have always been significantly fewer statistically than Christians, presumably due to the lower emphasis on the afterlife in most varieties of American Judaism. Nevertheless, Jewish belief in the afterlife rose from 17% among the cohort born in 1900–1910 to 74% among the 1970s cohort, a very significant jump. Perhaps Jews have understood that our culture asks us to answer "yes" to that question but not to spend much time thinking about it. In any event, Jews are still twice as likely as Christians to say that they don't know if there is a life after death.

The reasons for this finding are not as easy to figure out. Contact with Protestants was not a measurable factor (among those Jews who did not later convert). But immigrant status seems quite an important factor in rejecting notions of the afterlife for both Catholics and Jews. Perhaps the experience of immigration is itself so disruptive that it seriously affects notions of felicity in an afterlife for the immigrant generation. Among Jews, this may be because the Jews most likely to leave Europe at the turn of the century were those least impressed with Rabbinic exhortations to stay within the European religious community and not go to the United States, which they called "the *treyfer* (non-kosher) land." Those who went to the United States and later Canada called it *der goldener Medinah*, the Golden Land, showing that the Jews came to the United States to better their economic opportunities rather than to gain religious freedom. Most jettisoned their European habits of piety with few regrets. Education and denomination do make some difference in the present-day statistics; but the trend is clear across all groups. Jews with more traditional backgrounds are leading the way, but there is a significant rise among all Jews, as Reform Jews are only about 10% less likely to report beliefs in a life after death than Orthodox Jews. What differs is the kind of afterlife they envision. The mainline Jews are close to Protestants in their adoption of a spiritual afterlife; Orthodox Jews report a belief in bodily resurrection. In the second and third generation of immigrants, perhaps acculturation itself accounts for the higher correlation with Protestant views of heaven.

Greeley and Hout do not systematically test the hypothesis that American First Amendment rights promote competition in religion and thus are more successful at raising people's religious consciousness; but their findings are in consonance with this supply-side theory of American religious life. They strongly endorse a supply-side notion of American religious life, and it does make a certain amount of sense.

On the other hand, the items in their questionnaire concerning life after death are far more general and nonspecific than traditional Jewish and Christian doctrines of life after death. Their items are taken from the GSSs of 1983 and 1984, which contained 10 characterizations of the afterlife. The 10 items were as follows: (1) a life of peace and tranquility; (2) a life of intense action; (3) a life like the one here on earth only better; (4) a life without many things that make our present life unenjoyable; (5) a pale shadowy form of life, hardly life at all; (6) a spiritual life, involving our mind but not our body; (7) a paradise of pleasure and delights; (8) a place of loving intellectual communion; (9) union with God; (10) reunion with relatives. This covers a very wide group of conceptions of the afterlife and no one is expected to believe them all, especially as some of them contradict others.

Experimentally, we find that nearly all Christians think that union with God, peace and tranquility, and reunion with relatives are likely to await them, as well as many of the other descriptions of the afterlife above. Yet, few are explicitly part of the official Christian doctrine of resurrection. Many of them correlate highly with the immortality of the soul, which has been synthesized with resurrection in Christianity since the fourth century but is not a significant New Testament doctrine. Americans do seem more or less in agreement about these criteria, but there are some differences: Jews are slightly more likely than Christians to imagine a nonpersonal existence. Half of Jews but only one-fifth of Christians see a "vague" existence as likely. This finding seems intriguingly tied to Jewish ethnicity. It would be interesting to compare this with other groups segregated by ethnicity and questioned in an "ethnically aware" environment.

THE DEMISE OF THE DEVIL[14]

Another interesting phenomenon in American life is the gradual disappearance of any notion of hell in the liberal and mainline churches.[15] Many have seen this "demise of the devil" as a sign that we are losing our moral bearings, our sense of evil. On the other hand, one might just as easily argue that the demise of the devil is an indication that the United States is coming to terms with itself as a culturally plural country, since so many of us have lost our desire to carry out religious vengeance on our fellow-countrymen in the next world, ironically, just at the moment when so many fundamentalist extremists around the world are preaching our damnation.[16]

Jonathan Edwards, one of the founders of the Great Awakening and president of Princeton University, several times described the horrors of hell for Americans in his justly famous sermons. This descriptions is from "Sinners in the Hands of an Angry God":

> That world of misery, that lake of burning brimstone, is extended abroad under you. *There* is the dreaful pit of the glowing flames of the wrath of God; there is Hell's wide gaping mouth open; and you have nothing to stand upon, nor anything to take hold of; there is nothing between you and Hell but air; tis only the power and mere pleasure of God that holds you up.[17]

Americans of the eighteenth century were impressed with these images and motivated to strive even more fervently toward the good and eschew evil, though Edwards's own theology was based on the premise that God's will for each of us individually was unknowable. His Great Awakening was enormously successful. This vision of hell affected American's social behavior just as much as the desire for a just society stimulated Edwards to this vision. Vivid pictures of heaven and hell therefore seem to foster religious conversion, even within the same religion. That would certainly explain why fundamentalist and evangelical communities rely on them more often than the mainline churches. We shall have occasion to investigate this observation in greater detail in several different contexts.

Indeed, there is some evidence that the spike of interest in "gothic" or "supernatural" worldviews (for example, interest in vampires and vampire slayers, the occult, and space aliens) among teenagers is not so much lack of religious guidance as a teen rebellion against a strict fundamentalist or evangelical upbringing. These phenomena are common enough among teenagers and frequent subjects of teen-oriented entertainments. Commercial TV and films are full of experiences of aliens, angels, vampires, and demons. But they appear especially often among teens rejecting their own family's fundamentalism and evangelicalism.[18] There are even attempts by evangelical churches to capitalize on this teenage interest for the purposes of evangelization and confirmation of teen faith, with such evangelical tools as a "hellhouse," a Halloween walk-through depiction of the evils of nonevangelical moral codes, presenting evangelical religion as the solution to demonically controlled lives.[19]

Whatever the cause, there is a palpable change in American notions of the afterlife: very few of us think we are going to hell or even that we are in danger of going to hell, though our sizable minority of fundamentalists and evangelicals still trumpet it as the hallmark of faith and so maintain its usefulness as the place where the enemies of the faith should go.[20] Very few of us outside of the right wing conservatives take its existence seriously at all.

The lines of causation between our current lives and our hopes for the future are bidirectional. Our current lives affect our notions of the afterlife; our notions of the afterlife affect our behavior in this one. In our permissive society, this vision would probably be greeted with disbelief by most Americans and even by derisive laughter by some. Our desire to do away with hell is natural enough, but it may not be because we want to sin with impunity. It may just as easily be due to our loss of a sure sense that our individual religions are the only right ones. Because we feel our society's notions of equality are divinely endowed, we may be losing the easy surety that any American whose religion differs from us is automatically damned. That could be an indication that an incipiently multicultural society is forming in the United States as old parochialisms fade.

WHAT AMERICANS ACTUALLY THINK ABOUT HEAVEN

For the majority of Americans, heaven has become virtually a democratic entitlement. Surely we tend to project onto our view of a happy afterlife those things that we think are best and most lasting and virtuous and meaningful in this life while eliminating those things that we think are the most difficult, frustrating, evil, and inessential. The data are mostly from Christians, but the description of heaven is in some ways a projective test for all Americans, with adjustment for the specifically Christian doctrines. Here is a basic list of talking points, taken from Gallup and Castelli:

- The afterlife will be a *better life and a good life*.
- There will be *no more problems or troubles*. "No trials and tribulations.... worries and cares will vanish.... no worries, no cares, no sorrows. I think to be worried all the time would really be awful."
- There will be *no more sickness or pain*.
- The afterlife will be a *spiritual, not a physical realm*. "Totally spiritual... lack of physical limitations...there's not going to be a three-dimensional experience."
- It will be *peaceful*. "I think we'll be more peaceful because you really live your hell on earth."

- The afterlife will be *happy and joyful, no sorrow.*
- Heaven will be peaceful.
- Those who make it to heaven will be happy.
- They will be in the presence of God or Jesus Christ.
- There will be love between people.
- God's love will be the center of life after death.
- Crippled people will be whole.
- People in heaven will grow spiritually.
- They will see friends, relatives, or spouses.
- They will live forever.
- There will be humor....
- People in heaven will grow intellectually.
- They will have responsibilities.
- They will minister to the spiritual needs of others.
- Those in heaven will be recognizable as the same people that they were on earth.
- There will be angels in heaven. (pp. 47–48)

It is significant that few of the descriptions of heaven contain depictions of explicitly Christian doctrines. We see in these descriptions a significant ranking of values in American life this side of eternity. The first series of points deals with personal and familial happiness. The second expresses the importance of work and accomplishment and looking after others. Throughout, we see the American notions of the importance of meaningful work as vocation, personal identity, and personal growth and fulfillment, which would be very unusual in past European visions of heaven and incomprehensible in ancient ones. Significantly, among Americans, humor is often cited as an important component of heavenly life, arguably because we use humor to dispel tension over ethnic and regional differences. Indeed, our American notions of a competitive economy—positive growth, positive development, continuous education—are deeply enshrined in our contemporary notions of heaven.

This is a litmus text of American goals and values, transcendent and ultimate values as seen from our perspective in the early twenty-first century, even as it is a filter for the removal of those things that most keep us from achieving our goals and values.[21] If we also had a description of hell, we could see more clearly all the things that Americans feel are contrary to these values and how, given a heavenly economy, they should be punished. It is just as significant that we no longer excel in descriptions of hell or damnation. If we look at earlier conceptions of heaven and hell, we may be able to perceive similar comparisons with earlier social structures and policy. Dealing with other cultures' concepts of the afterlife historically will yield the same important information, but it will involve historical attention to details that are not nearly so well known or easy to discover.

We have seen that Americans—liberal or conservative, mainline church or sectarian, or even unchurched—have significant beliefs about the afterlife. Indeed, more Americans believe in an afterlife than believe in God. These beliefs range from the literal resurrection of the body to the immortality of the soul to deathless existence with flying saucers in the stars to nothing specific beyond the confidence that we will have something to enjoy. Most Americans have more conventional notions of an afterlife than those of a flying-saucer cult. The immortality of the soul, as opposed to the resurrection of the body, is inherent in most of our descriptions. Individuals within the mainline churches believe in an afterlife but they tend to feel comfortable with a range of individual opinions. They normally feel that their more conservative confrères have mistaken the literal biblical formulations for the underlying truths behind them. The conservative churches believe in the immortality of the soul and also in the literal resurrection of the body. They report that they believe it with certainty and that their liberal coreligionists are dangerously incorrect.

So in spite of our sophistication and pragmatism and our waning economic domination of the world, American culture is full of significant depictions of the afterlife, which we find virtually everywhere. We seem to live with them and the attendant contradictions that come from them virtually without difficulty, as have cultures everywhere in the past. Although some of us forcefully maintain that there is no afterlife, most of us take at least an agnostic and more likely a positive view toward survival after death.

We have entered a new millennium. Although it is entirely a calendrical convention invented centuries after the life of Jesus and not a true or accurate reckoning of the duration of time between ourselves and Jesus, we were obsessed with what might have happened as we reached the year 2000. We have even misunderstood our calendrical conventions: since the calendar started with the year 1, the real millennium came later, on New Year's Day 2001. Perhaps the odometers in our cars have confused our calendrical arithmetic. Was it the contemplation that the Y2K computer problem was not trivial, that our dependence on machines could bring a disaster of biblical proportions, if not exactly the one forecast by the seers of old? It was surely a result of our unremitting self-regard to think that by inventing a calendar we could force the hand of God to bring about the Consummation. One thing is certain: all of these notions were deeply involved in our traditional religious belief that time itself will end as the dead are given their final rewards and punishments.

Is fear the source of these contemplations of the end? Even the old saw that there are no atheists in foxholes is not true. The approach of death sometimes makes some people more convinced of the falsity of religious teaching about the afterlife. What seems to be universally true is that atheists are likely to keep their beliefs quiet at religious funerals. That would be impolite and cruel to the mourners. To object strongly in the presence of the grief stricken would itself be seen as grounds for insanity, since funerals demand decorum. Most of us think the decorum is justified, since the bereaved are truly suffering and should get what help we can provide: Even the doubtful or the disbelieving bereaved can find comfort in the rites of the occasion. Indeed, the public nature of the occasion tends to quiet people's personal doubts. Most people find the familiar language and ritual of funerals to be themselves consoling, if not immediately then after the grief has receded in their minds. We have a good social understanding of where we should use the language of departed souls, where the language of resurrection and millennial expectations, where the language of ghosts and goblins, and where the language of nothing at all. Society teaches us to keep these notions from contradicting each other. We shall look at previous cultures where similar practices can be found but are much harder to understand.

Our mass culture has only made these differing beliefs more available to us and has given us pictorial representations of them that would have been impossible only a few years ago. In my seminar on the afterlife, we annually list all the recent films that have been significantly concerned with the afterlife or depicted it in some graphic way. We usually fill the board with over a hundred movie titles in minutes. Children's cartoons are full of violence and also of depictions of ghosts and spirits, together with visual depictions of how cartoon characters survive their comic and very frequent deaths. Books, films, and TV talk shows are replete with depictions of near-death experiences (hereafter NDEs) and endlessly discuss whether or not they are demonstrations of the truths of the afterlife, as they appear to be. Sincere and very sane persons of impeccable credibility relate them to us with conviction. Popular TV programs like *The X-Files* or *Touched by an Angel* and popular films like *Ghosts* or *The Sixth Sense* have so successfully affected teenage as well as adult markets that they have spawned many imitators and have had a significant effect on American teen identity concepts, whether teens report that they are "Conservative," "mystical," "experimenters," "resisters," "marginal," or "irreligious."[22]

NEAR-DEATH EXPERIENCES

No topic has occupied American discussions of the afterlife so much as near-death experiences (NDEs), which have a number of common themes beyond the fearful emergencies that cause them—bright light, a feeling of warmth, a long tunnel, possibly a meeting with deceased family members, a reluctant return to painful existence. Those who have experienced them usually find their faith strengthened or confirmed and have left the American public significantly impressed.[23] The gift of their faith confirmed is also a revelation to us all, because the survivors seem to demonstrate life after death in a scientific setting. Even non-Christians have taken a significant interest in them.[24]

But can these NDEs really tell us scientifically what we want to know? Can there be any true scientific confirmation of a life after death if no one can actually visit the abode of the dead and come back with a verifiable traveler's report? We will look at reports of heavenly journeys throughout Western culture, weighing what the heavenly adventurers see when they are in heaven (as well as why their reports differ so much) and what truths they return with. We will try to evaluate how these relate to NDEs and if they have similar effects on society.

The important issues about God and the afterlife have been thought to be beyond confirmation or disconfirmation in the scientific sense. They are more like the question "What makes an action just or a sunset beautiful?" than they are like the question "Is there sodium in table salt?" The presence of an afterlife, like the existence of God, is not amenable to scientific analysis. Nevertheless, we are still required by science and by the use of our reason to eliminate unlikelihoods or impossibilities from our faith discourse. Because we cannot prove the existence of God scientifically, we are not thereby empowered to believe that the earth is flat or that the moon is made out of green cheese. Nor are we free to ignore the question, because a great many of the most important questions in life are of the type that is impossible to confirm or disconfirm.

Some of us have achieved certainty about these issues. Those who have evangelical faith and some of those who have experienced an NDE have also, characteristically, received an additional gift of confidence in the face of humankind's universal ultimate fears. But, given the enormous amount of discussion and literature that exists on these experiences, one unexpected thing that George Gallup has shown in his book *Adventures in Immortality* is how rare they actually are, compared to the population at large, and how rare is the typical experience of "confirmation" among the relatively rare NDEs themselves.[25] They are in far less evidence than our society's interest in them would indicate, from the seemingly numberless books that have featured them in one way or another. Even the argument that the occasional NDE in children proves that it is a real experience and not just a mirror of our social beliefs in a natural experience or a hallucination of some sort cannot be maintained.[26] Once we look at a selection of cartoon depictions of the afterlife and their presence in movies and books of all types, we can have no doubt about how the young can be socialized so quickly.

Although we cannot take any report as proof of the afterlife, we should take these experiences seriously. Belief in life after death is virtually universal in human experience. Very often, these notions come together with symbols of rebirth or regeneration.[27] Though a relatively small percentage of Americans experience NDEs, a mere fraction of 1%, this yields a rather large number in absolute terms—more than a million Americans. Furthermore, the notion that we can visit the dead or cause them to visit us, that we can go to heaven and see what is there, the notion that this visit will confirm our cherished earthly beliefs, is an extremely important and constant theme in world literature. In one sense all the accounts seem to promise verification but they have so far not met scientific criteria. We will need to study why people undertake these trips and how their means—whether they be NDE travel narratives or altered states of consciousness—affect the meaning taken from the trip itself.

Which afterlife would they validate? There are many different views of the afterlife available to us as Americans and citizens of the world. If the history of the belief was at least consistent and universal in Western experience, then we would know exactly what it was that Western religion preached. We would know that the great prophets of the West preached a single notion that is clear and consistent and easy to understand. In that case, we could say that our American experience was right or wrong, and if wrong, then we could return to our traditional truths, which at least have the underpinning of revelation.

WHAT HISTORY CAN TELL US

A belief in the afterlife can be said to be older than the human race, if Neanderthal burials are to be trusted. We see many pieces of evidence of Neanderthal religion in sites of the Mousterian culture. In particular, Neanderthals left flowers, grain, and other grave goods in their internments, which suggests that they felt the departed could use the implements sacrificed for them.[28] Assuming for a moment that we are justified in concluding that the Neanderthals are not exactly our species but a closely associated one (an assumption that is still hotly debated), the notion of an afterlife would precede humanity. Belief in spirits, both benevolent (as in departed ancestors) and malicious (as in ghosts) is virtually omnipresent in human culture, though these spirits sometimes share the stage with more sophisticated notions of a beatific afterlife.

"Sharing the stage" is an appropriate phrase. We have only to look at Shakespeare's *Hamlet* to realize how easily we accept the combination of traditional Christianity with belief in spirits and ghosts. The belief in spirits and ghosts functions in a number of ways in a society—including enforcing moral schemes, upholding various institutions, and guaranteeing appropriate burial of corpses.

The Bible, viewed historically, shows us how varied our views have been, even within Western traditions. That is made even more evident by studying the Quran as scripture. Even if we look at just one tradition—either Judaism, or Christianity, or Islam—we find that the view of the afterlife is fascinatingly varied. For example, we will see that the Bible itself at first zealously ignores the afterlife. When it does discuss the afterlife, it does so only to resolve very specific questions within its own culture. In fact, all the notions of life after death in the Hebrew Bible and afterward seem to be borrowed, to some degree or another. None of them were borrowed early or without prejudice.

Previous, shorter studies of the subject have shown the dichotomy between the resurrection of the body and the immortality of the soul. Scholarship clearly understands the immortality of the soul to be a Platonic Greek notion. Opinions about where the idea of the resurrection of the body comes from are mixed. Many scholars, especially in the first decades of the twentieth century, thought it came from Persia. The *religionsgeschichtliche Schule*, basing itself on newly translated material from ancient Iran, naturally saw it as a borrowing from Zoroastrianism. The neo-Orthodox school, which wanted to preserve it as a native Israelite belief, derived from specific experiences of tragedy, pointed to apocalypticism as a natural outgrowth of the prophetic tradition. Both were partly right and partly wrong.

Throughout twentieth-century scholarship, many have thought that the two beliefs—resurrection of the body and immortality of the soul—are logically uncombinable. More recently, scholars have shown that they combine easily and very thoroughly, so that the old distinctions do not hold. To the present scholar, all the previous studies are partly misled by their search for hypothetical origins that are no more than a matter of opinion. The most important thing for understanding the belief in the hereafter is not so much the origin of the notions but the way in which the notions are used within a specific society at a specific time, what the metaphors are being used to express about our human predicament.

THE KÜBLER-ROSS DILEMMA

Even academic research has fallen victim to this temptation. I think of the recent example of Elisabeth Kübler-Ross, who wrote *On Death and Dying*, as a salutary example.[29] This famous and justly praised book on the grieving process was a passionate defense of giving the dying the opportunity to face their own deaths in a constructive way, especially in American hospitals where knowledge that the patient was dying was often withheld from him or her. Kübler-Ross's study came directly out of this clinical setting, resulting from the clinical study of persons dying of cancer, and concluded that our medical procedures were designed to protect the feelings of doctors and caregivers rather than to allow the dying the dignity to deal with their impending deaths. The study maintained that when those who know that they will die soon are given the opportunity to grieve for themselves, some experience profoundly more honest, more meaningful, and less painful deaths. Kübler-Ross described the grieving process as a healing one, going from anger and denial through depression to somber acceptance. Kübler-Ross's observations struck a chord with everyone. Her analysis of the treatment of the dying in hospitals, with the techniques that were introduced as a result to encourage the dying through the grieving process, significantly changed hospital attitudes and therapeutic techniques, among both physicians and other caregivers.

Kübler-Ross's first book entirely concerned the process of dying and grieving; quite soon, however, her books began to argue that she had found sure evidence of life after death in her clinical settings, mostly in near-death experiences. It seems experimentally verifiable that people who have strong religious faith and who pray or meditate are at some advantage in the curing process as well as in the ease with which they reach acceptance of their own deaths. But her arguments immediately raised an issue directly contradictory to her earlier work: Is it better to stop denying the reality of death in a variety of religious ways as well as in our hospital practices? Is religious faith a denial of death or an affirmation of faith? Kübler-Ross's earlier work seemed to say that some kinds of denial, as, for instance, in a physician's behavior, also denied the patient the process of grief and transition that humans need to experience. On the other hand, her later work flatly stated that there is a life after death, that there is scientific proof of it in NDEs, and that it is beneficial for the spirit to consider the afterlife as one is dying. One wonders whether such a profound issue can even be satisfactorily addressed by confirmation and disconfirmation, or whether it is not more properly an issue of the patient's most basic orientation toward life. For some, religious faith will be comforting and for others not.

Then Kübler-Ross personally experienced yet another turn of events: a series of strokes, the last being as late as 1995, which left her facing the prospect of her own slow and debilitating death. Don Lattin interviewed her in 1997 and found her very unhappy about her situation, recanting her previous, more religious philosophy. She described her current state: "It's neither living nor dying. It's stuck in the middle. My only regret is that for 40 years I spoke of a good God who helps people, who knows what you need and how all you have to do is ask for it. Well that's baloney. I want to tell the world that it's a bunch of bull. Don't believe a word of it."[30]

It is bad enough that the person who had done most in the twentieth century to define the successful grieving process should herself fall victim to one of its most obvious pitfalls: "stage 2: anger" as she called it. She was widely reported to have recanted her observations about the afterlife, and worse still, to have admitted that she had cynically invented her certainty, both to enrich herself and to benefit her clinical work. Some say her religious belief was a kind of "stage 1: denial." Others say that her cynicism and admissions of fraud were the result of her depression, from which she has now recovered. Maybe so, but what does it say of her later reaffirmations?

Perhaps Kübler-Ross's experience points out that we all harbor affirmations and doubts in our mind and that both can be helpful or destructive.

But wherever the truth lies—if indeed, it can be put into the simple sentences—the story is a clear example both of our collective need for surety where none obtains and of individuals' ability to hold a series of conflicting ideas simultaneously. Let's be frank: both the faithful and the disbelieving rightfully have doubts and should have them. Faith without doubt is merely intolerance, merely fanaticism. Without doubt, faith turns to rabid fanaticism and inspires tragedies like the World Trade Center attack. Death anxiety is a strong and important reality and has important adaptive uses in human life. It is one thing that helps keep faith from becoming fanaticism.

DEATH ANXIETY

Shakespeare himself portrays death anxiety in *Measure for Measure*

'Tis too horrible! The weariest and most loathed world life
That age, ache, penury and imprisonment
Can lay on nature is a paradise
To what we fear of death. (*Measure for Measure*, act 3, scene 1; see also
    lines 128–32)

Poor Claudio says these abject lines in the same scene that he begins with heroic words about sacrificing himself to save his sister's honor: "If I must die, I will encounter darkness as a bride and hug it in mine arms" (3.1.83–85). In this briefest moment, Shakespeare risks our respect by portraying his character suddenly turning cowardly in contemplating the horrors of death and hell. The greater risk provides us with a deeper truth about our humanity.

Modern idiom is much poorer than Shakespeare's. He shows us that death anxiety infects everything we do as humans, even when we are trying to be brave. It is part of the human condition; indeed, it seems a consequence of self-consciousness itself. It is a price we pay for being aware of ourselves as beings. Whether it is better to face this cold end without the benefit of religious understanding or to adopt religious views of the afterlife is still very much an open question, which is where Shakespeare leaves it. Which is the true denial of death?

THE TRANSCENDENT AND DOUBT

The consensus of liberal theologians has for a long time been that the existence of God, hence the validity of religion, is not susceptible to ordinary scientific notions of confirmation and disconfirmation.[31] One person looks at a sunset and sees the handiwork of the creator; another sees merely the particles of pollution adding color to the sky. Neither can erode the confidence

of the other, because neither perspective is subject to confirmation or disconfirmation. The perspective is, rather, something more fundamental about
personal orientation to meaning in the universe. The existence of God is an
aspect of our understanding of the meaning of existence—along with justice,
love, beauty, and a host of other human values—not something that can be
scientifically verified.

Life after death, at first, seems quite a different proposition. The major
pictures of life after death in the world's cultures are propositions and claims
about what are believed to be objective places. They do not have the unifor-
mity or cultural universality of the question of the existence or nonexistence
of the transcendent. Yet, when subjected to historical analysis, which shows
that the afterlife is constantly in flux and constantly being accommodated
to social, political, and economic necessities in the society, the propositional
value of any particular heaven grows much less important than the general
claim that an afterlife exists at all.

So, in the end, the afterlife is another way to express the same transcendent, nonconfirmable issue of God. The afterlife is particularly important to
religions that organize themselves as missionary religions and not nearly
as important to religions that do not. Instead, the very speculation that an
afterlife exists seems like a human need and an ideal—again, like love, beauty,
or justice—that exists in our minds rather than the world and gives a sense
of meaning to our lives. Like beauty and justice, life after death is no less
important for being unverifiable.

This is not a pleasant thought; nor is it a view that most people will appreciate easily. Most people will prefer to live within the system of beliefs
that they inherit. The very variety and change of our notions in the afterlife
speaks against any literal truth. The inherent implausibility of any one depiction of an afterlife based on the variety of contradictory notions has certainly
brought naive notions of the afterlife into question. But implausibility alone
does not actually reach the deep issue of the reality of a personal afterlife or
its potential meaning and significance in human existence. It has not even
ended speculation about the soul's afterlife.[32]

Physicians have placed word generators high up and facing ceiling-ward
in operating rooms so that an out-of-body patient can read and report on
them, thus confirming the actuality of the experience. To date none have
done so. We may suspect that none ever will. For one thing, difficulties in
confirmation occur because the EEG and other instruments used by doctors
are not designed for the sensitivities that this research demands. The brain
may be functioning deeply even when ordinary instruments can detect no activity. This conclusion is buttressed by the ability of various disabilities and
drugs to simulate out-of-body experiences: the bright light, the long tunnel,
and the feelings of euphoria.[33]

All of these experiments show that concrete, material proof of immaterial
hopes is not possible. The body does decompose and no one has convincingly

demonstrated that it can recompose, or even if it did, that it could be reanimated with the same consciousness, though many such miracles have been claimed in the last two millennia. Furthermore, it seems unlikely that a reanimated and reassembled body would really be ourselves, if our experience is as unique as we normally think it is. Proof of resurrection is never likely to be so easily demonstrable. Instead, perhaps we should take comfort in the fact that we have doubts. Doubts complete faith and keep it from becoming fanaticism.

THE SOUL AND THE AFTERLIFE

Heavenly journeys and NDEs have constantly reinforced notions of the immortality of the soul and testified to the reality of resurrection. But they cannot demonstrate them. Finally, in Neoplatonism and Augustine's thought, our very interior lives became the key to understanding how the material world and the intelligible world could affect each other. Though there is nothing inherently less plausible in the resurrection of the body at the end of time than in the immortality of the soul, it is the latter that has triumphed in Western philosophy in the last two hundred years. Again, social forces help explain this victory. It is the notion of the immortality of the soul that fits most closely with our current experience of ourselves. The democratic West is based upon the internal experience of self-consciousness and the conviction that this individual self-reflection is the basis and definition of a unique, even a transcendent self. It valorizes that personal experience as transcendent, saying, in effect, that the examined life transcends our short span of years.

In the eighteenth century, Moses Mendelssohn thought that the immortality of the soul could be demonstrated rationally and did so in his essay *The Phaedon* (named for Plato's *Phaedo*), but he felt that resurrection was a religious doctrine that could only be accepted by faith. Most Americans are convinced of the same without relying on proof; it merely makes better sense of their individual experience.

In an earlier time, the church fathers stressed the exact converse: Only resurrection preserves the uniqueness of each life and the confidence of its historical purpose while the immortality of the soul ultimately implies the survival only of the ideas themselves and trivializes the historical existence of the individual. Each has been used to confirm that true individuality survives after death. But a demonstration of the truth of either proposition—immortality of the soul or resurrection of the body—has never actually been accomplished. In this scientific climate, it would take a miracle of staggering importance. Furthermore, Judaism, Christianity, and Islam all demand that we hold both propositions simultaneously, insisting that both are true, in spite of their many seeming contradictions.

In the history of Western thought, the immortality of the soul now seems more plausible for a number of reasons. First, the passage of two millennia since Jesus' birth without the arrival of the final consummation, without the apocalypse he predicted, raises doubts about the vision of the end. Many, many plausible times for the end have come and gone, leaving the predictors either disillusioned or not, but always bereft of the end. Every time a convenient number rolls by on the calendar, humanity renews its faith in the end of time. It takes little insight to see that we are more in danger from ourselves than we are from an irate divinity. Or is that not two ways of saying the same thing? The immortality of the soul has a number of inconveniences with regard to contemporary thinking: It is terminally dualistic. It denigrates the body and probably artificially distinguishes our rational powers from animals. But these inconveniences do not disprove the afterlife; they merely tell us we need to reconceptualize it.

A relatively new American possibility is that we each get what we think we will get. It certainly is a frequent statement of American multicultural life. This new ideal has much affected the popular imagination; it was, for example, the premise of the film *What Dreams May Come*. Even hell is nothing but the self-generated setting of the soul's despair. With appropriate "therapy" in the afterlife, even suicides and sinners can be rehabilitated to partake of whatever heaven they best imagine.

This was, in a way, the vision of Origen and Gregory of Nyssa. They too lived in a culturally plural world. But regardless of where the idea came from, nothing could be more twenty-first-century American. It reflects our American experience of living in fairly close contact with people whose most intimate religious beliefs and values differ significantly from our own. It offers the comfort that we all get what we want; therefore we are all correct, all validated, all justified. It further posits that even the dead need to work on self-realization, the idle dream of the Hollywood rich, who can finally finish their therapy in the next world.

On the other hand, while the special effects were amazing, *What Dreams May Come* was not a wildly successful film. Maybe this particular culturally plural Hollywood ending is not yet as successful as the more traditional religious one. Or maybe it is so completely assumed by liberal and mainstream America that stating it was boring and did not add much to our personal quest for meaning. Or maybe it was just Hollywood's heaven and not America's heaven. Or it may be that this articulation of self-realization is too naive but that a more sophisticated form of it will satisfy the mind.

Modern America, Christian or not, has ineluctably retreated to the position of the pagan philosophers of late antiquity: Our souls are immortal by nature; all will be saved; it may just take some souls longer to figure out that altruism and moral behavior are what guarantees salvation—or, alternatively, that it is really self-realization that guarantees our salvation. Either seems acceptable as a statement of the distinctively American hereafter, because each validates quintessentially American values in this life.

In any event, the fear and reality of hell have almost entirely disappeared in America, except among the fundamentalist and evangelical sects, which seem closer to the millenarians sects of long ago than the mainstream of American life. AOL (America Online) regularly polls its subscribers about their beliefs in the afterlife. They are, granted, not a cross-section of Americans; they are far more privileged and more conservative than average Americans. Almost all who choose to answer the surveys (a self-selected group within a self-selected group) believe in the afterlife and about 90% consistently say they expect to see it. Indeed, some such general notion would fit our current notions of cultural pluralism, as all the major religions of America, including Hinduism and Buddhism (after its fashion), to say nothing of postmodern religion, also affirm a belief in a consciousness that survives death.[34]

CONSCIOUSNESS AND THE SOUL

Consciousness is the truly mysterious obsession of modern Western philosophical inquiry. Technical progress has not brought us much closer to understanding it, though research into the physical action of the brain has dethroned our surety of the self's importance. Although the history of philosophy for centuries has been devoted to a description of the soul and the self, both in the West and the East, it still remains the perennial subject of philosophers, religion, and poetry all over the world, with little hope of achieving a consensus soon. Nor have I proposed here to resolve any of the difficult problems attendant even to describing consciousness, much less defining it. But I am stating that the afterlife is a mirror for what each society feels is transcendent in its individuals' lives. In the modern period, the self has come more and more to be identified with the immortal soul. Personal consciousness is divine in our society because we value it so much.

Now, we see that the afterlife must be placed with the conception of God itself as something that is not available technically for confirmation or disconfirmation. Like statements about God and statements about ultimate concerns, it cannot be verified. Most scholars have stopped trying to demonstrate that God exists, leaving that question to a realm of discourse that has nothing to do with confirmation and disconfirmation. It is time to put our notions of an afterlife there too, realizing that our attempts to demonstrate it from near-death experiences are mistaken, as they only hold up a mirror to our own hopes and values. Indeed, the connection between the afterlife and religious truth seems more inherent in surviving varieties of Christianity than it is either in Islam or Judaism, where there is, in general, less discussion of the issue at all.

That is not saying that the afterlife is unproved; it is saying that *it is in principle unprovable.*[35] Thus, when Stephen T. Davis says that he concludes that the theory of resurrection is a viable option for Christian belief, just as the theory of temporary disembodiment is, he is making a statement about his belief in the entire Christian worldview and its continued importance in his life, as well as in the lives of his readers.[36] In doing so, he is affirming that his notions of God, history, and the afterlife are probably so intertwined that one is incomprehensible without the others. We can probably thank Plotinus and Augustine for that synthesis. Indeed, it may be that any Christian's orientation toward the afterlife is equally as true as but not in any way intersecting with, let us say, any Tibetan Buddhist's vision. They are both coherent views of truth, but we have no way of establishing their correspondence with anything, except with a certain culture's understanding of reality.

NOTES

This article has been adapted from *Life after Death: A History of the Afterlife in Western Religion* by Alan F. Segal. Copyright © 2004 by Alan F. Segal. Used by permission of Doubleday, a division of Random House, Inc.

1. Tertullian, *de resurrectione carnis*, 1. Available English translation: Souter, Alexander. *Tertullian—Concerning the Resurrection of the Flesh.* London: SPCK, 1922.

2. Many pastors—whether they be priests, ministers, or rabbis—have reported to me that their congregants report a belief in the resurrection of the body but that what they mean by it is the immortality of the soul. We shall spend a fair amount of time distinguishing between these two confusing notions in early Christian and rabbinic texts.

3. The Gallup organization's work is one of our most significant descriptive tools for American religious life. Since the U.S. Census is not allowed to ask questions about religion, George Gallup Jr.'s continuing interest in our religious life has provided researchers with major and significant measures of our religiosity. See George Gallup Jr. and Jim Castelli, *The People's Religion: American Faith in the 90's* (New York: MacMillan, 1989).

4. Gallup and Castelli, *The People's Religion.*

5. See Alexis de Tocqueville, *Democracy in America*, vol. 2, bk. 1, chaps. 5–7: Available English edition: Alexis de Tocqueville: *Democracy in America and Two Essays on America*, trans. Gerald E. Bevan. (New York: Penguin Classics, 2003). vol. 2, bk. 1, chaps. 5–7: "How Religion in the United States Avails Itself of Democratic Tendencies," "The Progress of Roman Catholicism in the United States," and "What Causes Democratic Nations to Incline toward Pantheism."

6. Gerhard Lenski, *The Religious Factor: A Sociological Study of Religion's Impact on Politics, Economics, and Family Life*, 1961 rev. ed., reprint (Garden City, N.Y.: Anchor, 1963).

7. Gallup and Castelli, *The People's Religion*, p. 54.

8. As well as the Gallup poll and the American Institute of Public Opinion (AIPO), my information comes from Andrew M. Greeley, *Religious Change in America* (Cambridge, Mass.: Harvard University Press, 1989) and uses sampling from the National Opinion Research Center (NORC, operating out of the University of Chicago, with which Greeley has long been associated). NORC also sponsors the General Social Survey, used below.

Gallup, for example, used AIPO to measure the strength of religious beliefs and practices in the United States and Europe by collecting data on six questions designed to measure doctrinal behavior and emotional religiosity: weekly church attendance, belief in a personal God, importance of God in daily life, belief in life after death, obtaining comfort from religion, and agreement with the statement that the country's churches answered people's spiritual needs. By combining the affirmative answers and dividing by 100, AIPO constructed each country's "Religion Index." Here are the scores: Ireland 73; United States 67; Northern Ireland 65; Spain 51; Italy 43; Belgium 39; West Germany 37; Norway 36; Netherlands 36; Great Britain 36; France 32; and Denmark 21.5.

9. Douglas P. Crowne and David Marlowe, *The Approval Motive: Studies in Evaluative Dependence* (New York: Wiley, 1964).

10. Religion has other functions as well. It is important for people in a capitalistic society to appear trustworthy and honest; religious piety, hence church attendance, is highly correlated with these values in the American psyche. We surely wish to attend church for other reasons too, not the least of which is that we really do strive to be trustworthy, honest, and religious. From one point of view, this piety may merely be another way of stating the social utility of religion in a democratic and capitalistic society. But virtually all successful persons in the United States report that they seek to live up to transcendent and religious goals in their everyday lives and attribute their success to their values. Being religious has other measurable positive effects on our business lives. In suburban settings, we surely rely on church membership for networking about career, child rearing, and friendship making, far more than Europeans do. So it is no wonder that we want to attend church so much, regularly telling people and ourselves that we attend more often than we actually do.

11. Stephen L Carter, *The Culture of Disbelief: How American Law and Politics Trivialize Religious Devotion* (New York: Basic Books, 1993).

12. Robert A. Neimeyer and David Van Brunt Neimeyer, "Death Anxiety," in *Dying: Facing the Fact*, ed. Hannelore Wass and Robert A. Neimeyer, 3rd ed. (Bristol Pa.: Taylor and Francis, 1995), pp. 49–88, esp. pp. 64–66.

13. See Andrew M. Greeley and Michael Hout, "Americans Increasing Belief in Life after Death: Religious Competition and Acculturations," *American Sociological Review* 66 (1999): 813.

14. The heading is taken from Susan Garrett, *The Demise of the Devil* (Minneapolis: Fortress, 1989), which is a very competent analysis of the meaning of magic in Luke-Acts. The title is quite relevant to the American context as well.

15. George Gallup Jr., *Adventures in Immortality*, with William Proctor (New York: McGraw Hill, 1982), pp. 55–66.

16. *Pace* Andrew Delbanco, *The Death of Satan: How Americans Have Lost the Sense of Evil* (New York: Farrar, Strauss, 1995); see also Jerry L. Walls, *Hell: The Logic of Damnation* (Notre Dame, Ind.: University of Notre Dame Press, 1992).

17. Quoted in Walls, *Hell: The Logic of Damnation*, p. 1.

18. Lynn Schofield Clark, "Angels, Aliens, and the Dark Side of Evangelicalism," in *From Angels to Aliens: Teenagers, the Media, and the Supernatural*, ed. Lynn Schofield Clark (New York: Oxford, 2003), pp. 24–45. Clark attributes this correlation to the elaborated supernatural world that is commonly taught in evangelical families. Even when the teens reject the content of that world, they often refill it with new and more popular content.

19. See the documentary *Hellhouse*, directed and produced by George Ratliffe. For an account of the popularity of exorcism in American life, see Michael Cuneo, *American Exorcism: Expelling Demons in the Land of Plenty* (New York: Doubleday, 2001).

20. See, for example, *Newsweek* polls of November 1, 1999, as well as previous ones reported for the issues of November 13, 1995, April 8, 1996, and September 22,

1997. These findings are reproducible cross-culturally. Florian and Kravetz conducted a study of 178 Israeli Jews that correlated fear of personal death with religious practice. Although moderately religious respondents scored higher on some dimensions of death fear (e.g., concern over the consequences of one's death for one's family and friends), highly religious subjects scored highest on others (e.g., fear of punishment in the afterlife). Religious faith seems to assuage some anxieties and raise others. See V. Florian and S. Kravetz, "Fear of Personal Death: Attribution, Structure and Relation to Religious Belief," *Journal of Personality and Social Psychology* 44 (1983): 600–607.

21. Transcendent values are those values to which we give ultimate significance. The theological term originally described God—that he was necessarily greater than the universe, therefore transcending it. This protected us from thinking that God was the same as the universe. The converse term in traditional theology is God's immanence, His presence in all of our lives. Both were necessary to achieve even an outline of what Jews, Christians, and Muslims normally think of God.

22. See the interesting paper by Lynn Schofield Clark, "U.S. Adolescent Religious Identity, the Media, and the 'Funky' Side of Religion," unpublished paper, Center for Mass Media Research, University of Colorado at Boulder.

23. See Raymond A. Moody, *Life after Life: The Investigation of a Phenomenon—Survival of Bodily Death*, with Elisabeth Kübler-Ross, 2nd ed. (San Francisco: Harper, 2001); Dr. Melvin Morse, *Closer to the Light: Learning From the Near-Death Experiences of Children* (New York: Ivy Books, 1991), also *Transformed by the Light: The Powerful Effect of Near Death Experiences on People's Lives* (New York: Ballantine Books, 1992).

24. The Tibetan Buddhist community in the United States has seen in them confirmation of the truth of a number of phenomena that are described in their religious writings. In particular, the bright light is well documented in the *Bardol Thodol*, the so-called *Tibetan Book of the Dead*.

25. Gallup, *Adventures in Immortality*, pp. 1–54.

26. See Morse, *Closer to the Light*.

27. See, for example, Maurice Bloch and Jonathan Parry, ed., *Death and the Regeneration of Life* (London: Cambridge University Press, 1982).

28. See Mike Parker Pearson, *The Archaeology of Death and Burial*, 3rd ed. (College Station, Tex.: Texas A & M Press, 2002), pp. 53, 147–51. This does not absolutely prove that they believed in life after death. They may just have been observing a taboo or a gift-giving rite. But the chances are that some kind of continuity of personality on the other side of the grave was responsible for the inclusion of these grave goods. This inclusion seems at least to say that the corpse continues to share in the social life of the community; so in that way, even without a notion of a soul or spirit, the corpse continues to function as a human life.

29. Elizabeth Kübler-Ross, *On Death and Dying* (Toronto: MacMillan Company, 1969). There were many important books that tried to counter society's "denial of death" with a more honest appraisal, constituting a kind of "death awareness" movement. See Ernest Becker, *The Denial of Death* (New York: Free Press, 1973); Philip Ariès, *Western Attitudes toward Death* (Baltimore: Johns Hopkins University Press, 1974); *Dying: Facing the Facts*, ed. Hannelore Wass (New York: Hemisphere, 1979).

30. See "Expert on Death Faces Her Own Death: Kübler-Ross Now Questions Her Life's Work," *San Francisco Chronicle*, May 31, 1997, Lexis-Nexis Academic Universe: General News Topics. My thanks to several students who have investigated this story in the past few years, especially Elise Cucchi of Williams College.

31. See, for example, the helpful book by Malcolm L. Diamond, *Contemporary Philosophy and Religious Thought: An Introduction to the Philosophy of Religion* (New York: McGraw Hill, 1974).

32. An Internet news article of July 4, 2001, "Scientist Says Mind Continues after Brain Dies," written by Sarah Tippet for America Online, reviews the research of Sam Pamia, a physician in Southampton, England, who has studied the NDE with an eye to demonstrating that the soul survives death. Pamia interviewed 63 heart attack patients who were deemed clinically dead but were revived. Of these, 56 had no recollection of the periods of unconsciousness, and seven reported memories. Four were labeled NDEs, because they reported lucid thinking, reasoning, moving about, and communicating with others after doctors determined that their brains had stopped functioning. Pamia is convinced that these experiences provide evidence of an afterlife.

33. See, for example, Carlos Alvarado, "Out-of-Body Experiences," *Varieties of Anomalous Experience: Examining the Scientific Evidence*, ed. Etzel Cardeña, Steven Jay Lynn, and Stanley Krippner (Washington, D.C.: American Psychological Association, 2000), pp. 183–218.

34. Since Plato established the relationship between the soul and intellection, by tying his proof for the immortality of the soul to memory, we have gradually developed our notions of consciousness through the acquired intellect of medieval philosophers to our general American notion that the immortal soul contains our self-consciousness. That would have surprised the ancient pagans. Indeed, the experience of separating the soul from the body—an experience thought quite ordinary in the ancient world, as it explained sleep among other things—was thought to be a simple demonstration of the truth of the immortality of the soul. If the soul could exist without the body in life, nothing prevented it from existing without the body after death. It all seemed clear enough then. But Platonic reincarnation demanded that the soul did not carry our personal memories with it, only our knowledge of the basic categories of thought.

35. *Pace* John Hick, *Death and Eternal Life* (New York: Fordham, 1978) and others.

36. See *Death and Afterlife*, ed. Stephen T. Davis (New York: St. Martin's Press, 1989), p. 131. This book also contains articles and responses by Nielsen, Hick, Badham, Glucklich, Griffin, Hughes, Cook, and Irish. It provides a very interesting dialogue about the nature of faith in resurrection in the modern world. See also Stephen T. Davis, "Physicalism and Resurrection," in *Soul, Body, and Survival: Essays on the Metaphysics of Human Persons* ed. Kevin Corcoran (Ithaca, N.Y.: Cornell University Press, 2001) as well as essays by Lynne Baker, John Cooper, Kevin Corcoran, John Foster, Stewart Goetz, William Hasker, Jaegwon Kim, Brian Leftow, E. J. Lowe, Trention Merricks, Timothy O'Conor, Eric T. Olson, and Charles Taliaferro.

CHAPTER 4

LIFE EXTENSION: PROPONENTS, OPPONENTS, AND THE SOCIAL IMPACT OF THE DEFEAT OF DEATH

Kevin T. Keith

I don't want to achieve immortality through my works. I want to achieve immortality by not dying.

—Woody Allen

The finitude of human life is a blessing for every individual, whether he knows it or not.

—Leon Kass

It is always a shock to get what we ask for. In the unreflective rush of modern postmodern science, dreams are achieved with unsettling ease. One candidate dream is the quest for immortality.

That phrase itself, "the quest for immortality," its embarrassing pretension a kind of throwback to Victorian natural-philosopher hubris, underscores how close we've come to the impossible. Science once gloried in stolid, methodical methodology, progress made one deliberate step at a time. The grand "Eureka!" was more legend and romance than real science; everyday lab work is the quiet clarification of small problems in small fields. But the shocking power of contemporary science has awakened dormant dreams and birthed futures quite old-fashioned in their grandeur. The entire human genome in a memory bank, "the theory of everything," babies conceived hither and gestated thither: science is dreaming big again.

As medical power increases, it seems possible not merely to mitigate the most threatening diseases but to eliminate, or at least stave off, disease itself, and with it the debilitation that once seemed the inevitable burden of advanced age. Scientists are now talking seriously of extending the human life span—that is, of finding, and possibly eradicating, the inherent limit to human longevity, which, they claim, we have so far failed to reach only because of the unnatural intervention of natural death.

Whether this hope will be borne out remains to be seen. That the attempt would be made, however, that we must now seriously contemplate how to, and whether to, and whether we really want to, sentence ourselves to more of the future than any human yet has faced, forces us to raise questions that have hitherto enjoyed the luxury of irrelevance.

THE DREAM OF LIFE, THE FEAR OF DEATH

Death, be not proud.... Death, thou shalt die.

—John Donne

Many cultures have expected life after earthly death—whether by rebirth, by transcendence to an eternal realm, or as reward or punishment at the hands of the gods. That this should be such a common theme underscores the severity of the problem of death—not that we *can* die but that death has been seen as *insurmountable*. To beat death, to cheat death, required not *not-dying* but *dying and living on*. For prescientific cultures, afterlife was the only path to eternity. Physical immortality was a concept unknown or applicable only outside the human sphere (gods were immortal; ordinary humans, by contrast, stood so far bereft of this status that they were *referred to as*... "mortals").

The hope of an afterlife may thus be seen as a surrender to the inevitability of death, a last best hope when a more immediate, and possibly more enjoyable, physical immortality eludes. (No need of an *after*life if one does not intend one's life to end.)

If an eternal future is what is sought, it would seem preferable on probabilistic grounds alone to continue a life in the mundane, physical realm, rather than gamble on the unknowns of the unseen.[1] Immortality in the fleshly realm offers the promise of a familiar (and presumably desirable—else why fear death?) mode of living, in familiar surroundings; the afterlife carries the attendant risk that one will wind up in an eternity not to one's liking. All things considered, then, the best way to live forever is not to die. The catch, of course, is that to achieve immortality one must find a way to beat some very long odds. Few achieve this. In fact, every person known to have attempted it is known to have failed. The ubiquity of death makes dreams of the afterlife a highly popular insurance policy.

That may be changing. An eternity of life *in this life* has come to seem more possible than before—having stepped, perhaps, from the level of fantasy to that of science fiction, one notch closer to fact. The thought of extending physical life to the point that it promises the benefits of the eternal afterlife has shed its trappings of lunacy and quackery. Serious scientists now speak of immortality, and serious moralists now cluck at imaginings that would have been ravings only a few years ago. The denial of death has emerged from its embarrassing status as plot or symptom. It is now a goal, a plan, a research program, a *project*.

Curing Death

The factual observation that death is a natural process—resulting either from physiological malfunction or the body's inherent mechanisms of senescence—gives rise to the perfectly logical suspicion that if those processes could be slowed or mitigated, death itself could be "treated" just as any other bodily ailment. Denial of death, in this way of thinking, is a denial that death is an inevitable and implacable finality—not a mere failure of the life process but a distinct and final "stage" of life, an unavoidable stage that punctuates, and terminates, all other stages. Instead, death, denied, is a *disease*, a *treatable condition*. Death is perhaps a serious disease—no need to minimize it—but no different in principle, to the scientifically ambitious thinker, from any other severe derangement of organ function.

As a disease, death can be—and, one might think, surely should be—*cured*. Denial of death has thus moved from a dream to a practical goal—a goal that, in its simplest form, envisions death as a kind of medical specialty: not the endpoint of a failed treatment but the disease being treated, perhaps someday eliminated, itself. For if presenescent morbidity can be eliminated, why not senescence, too? If medicine gives us control of our bodies' responses to the degradations of disease and injury, why can it not give us control of the internal mechanisms of wear and decline? Why should our bodies *ever* wear out?[2]

Death denied in this way would be a denial of the idea that every life reaches an endpoint as a natural result of the processes of living. It would remove the inevitability of that endpoint and remove the terminal implications of the concept of a "natural" human life span. There are many people dedicated to doing this. Denial of death is no longer a mindset. It is a program, a goal, a science, and an industry.

Sowing the Wind

The field is not new—antioxidation strategies for preventing cell aging have been proposed since at least the late 1950s. It is growing rapidly, however. There is now an International Association of Biomedical Gerontology (IABG), which has been holding annual conferences on life-extension technology for 15 years. A remarkably broad, profit-minded life-extension industry has also quietly grown up, involving academic scientists and cutting-edge commercial-science firms. None is yet ready to market anti-aging therapies or life-extension treatments, but the range of serious players is testimony to the perceived possibilities the field offers. They include the Defense Advanced Research Projects Agency (DARPA), the military cutting-edge technology program; Advanced Cell Technologies (ACT), (in)famous for producing the first cloned human embryo for stem cell research; Geron Corporation, a high-profile biotech firm specializing in anticancer treatments based on stem cells and telomerase; Human Genome Sciences, another biotech firm pursuing genetically engineered pharmaceuticals based on human proteins; and researchers at numerous academic facilities, including the University of California, Irvine, the University of California, Berkeley, Stanford University, Cambridge University, and others.[3]

The term "engineered negligible senescence"—meaning a state in which medical treatments and biotechnology have reduced age-related disease to the point at which there is no statistically detectable change in a population's death rate with the increasing age of the population—was coined almost 20 years ago by Caleb E. Finch of the University of Southern California.[4] A landmark paper in 2002, coauthored by a team of scientists from across the United States and England, proposed "SENS" ("Strategies for Engineered Negligible Senescence") as a practical program for which they held the expectation, "within about a decade, of substantive progress toward that goal."

> In each case [of necessary avenues of research] we anticipate that adequately funded efforts to develop such technology have a good chance of success in mice within ten years...; moreover, we argue...that translation of it to humans may occur rapidly thereafter.[5]

The scientists go further, suggesting that it is not merely possible to prevent aging for healthy adults but that *reversing mammalian aging is not necessarily any harder than dramatically postponing it.*[6] Thus today's oldsters, if they are lucky enough to make it past the point at which aging is finally subdued, may be able to look forward to an essentially endless life of rejuvenated health and youth as well!

The figurehead of the scientific longevity movement—active in research but more active in cheerleading his fellow researchers—is Aubrey de Grey of Cambridge University and the IABG. De Grey, the architect of the SENS movement, thinks the technical challenges it presents will be met faster than critics expect. He points out that only a relatively minor, but consistent, incremental decrease in age-specific mortality rates would produce "actuarial escape velocity"—a situation in which the average person's probability of death in a given year falls faster from cumulative scientific progress in anti-aging than it rises from that person's own biological aging. De Grey calculates that this point will be reached if science manages to reduce

the risk of death by 10% per year on a continuous basis. Even a total reduction of only 30% altogether would give the average person an extra 20 years
of life, during which science is likely to achieve a second 30% reduction, and
so on.[7]

An even more sanguine opinion, however, holds that merely making old
age more likely could, by itself, open the door to a potentially limitless continuation from there onward. Applying engineering principles, Leonid Gavrilov and Natalia Gavrilova point out that the graph of increasing human
mortality with age closely models the curve of increasing failures of technological systems, which is well known to engineers. Both graphs exhibit a
characteristic "late-life mortality leveling off"—a plateau in the death rate
in old age, beyond which increasing age does not increase one's chances of
dying (though of course the absolute death rate in a given year is still high).[8]
This suggests that, if the direct causes of death in old age—disease, accidents,
strokes, etc.—could be controlled, just getting older would not, itself, result
in death for biological organisms any more than it does for well-maintained
machines:

> There is no fixed upper limit to human longevity—there is no special
> number that separates possible from impossible values of a life span. This
> conclusion flies in the face of the common belief that humans have a fixed
> maximal life span and that there exists a biological limit to longevity.[9]

Gavrilov and Gavrilova also argue that the mathematics of engineering failure processes suggest that low rates of "manufacturing error" in biological
systems (i.e., improving health in the early years of life, in preparation for the
periods of increasing damage with aging) will have a dramatic increase in
late-life mortality irrespective of major changes in basic human biology:

> Even small improvements to the processes of early human development—
> ones that increase the numbers of initially functional elements—could
> result in a remarkable fall in mortality and a significant extension of
> human life.[10]

Taking a longer view, technology visionary Ray Kurzweil and longevity
specialist Terry Grossman see a multistage progression, from the current,
groping efforts to full control of aging and debility—what they describe as
three "bridges" to an immortal future. The first "bridge" is life extension
using the best available knowledge, to allow the current generation to last
long enough to be on hand when true control of aging is finally achieved.
The second bridge takes those alive at that time through the process of aging
control and the revision of all life-threatening disease or degenerative processes. This would represent "immortality" in a limited sense. But Kurzweil

and Grossman are ambitious even for a field grounded on expansive visions of the future. Immortality is not enough for them. Its main significance is merely that it will serve to keep all those who benefit from it alive indefinitely, until technology progresses to the point at which the third bridge—"the nanotechnology–Artificial Intelligence revolution"—is crossed to "enable us to rebuild our bodies and brains at the molecular level."[11]

Reaping the Whirlwind

In among the cautious engineers, sober biologists, and technologically savvy visionaries, however, the life-extension field is rife with dreamers who range from outright cranks and opportunists to more influential figures whose intentions, and apparently sincere expectations, can give pause to the most sanguine futurist.

The Extropy Institute is a life-extension-promotion outfit that sponsors an annual conference attended by mainstream researchers. At a 1999 conference,

> [The]Extropy Institute's founder, a chiseled, ponytailed philosophy PhD named Max More, confidently declare[d], "This is the fourth revolution in our history—the ultrahuman revolution.".... More's wife, an artist and bodybuilder named Natasha Vita-More, sketch[ed] out a future in which people will enjoy multiple sex organs, polymer skin that changes color like a mood ring, and virtual reality eyeball implants....
>
> "Maybe I can look like a Renaissance painting for a while, or maybe a pointillist image, or maybe Cubist, like a Picasso," she [said]...."Our future bodies will have streamlined muscles in all sorts of interesting shapes— new types of limbs, new types of carved skeletal structures."[12]

The life-extension industry also suffers from its unwelcome association with quack medicine peddlers and scam artists who prey on the gullibility of a scientifically ignorant public, raising false hopes while touting worthless products. Fad therapies and snake oil have flooded the alternative medicine market, embarrassing researchers who do not want serious science associated with such schemes and who are afraid that funding and public acceptance for their work will be hampered by the sideshow excesses that accompany it. In 2002, a statement signed by 52 researchers on aging was published in a scientific journal, declaring that "the [anti-aging] products being sold have no scientifically demonstrated efficacy, in some cases they may be harmful, and those selling them often misrepresent the science upon which they are based."[13]

The scientific community is equally wary of its own members who show an awkward degree of enthusiasm for immortality. It is often remarked that proposals to the NIH Office of Aging Research have to carefully avoid using the word "longevity" and instead claim to be aimed only at reducing disease-related mortality. A group of leading researchers also noted that "any positive remark about the feasibility of [successful longevity treatments] risks two undesirable reactions: in the public the engendering of unwarranted optimism, and in the research community the pigeon-holing of oneself with snake oil–peddling charlatans."[14]

Aubrey de Grey has argued to his colleagues that scientists working on life extension or immortality should come out of the closet (so to speak) and encourage the public to take an interest in this work by offering tentative timescales on which the practical extension of life and retardation of aging can be expected to become available, in part to enable members of the public to plan their own health strategies to survive until that time, and in part to pressure governments for necessary funding and programs to achieve it.[15] He also notes that a majority of his IABG colleagues disagree.[16]

LIFE EXTENSION

> Immortality is not a gift,
> Immortality is an achievement;
> And only those who strive mightily
> Shall possess it.
>
> —Edgar Lee Masters

It is clear enough, then, that something is underway—something significant, possibly life changing (in the most broadly literal sense), and already carrying with it snares and pitfalls of human perfidy or technological mishap. Just what that is, and what it portends for individuals—perhaps the species—requires serious consideration.

Terminology

We must pause here to review the practical grounding of these dramatically big dreams. There are various avenues by which death is being given the scientific bum's rush, and various means by which its denial may be obtained. Some clarifying terminology, and a review of the currently promising avenues of research, are needed.

It is as well to admit at the outset that "immortality"—though that word is used—is not truly on offer. What is conceivable in practical terms is, at best, effective control of the natural processes—disease and inherent debility—that commonly lead to death. Control of morbidity in this sense could conceivably eliminate these processes, and thus eliminate both the inevitability of senile debility and the statistical certainty of fatal diseases—it could, that is, remove any natural inevitability of mortality. But no such program can encompass all possibilities; death by violence or accident would always be a danger, and even death by untreated disease or unique genetic defect would remain possible. Thus everyone would face some possibility of death even if no "natural" source of death were to be feared—and, probability being what it is, everyone would eventually roll the mortal snake-eyes in life's mandatory crapshoot.[17]

We must therefore distinguish between the attempt to extend the *average* human life span by reducing debilitating disease, the attempt to extend the *maximum* human life span by preventing or delaying natural senescence, and the attempt to actually *remove the possibility of natural death entirely* through as-yet-unknown technologies.

In the literature of the field, both an increase in average life expectancy and an increase in maximum human life span are often referred to as "life extension," while the elimination of all natural sources of death is sometimes referred to as "immortality." The attempt to extend life span by the specific means of slowing, but not eliminating, the natural process of aging is known as "age retardation"; there are other proposed methods of life extension, however, that aim to eliminate aging entirely. Finally, the increase in the total *healthy* years of life, without increasing the total overall life span—the use of technology, that is, to maintain health as long as possible and restrict morbidity to the later years of a life of otherwise normal length—is often referred to as "morbidity compression."

The Second Half of Life

The most likely and most direct program of life extension focuses on simply increasing the average life span of the normal human being. Remarkable results in this line are available from relatively modest technological investments. The average life expectancy of a resident of the United States increased from 46.3 years to 74.3 years, for males, and from 48.3 years to 79.7 years, for females, between 1900 and 2000—a gain of about three years of life expectancy per decade, in other words.[18] The American Academy of Anti-Aging Medicine notes that "this advance can be generally attributed to improvements in sanitation, the discovery of antibiotics, and medical care. Now, as scientists make headway against chronic diseases like cancer and heart disease, some think it can be extended even further."[19] The Centers for Disease Control—traditionally a cautious organization—declares:

> The United States is on the brink of a longevity revolution....Although the risk of disease and disability clearly increases with advancing age, poor health is not an inevitable consequence of aging. Much of the illness, disability, and death associated with chronic disease is avoidable through known prevention measures.[20]

In other words, the 30 years of extra life granted the average American over the last 100 years are the product of medical and social improvements that we now think of as fairly ordinary, and, more significantly, *that were not developed for the purpose of extending life span.* That death is a disease is shown most clearly by the convenient, but remarkable, fact that, *in curing disease, medicine put death off by 30 years* for the average person, while also extending the range of healthy, productive life—and this in only the first decades of truly effective scientific medicine and antibiotics.

This "easy" way to life extension—by reduction of natural morbidity— reveals the natural maximum human life span, currently thought to be about 120–25 years.[21] With disease elimination and morbidity compression, this would make available 40–50 years of good health in the "second half" of life that most people today never see.

Who has not said "If I could only go back and start over…"? If the dreams of the mainstream anti-aging researchers bear fruit, it may finally be possible to "live your life over again," or at least to live another life when your three score-and-ten are done with, and manage to do some of the things you wish you had done the first time around.

Under that scenario, one would cheat death entirely in one's first life. Seventy years of age would not be the beginning of the end, but merely early middle age; decline, debility, and the fading of one's capacities would be as far off for a 70-year-old as they are for a 20-year-old today. And, if 50 years of healthy adulthood seems today like a full life, then to live out that 50 years and have 50 more still to come, with no likelihood of immediate death or decline, would be essentially *to live through an entire life* and move on to the next one, *without dying!*

The Means to the End of the End

On closer inspection, it is apparent that this dramatic 30-year gain is largely the result of eliminating common causes of infant and childhood mortality, which have a large statistical impact on the population-wide average age at death. There are limits to how much can be gained from disease reduction alone, however. Late-life disease has a lesser impact on the life expectancy of adults; extending maximum life expectancy for those of adult years through reductions in disease-related morbidity alone would therefore require unrealistic advances.

S. Jay Olshansky, who has been tracking changes in average age at death in the United States for over 15 years, notes that

the vast majority of this increase in life expectancy from 47 to about 77 through 80 [years] now for females in the United States, is a result of declines in infant, child and maternal mortality. That can only be achieved once for a population. Once it is then achieved, the only way to achieve another increase in life expectancy like that is to influence the elderly....

If, indeed, we were to find a cure for cancer, for example, life expectancy at birth would rise by about three and a half years. Life expectancy at birth would also rise by about the same amount, three to three and a half years if systemic heart disease was hypothetically eliminated. And if we eliminated all cardiovascular diseases, diabetes and all forms of cancer combined, life expectancy at birth in humans would rise up to about 90. So you have to believe that we will be experiencing rather dramatic reductions in mortality in order to yield these very high life expectancies. A life expectancy of 100 required about 85 percent reductions in all causes of death at every age.[22]

Thus, it is evident that, while mainstream medicine and related improvements in health across the population have had a dramatic impact on *average* life expectancy at birth, they have had little impact on *maximum* life expectancy or life expectancy for those who survive to reach their 70s. These advances have not addressed the inbred limits (if any) to the human life span, but rather the phenomena that most commonly prevent those limits from even being reached.

Other approaches to life extension are in the offing, however. Steven Austad, a leading researcher in longevity, confidently proclaims that limited life extension is currently doable, and that more dramatic alterations in the mortal course will be possible with future developments:

In the near term using traditional medicine, I think...that we will get a few additional years, whether it's going to be five, whether it's going to be ten, whether it's going to be three, I think we'll find out. Longer term as the sorts of therapies that I've been talking about that work in animals actually get extended to humans...I think it's easily possible that we'll get a few additional decades of human life expectancy....

The last question, are there hard physiological barriers on the maximum human life span? I will say we don't know, but I [have] some animal data that I think suggests that there are not.[23]

Sherwin Nuland, on the other hand, argues that longevity is less desirable than simple compression of morbidity, and that we should focus our resources on the latter:

[Biotechnological revisions of the human condition] are not the problems American medicine should be struggling with. Its proper task is not the prolongation of life beyond the naturally decreed maximum span of our species...but its betterment. And if anyone's life needs betterment it is surely the elderly man or woman still living well beyond the years of vigor

and productivity because the benisons of public health and biomedicine
have made it possible.[24]

Needless to say, each of these scenarios is far-fetched, but each is the focus
of an active research program. The practical control of bodily functions that
science commands increases almost by the day. Advances on all of these
fronts are all but inevitable—as are the consequences of those advances.

Nuts and Bolts

How is all this to come about?

Morbidity compression, as previously noted, is the logical result of the
control of ordinary pathology. True life extension, however, requires as yet
speculative, but surprisingly promising, research into a number of common
pathways to cellular-level mortality and organ-system degradation—
the processes by which the body runs down even if it is not killed by outright
pathology.

Current Research

Aubrey de Grey's group identifies seven biological mechanisms that, if adequately controlled, are all de Grey thinks necessary for retardation of aging.
He points out that each of these was first identified at least 20 years ago, and
no other major degradation pathways have been identified since then, suggesting that no others are likely to be found. The list includes:

- Cell mass loss;
- Cellular senescence;
- Chromosomal mutations and cancer;
- Mitochondrial plasmid mutations;
- Lysosomal "junk";
- Amyloid plaques in neural tissue;
- Extracellular structural protein cross-linking.[25]

For each of these problems, de Grey blithely proposes a technological fix—
sometimes radically esoteric (hiding a redundant copy of the mitochondrial
genome in the chromosomes in the cell's nucleus; genetically engineering the
telomerase gene entirely out of the human species to eliminate all cancers,
and then rejuvenating the body with periodic injections of telomerase-enabled
stem cells for tissue growth), sometimes merely optimistic (new drugs to
dissolve amyloid buildups). The handwaving quality of these solutions, and
de Grey's breathless indifference to their enormity (permanently restructure
an entire, distinct part of the human genome?) tends to undermine his assurances that "all of [these techniques] are likely to be feasible in mice within

a decade (presuming adequate funding), and may be translatable to humans within a decade or two thereafter."[26] Nonetheless, none of them is absurd, and all are the subject of active research programs. The "10 years in mice" prediction is taken seriously by others in the field.

The President's Council on Bioethics, in surveying the range of necessary and possible treatments for aging for their symposium on the ethics of such treatments, comes up with a similar list of prerequisite techniques for life extension:

- Muscle enhancement;
- Memory enhancement;
- Antisenescence through caloric restriction;
- Genetic engineering to combat mutations;
- Cell-loss prevention through antioxidation (anti–free radical) therapy;
- Antisenescence through hormone treatment;
- Antisenescence through telomere manipulation.[27]

The similarity to de Grey's list is obvious, although the treatments recommended in some cases are different.

It appears, then, that the scientifically informed community has converged on a practical and manageable research project on aging retardation. Nothing guarantees success, but the field is well defined, long active, and takes itself seriously enough to be now engaged in a debate over *when* its own success can be expected.

Wishful Thinking

Other technological bids for immortality involve rather grander flights of fancy. In the time-honored way of wishful futurists, seekers of immortality seize upon each new scientific advance, or fad, as the solution they have been waiting for. Some visionaries see "science"—the grand enterprise itself, not just some particular piece of knowledge or technology—as guaranteeing its own eventual triumph over the mundane physicality of an imperfect world:

> According to models that Ray [Kurzweil] has created, our paradigm-shift rate—the rate of technical progress—is doubling every decade, and the capability (price, performance, capacity, and speed) of specific information technologies is doubling every year. So the answer to our question ["Do we have the knowledge and the tools today to live forever?"] is actually a definitive yes—the knowledge exists, if aggressively applied, for you to slow aging and disease processes to such a degree that you can be in good health and good spirits when the more radical life-extending and life-enhancing technologies become available over the next couple of decades.[28]

In a similarly hopeful vein, much of today's headline-setting science has been confidently cited as the breakthrough that—"any day now"—will make life extension and the final defeat of death a reality:

- "Nanotechnology"[29] will provide intracellular robots that systematically clean up tissue damage and repair malfunctioning biomolecules—what the body can't do for itself will be done by an invisible corps of indwelling majordomos and repair techs...or something.
- The Human Genome Project will unlock the secrets of our inherited bioprocesses—including the mechanisms of senescence and of many diseases. Once we have that knowledge in hand, the next step will surely be obvious.[30]
- Stem cell research, not surprisingly, is the latest great hope for the evermore. There is perhaps a symbolic suggestion of eternal youth lurking in cells taken from embryos or umbilical cord blood, not to mention their notable property of immortality (in the technical sense—they can be maintained permanently in tissue culture flasks). At any rate, the oft-made promise that stem cells will provide a source of rejuvenated tissue for debilitative conditions is reason enough to hope that further such applications would stave off any form of tissue damage, perhaps forever.
- And, for those of us unlucky enough to be born on the cusp of glory—late enough to see the promised land of immortality, but too soon to get there ourselves—cryogenics[31] will preserve our corpses until highly advanced and highly altruistic citizens of the future perfect techniques for reconstructing personalities and memories from the slush of an old, frozen brain—and then choose to invest the money and effort needed to do so.

Though far more speculative than the others, these radical technologies are also the subjects of active research programs. Thus, maximum-age life-extension technologies run across a spectrum from the merely far-fetched to the entirely fictional, but it is difficult to say what is too amazing—or too crazy—for so grand an enterprise.

The World of Tomorrow

With this much technological progress in the pipeline, clearly we are living in the end times. Immortality is but an R&D cycle away. Given any luck at all, we will be the last generation to face death, the first to face deathlessness. For all their eager adherents, however, and all the promise they—perhaps legitimately—show, there is no guarantee that any of these nascent technologies will bear fruit for the current generation of immortality seekers. How bitter to be a member of the *next-to-last* generation to face death!

What these exercises in hope and hype have in common is the expectation that...*somehow*, in some unknown, but almost-visible way...technology will prevail over the most insurmountable barrier known. For the technological main-chancers of the life-extension community, it is a given that some breakthrough—"just around the corner"—will solve the last remaining problems and open the future to whoever wants to take it.

This roll-the-dice approach to life extension requires more than just a drive to deny death; it requires a complementary positive expectation regarding the development and benefits of technology. Mainstream life extension—mortality reduction and morbidity compression—focuses on existing technology, with its too-obvious gaps, limitations, and side effects. Anyone counting on familiar technology—improved antibiotics, say, or new hormone pills—to give them the future has to be aware of the practical limitations on what is likely to be achieved by such means. The full-gone futurist, though, has the luxury of boundless optimism, unburdened by any inconvenient contrary facts, or any facts at all.

THE DENIAL OF DEATH

To venerate the simple days
Which lead the seasons by,
Needs but to remember
That from you or me
They may take the trifle
Termed mortality!

—Emily Dickinson

Why, then, all this chasing after more years and more science to bring more years?

Denial and Affirmation

We speak of "denial of death," but medico-technological life extension takes that concept rather literally. Fear of death, and its denial, are cultural characteristics that manifest in many ways, often behavioral: irrational risk taking, harrowing medical treatments in hopeless cases, an imbalance of medical resources expended in the final months of life, a cultural emphasis (in the West, at least) on an absurdly impossible ideal of youth. In all these cases, though, death is *denied* essentially by pretending that it will not happen or will happen only to other people. Death itself—death as a phenomenon—is left untouched; its denial is an act of wishing-away, of the closing of one's eyes. The seemingly obvious, direct approach to the denial of death—that of *refusing to die*—is actually one of the less common ones. Like the weather, everyone talks about death but few do anything about it.

It requires not merely a tremendous aversion to death but a complex of attitudes and expectations—about technology, medicine, the "natural" course of life, and much else—to see death as *optional*, as a problem to be *solved* rather than delayed or denied. Denial of death in the traditional guise—denial of death as a refusal to *acknowledge* death—seems to be an essentially conservative impulse. what is desired is the continuation of the here and now, the avoidance of a disruptive finality. One wants not to be much, much older, but rather young forever; not to undergo more and better medical treatments, but never to need medical care. Denial of death by way of technological life extension, by contrast, is a more expansive undertaking: *more* of more of the same; this life, yes, but ever so much more so.

Continuing that thought, a paradox appears in distinguishing these two modes of denial of death. The conservative mode—pretending death is irrelevant—often causes death through risky behavior or a refusal to respond appropriately to danger. The expansive mode—overcoming death with technology—requires an explicit acknowledgment that death is a reality, in order to achieve the technological change that constitutes its denial. Each mode incorporates its own contradiction: the denial of death that leads to death, the acceptance of death that overcomes it.

The technological denial of death, then, is not in the nature of a running away or a fearful wish for immunity; it is a kind of acceptance of a challenge, a task imposed by humanity's most implacable enemy and offering (as such technological challenges do) the reward of continued opportunities to meet further challenges. This is not to suggest that those who seek life extension through medical technology are engaged in mere game playing; presumably they are motivated to defeat death because, in fact, they really don't want to die. But that desire manifests itself, for the technologically inclined immortalist, as an active project to change the terms on which life is lived, to fix the bug in the system that otherwise inevitably causes it to crash.

It would be much too glib to posit specific psychological motivations underlying one or another mode of response to death. The point is merely that there is a distinct difference—if not of motivation, then of intention in action—between wishing one did not have to die and undertaking an actual practical program to make death obsolete. The latter is a peculiarly aggressive form of denial (and one that, *Frankenstein* notwithstanding, became a plausible dream only in the late twentieth century).

The Fear of Death and the Love of Life

This analysis is not universally received, however. The President's Council on Bioethics traces the desire to prolong life to the fear of death:

> The fear of death, that ultimate and universal fear, surely has a hand (even if only implicitly) in motivating the search for ways to slow the clock. Death is nature's deepest and greatest barrier to total human self-mastery....Our

subjection to death—and our awareness of this fact—is central to what makes us human ("mortals") rather than divine, and it makes us fearful and weak and constrained.[32]

There is certainly an intuitive appeal to this perspective: what could motivate us to go to such lengths (remaking our genes? nano-robots? cryogenic hibernation?) to gain more time on earth *other than* a fear of the alternative? What but desperation could justify such desperate measures?

But the language of life-extension advocates does not betray fear so much as excitement and anticipation; death, to many in the field, appears not to be an awesome transition but a regrettable waste. Since almost no one *wants* to die (including opponents of life extension, who value death but are content to wait for it), the thinking seems to be that no one should *have to* die—and anyone who does die, whether through lack of technological alternatives or the refusal to use them, has forfeited the one thing that makes all other things worthwhile.

A telling point in the council's statement, above, is the pejorative use of the phrase "total human self-mastery." For visionaries like de Grey, who intends to physically reconfigure the human genome, for technocratic futurists like Kurzweil and Grossman, who want nothing less than a new form of computer-enhanced human intelligence, for gushing bio-artists like Vita-More who foresee a carnival of colored and sculpted human bodies, total human self-mastery is both a goal and a tool. And that distinction—that difference in perspective, between seeing the audacious control of human bodies and human nature as an act of impiety or hubris and seeing it as the next step forward on the continuing drive toward human betterment—may explain why the flight from death need not be driven by the fear of death.

For many of its most vocal proponents, it seems motivated more by an almost irrepressible enthusiasm for all that may be possible once the limitations and frustrations imposed by our lack of total human self-mastery are overcome. Certainly these deniers of death show no signs of being "fearful and weak and constrained" in the face of death. This suggests, too, that the fear of death is *not* an "ultimate and universal fear"—its place is taken by other, richer and more welcoming emotions among those who, when they gaze upon immortality, take *life* and not *death* as the object of that gaze.

For the life-extensionists, then, denial of death is their stock-in-trade, but that denial springs from a vision that looks beyond death to the possibilities inherent in a world from which death has been removed. Traditionally, transcending death meant achieving an afterlife of whatever sort—it meant, that is, *dying*. But for today's technological transcendentalists, going beyond death means removing death as an obstacle so that time and energy—much more time, much more energy—can be focused on more important things.

Life as a Consumer Commodity

What of the members of the public who may make use of this technology if it is perfected? In choosing the means to deny death to themselves, what are they seeking and what are they hoping to avoid?

At first glance, at least, we may imagine that the average person would choose treatments to achieve immortality for the same reason that the average person chooses treatments to prolong dying during a terminal illness: they *don't want to die*. We do not need to posit psychopathologies of fear or denial to explain such a choice; the thing virtually explains itself. Whatever good there is is found in life; to cling to that good—and why not?—means to cling to life and to reject its termination. And so we seek what means we can to live when death looms.

This is not to say that the fear of death is not a real phenomenon, nor a common one; surely it is the former and likely it is the latter. Nor even is it to say that fear of death does not serve a protective purpose under many circumstances; no doubt it does. But one may choose life without being especially fearful of death; one does not need to fear it not to *prefer* it when a choice is available. For consumers of life-extension technology, then, immortality may hold the positive allure that it seems to for its researchers and professional proponents; immortality is a denial of death by way of an affirmation of its alternative, a positive evaluation of what will continue without death, rather than a negative statement about what will end with it.

So, denial of death is certainly a prominent aspect of the search for immortality—how could it not be? But this denial seems to play out in ways and forms different from the stereotype of fear and pathological obliviousness. The act of denial by way of technological life extension requires an aggressive and open-eyed *engagement with* death, a literally scientific scrutiny of death's ways and mysteries until no more mystery remains and its ways are mastered and overcome. The individual motivations of the seekers, dreamers, main-chancers, and visionaries who pursue this project are unknown and, no doubt, various—but they seem to have little to do with "ultimate fear"; these pioneers certainly recognize no irony and no fault in the attainment of "total human self-mastery."

The Future of Denial

Has the prospect of immortality emptied the concept of denial of death of its own meaning, then? When death's pale horse has been put out to pasture, and life in abundance is for the taking, what is there still to deny?

Death looms throughout mortal life. Death is the motivation for life extension, obviously, and, given that it can never be truly eliminated, it will be as real to our "immortal" descendants as it was to us or our short-lived forebears. What will change, if significant life extension is achieved, is its immediacy.

Generation will succeed generation as before, but with centuries, perhaps, between them; one's acquaintances will pass away as their allotted time closes, but once a decade, maybe, or once a century. Death as a near and present danger will recede; future generations may view today's epidemic of fear and denial of death as we, today, view our ancestors' panic over smallpox and whooping cough: a nearly incomprehensible hysteria over a mortal danger that, in retrospect, proved amenable to medico-technological control. Death may be seen as significant but not likely; a serious matter but not a priority.

In that environment, denial of death as a practice would be unremarkable; future generations will have denied death in the way in which our own denied smallpox—by defeating it and then mostly forgetting about it. In that environment also, denial of death as a psychological state, still less a pathology, would be unknown—like denial of childbed fever or denial of gout—a needless worry over a real but somewhat quaint and old-fashioned condition.

This technology, if it succeeds, bids fair not just to remake our lives but to recontextualize, and thus redefine, death as a phenomenon and as a biological/sociological constraint upon our species. What we understand death to be, what impact the mere thought of death has on us, must be different, and likely much less profound, when death looms no more in the landscapes of our lives and every prospect pleases.

LIFE EXTENSION AND THE WAYS OF BEING HUMAN

> Quantity has a quality all its own.
>
> —attributed to Stalin

If our faith in science's promise is well placed, we can expect the dangers of diseases of many kinds to lessen, the impact of malnutrition and preventable diseases to disappear, and the average age at death to increase toward its natural limit or even without limit. The more dramatic sources of life extension—the nanotechnology and cryogenic freezing and such—may make us shake our heads at the scope and the power of our technology, but we are used to having that reaction by now, and in much less revolutionary contexts. The fact that life extension—*if*, we must remind ourselves, *if* it works—is *not* magic may lead us to overlook how revolutionary it might be.

Our society, in fact most human institutions, are implicitly constructed around the constraints of the traditional human life span. What we take to be "normal" life—the sequence of steps and stages of a life, the relations between generations that make them possible, the social and economic institutions in which they are played out—is geared to the pace and scope of what we now take to be a "normal" life span. We cannot live 120-year, or 200-year, or still less *indefinite* lives in a society that expects a predictable succession of generations every 75 years or so.

Understanding the full enormity of life extension—not merely how it responds to our inclination to deny death, but how it may push us to embrace another kind of life entirely—is necessary to understanding not only that denial but, as will be seen, how the promise of extended life might seem false to some. To understand what we are choosing in choosing extended life, we must come to terms with the many changes it would wreak on the lives we would be giving up.

Balancing the Stages of Life

Most obviously, the progression through stages of life would be drastically altered. Humans are already noteworthy for our prolonged social adolescence. Extended periods of education and job training, and delayed reproduction, have pushed the length of time between the birth of one generation and the birth of its own offspring close to 30 years in industrialized societies. That is, almost half the normal life span is spent preparing for generational independence, even as the age at puberty in industrialized societies has been dropping. Many people now do not finish raising their children until they (the parents) are in their 50s or even their 60s. Humans are thus accustomed to spending a significant fraction of the first half of their lives preparing for adulthood and parenthood, and most of their adult years raising and supporting their children.

However, if the average period of adulthood were prolonged from about 40 years to well over 100 years, the balance between stages of life would shift dramatically. Assuming that biological adolescence is not greatly altered, then the preparatory phase of life, which now occupies most of the first half of life, would shrink to only a small fraction of one's total life span, and the long middle years would dwarf both the youth and child-rearing phases. "Empty nest" parenthood, when the children have finally grown and left the home, would begin in early middle age, not closer to retirement age as is now common.

Family dynamics would be greatly altered. Parents would coexist with their adult children for 100 years or more. Assuming that reproduction occurs between the ages of 30 and 40, as it now often does in industrialized countries, then with an average life span of only 120 years one would begin to see extended families of four or even five generations as a common occurrence; much more extended families would occur with longer life spans. Overall family size, now dropping dramatically in most developed countries, would increase, but largely as a result of adding more older members, not more children.

The retirement years would have to be carefully considered as well. If retirement comes at an age above—possibly far above—100, then one would be retiring when one's children are themselves greatly advanced in years. We might see 120-year-old retirees being supported and cared for by (reasonably healthy) 90-year-old children. If life spans increase to 200 or more years, the possibilities become even more staggering. The implicit contract for mutual assistance that currently binds successive generations would have to be rewritten—but how is not clear.

Not only would these changes occur, but their impact would be felt rapidly—long before the technologies themselves were fully implemented, or those who benefited from them actually entered the extended years the technology granted. Gregory Stock points out that the mere knowledge that such changes were underway would cause shifts in people's planning of their lives and their expectations for the future—shifts that would influence the design and function of social institutions today, in anticipation of the impact of extended life tomorrow.[33]

The Economic Impact of Advanced Age

Possibly the most talked-about implication of potential changes in average human life span is the strain it would put on the systems by which humans make their livings and support their families. The logistics of earning a living wage and preparing for retirement would surely be changed. The balance of economic interests across generations—the increasing numbers of older family members, the shift to a society in which the elderly greatly outnumber the youth, the relative need for and access to economic resources of the younger and older generations, and the social institutions that address the needs of the differing generations—would be drastically altered.

In part, these effects hinge on the exact form the extended period of life would take. The discussion above assumed that an extended life span would mostly take the form of extended years of robust and productive life—an extended healthy middle age. But there is no guarantee of this. It is perfectly possible that the scientific advances leading to extended life will allow the maintenance of basic bodily functioning but not prevent mental or physical debility, thus leading to an extended old age of senility or medical dependency. Extended life may thus take one of two roads: extended years of productive working life, or today's 40-year working span followed by extended years of debility and increasingly intensive, but effective, life support.

A very long working life could mean that most people would have a fair degree of financial security as they approached their declining years. The last 50 or 60 years of working life might provide ample discretionary income and the opportunities it brings; a longer period of high earning might also allow for retirement proportionally earlier in life.

The alternative possibility is that the "extra" years would accrue mostly during the period of old age, as individuals continue getting older and weaker, requiring more and more aggressive medical support and consuming increasing resources of caregiving funds, technology, and time. This could provoke difficult decisions about limitations on care for the elderly, or even limitations on access to the life-extension technology, driven by the financial impossibility of meeting the needs that the widespread use of such technology would create. (Aubrey de Grey casually dismisses this possibility: "[Advanced life-extension technology] will bring about the greatest economic change of all in society: the elimination of retirement benefits. Retirement benefits are for frail people, and there won't *be* any frail people.")[34]

In addition, the discussion so far has not considered secondary effects, but they are likely to be significant. Life extension, by changing the temporal profile of a human life, must necessarily change the social context in which it is lived, and the social institutions through which people interact. People who have benefited from life extension will not only live longer—they will live in a world filled with people who live longer and who will create, without even intending it, institutions and social patterns fitted to those longer lives. That world will not be the same as ours—and so we cannot extrapolate from this world to that and assume that longer lives are the same as shorter lives "but more so."

Employment prospects for the long-lived elderly are also significant. In the best-case scenario outlined above, long working lives at full productivity would provide a workforce of unprecedented experience and vision. Possibly this workforce would serve as "excess capacity," available for new projects and unheard-of entrepreneurial undertakings that would expand the overall economy to unprecedented levels of production. Possibly, however, this workforce would depress the labor market, leading to lower wages and decreased security for all workers, who could always be easily replaced by an older worker needing to accumulate funds for retirement. In the worst-case scenario, longer-lived citizens who do not maintain their economic productivity as they age will require massive resource redistribution to meet their needs for care and support.

Our current economy, composed of the collective activity of humans with 75-year life spans and 50-year working lives, can be nothing like an economy populated by humans with 150-year life spans and 100-year working lives (to say nothing of 300-year life spans and 200-year working lives). The less-attractive scenario—an economy of humans with 50-year working lives followed by perhaps 75 years of economically unproductive aging—is at best a grim parody of our current system.

Another economic concern related to the use of life-extension technology is the question of equal access to its benefits. Such technologies are likely to be very expensive, certainly in the early years of their use, possibly always.

This portends particularly vicious inequities, whereby the advantages of class and clout convey not merely an easier life, but life itself. (This is, of course, already true in respect of access to expensive treatments for severe diseases, and even in respect to basic health care and sanitation for many people in underdeveloped countries, but it seems an especially stark distinction between classes when the inconvenience the affluent are privileged to escape is mortality itself.)

Lack of access to the necessary treatments is only one issue, though. Another is the plight of the short-lived in a world transformed to meet the needs of the immortal. Will education or jobs be "wasted" on those who can make use of them for only a few decades rather than centuries? Will today's medical technologies be maintained and provided to the short-lived population when they have become obsolete for the eternally healthy, and socially dominant, population of immortals?

It is easy to imagine that, when the life-extension revolution comes, its benefits will become available all at once and to the whole world—that we will all enter that transformed future together and on equal terms. But such has been the case for no other technological revolution in history. And no other technological revolution has had such a sweeping, worldwide impact as this one promises.

It is possible—barely—to imagine what an extended life might be like. It is almost impossible to imagine what the world in which such a life would be lived must become.

The Value of Time

There may be a way in which the value of time will be altered in a greatly extended life span—year following year unnoticeably when years are as minutes in a shorter life. Paradoxically, time may be both cheapened and made more precious by the having more of it—cheapened, like any commodity, by surplus, but increased in total value by sheer quantity.

It is easy to see how the pace of an endless life could slow to an unproductive drag. Few projects would take on real urgency (they can always be finished next century). The characteristically desperate drive of the ambitious, racing the winged chariot to accomplish much living in little time, would be literally a mental illness in a world in which there is almost never too little time for anything. It would be difficult to muster the drive to complete even ordinary tasks. If lack of time is the impetus for productive effort, the lack of the lack of time may remove that motivation.

Yet there is a way in which endless time takes on a significance greater than can be imagined for time today. Death in a long-lived life, it was noted above, cuts off much more time and experience than in a life with a closer and more limited temporal horizon. Time, for those with all the time in the world, must be all the more jealously guarded against loss. For when one loses so very much in death—cutting off not a few years or a few decades, but a few *centuries* of potential life—it would be hard not to rage at the dying of that light.

Human Relationships

Relationships—both romantic and otherwise—would have to change dramatically upon the adoption of extended life. It has been suggested that today's relatively high divorce rate is partly the product of longer life spans and more equal ages of men and women at marriage.[35] This phenomenon can only exacerbate with greatly extended life spans; it is hard to imagine many marriages lasting from the mid-20s to the mid-120s, to say nothing of two or three *centuries*.

"Serial monogamy"—sequential serious relationships before marriage, and multiple marriages—is often described as the *de facto* practice of today's adults, but the ending of each such relationship has an air of failure about it. With life spans greatly exceeding the realistic span of most monogamous relationships, it is possible that serial monogamy would become a norm for relationships; each new relationship would be expected to come to an end at some foreseeable point in the future, and relationships could be planned with this eventuality in mind.

Other changes would be more subtle but even more inevitable: the nature of marriage as 100-year anniversaries become commonplace; the relationship between marriage and child rearing in marriages lasting many times longer than needed for that purpose; the relationships between parents and children as the generational difference between them shrinks to only a small fraction of their respective lives; the understanding of culture and social roles as children grow up in a society in which the majority of residents are 100, 200, or more years older than them; the understanding of friendship over spans longer than most people could be expected to maintain stable personal identities.

Each of our relationships is marked and formed, in some way at least, by death. Children see their parents die, often well before their own life's path is fully established. Siblings must remake their relationships to one another when their parents have died. Parents plan for their own deaths—with wills, insurance, and the other impedimenta of mortality—as part of their obligation to provide for their children. Friends see friends die over the years, and the incremental severing of one's friendships is a rite of old age. Death sets the pace of the sequence of generations, also. Each passing decade sees the child significantly more independent while it sees the parent significantly closer to death, and these changes define the changing relationship between the two.

How will all these relationships play out if the period of independent maturity extends for 100 or 200 years? Parents and children 30 years apart in age in the context of a 300-year life span will have much more in common with each other than either would have with the truly old or the truly young. For the first time, parents and children will be at the *same* stage of life, and in that perennial, robust middle age they will live through centuries of shared experience.

Whatever happens, how we understand relationships must change in the context of lives wherein death does not loom. The norms we have for relationships—what we think marriage is, or friendship is, what we believe children owe to their parents and vice versa, how we expect the succession of generations to take place, the proper hierarchy of respect and devotion we perceive between generations—must change as well. This will likely be awkward for the first few generations facing such challenges with no tradition to guide them; it may even be offensive to some who see moral significance in contemporary patterns that are in fact merely dictated by temporal contingency. It is no small thing, however conceived.

THE REJECTION OF LIFE EXTENSION

Contra naturam, the defiance of nature, used to be a sufficient argument for those who were not persuaded by *contra deum*, provoking the wrath of God....The ultimate question is how far we may go in defying nature without undermining our humanity....What does it mean for human beings, who are defined by their mortality, to entertain, even fleetingly, even as a remote possibility, the idea of immortality?

—Gertrude Himmelfarb

Extended life would be a complicated business, it is clear enough. But surely it would be worth whatever costs it may carry with it? We mortals fight so very hard for whatever incremental extension of life we can achieve in even the last debilitated days of our doomed tenure on earth, what would we not endure for a doubling, a tripling, a *limitless* extension of the best part of our lives? When the alternative is, literally, nothing at all, centuries of something must be a bargain at any price, no?

Perhaps not. There is at least a dedicated body of nay-sayers, aghast not just at the burdens and complexities of extended life but at the very possibility of it in any form or manner. For some, life as we now know it, mere mortality with all its limits and disappointments, *is* life as it should be, perhaps is meant to be. To tinker with life-as-it-is, to create life that is other than life-as-it-is, is to transgress against life itself. It is *immoral*, in one way or another, to fail to die, indeed, to live any life that is not life-as-it-is.

There may be practical exigencies encouraging such a conclusion. Though Colorado Governor Richard Lamm raised hackles in 1984 by suggesting that the elderly had "a duty to die and get out of the way with all our machines

and artificial hearts and everything else like that,"[36] the utilitarian calculation behind his claim was clear enough. Or it may be that the combination of
high cost and low likelihood of success simply makes life extension research
a bad investment, like cold fusion or supersonic airliners—desirable but impossible to justify. There is also a strong argument from economic fairness:
since the resources required to develop and implement life extension could
be very great, and the necessary treatments are likely to be very expensive,
investing in an extensive developmental program that will benefit only the
affluent, and to such a disproportionate degree, may be a very unfair use of
those resources. But these prudential considerations are not the only source
of opposition to playing in the fields of the Lord.

There is a coordinated body of conservative reaction to life extension that
sees it as bad in itself—wrong even if it were affordable, even if the practical
objections to the program could be answered. The motivations for such a
stance are various: a natural-law vision of mortality as normative; a sectarian
religious perspective that sees any alteration in God's plan as blasphemous
or counterproductive; the general conservative suspicion of newfangled technologies and social disruption; and perhaps others.

This opposition sees the mortal framework we inherit and inhabit in our
unmodified forms as definitive of human personhood—the standard way of
"being human" is taken as establishing a stipulative definition of "human
being." The artificiality of life extension is then an unmistakable affront to
this definitive way of being human. The eventual success of the technology
would in no way obscure the insult.

If life extension comes through some sort of medical treatment, presumably provided to each person in infancy or youth as a form of inoculation
against mortality, the fact that the treatment is necessary, that each individual's biology must be manipulated to stave off the inherited inevitability of
a normal life span, underscores the imposition being made upon nature and
upon human nature. If it takes the form of germ-line genetic engineering—
the manipulation of the genes to create a new, inherited biology possessed
of lengthy or unlimited life—that distinct and unmistakable revision of the
genes, even though passed down to subsequent generations with no further
direct intervention, remains visible to genetic analysis like an indelible tat-
too, as fake as the globular breast implants and linear noselines of today's
fashionable surgical monstrosities. There is no way to alter the biological
boundaries of human lives without altering the human beings who inhabit them, altering them, as alteration must do, into something other than what
they were—and what is a human being who has been made *other*? What can
that being be but *non*-human? To those who place great store in not being
non-human, non-human being is no prize.

So there are reasons to rejoice at the prospect of endful human life—
reasons to reject the rejectionism of endless non-human life, endless fleeing

from what humans must be to be human. And there are those who do so rejoice, do so reject.

Criticism of Life Extension as a Program

Some are concerned that, inasmuch as every technological advance brings with it its own problems, life extension resulting from technological advances in particular areas would create unprecedented difficulties in other, related areas. For instance, biologist Steven N. Austad testified to the President's Council on Bioethics that

> If we continue to increase longevity by the sort of disease-based advances, which we've become so good at making over the last century,…we could be facing a major social catastrophe, and I'll just give you one example of that. Neuroscientists and my friends in the Alzheimer's Disease community tell me that approximately 50 percent of people over the age of 85 have some sort of disabling dementia. Therefore, as more and more people, as a larger fraction of the population reaches this age, we could be faced with the possibility of a vastly expanding population of people who need 24 hour a day nursing care.[37]

Leonard Hayflick, a key figure in the biology of senescence, also argues on practical grounds that life extension is both unlikely and a mistake:

> Probably the most telling argument…is the stupid question, Why do you want to do it in the first place? What is the benefit? People have this underlying, tacit belief that increasing human longevity, or curing aging, or however you want to characterize it, is a good. They've never asked themselves or never described what that good is. And I challenge *all of them* to provide a single scenario that makes sense. Any scenario they're liable to describe will come closer to science fiction than probable scientific reality.[38]

Ethicist Daniel Callahan takes a similar view, seeing the sweep of biological and sociological changes required to make extended life possible as an insurmountable practical barrier to achieving it:

> The truly intimidating feature of a greatly extended life span, much less earthly immortality, is that just about everything else in human life would have to be changed to make it worthwhile. We would need, in effect, nothing less than a glorified body, one where each and every part and organ functioned perfectly, resistant to wear and tear. We would no less need an analogous social order that was perfect in its own way but that, at a minimum, did not kill us by war and violence or spoil life by meanness and other forms of private misery.[39]

Leon Kass, director of the President's Council on Bioethics and the most vocal opponent of radical biotechnology in general, worries that technological progress in itself is a danger:

> Would [new biotechnologies] serve the pursuit of happiness, or would they devalue it? And would they serve our aspirations beyond happiness—for goodness, virtue, and dignity? Will the new means simply serve the old ends better, or will they reshape our desires to fit only what these new means can deliver? . . .
>
> We want longer lives—but do we want them at the cost of living carelessly or shallowly with diminished aspiration for living well, and at the risk of becoming people so obsessed with our own longevity that we care little about the next generations? . . . We want all the extra advantages that biotechnology has to offer—but do we want to live in a world in which "advantage," and much of life itself, has come to have a biotechnological meaning?[40]

Kass also refers to "potential deformations of our desires"—this, together with the fear of "reshap[ing] our desires," makes it clear that Kass feels it is wrong not merely to want certain things but *to become the kind of person who would want those things.* Pursuing longevity to the point at which one begins to value being long-lived is, for Kass, a transgression against human nature, by way of cultivating a desire to be other than properly human in nature.

Kass suggests that a modest goal would be to seek a "reasonable" number of extended years of life, but he predicts that no one would be satisfied with that:

> How many years is reasonably few? . . . If we can't immediately land on the reasonable number of added years, perhaps we can locate the principle. What is the principle of reasonableness? . . . We have no answer to this question. . . .
>
> Under such circumstances, lacking a standard of reasonableness, we fall back on our wants and desires. Under liberal democracy, this means on the desires of the majority. . . . I suspect we know the answer: The attachment to life—or the fear of death—knows no limits, certainly not for most human beings. . . . We want to live and live, and not to wither and not to die. For most of us, especially under modern secular conditions in which more and more people believe this is the only life they have, the desire to prolong the life span (even modestly) must be seen as expressing a desire *never* to grow old and die. However naïve their counsel, those who propose immortality deserve credit: They honestly and shamelessly expose this desire.[41]

For Kass, then, certain desires are both disreputable and inevitable. Humanity can be saved from its most degrading impulses only by making those shameless desires unattainable.

The practical difficulties of actual implementation aside, Daniel Callahan seems to perceive an inevitable malaise resulting from extended life—a future that would be unbearable because it cannot be otherwise, human nature being what it is even after human bodies become what they are not:

[The tedium of immortality] is not an inspiring picture. But don't worry, the optimists seem to be saying, we can deal with that. Such optimism ignores one fundamental problem, hardly ever alluded to, that of the social, not biological, pathologies that have in the past and in the present ruined so much of life and brought about so much misery and so many deaths. I believe that sickness and biological death represent a lesser evil than those we human beings bring upon ourselves.[42]

Callahan seems to expect that any radical technology such as life extension *must turn out badly*, simply because the "social pathologies" so common to the human species will ensure it. It is not clear on what basis he presumes this, though. He is certainly right that humans bring much bad on themselves and each other; perhaps he is right that human societies inevitably harbor "misery" and "ruin" (surely history suggests it would be foolish to expect anything else). But it is not obvious why the social pathologies of a long life would be worse than the pathologies of a shorter one—that a generation of human beings, living, say, 750 years, would suffer more, cumulatively, than 10 generations of short-lived humans over the same span of time. Still, that the future could be worse than we hope is hardly an implausible suggestion.

Leon Kass has similar practical concerns:

How will growing numbers and percentages of people living well past one hundred affect, for example, work opportunities, retirement plans, hiring and promotion, cultural attitudes and beliefs, the structure of family life, relations between the generations, or the locus of rule and authority in government, business, and the professions? Even the most cursory examination of these matters suggests that the cumulative results of aggregated decisions for longer and more vigorous life could be highly disruptive and undesirable, even to the point that many individuals would be *worse off* through most of their lives, and worse off enough to offset the benefits of better health afforded them near the end of life.[43]

Indeed, several people have predicted that retardation of aging will present a classic instance of the Tragedy of the Commons.[44]

These attitudes do not sit well with all proponents of the limitless future. Robert Bradbury, member of the visionary Extropy Institute, complains that

We have to deal with human naturalists, those people who think it is non-human to live 200 years, or the religious deathists, who have a significant amount of power by having the key to the Pearly Gates, so to speak, and the limits-to-growth camp, and, of course, the bureaucratic fearmongers like the Social Security Administration![45]

Fellow Extropian Natasha Vita-More refers to people who prefer to retain the natural functions and limitations they were born with, and forego enhancing their bodies with biotechnology, as "humanish—you know, like Amish."[46]

Kass and his followers may not regard these condescending descriptions as insulting, however. Much of the go-slow rhetoric heard on this subject *is* distinctly religious in tone (though the President's Council does not adopt religious justifications for its official positions). Harking back to earlier and simpler times is also prevalent. Kass himself has written, in other contexts, of the harms of the birth control revolution and the benefits of formal "courting" (rather than unsupervised dating) for young couples. Fellow council member Francis Fukuyama has warned against a "post-human" future. References to *1984* and *Brave New World* are rife in their writings and in the official publications of the council. It is not too much to say that the anti-post-human opponents of life extension are not unbridled enthusiasts of progress for progress's sake.

The practically grounded objections—that life extension will disrupt society or even make it unlivable, that it will destroy our economies, mire us in interminably pointless lives of mere endurance, sever us from our purposes as human beings, or embroil us in ethical transgressions of other kinds on our way to the goal—could in principle be met; for every practical objection there is, conceivably, a practical solution. But since many of the objections have to do with the results of complex future developments, it can be argued that it is irresponsible to pursue a program that we cannot guarantee will not destroy the best things about our lives, even if we also cannot prove that it will. As for the ideological objections, though subjective, they are heard from a range of politically connected conservatives and have served to raise the question whether any individual researcher, or generation of researchers, has the right to change the future for every generation to come.

The implication of both these kinds of concerns—that life extension will prove a Pandora's box of social disruption, and that it is an unrighteous (and possibly irreversible) mucking about with the central identity of our species—is that the research should not be pursued. Some of its effects may be known only when they manifest themselves—only when it is too late to turn back the clock—and if they truly are outcomes we dare not risk, then any action that portends such outcomes is one we dare not take.

Natural Death, Unnatural Life

This rejectionist stance, however, is not the only reason for opposing life extension research. For some, there is a perceived good in death, or at least in accepting the fact of death, given that dying is part of how we must understand ourselves as human beings. Death is not just something we are stuck with as humans (and therefore must endure, because we are obliged to respect and maintain what it is to be human), but something that makes possible the good that we find in our lives.

Leon Kass is convinced that mortality is central to human identity and, moreover, to human well-being in itself:

> This is a question in which our very humanity is at stake, not only in the consequences but also in the very meaning of the choice. For to argue that human life would be better without death is, I submit, to argue that human life would be better being something other than human. To be immortal would not be just to continue life as we mortals now know it, only forever. The new immortals, in the decisive sense, would not be like us at all. If this is true, a human choice for bodily immortality would suffer from the deep confusion of choosing to have some great good only on the condition of turning into someone else. Moreover, such an immortal someone else, in my view, will be less well off than we mortals are now, thanks indeed to our mortality.[47]

He goes further than that, in fact, to argue that death is *good in itself:*

> My question concerns the fact of our finitude, the fact of our mortality—the *fact that we must die*, the fact that a full life for human beings has a biological, built-in limit, one that has evolved as part of our nature. Does this fact also have value? Is our finitude good for us—as individuals?[48]

Kass answers his own questions by listing a number of potential problems with immortality: boredom and tedium, the lack of "seriousness" in an immortal life ("to know and to feel that one goes around only once...is for many people the necessary spur to the pursuit of something worthwhile"); loss of beauty ("mortality...may be the cause of our enhanced appreciation of the beautiful and the worthy and of our treasuring and loving them"); and degradation of character or virtue ("Through moral courage...we rise up above our mere creatureliness, for the sake of the noble and the good....The immortals cannot be noble.").[49] Death then either forces us to the recognition of what is morally worthy, or makes it possible to achieve it.

Noted future-fearer Francis Fukuyama proclaims that

> The most significant threat posed by contemporary biotechnology is the possibility that it will alter human nature and thereby move us into a "post-human" stage of history. This is important...because human nature exists, is a meaningful concept, and has provided a stable continuity to our experience as a species....Human nature shapes and constrains the possible kinds of political regimes, so a technology powerful enough to reshape what we are will have possibly malign consequences for liberal democracy and the nature of politics itself.[50]

Life extension is one possible source of these dangers, for Fukuyama. The particular dangers he sees in it are largely the demographic and economic impacts discussed earlier, but, he notes, "learning to meet... social obligations is a source of both morality and character," which would be diminished by an extended old age when work and child-rearing duties were behind one.[51]

Since human nature (and the lives it condemns us to lead) defines the moral good for human beings, it is vital, for Fukuyama, to avoid changing that nature. Tinker too much with the sullied flesh in which our natures go about their business, and the interface between that nature and the world changes, the kinds of lives it makes possible, or inevitable, change also, and in the end human nature—what it is possible to be while being human— changes. Becoming what we were not, we leave off being what we were—thus our "posthuman" future. Human beings who live too long are not just im- mortal humans—they are immortal *non*-humans. Lacking "human" nature, they then lack human rights.

> What is it we want to protect from any future advances in biotechnology? The answer is, we want to protect the full range of our complex, evolved natures against attempts at self-modification. We do not want to disrupt either the unity or the continuity of human nature, and thereby the human rights that are based on it.[52]

In a similar vein, council member William Hurlbut believes that there is a proper pace of life, and that deviation from it deranges life's meaning or "aesthetic" quality:

> It seems to me that if you play a symphony much slower than normal, it won't be very good any more, that there comes a point where you've lost the artistic coherence of the thing.[53]

Within the most prominent and influential advisory board to have consid- ered life extension as a general program, then, there is a concerted feeling that it should not be pursued, not merely because of particular consequences it may have, but simply because extended life would be different from the lives we currently lead.

This anti-change stance exhibits a strange arbitrariness, however, that other members of the council have noted. Philosopher Charles Sandel pointed out that some of the predicted social effects of an extended life span have already occurred, as the average age at death increased from 48 years to 78 years over the last century, without causing concern. The objection that a further increase would be somehow unwarranted is thus an implicit claim that the changes over recent decades were "just right" but that any further changes would, for some reason, be wrong:

> Are the background conditions in human self-understandings for the vir- tues just about right now at 78 years of the average life span, or such that

they would be eroded and diminished if we extend it to 120 or 150, or 180[?] But that would be odd if they were just right now.

Is it the suggestion that back when it was 48, rather than 78, a century ago...the virtues we prize were on greater display or more available to us[?] And if so, would that be reason to aim for, or at least to wish for or long for a shorter life span, rather than a longer one?[54]

Charles Krauthammer, himself conservative by inclination, acknowledges that this is an unworkably dubious proposition, either retroactively or prospectively:

Given the choice, if people [had] been asked the question we are asking 100 years ago, I think they would have said let's try to extend life expectancy and see how it develops. And I would say that on balance, it's been a pretty good experiment, and the species has done rather well.

I would find it very hard to argue against—it's beyond hard. I think it would be odd if we were to as a body begin to argue against or question the value of this enterprise. I think the best that we can do is to say here are the problems which might arise. Let's start thinking about them.[55]

And the council itself—apparently prodded by Sandel—in its official report disavowed any inclination to roll back the clock on infant mortality.[56] So the objection that life span change should be opposed *because it is change* is undermined by the general social embrace of the same changes cumulatively over the past 50 years.

Yet this sense of hesitancy—that the fact that the future is unknown might be reason not to seek it—pervades the council's deliberations and publications. Dissenting member Rebecca Dresser noted this in discussion and pointed out the option of a more optimistic perspective on the changes that, after all, scientific progress is intended to produce:

I do think that this [council staff's background] paper has an inherent tone of conservatism, and we live in the best of all possible worlds. And I notice that at the beginning you said the case in favor of living longer hardly needs to be made in detail, and so if we focus more on the drawbacks than the advantages, it's not because the advantages are not lacking. But I think that that's one thing that gives it this tone of well, let's—what we have now is the best, and let's think about all the bad things that would happen if we changed it. So I mean, I think we should concede that—just think of the opportunities for human flourishing that would expand.[57]

In the end, with all arguments of this type—that change is to be resisted because it might be for the worse—their force arises entirely from one's willingness to accept the assumptions and values that drive them, or, one might say, to succumb to the fears and hesitancies they embody. If one is a pessimist about the future, or about humanity's ability to exercise wise and practical choices over its own course through history, then grandiose plans to remake the bounds of human life would surely seem reckless or even immoral. If one is not possessed of a restrictively idealized view of human nature, or regards it as part of the human project to remake that nature as needed (as arguably we have done through economics, medicine, and perhaps the mere fact of civilization in general), the objections above lose much of their force. But this is not to say they are merely empty opinionating.

There *is* a certainty of comprehensive social restructuring if the entire human species were to shift to a life span many times longer than currently possible. There is a real accompanying danger that this disruption would prove unmanageable, destabilizing, or simply unbearable for those who have to live with it. And, on practical grounds alone, one should not take lightly the prospect of fundamentally altering basic human biology, nor of forcing an artificial evolution into a form of life that would be in some respects unrecognizable as that of the human species as we now know it.

Whether one regards the replacement of our species with an upgraded version of itself as inherently immoral, or merely a daunting step into the unknown, depends again on one's values and assumptions about what it means to be the kind of humans we currently are. But no one can deny that doing so would be a portentous undertaking. The breezy assurance of the de Greys and the Vita-Mores who race to that Nietzschean blind leap forward seems to demand the tempering of cooler, less excitable voices.

THE DENIAL OF THE DENIAL OF DEATH

> Is the purpose of medicine and biotechnology, in principle, to let us live endless, painless lives of perfect bliss? Or is their purpose rather to let us live out the humanly full span of life within the edifying limits and constraints of humanity's grasp and power?
>
> —President's Council on Bioethics

Given the real concerns raised by the possibility of life extension, and acknowledging the sincere beliefs in a permanent and morally significant human nature that conservative critics hold, it is not surprising that the life-extension project would be rejected in some quarters. This rejection is aimed as much at the goals and values of the life-extension community as it is at the possible consequences of their efforts. Life simply *should not be extended*, in the minds of the most fervent opponents of such a plan; to do so transgresses moral norms defining life as it should be, and humanity as the subject of such life. Whatever else may follow, good or ill, is the product of a program tainted at its birth with values and intentions not merely arresting in their boldness but iniquitous in their lack of humility.

A Duty to Die

Leon Kass makes his stand on mortality clear in a religiously themed essay in which he argues that true immortality is the perpetuation of multiple generations, not of a single life. He argues unambiguously against life extension for those reasons:

> Unqualified endorsement of medical progress and the unlimited pursuit of longevity cannot be the counsel of wisdom.…
>
> Confronted with the growing moral challenges posed by biomedical technology, let us resist the siren song of the conquest of aging and death.[58]

From this perspective, prolonging a single generation's tenure on earth is both selfish and, in some way, a failure of our responsibility to bring new generations into being. For Kass, life extension is an offense to God. But in addition to that, it is a distortion of the normal course of a human life. He does not deny that medicine can offer much, and is likely to achieve much; he speaks of "medical *progress*" and "the *conquest* of aging and death." But he does not regard such progress as a good thing but rather the opposite—morally worse the greater its achievements in the technical realm. For Kass, nothing fails like success.

Kass also proposes a rather dubious psychological explanation for the desire for immortality:

> Why do human beings seek immortality?…Is it really first and most because we do not want to die, because we do not want to leave this embodied life on earth or give up our earthly pastimes, because we want to see more and do more? I do not think so. This may be what we say, but it is not what we mean. Mortality as such is *not* our defect, nor bodily immortality our goal. Rather, immortality is at most a pointer, a derivative manifestation, or an accompaniment of some deeper deficiency.…
>
> The Bible also teaches of human aspiration.…We are not as God; we are naked, weak, not-self-sufficient, possessed by powerful and rebellious desires that we can neither master nor satisfy alone. We are ashamed before ourselves, and we hide from God.…The expulsion from the Garden [of Eden] merely ratifies our estrangement from God and testifies to our insufficiency, of which our accompanying mortality is but a visible sign—or perhaps even God's gift to put an end to our sad awareness and deficiency.[59]

A proper conception of human nature, then, emphasizes our limitations. What is most important about us as humans is the fact that we are so relentlessly confronted with the frustrations of our imperfect flesh, and that those imperfections highlight our dependency on God. Attempting to repair the defects or incompleteness of our bodily natures is both impious and wrongly directed. We are expected to hope for better things *and not achieve them,* so as to make ourselves more fully aware of our inadequacy before God and of God's generosity in overlooking it. To strive against the limits of our earthly lives *and actually succeed in transcending them* is ingratitude, and perhaps blasphemy.

The President's Council on Bioethics—Kass here in his secular guise—takes a similar tack without the explicitly Christian trappings. The Council seems to regard change itself as inherently immoral. Considering changes to the "shape" of a life, the Council identifies as ethical issues the fact that "the animated shape of a whole life affects how we live every portion, and altering the shape of that whole might therefore have far greater consequences than merely giving us more time," and that "moving the [endpoint] of a human life span could alter human attitudes and dispositions toward mortality and toward the whole of life."

The objection here is familiar, though not couched in religious terms. There is a good in our inherent limits as we now know them, and changing humanity or human lives so as to ameliorate those limits necessarily deprives us of that good. In seeking the apparent benefits of longer life, we sacrifice not only the life we now live but the life we are *supposed* to live—and the deaths we are supposed to die.

The Benefit in Dying

At times the council argues that aging *is* that positive good of which increased longevity would deprive us—not just that there is good in a life that includes aging, but that the process of aging, and its endpoint in death, are to be valued in themselves:

The very experience of spending a life, and of becoming *spent* in doing so—that is, the very experience of *aging*—contributes to our sense of accomplishment and commitment, and to our sense of the meaningfulness of time's passage and of our passage through it. Being "used up" by our activities reinforces our sense of fully living in the world. A life lived devoid of that sense, or so thoroughly removed from it as to be in practice devoid of it, might well be a life of lesser engagements and weakened commitments—a life other than the one that we have come to understand as fully human.[60]

Age-retardation technologies make aging both more manipulable and more controllable as [being] explicitly a human project, and partially sever age from the moorings of nature, time, and maturity. They put it in our hands, but make it a less intelligible component of our full human life.[61]

Here we have a central human good, ineluctably tied to aging, that does not depend for its perception on particular religious beliefs or even a given set of values about human temporality. Everyone ages, and everyone *experiences* aging as they do so—to give that up is, for everyone, to give up a part of their lives, a part of what makes them who they understand themselves to be and makes their lives what they understand them to be. Death, too, is a universal experience, and thus a characteristically human one. The council's argument is thus applicable to—and appreciable by—anyone, whatever their personal feelings about aging or life extension.

It is not obvious, though, that that consideration leads to the pessimistic conclusions favored by the council. Joseph Margolis agrees that death is significant because of the consequences it has for the boundaries of our lives—but no more than this:

> The significance of death lies in its affecting whatever we take to be significant in life itself. Being the limit of life, death colors every serious engagement....
>
> The significance of death lies in our appreciation, living, that we pass through the successive moments of our life but once...and that that sequence has a distinctly short, finite limit. In this sense, the significance of death is simply the finitude of life self-consciously infecting action and reflection.[62]

For Margolis, death is something we cannot not be aware of, and thus something that unavoidably influences how we live our lives. But he is silent on whether we must accept the limitations that death imposes on those lives, still less embrace them.

The idea that dying is itself a good to be sought (at the right time) springs from a sense that there is some correct arc to life, of which dying is a part—that to refashion that arc, or "shape," is to reject something fundamentally of value. Dying, or at least dying *while conscious of one's dying*, being so quintessentially human an enterprise, is a milestone human endeavor, like undergoing puberty or falling in love—fraught with significance, not always comfortable, but not to be missed. But as Margolis points out, we can acknowledge that dying is an important event without agreeing that it is a desirable event. Death seen in this light may be more like cancer or a broken heart—fraught with significance, yes, but all the better if avoided.

Our Pre-Post-Human Now

William F. Buckley Jr. once famously declared that a conservative was one who "stands athwart history, yelling Stop." Conservative critics of life extension have lived up to this claim with remarkable literal-mindedness.

The call to "resist the siren song of the conquest of aging and death" can be an attractive invitation only to one who wants no part of the future, and still more wants to be sure that others do not make the mistake of rushing into it themselves.

What drives this obstructionism, clearly, is a sense that things are, if not exactly fine, then *right*, as they stand—that to deviate too much from the fate we inherit as human beings is to give up what we are *supposed* to be for what we *choose* to be, and on only the flimsy authority of our own preference. This does not require an assertion that human life is perfect, or even unimprovable, as it is most commonly lived today (Kass, recall, offers the *imperfections* of life as a reason for not changing). It does, however, require the belief that human life as we now know it is in some way appropriate for us.

Part of this may be a rejection of, in Fukuyama's phrase again, a "posthuman future." A common science-fiction horror scenario is the destruction of the whole human race, its replacement by an alien species. To proponents of our all-too-human present, the idea of the "trans-human" or the "posthuman" must seem very like this fearsome fantasy.

Creatures who live for centuries, perhaps forever; generations giving birth to the minimal number necessary to replace themselves, and no more, and at intervals of hundreds of years; societies with almost no children, organized to funnel resources upward across the generations; vigorous ancients terrified at running the slightest risk of death: such a race would stagger us with its incomprehensible values and strange fascination with endless stretches of time put to such arid purposes. Yet this race would be our own, if we choose to leave behind what we are and become what we, today, cannot recognize as ourselves. Those alien humans, demanded by an aging modern to justify their destruction of human *being* as it is to us, could only reply, like Prince Hal: "I know thee not, old man....Presume not that I am the thing that I was." One who recoils at the end of humanity as it is might not be much comforted by the thought that humanity's replacement was merely our own species remade.

The denial of the denial of death, then, is motivated both by an enthusiasm for death in itself and by a horror of the loss of those aspects of humanity that are tied to the inevitability of death and its relative likelihood. Death is a threat to what is good in life, to be sure, but it is also one of the parameters that make life what it is. The emphasis on "struggle," "limitation," "weakness," and "fear" in the writings of opponents of life extension speaks to the degree to which they see life's meaning, or the basic nature of humanity, as tied to the constraints imposed by the fact of death. For them, living an immortal life may seem like playing tennis without a net—a self-indulgent exercise that, offering no opportunity for failure, offers no opportunity for victory. Worse, it is living a life different from the one we live now, therefore lacking some of the goods we find in our present lives and leading us to some new state which we carelessly leave our selves behind to reach. All human good is lost, then, if it is true that "human" is defined by what we are in the here and now, and especially so if death is one of those goods.

From whatever perspective motivates this clinging to the now, only one course is possible: to stand athwart the remaking of humanity yelling "Stop." For that remaking is a one-way proposition—once done it will not be undone any more than we would now choose to go back to life spans of 48 years and high infant mortality. What may be lost in the transition to endless futures will be lost forever. Defenders of the human race as it now is must thus prevent that fateful step, now and forever, to preserve what they value; lose that battle once and they have lost it for all time. In this light, it is easier to understand the fervency of their opposition, whether or not one accepts the premises and presentiments that motivate it.

CONCLUSION

"O brave new world that has such people in it. Let's start at once." "You have a most peculiar way of talking sometimes," said Bernard, staring at the young man in perplexed astonishment. "And, anyhow, hadn't you better wait till you actually see the new world?"

—Aldous Huxley

This prophesied new world...could rather resemble the humanly diminished world portrayed in Aldous Huxley's novel *Brave New World*, whose technologically enhanced inhabitants live cheerfully, without disappointment or regret, "enjoying" flat, empty lives devoid of love and longing, filled with only trivial pursuits and shallow attachments.

—President's Council on Bioethics

[There is a] kind of soft tyranny envisioned in *Brave New World*, in which everyone is healthy and happy but has forgotten the meaning of hope, fear, or struggle.

—Francis Fukuyama

We are compelled to decide nothing less than whether...we are going to say yes in principle to the road that leads to the dehumanized hell of *Brave New World*.

—Leon Kass

O, wonder!
How many goodly creatures are there here!
How beauteous mankind is! O brave new world,
That has such people in't!

—William Shakespeare

Life extension technology has come further than many realize—to the point that it justifies a practical scientific project and a plausible concern for its possible consequences. Given the searching implications it has, not just for the length but the pace, tenor, and social context of human lives, and given also that the provision of such technology will produce social changes that are unlikely to be undone, important questions must be answered before those changes are made.

For those pursuing or advocating the technology, those questions have been answered; that they themselves approve of the changes in store is reason enough for them to devote effort to making life extension possible—after which they can present the world a *fait accompli* and let the consequences pile up as they may. For the critics, that prospect is itself a reason to slow or halt this work until a social consensus about its applications can be generated; naturally, they want that consensus to be the one they favor.

The competing visions of those who battle death and those who battle those who battle death are perhaps not as deadlocked as they may seem, however. In working through the implications of each, we may see a way clear to understand the power that technology is bringing us, and what our responsibilities in using it are.

Foreseeable (?) Consequences

Concerns for the practical consequences of life extension have their force, but that is not to say they are decisive.

One point that has not been explicitly emphasized by the critics, but which dovetails with their concerns over irreversible changes in basic human nature, is that the consequences of life extension, if it is allowed to go forward, will be imposed upon most human beings alive at that time without their consent or consultation. The world will simply become a different place, better for those who embrace the change and can afford to avail themselves of its benefits, but increasingly alien, possibly hostile, to those who prefer the old ways or who cannot afford or are not offered the technology necessary to keep up with the new.

Viewed in this way, the offering of life extension—even if the technology, in its basic biological aspects, is proven safe—is a kind of unplanned experiment with the whole of humanity as subjects. Almost no one will be given a chance to consent, and, once the technology has become widespread enough to change basic social and economic patterns, no one will have the option of refusing to participate. The economic disruptions resulting from the technology are similarly unilateral and unavoidable. Given the likelihood that life extension will remain a luxury for most of the world even long after it has become commonplace in affluent cultures, there will almost certainly be a "life span underclass" of short-lived people enviously struggling against biological deadlines to which their more fortunate fellows are immune.

So, then, the side effects of life extension will likely be imposed without recourse on those who cannot access the direct benefits of that technology or who prefer not to do so. This would seem to invoke the principles of caution and of informed consent.

But this may be going too far. Although we insist on the principle of informed consent for patients and experimental subjects considered individually, we do not apply it to species or cultures.

We have never eschewed, and rarely even limited, any revolutionary technology because of its possible social impact, or even because it would "alter human nature." We have never been much embarrassed by the consequences to the worst off of advances in technology or shifts in economic and sociological patterns; still less have we hesitated to endorse technologies widely desired for their general benefits, even when their side effects became evident. We did not demand informed consent before imposing 78-year life spans on a world used to a 48-year average, and we do not now regard the twentieth-century development of antibiotics, childhood immunizations, and ample nutrition as a bad thing, certainly not as an immoral medical experiment. In light of a long history of uncritical embrace of the new, the claim that we must halt work on life extension—when we did not halt so many other life-changing, society-changing, perhaps *human-nature-changing* technologies and did not wait to insist upon universal access to or equitable distribution of the new products—seems more like special pleading for a favored cause than an invocation of recognized moral principle.

John Harris reviewed many of the standard arguments against immortality for the New York Academy of Science's monograph on aging research. He argues, broadly speaking, that the social disruptions that may result from life extension or immortality are overstated, and that the fact that technology raises challenges is not by itself a reason to refuse to use it. He too notes that we have had no such qualms in the face of other technology-driven social revolutions in the past.[63]

Stephen Hall, who has extensively documented the history of the life-extension field and of opposition to it, makes a similar point when he says,

In the absence of such consensus [that life extension clearly violates widely-held social norms], however, in the face of an uncertain future about which we might respectfully have different interpretations and expectations, the social and political impulse to ban represents not moral decisiveness, as some would have us believe, but a form of moral insecurity. It nourishes itself on a kind of pessimism about the human condition, a lack of faith that we can understand and use our newfound powers wisely, a lack of faith that we can discriminate between desirable uses and undesirable misuses[,] a lack of social and political faith that we can, if necessary, adapt to unpredictable consequences that might inadvertently ensue.[64]

Going further down this road, John K. Davis considers the refusal to adopt life-extension technologies on the grounds that it is unfair for some to outlive others who are not as privileged, and dismisses it outright as "collective suttee."[65] He predicts that "life extension may well be too costly for the world's haves to provide it for all the world's have-nots even if they really try," but then argues on greatest-benefit grounds that depriving the "haves" of this opportunity would not produce any offsetting advantage for the "have-nots," who will not enjoy it in any case, and therefore is unjustified. This smacks somewhat of "damn the torpedoes"—and I presume Davis expects himself to wind up in the privileged group if the technology becomes available soon enough, making his indifference to consequences less than heroic—but it is more forthright than an argument that we must halt this particular technology, and *only* this one, to satisfy requirements of equality and social stability that we do not, in fact, recognize as moral constraints in any other area.

Taking a different approach, Gregory Stock argues from simple practical considerations that prior planning for demographic shifts resulting from technology use is a waste of time—that the specific contingencies of the technologies, the subtle factors determining how, and by whom, and in what manner they are used, are impossible to predict but in the end are what determine the actual impact the technology will have. From this perspective, moral hand wringing over the unforeseeable consequences of particular courses of action is pointless, since *everything* about the future is unforeseeable.

So, concern about practical outcomes is understandable, but we have seemingly agreed as a society that it has not force enough to halt our adoption of technologies *other than life extension*. Perhaps life extension is the point where moral lines must be drawn, but it seems easier to conclude that any such line drawing must rest on a more universal principle.

Human Nature, Human Artifice

Another significant concern is the question of human nature: are we transgressing a moral imperative to remain as we are, in seeking a future so very much at odds with what we are today? Conservatives of the Kass/Fukuyama school certainly think so, but here again it is not clear how plausible those claims turn out to be under scrutiny.

There is a logical paradox in imagining an "unnatural human nature." From the perspective of future generations, long life, low birth rates, and endless days devoid of urgency would *be* human nature in the only way they knew it. Surely long-lived humans would be aghast at the suggestion that they should cut their lives to but a fraction of a century, and race through them desperately keeping a deathwatch on themselves as they struggled to complete a paltry few of the plans and projects they regard as natural to a naturally long life. From their respective standpoints, short-lived and long-lived humans would each regard their own way of being as definitive of "human nature," and the other as false or distorted. (The artificiality of extended life makes no difference; our current life span is a product of the nutritional, sanitation, and medical advances of recent centuries, but we do not regard it as unnatural for that reason.) Is either of these perspectives correct? Which is truly "human" and which is merely, and wrongly, (as it may be) "pre-human" or "post-human"?

Today's conservative designates the humans of the late twentieth century the type specimen of humanity for all time, and assesses life extension accordingly: morbidity compression is a laudable goal, allowing everyone to achieve the maximum to be had within the constraints we now face; extension of maximal age, though, is a revision not just of *what we achieve as we are*, but of *what we are*, and that is out of the question.

Gregory Stock argues to the contrary that our "intuitive" response to life extension depends in part on how the technology is packaged. We may picture longevity seekers as selfishly clamoring for more of the limited time and space that earthly life has to offer, and thus crowding others out, but if longevity became the norm, those who lived for centuries would no more be crowding out the coming generations (who, in their turn, would also live for centuries) than do today's 78-year-olds crowd out succeeding generations with their own life spans of 78 years.[66] There is no obviously correct rate at which the generations must pass away.

Adopting a more welcoming standpoint, then, it is possible to see the entire history of the human species as an extended project in making and remaking our nature through technology, as agriculture allowed organized social groups to evolve in complexity, diets changed, social customs and mores became ever more egalitarian, sexual practices were liberalized, life span lengthened, age at menarche dropped and age at first childbirth increased, skirts rose and fell, and our life spans, lifestyles, and psychologies reeled from one upheaval to the next. (Presume not that we are the thing that we were.)

Considering only Freud and Kinsey, we cannot escape recognizing that what "everyone just *knows*" about human nature is both malleable and open to debate. As noted above, we have not slowed to bemoan the loss of the old ways at any point along this historical pathway of technological self-definition; there is no reason the next step along it should be more horrifying than any previous one.

At any rate, human nature has endured and adapted, whatever we have done to it—and has seemed natural to us at each step of the way. An argument can be made that it is within human nature to change our nature. How and whether to do so are still difficult questions, but if the foregoing claim is true, it cannot be the case that we must not change our nature; we cannot help doing so, and we have done so with success almost any time the opportunity presented itself.

If we are to heed the conservative call for the abnegation of our future selves, we must be willing to endorse a static view of human nature. The futurists' expectation, to the contrary, appears to be that that nature is fluid, or even open to direct and conscious intervention. Vita-More's grandiose visions of bodies as sculpturable modules, Ray Kurzweil's breathless dream of nano-computer-enhanced brains, Aubrey de Grey's casual prediction of 5,000-year average life spans, make perfectly clear how comfortable the more visionary proponents of life extension are with radically postmodern human natures.

Fundamentally, then, the controversy over human life extension recapitulates a standing controversy over the malleability of human nature and the wisdom of tinkering with it. At the level of basic values there are two camps whose members largely agree on what the consequences of life extension could be but have incompatible views of whether they are good or bad.

The Goodness of Nothingness

Most startling, perhaps, and most challenging to the seemingly obvious allure of longer life and freedom from disease, is the claim that death itself is a human good.

The religious motivation for such a claim is obvious to those in the Christian tradition: death is the gateway to heaven, and delaying death artificially is implicitly a rejection of God's summons to heaven as well as a loss for the one who refuses to go there when given the chance. Kass's invocation of humanity's faults in the eyes of God, and his description of death as the gift of release from those faults and imperfections, assign death a positive value that can only make sense from a Christian perspective. It is possible to imagine lives that are "worse than death"; however, only in the light of a doctrine that all humans are "fallen," that God grants entry to an afterlife beyond death, and that that afterlife is infinitely better than the degraded lives we live on earth, can one imagine that *every* human life is worse than death.

Not everyone takes so pessimistic an attitude. In fact, there is a long philosophical literature on the puzzle of fearing death: if death is nothingness, what is to be feared? Philosopher Thomas Nagel considers arguments that death cannot be bad (either because one does not consciously *know* one is dead, or because eternal non-being is not in itself harmful, or for other abstruse reasons). He ends with the rather self-evident observation that death is harmful because it deprives one of what is good about being alive. He then notes that, nonetheless, everyone dies and most deaths are not considered tragedies—it is only those that cause some peculiar loss that are regarded as especially bad. ("The death of Keats at 24 is generally regarded as tragic; that of Tolstoy at 82 is not").[67]

Thus, for Nagel, death in itself is not bad, but the loss caused by death is bad, and the greater that loss the worse it is. "Normality seems to have nothing to do with it, for the fact that we will all inevitably die in a few score years cannot by itself imply that it would not be good to live longer."[68]

Here we have two contrasting views of death. For Kass, it is being condemned to continue experiencing the (contemptible) goods of life that is the worst punishment; for Nagel, it is the loss of those goods. For Kass, death is a good by way of throwing life's other goods into relief, and by allowing a transition to a greater good beyond; for Nagel, life is the locus of all good, and death is its termination. Nagel's position also, perhaps, goes far toward explaining the fear of death: we need not fear being dead (a paradox, since we cannot consciously experience it), but we can fear the loss of good we know death will entail.

As Nagel points out, "If the normal lifespan were a thousand years, death at 80 would be a tragedy. As things are, it may just be a more widespread tragedy."[69] Thus, the claim that relatively short life spans are "natural" cannot be a reason for not extending them: in fact, we are all doomed to a tragically young death at 80 or before—the more tragic if it happens that we can extend our lives but fail to do so.

Limitless Enthusiasm for Limitlessness

We have considered above most of the conservative objections to life extension, revisiting them from alternative perspectives and value sets. But we should end where we began, with the visions that brought this issue into being in the first place and raised the portentous possibilities with which both sides now grapple.

If the conservative position seems both obstructionist and pessimistic, it must be recognized that the advocates' positions can easily give reason for alarm. Unilaterally remaking an entire species—perhaps remaking the bodies and the lives of individual members of the species *while they are still using them*—and ushering in a new world, new ways of being, which some may not have asked for or endorsed, is a staggering prospect. One expects a sense of humility, of the enormity of the actions proposed, of the responsibility for good and for ill that the agents of this change take upon themselves. Instead, the gold-rush of profit seekers, frauds, and carnival-barker evangelists braying their glib promises of utopian eternities of ease and indulgence who are ushering in the biological millennium is disconcerting at the very least.

Why *should* entrepreneurial techno-enthusiasts be allowed to push the human species over so precipitous a cliff? Though it is true, as noted above,

that humans have taken in stride innumerable technological and sociological "revolutions" in the past, including some that have materially impacted
human health and longevity, it has to be admitted that the change from sub-
100-year life spans to (conceivably) supra-1,000-year life spans dwarfs any
previous self-mediated change in human biological capacity at least since
the development of language. And this change will come about, if it does,
through the virtually unsupervised efforts of no more than a few hundred
(at the most influential levels, a few dozen) driven technologists indifferent
to the objections or fears of the rest of the human species. We have taken
our lumps from over-eager scientists in the past—nuclear weapons, chloro-
fluorocarbons, and PCBs are all cases in point—but never on such a scale.
Perhaps the nay-sayers have a point in cautioning against unilateral and irreversible action in advance of a general consensus.

Perhaps, on the other hand, there is a different imperative at work. Beyond
questions of absolute or relative human nature, of benefits and harms, of
consequences to society and the economy, and even of the right to proceed
where others' values and interests are at stake, there may be the simple phenomenon of change as an inescapable feature of a complex physical world.

Nothing abides—that, perhaps, is the only unambiguous lesson of history and of evolution. The conservative impulse is doomed in the end, not
simply because social forces eventually overwhelm attempts at restraint, but
perhaps more fundamentally because all things must come to an end, and be
superseded by whatever reconfiguration fits the time and context best.

Whatever human nature may be, what we know about it is this: it responds
to circumstance, and circumstances change. Whatever we may hope our economic system or our social institutions may make possible for us, what we
can predict of them is this: they will be different in the future, and different
again after that. And what we know of our biology and the lives it leads us to
is this: we can change it and will, in some way, and those changes will have
consequences, and we will thereby live new lives in new circumstances.

This is not a plea for nihilism about the consequences of change, or for
a refusal to plan because all plans are in vain. They are not. But it is a suggestion that the fundamentally conservative position—to yell "Stop" because
what we have now is what we are meant to have forever—is both wrong-
headed and futile. What we have now we will not have forever; *therefore* the
fact that we have it now is not by itself a reason to keep it.

Whatever new future this technology brings may be good or it may be
bad, but if it is bad it will not be bad *because it is different*. The likely consequences of the technology are momentous, but lower birth rates, longer
generational succession times, hyper-extended families, overlapping generations, and all the rest may be good or bad, but if they are bad they will not be
bad *because they are different*. Whatever decision we make about life-extension
technology or any other possible advance, the future will be different from

the present, but it will not be bad *because it is different.* (And, perhaps sadly but no less truly, the future will be made by particular events and acts on which the vast majority of earth's citizens are not consulted and cannot either help or hinder.)

This consideration forces the debate back onto the practical merits of the competing visions of the human future: the mortal and the immortal. Perhaps there is something to be said for the former, but death has historically been a tough sell. Very likely, most of those who have the chance at extended life will take it—unreflectively, perhaps, but no more so than do they leap into any other major decision. And if that chance becomes widely available, eventually enough people will take it to force all the long-range consequences, social rearrangements, economic redistributions, and personal-relationship mutations that have been predicted, and no doubt much more besides. In choosing longer life we choose different lives, and, life, technology, and the thrill of the new being what they are, many will likely make that choice gladly if the dreamers and tinkerers succeed in making it available.

The technological denial of death—a denial of death that simultaneously asserts a denial of the fear of death, by making it obsolete—is almost inevitable, if only because the affirmation of life is so universal. The call to reject that affirmation, deny the denial of death, affirm the limitations of life out of an affection for the suffering they cause, is likely to be swept aside by the rush to a future of fewer limits and limitless prospects, where death shall have no dominion.

NOTES

1. Pascal's Wager intrudes here: if you assume the afterlife is eternal perfection, then of course the gamble is more attractive; Pascal apparently never considered the possibility of embracing the afterlife and still winding up in "the bad place."

2. The question of "senescence"—the natural decline of a biological organism over time, through inbred mechanisms of aging and death—is itself controversial. Nonmammalian species are known to exhibit senescence—they simply will not live beyond a specified period, even in a nurturing environment. For single-celled organisms, this results from "telomere shortening"—the step-by-step reduction in the end-segments of chromosomal DNA during successive cell divisions; after a certain number of such divisions (called the "Hayflick limit," after the scientist who described this mechanism), the telomeres are too short to permit DNA replication, and the cell dies. In mammals, however, the question seems more complicated. Telomere shortening was confidently predicted to pose a barrier to mammalian cloning, but it has not done so. Also, some species, notably mice, can be forced into extremely long life spans, far in excess of what appears to be their natural age limit, in particular by imposing a drastic reduced-calorie diet. In the end, senescence in humans is still poorly understood. Though many scientists—notably Hayflick—expect there is an upper limit on human age, some researchers on aging predict that no absolute maximum for human age will be found; others predict that such a limit exists but will be overcome with more radical future technologies.

3. Brian Alexander, "Don't Die, Stay Pretty: Introducing the Ultrahuman Makeover," *Wired* 8.01 (January 2000).

4. Caleb E. Finch, *Longevity, Senescence and the Genome* (Chicago: University of Chicago Press, 1990).

5. Aubrey D.N.J. de Grey et al., "Time to Talk SENS: Critiquing the Immutability of Human Aging," *Annals of the New York Academy of Sciences* 959 (2002): 452–62.

6. Ibid., emphasis in the original.

7. Aubrey D.N.J. de Grey, "Escape Velocity: Why the Prospect of Extreme Human Life Extension Matters Now," *PLoS Biology* 2, no. 6 (2004): e187.

8. Older people, even if healthy, are more likely to die in a given year than younger people, due to the natural mechanisms of aging and the older body's more limited resources for recovery from illness or injury. Even if all overt diseases, but not the process of aging itself, were eliminated, individuals would still die from the contingencies of aging and the unavoidable risks of living in imperfect and fallible bodies, and older individuals would be at the greatest risk. So, incrementally reducing the risk of mortality from disease, even at a rate faster than the increasing risk of mortality from aging, would not eliminate older people's relatively higher risk of death compared to that of younger people, although it would reduce the risk in absolute terms. It's better to be young and healthy in a world free of cancer and heart disease than it is to be old and frail in a world free of cancer and heart disease—even though both age cohorts benefit from the elimination of those diseases. Thus, the elderly are not guaranteed a life span long enough to see the day that true anti-aging and functional immortality are reached, even if the major causes of adult pathology are eliminated. (But see the following discussion for a contrasting opinion.)

9. Leonid Gavrilov and Natalia Gavrilova, "Why We Fall Apart: Engineering's Reliability Theory Explains Human Aging." *IEEE Spectrum (NA)*, September 2004.

10. Ibid.

11. Ray Kurzweil and Terry Grossman, *Fantastic Voyage: Live Long Enough to Live Forever* (Emmaus, Pa.: Rodale, 2004) 15.

12. Alexander, "Don't Die, Stay Pretty."

13. S. J. Olshansky, L. Hayflick, and B. A. Carnes, "Position Statement on Human Aging," *Journal of Gerontology Series A: Biological Sciences and Medical Sciences* 57, no. 8 (August 2002): B292–97.

14. Aubrey D.N. de Grey, John W. Baynes, David Berd, Christopher B. Heward, Graham Pawelec, and Gregory Stock, "Is Human Aging Still Mysterious Enough to Be Left Only to Scientists?" *BioEssays* 24, no. 7 (2002): 667–76.

15. de Grey et al., "Time to Talk SENS"; Aubrey D.N.J. de Grey, "Biogerontologists' Duty to Discuss Timescales Publicly," *Annals of the New York Academy of Sciences* 1019 (2004): 542–45.

16. Aubrey D.N.J. de Grey, "Report on the Open Discussion on the Future of Life Extension Research," *Annals of the New York Academy of Sciences* 1019 (2004): 552–53.

17. The 2002 age-adjusted death rate from accidental causes was 35.5 per 100,000. Centers for Disease Control, "Deaths: Preliminary Data for 2002," *National Vital Statistics Reports* 52 (13), Table B, http://www.cdc.gov/nchs.data/nvsr/nvsr52/nvsr52_13.pdf (accessed January 12, 2005). Assuming that only accidental deaths would occur with effective life-extension technology, this rate, if it persisted, would give an average age at death of only 1,963 years; if suicides and homicides also continued at present rates, long-lived future citizens would die, on average, after only 1,333 years. Hardly "immortality."

18. See United States Life Tables, 2004. NVSR Vol. 56, No. 9. 40 pp. (PHS) 2008-1120, Table 12, http://www.cdc.gov/nchs/data/nvsr/nvsr56/nvsr56_09.pdf (accessed July 30, 2008).

19. Aging Under the Microscope: A Biological Quest, Chapter 1, "Posing Questions, Finding Answers", http://www.nia.nih.gov/HealthInformation/Publications/AgingUndertheMicroscope/chapter01.htm l (accessed July 30, 2008).

20. Healthy Aging for Older Adults, http://www.cdc.gov/aging/ (accessed July 4, 2004). Note: by "longevity," the Centers for Disease Control seems to mean merely that the average age of the U.S. population is increasing due to the baby boomers moving out of middle age. The CDC does not appear to expect or advocate an extension in the maximum human life span. However, a significant reduction in the death rate due to chronic illness would increase the average age at death, even if it did not increase the maximum life span.

21. The idea of a 120-year human age limit arises from the fact that the examples of extreme longevity in humans seem to end around that age: that is, there are a few rare, documented cases of humans living beyond 120 years, but none beyond 125. Although the age/frequency curve is extremely low at that point, it does not tail out forever as a truly random curve would do. This suggests that there is a "hard cutoff" at that age. However, the number of cases of death near or above 120 years is so low (with reliably confirmed cases nearly nonexistent) that any such conclusions are speculative at best. Humans may be encountering senescence above 100 years, or they may simply be falling prey to increasingly lengthy odds of remaining fit and disease-free at that age. It is hard to tell.

22. S. Jay Olshansky, testimony of December 12, 2002, to President's Council on Bioethics hearings on "Adding Years to Life: Current Knowledge and Future Prospects," Session 2, http://bioethicsprint.bioethics.gov/transcripts/dec02/session2.html (accessed December 30, 2004).

23. Steven N. Austad, testimony of December 12, 2002, to President's Council on Bioethics hearings on "Adding Years to Life: Current Knowledge and Future Prospects," Session 1, http://bioethicsprint.bioethics.gov/transcripts/dec02/session2.html (accessed December 30, 2004).

24. Sherwin B. Nuland, "How to Grow Old," in *The Best American Science Writing 2004*, ed. Dava Sobel (New York : ecco Press, HarperCollins Publishers, 2004).

25. Aubrey de Grey, "SENS (Strategies for Engineered Negligible Senescence)," http://www.gen.cam.ac.uk/sens/ (accessed January 13, 2005).

26. Ibid.

27. President's Council on Bioethics, *Beyond Therapy: Biotechnology and the Pursuit of Happiness* (New York: Dana Press, 2003) 189–203.

28. Kurzweil and Grossman, *Fantastic Voyage*, 3.

29. Nanotechnology is the science of designing artificial mechanisms on the scale of individual molecules, which could then be used to perform tasks inside the body or even inside individual cells, such as repairing molecular damage or enhancing biological functions.

30. It is known that remarkably small genetic changes can produce dramatic life extension in animal models. Once it was assumed that genetic control of aging would be an extremely complex process—like genetic control of intelligence or physical appearance or suchlike. In fact, multiple single-gene changes have been identified, any one of which significantly increases longevity in their respective species, with retained robust physical ability. Over 50 such genes have been identified in nematodes (a standard life-extension experimental subject) and at least half a dozen in mice; more are expected. These genes are not necessarily identical to human genes, but it is likely that similar mechanisms exist. Cf. Austad, testimony of December 12, 2002, to President's Council on Bioethics hearings.

31. Cryogenics is the practice of infusing a newly dead body with a solution that replaces most of the water in the tissues, and then storing the corpse indefinitely at

the temperature of liquid nitrogen. The embalming solution reduces cell damage from the formation of ice crystals, but, inasmuch as the body is already *dead* when the process is performed, and there is no known way to return the tissues to their natural state or undo the damage that does occur, let alone reverse the process of death that has already occurred, the technique offers no hope that the dead person will be any better off when they are warmed than they were at the time of cooling. The entire process is premised on the hope that some future technology will be invented that will allow for the reanimation of super-cooled dead bodies. Naturally, cryogenics organizations offer no guarantees that anyone in the future will undertake that part of the project.

32. President's Council on Bioethics, *Beyond Therapy*, 182.

33. Gregory Stock, *Redesigning Humans: Our Inevitable Genetic Future* (Boston: Houghton Mifflin, 2002), 87–88.

34. Aubrey D.N. de Grey "Escape Velocity: Why the Prospect of Extreme Human Life Extension Matters Now," *PLoS Biology* 2, no. 6 (2004): e187, emphasis in the original.

35. With women no longer marrying in their teens to men sometimes generations older than themselves, the once-common sight of a woman widowed four or five times in succession by men much older than her has disappeared. Women and men both now enter marriage at a time when they can look forward to 40–50 more years of healthy life—but, until about World War II or afterwards, human history had never seen a generation in which that was true. Thus, today's divorces after 5, 10, or 20 years of marriage may be partly the product of the "natural senescence" of relationships that would previously have ended in death after about the same length of time.

36. Richard Lamm, speech, March 27, 1984, as reported in the *New York Times*, March 29, 1984, http://query.nytimes.com/gst/fullpage.html?sec=health&res=9E 01E5D91E39F93AA15750C0A962948260 (accessed July 30, 2008). Interestingly, Lamm cited Leon Kass (see below) as the direct inspiration for this statement.

37. Austad, testimony of December 12, 2002, to President's Council on Bioethics hearings.

38. Leonard Hayflick, quoted in Stephen S. Hall, *Merchants of Immortality: Chasing the Dream of Human Life Extension* (Boston: Houghton Mifflin, 2003), 9, emphasis in the original.

39. Daniel Callahan, "Visions of Eternity," *First Things* 133 (May 2003): 28–35.

40. Leon R. Kass, foreword to *Beyond Therapy: Biotechnology and the Pursuit of Happiness* (New York: Dana Press, 2003).

41. Leon R. Kass, *Toward a More Natural Science: Biology and Human Affairs* (New York: Free Press, 1985), 305–6, emphasis in the original.

42. Callahan, "Visions of Eternity," 28–35.

43. Leon Kass, "L'Chaim and Its Limits: Why Not Immortality?" *First Things* 113 (May 2001): 17–24, emphasis in original.

44. Kass, *Toward a More Natural Science*, 303, emphasis in the original.

45. Alexander, "Don't Die, Stay Pretty."

46. Ibid.

47. Kass, "L'Chaim and Its Limits: Why Not Immortality?" 17–24.

48. Kass, *Toward a More Natural Science*, 308, emphasis in the original.

49. Ibid., 309–10.

50. Francis Fukuyama, *Our Posthuman Future: Consequences of the Biotechnology Revolution*, (New York: Farrar, Straus, and Giroux, 2002), 7.

51. Ibid., 70.

52. Ibid., 172.

53. William Hurlbut, comment in President's Council on Bioethics hearings on "Beyond Therapy: Ageless Bodies?," March 6, 2003, Session 2, http://www.bioethics.gov/transcripts/march03/session2.html (accessed December 30, 2004).

54. Charles Sandel, comment in President's Council on Bioethics hearings on "Beyond Therapy: Ageless Bodies?," March 6, 2003, Session 2, http://www.bioethics.gov/transcripts/march03/session2.html (accessed 12/30/2004).

55. Charles Krauthammer, comment in President's Council on Bioethics hearings on "Beyond Therapy: Ageless Bodies?," march 6, 2003, Session 2, http://www.bio ethics.gov/transcripts/march03/session2.html (accessed December 30, 2004).

56. President's Council on Bioethics, *Beyond Therapy*, 224–25.

57. Rebecca Dresser, comment in President's Council on Bioethics hearings on "Beyond Therapy: Ageless Bodies?," March 6, 2003, Session 2, http://www.bioethics.gov/transcripts/march03/session2.html (accessed December 30, 2004).

58. Kass, "Why Not Immortality?" 17–24.

59. Kass, *Toward a More Natural Science*, 312–13, emphasis in the original.

60. President's Council on Bioethics, *Beyond Therapy*, 212.

61. Ibid., 217.

62. Joseph Margolis, "Death," in *Ethical Issues in Death and Dying*, ed. Tom L. Beauchamp and Seymour Perlin (Englewood Cliffs, N.J.: Prentice-Hall, 1978), 360–61.

63. John Harris, "Immortal Ethics," *Annals of the New York Academy of Sciences* 1019 (2004): 527–34.

64. Hall, *Merchants of Immortality*, 355.

65. John K. Davis, "Collective Suttee: Is It Unjust to Develop Life Extension If It Will Not Be Possible to Provide It to Everyone?" *Annals of the New York Academy of Sciences* 1019 (2004): 535–41.

66. Stock, *Redesigning Humans*, 90.

67. Thomas Nagel, "Death," in *Mortal Questions* (Cambridge, Mass.: Cambridge University Press, 1979), 9–10.

68. Ibid., 10.

69. Ibid.

CHAPTER 5

COVERING (UP?) DEATH: A CLOSE READING OF *TIME* MAGAZINE'S SEPTEMBER 11, 2001, SPECIAL ISSUE

Christina Staudt

One cannot look directly at the sun or at death.

—La Rochefoucauld

On the morning of Tuesday, September 11, 2001, *Time* magazine picture editor MaryAnne Golon received a call urging her to drive immediately to Manhattan to begin work on a breaking news story—an airplane had hit the World Trade Center. Before she could make her way into the office, she learned that terrorists had hijacked four passenger planes. Two had been deliberately flown into the Twin Towers of the World Trade Center, causing their collapse within the hour. A third plane had crashed onto the Pentagon and a fourth—apparently also destined for a target in Washington, D.C.—had gone down in Pennsylvania. The attacks appeared to have taken more than 5,000 lives.[1]

How did Golon and her colleagues at the country's largest pictorial news magazine deal with death on such a massive scale? The short answer is *furtively*. In *Time*'s 9/11 special issue, which appeared on newsstands within 72 hours of the momentous event (September 14, 2001), the dead are barely noticeable. *Time* magazine had not always shied away from the topic of death. A cover story on "Death in America" in September 2000 featured photographs of dying Americans and discussed their stories in detail. Casualties of grenades and suicide bombers were not uncommon in the magazine's reporting on war and conflict. Those who died on September 11, 2001, however, were treated differently. Among 30 pictures, only two directly portray those who succumbed, and in one of those two the dead person is not the primary focus. In eight, the dead are implied but not visible. The other 20 shots have the lens directed on tangential motifs, as if a straightforward viewing of the dead might be too blinding.

Such media evasion of mass death is usually suspect, indicating politically motivated, official censorship, exemplified in its extreme, in the lack of news coverage of the 30,000 people who "disappeared" during the military junta in Argentina between 1976 and 1983. But the steering away from publishing a country's perished citizens can be politically motivated by those in authority even when the reasons are less sinister than in a brutal dictatorship. Many journalists have voiced their dissatisfaction with the policy of the George W. Bush administration in not allowing photographs of American war dead returning to American bases after having been killed in Iraq or Afghanistan; this control of the representation of the dead is seen as an attempt to "spin" the public's perception of the wars. However, when *Time*, a commercial news magazine, chose to omit images of the dead from its first report of the September 11 attacks, the inferential denial of death was in all likelihood a form of editorial death management in the service of its readership.

The magazine-buying public voted its approval of the coverage by making the 9/11 special issue the best-selling issue in *Time*'s history. In addition to mailing the volume to its four million regular subscribers, *Time* printed 500,000 copies for sale at newsstands. Two hundred and fifty thousand copies were sold within hours, the rest within the next few days. *Time* continued to print copies of this issue for the remainder of 2001 and into 2002. By March 2002, 3.2 million single copies had been sold, almost 10 times the number for the previous most popular issue in the history of the magazine. Sales continued through telephone and online orders into the following years. Readers also showed their appreciation by sending an unprecedented number of complimentary letters to the editors of *Time*. Many of those who own the issue consider it a collector's item. Libraries kept it on special reserve for months or imposed other restrictions on its circulation. In May 2002, the American Society of Magazine Editors (ASME) awarded the special issue the top prize in the single-topic issue category for 2001.

What may have been the connection between the implicit denial of the dead and the popular success of this issue? If, in this massive disaster, *Time* did not focus on the thousands of dead, what did it report on and to what end? Whose purpose(s) did the omission of the dead serve?

GIVING FORM TO SEPTEMBER 11

The concept "9/11" is changing and unstable, with a continually redefined meaning in relation to political and cultural life in the United States and the world. Individual and collective memories are managed and manipulated to serve a range of purposes in political rhetoric, court cases, 9/11 Commission hearings, commemorative art and building projects, academic theses, and other forms of representation.

Arguably, representation is the means by which reality is created—given form. Individuals tend to create or embrace definitions of reality that offer them means of control and venues for coping and interacting functionally with the world around them. Representations interpret and edit the world they depict or describe; they bring about order, inform, and give rise to emotions. They make it possible for society to grasp and communicate ideas, manage life, and promote beliefs and desires; those in charge of the representations wield the power to make their reality appear true (see Goodwin and Bronfen 1993; Watzlawick 1976).

In the contemporary world, the media provide a substantial part of the representations that people encounter. They produce social spaces for discourse and participate in dictating visions of the time. Media reports help formulate opinions, create worldviews, and construct identities (e.g., of heroes and of national belonging). The media create, hone and even alter memories of events by selecting what aspects to highlight. In a free society, media outlets are an integral part of their environment, playing an interactive role with society, simultaneously reflecting, forming, and expressing the community in which they thrive.

A variety of outlets—television, radio, print media, and the Internet—participated in forming, and continue to mold, the public and personal histories of September 11, each TV station, newspaper, blog, and "e-zine" engaging selectively with what mattered, and matters, to its producers and consumers. The information gathered, subsequently edited, and finally disseminated in words and pictures provides the substantial fodder for the creation of our national memory of "9/11" and of our remembrance of those who died. For those with no personal connection to the events, the media reports may be the only points of reference. *Time* magazine participated in this project in harmonious tune with its readership. Like all other media productions, *Time* magazine's 9/11 issue is inextricably linked with the culture in which it was produced. It was, and is, permeated and constituted by the concerns, beliefs, and practices of its environment. Its representations show how mainstream America would like to define itself in a deadly crisis and reveal how the events of September 11 were appropriated to promote certain values dear to this population.

According to Ernest Becker (1973), all personal and societal representations can be seen as propelled by a creative instinct that is rooted in a fear of death, while Richard Stamelman (1990) has proposed that "dispossession makes possible the creation of images, and negatively, as embodied in absence, death, and loss, animates the quest of writing and other forms of configuration" (x). Whether or not one agrees with these premises with regard to the origin of creativity, a willingness to subscribe to them while viewing *Time* magazine's September 11 issue adds an important dimension to the understanding of its configuration. Studying a group's collective attitude toward death offers an opportunity to "rediscover people and to catch them in their reactions to an event which allows no exceptions" (Vovelle 1990, 64). In the special issue we see mainstream America as it has created itself in the face of unspeakable loss: a nation full of spirituality, compassion, and patriotism.

The motif, mood, and placement of individual pictures, their accompanying captions, the graphics, the thrust of the textual story, and the overall layout reveal the *Time* editors' collective vision of September 11. The personal intentions of individual photographers and graphic artists who contributed material are subordinate to the overall composition of the issue. The intention of the editors, however, does not constitute the magazine's final construction of September 11. That process is not complete until the magazine reaches its readers, who interpret it in their personal contexts.

CONNECTING WITH READERS

In a world where news, entertainment, and commentary are dominated by television and the Internet, the illustrated weekly news magazine holds a niche position. *Time*'s main competitors are *Newsweek* and *U.S. News and World Report*. According to Mediamark Research and Intelligence (MRI), reporting in May 2002, in an average week *Time* sold 200,000 copies at newsstands and four million issues arrived in the homes and offices of subscribers. *Newsweek* and *U.S. News and World Report* had 3.3 million and one million subscribers respectively. Many copies are read by more than one person with the readership per copy varying from issue to issue. Based on data reported by Time, Inc. and compiled by MRI, the average number of readers is close to five per copy of *Time* (data from in 2007). *Time* is frequently quoted in other mass media, further expanding its sphere of influence beyond its core readership.

The weekly news magazines offer a specialized service by giving a manageable summary of the events of the previous seven days and covering issues of interest to their readership. *Time* magazine surveys a broad segment of life in America and abroad under headings such as "world," "business," "society," and "arts." It also includes opinion columns, obituaries, and letters to the editor. The cover story is usually an investigative piece on a salient topic. All three news weeklies produced September 11 issues. However, as part of a giant media conglomerate, *Time* was able to find printing press capacity in other sectors of its parent company and delivered its issue several days ahead of the other news weeklies. It had by far the greatest circulation, making it the chosen vehicle for this study.

Time's readers are not definable by political party or by narrow socioeconomic class. They represent a geographic and ideological cross section of middle- and upper-middle-class Americans of higher than median age, income, and education as compared with the total U.S. population [extrapolated from US Census data (2000) and the Mendelsohn Affluent Survey (2002)]. Established in 1923, *Time* placed itself in the American public discourse as "a weekly news-magazine, aimed to serve the modern necessity of keeping people informed." Organized and effective presentation was a key component from the beginning. "*Time* is interested—not in how much it includes between the covers—but how much it gets off its pages into the minds of its readers." The editors prided themselves on neutral and objective reporting (Mott 1968, 295).

    Time's editors see the magazine as speaking to and for mainstream America and as giving a picture of mainstream America to the 1.5 million who subscribe to *Time* from abroad (American expatriates as well as foreigners). Nancy Gibbs, the senior editor who wrote the cover story for the September 11 issue, sees *Time* not as a primary news source but as a place where issues are put on the table and where news is explained and made manageable (personal interview, Gibbs 2002). *Time*'s picture editors MaryAnne Golon and Michele Stephenson contend that *Time* is doing more than just summarizing the events of a week (personal interview). They recall several occasions when *Time*'s attention to a particular set of facts or issues became part of a headline story in major newspapers and on TV. James Kelly, the managing editor at the time, summarized his view of *Time*'s purpose in his announcement of the nomination of the 9/11 issue for the 2002 ASME award: "We all [he and his staff] have one goal in mind: to bring you the best-reported, best-written, best-looking magazine every week" (Kelly 2002, 6).

    People seek out a magazine or newspaper that satisfies their need for information and entertainment in a serviceable format, and *Time*, like other media, has an evolving and reciprocal relationship with its readership. "Maintaining a regular readership means offering readers a recognizable position in successive numbers that is creating a consistent 'reader' within the text by its reading practice of the press itself" (Sinnema 1998, 20). *Time* received many hundreds of e-mails from readers all over the United States and in many foreign countries on September 11. By the end of the week, the number had reached 1,500. Such communication is one reason why *Time*'s editors feel they know and understand the sentiments of their readership. As in all media outlets, *Time*'s editors structure a "dominant position from which to read" (Beetham 1990, 9–32). *Time*'s "dominant position" is so imbued with broadly based American values that, when asked about the magazine's bias, readers' typical responses are that *Time* is "neutral," "objective," and "inoffensive." In an informal survey, questions about a "cover-up" of the dead or about self-censorship by *Time* were either met with incomprehension or rejected as irrelevant.[2] Working within this mostly nonprovocative ideological purview, *Time*'s editors create a product they believe will stimulate and please their

readers and will nurture the relationship with them. How the story of September 11 needed to be told to resonate effectively with *Time*'s readers was
instinctively understood by veteran editors, based on the magazine's established "dominant position."

LAYOUT OF THE *TIME* 9/11 ISSUE

Presenting the Facts While Omitting the Dead

To MaryAnne Golon (2002) the obvious choice for the cover of *Time*'s
special issue was the burning Twin Towers. (*Time*'s director of photography,
Stephenson, was on vacation on September 11, and the primary work of organizing and selecting the pictures for the issue was handled by MaryAnne
Golon). The hits on the towers were the most dramatic aspect of the day. The
sight was shown on television repeatedly for days, and the editors predicted
correctly that this would become the primary icon of September 11. The
particular image chosen for the *Time* cover places the viewer on the street
below the towers, in close proximity to the falling ashes and burning debris,
and brings the reader right into the action.

The deaths of thousands of people are implied in this image but its meaning goes beyond the demise of the victims. The image elicited a close to
unanimous reaction of horror and condemnation among Americans. Many
others around the world concurred, but no image has a predetermined, universally accepted meaning. The burning towers gain meaning in relation to
the experience of the viewer and to the ideological mindset of the culture in
which the picture appears. Some groups in the Middle East celebrated at the
sight of this image. The meaning is fabricated in the minds of the viewer. A
picture, like a text, "manifests the various ways in which the reading subject knows the world, relies upon many of the same assumptions about the
way the world operates, and thereby functions according to a set of meanings already comprehensible to those readers who picked it up" (Sinnema
1998, 26).

At the core of the American people's reaction was the knowledge that the
event was real and intentional. Had the fateful collisions been accidental, the
impact of the picture would not have been as wrenching. The shock induced
by fiction is of a different ilk (see Zillman and Bryant 1985). Americans
learned that an obscure and hateful group that prays for the eradication of
the United States had engineered the attack with members who were willing
to commit suicide to achieve the group's evil objectives. The viewer was not
only witnessing burning office towers but also an assault on U.S. soil with no
parallel since at least as far back as Pearl Harbor and arguably since the War
of 1812. From the beginning, pundits and politicians referred to the events
as "war," a war fought on the home front against a fanatical enemy hiding in

our midst. Attention to the dead was pictorially deferred by *Time* until the
viewer had begun processing this monumental crisis.

The image on the inside cover of the special issue, next to a letter from the
magazine's managing editor, is a black and white photograph of a crowd running from Ground Zero, as the impact zone came to be known. MaryAnne
Golon said that the editors did not consciously select a black and white picture as the introductory image. ("It just seemed like a powerful beginning.")
In response to the suggestion that a black and white photograph in today's
world of multichromatic imagery places the viewer at a distance from the
action, Golon countered that black and white photography also suggests a
documentary film with a truth claim. Anecdotal evidence suggests that many
agree with Golon. A black and white image is an alert to the senses and connotes serious news. The blooded and dust-covered people in the image hold
hands as they run to safety, conveying that they are injured but have escaped
death and are offering support to each other. The picture introduces *Time*'s
main theme in the 9/11 issue: Americans have encountered extreme pain and
distress but will survive by working together.

The cover picture functions as a headline to the story; the introductory
scene in black and white promises authenticity and the subsequent images
unfold the story. The four sequential pictures, titled "The Second Strike,"
spread over the next two pages, show one of the airplanes hitting the south
tower, in a recapitulation of everyone's initial shock at the news of the morning on 9/11. That *Time* chose to picture the attack on the second tower
rather than the first was purely an aesthetic decision. The magazine had
access to video-filmed imagery of the first impact, but when the individual
frames were developed for magazine print purposes, the quality could not
compare with still photography. Seven frames from the video were developed
and printed, for the record, further into the issue. The scene of the assault on
the towers was replayed on television all day on September 11 and frequently
during the following days. Most of *Time*'s readership would have been familiar with it by the time the special arrived in their hands. Nevertheless,
the pictures hold unique narrative power. They show the course of events
in stages that can be perused individually and at length if the viewer wishes.
The psychological impact of each frame is sustained, unlike the frames of
a film strip moving in real time and disappearing into the ether. "Nonstop
imagery (television, streaming video, movies) is our surround, but when it
comes to remembering, the photograph has the bigger bite. Memory freeze-
frames; its basic unit is the single image. In an era of information overload,
the photograph provides a quick way of apprehending something and a compact form for memorizing it" (Sontag 2003, 22).

The first of the four photographs serves to create dread in the heart of the
viewer. The tiny airplane over the skyscrapers of Manhattan is innocuous in
size, but because we know the outcome, it packs enormous, menacing power.

The north tower, already on fire, gives credence to the idea of the airplane as a missile threatening the south tower. The second image, showing the plane just before impact, anticipates the imminent disaster and brings the accumulated tension in the viewer to a climax. The last two pictures function as a follow-through that releases the suspense but also leaves no opening for escape. The disaster is complete.

The images have no frame but cover the pages of the magazine all the way to the edges on three sides. They are grounded by a black band at the base, which contains a caption in eye-catching red capitals and a brief sentence in white text. As is common usage in *Time*, the sentence following the caption does not have a period at the end. In the context of this event, the lack of a period suggests the uncertainty of a story in progress, one as yet lacking an ending. The unframed picture is standard for *Time*. The format conveys that the image pictured describes something that is continuous in a larger world and has implications beyond what is described on the page.

Golon mentioned that *Time* had received some criticism for overwhelmingly featuring the Twin Towers in this issue. The assault on the Pentagon, shown in a picture entitled "Ready, Aim," shares a spread with a portion of the text far inside the issue. There is no picture of the airplane that was downed in Pennsylvania. But *Time* probably got it right in the eyes and minds of most readers. The Pentagon is a symbol of the American military, while the Twin Towers were a symbol of America's economic might and reach, an emblem of a way of life based on capitalism and a free market. The Twin Towers symbolized America's values, whereas the Pentagon symbolizes the vehicle for defending those values. The attack on the Pentagon was an attack on the armor of the nation, while the attack on the towers was an attack on its heart.

In confronting the pictures of the airplanes hitting their targets, the reader did not learn anything new about the events. Nor was he or she likely to find redemption or comfort in these reminders of the enormous damage the terrorists had wrought. These were blunt recapitulations of a shocking and, although few people openly said so, humiliating event for which America was mentally and emotionally unprepared. In spite of what retrospectively came to be seen as substantial warnings, the assault came as a total surprise. A collective sense of horror amplified by degrees of grief, fear, and anger prevailed in the country. To pictorially relive the catastrophe in such an ambience may seem almost masochistic on the part of *Time* and its readers and of all the media and members of the public that indulged in kindred reports. However, the horrifying imagery, presented repeatedly in similar form in a multitude of venues, served as a vehicle for coping with the aftermath. People were forced to recognize the underlying truth that the superpower of the world had been unable to defend itself on its own territory, with horrendous consequences. Conventional wisdom suggests that the first step in a recovery process is to face the truth honestly; grief counselors often recommend to clients that they should tell and retell their experience of a loved one's death in order to come to grips with it. Similarly, the straightforward, descriptive pictures in *Time* could help the readers take the first step toward coming to terms with a momentous national tragedy. This series of images, showing the airplanes' impact on the Twin Towers, visually discloses the deadly terrorist act while leaving the literal and excruciating truth of the resulting mangled bodies to the imagination. It is simultaneous acknowledgment and denial, a not uncommon strategy in the encounter with death (see Sherry R. Schachter, "Cancer Patients Facing Death," chapter 2 in this volume).

"Fleeing the Cloud" depicts a group of men close enough to the impact area to be at physical risk. A deadly cloud of smoke chases them as they run down the avenue with intent focus on saving themselves. As in the black and white introductory picture, death threatens but life prevails. Again, *Time* chose an image that was arousing and moving but tended toward hope rather than despair. Like most of the photographs in this issue, "Fleeing the Cloud" is spread over two pages. This keeps the reader's attention on one subject at a time and suggests the monumental dimensions of every subject depicted. When Golon selected "Fleeing the Cloud" as a potent descriptive image of what it was like to be in the middle of the action, threatened by smoke and fire, she did not see the billowing cloud as having connotations of nuclear bombing. Some of those informally interviewed about their impressions of the special issue felt that the caption "Fleeing the Cloud" evokes the possibility that this could have been a nuclear attack. While the picture allowed the viewer to imagine a flight to safety, it also augmented the fear of death by suggesting that a "dirty-bomb" attack by a rogue group was potentially a greater risk than had previously been believed. (For an elaboration of the psychological complexities of fantasies of risk and safety, see Jerry S. Piven, "Death, Terror, Culture, and Violence," chapter 7 in this volume.)

Time told the story of the day in text and graphics, as well as in pictures. The sequence of the different forms of reporting creates a viewing/reading rhythm that moves the reader into different mental and emotional states by offering a variety of modes and venues with which to process the difficult material. The shifts make the experience of leafing through the magazine both richer and less emotionally taxing. The graphics describing the attack are analytical and require a cerebral engagement. The illustrated charts offer a respite from the emotional onslaught of the photographs and an alternative way to examine and stay involved with the topic of 9/11 without facing the dead.

The first graphic, "Twin Terrors," appears more than halfway through the issue, when the reader is reeling from exposure to 16 emotionally demanding photographs. It explains the technical aspects of the collapse of the Twin Towers. The American public found the purported motivation for the attack difficult to comprehend. The terrorists' religious zeal seemed arcane and illogical. In contrast, the material collapse of the buildings was based on the laws of physics and made clear sense, a welcome relief for the reader who strained to find a nugget of the rational in the havoc.

The graphic depiction of "Paths of Destruction" serves a similar purpose: it breaks up the text and offers a summary and sense of order in the midst of the turmoil. The charted courses of the planes, the timetables and the maps of the affected areas in New York City and Washington give the reader something sensible and recognizable. With so many unanswered questions and so much uncertainty about who the perpetrators were and whether the country would be hit again, the ability to say anything with certainty provided comfort. To lay out the known facts is a practical way to begin to decipher a difficult situation. *Time*'s graphics provided the beginning of such organized fact-finding. However, there were some facts that the reader preferred not to face.

Crossing the Line

Golon feels that through her many years at *Time* she has learned to select images that appeal to her readers and serve their needs and their reasons for subscribing to the magazine. In this crisis, she said: "I just went to work. We are like soldiers. We are an experienced team and we have done our work until it is almost automatic. We are well trained and now we went into battle." She said she has a "gut feeling"—an intuition—about what the audience considers good taste, and usually she can accurately gauge the reaction to controversial coverage.

She and the other editors made one misstep in the special issue, the picture that was given the caption "The Long Fall." It shows small dark human forms silhouetted against a pale sky falling alongside an imposing steel and glass structure that fills the page from top to bottom. Perhaps a metaphor for how small individual human beings are in relation to the enormity of this event, it portrays one of the most harrowing occurrences of the day: people voluntarily jumping out of the burning towers rather than being trapped in circumstances beyond their control. This photograph, recording a final defiant assertion of free will or a desperate act in the grip of panic, is the magazine's only image of those who would die. Mindful of its audience, *Time*'s editors deliberately and on principle chose to avoid pictures of fatalities in the special issue, and they debated the inclusion of the "Long Fall" at length. In addition to a concern for the general viewer, the feelings of the relatives of the victims were a consideration. (The claim of authority over the representation of the dead would later become a contested issue among the victims' families, city officials, and real estate interests.) The editors finally decided to use the photograph, because, in Golon's words, "it was an important part of what had occurred that day."

It is the only picture, according to Golon, that the editors would not include if they could remake the issue. "This is one of the few images for which
we have received public criticism. When the time came to do *Time*'s 2001
commemorative edition, Kelly [*Time's* managing editor] made it clear that
this photo should not be repeated. It had been a close call and there was no
reason to tread there again." By "a close call," Golon meant that *Time* had
been on the brink of risking the readership's trust in the editors' good judgment. Jeffrey Goldstein has noted that "the viewing of violent images loses
its appeal when the viewer does not feel relatively safe" (1998, 219). The context of the falling bodies plays a crucial role in the viewer's reception of the
image. *Time*'s readers felt vulnerable in the days after the attack and did not
need or wish to exacerbate their anxiety by considering the consequences of
the act they witnessed in this image.

"Long Fall" is a subtle rendition of death without the gore of mangled
corpses, but the imagination follows the jumpers to the ground and encounters their smashed bodies in the mind's eye. With this picture before them,
readers were brutally confronted by death, and death's undeniable presence
aggravated the pain in their wounded psyche. Americans preferred not to
look. The picture is aesthetically exquisite, with the geometric shapes of the
building balanced by the organic shapes of the bodies flowing through the
sky. Its beauty was surely one of the reasons it was included, but this did not,
for most readers, compensate for the morbid content. The graceful bodies
and sheer beauty of the image may even make it more horrifying than a collection of mutilated bodies. Psychological terror is embedded in "The Long
Fall" just as Hitchcock films create fear and suspense by suggestion and implication rather than by graphic description.

Masking Death with Beauty

The aesthetic appeal of "The Long Fall" probably contributed to the accu-
sations of exploitation of the dead. The intersecting of death and aesthet-
ics has no single outcome even given a single viewer and similar motif.
Depending on the circumstances, a beautiful, sensitive portrayal of a dead
person may lend dignity to the death or may seem callous in the way it calls
attention to its own artistry rather than to the sad reality portrayed. Often
both aspects can be simultaneously present. In *Time*'s 9/11 issue, the artistry
of many of the photographs mitigate the impact of their death-imbued subject matter. In several, the dead are literally hidden under a beautiful surface,
denying the viewer (or, should we say, protecting the viewer from) the unvar-
nished appearance of death. By stirring her aesthetic sensibility, the images
coax the viewer into considering formal properties and intriguing compositions as well as the gruesome content. The photographs transform reality
into art and facilitate the denial of what lies behind the motif.

The picture "Makeshift E.R." has at its center rescue workers helping a victim, as its caption suggests, but the surreal quality of the scene seduces the viewer into lingering over the image to search out the details. In a street covered in smoke and debris, the eye discovers the faintly outlined steel shafts of one of the towers, a row of American flags, a green traffic light absurdly beckoning, and scattered rescue workers engaged in various tasks. Disturbed and fascinated by the extraordinary physical deconstruction of downtown New York, the reader is enticed to investigate the scene and absorb its minutiae. Death is a secondary focus in this chaotic and complex composition.

"Ash Tuesday" is a haunting photograph of a landscape blanketed in yellow dust, seemingly far removed from any city. Its otherworldly quality invites quiet contemplation and soothes the psyche. The caption, an accurate description of the monochrome landscape caused by the disaster, suggests a link to the Christian calendar. Ash Wednesday, the first day of Lent, is the beginning of 40 days of atonement and sacrifice. The three men covered in dust and ash may be interpreted as being on a similar journey. The dust may conjure up biblical references to that word, such as descriptions of Hebrews putting dust or ashes on their heads when they mourned (Josh. 7:6; Isa. 47:1; Lam. 3:29), the fact that dust denotes the grave and death (Gen. 13:16; Job 7:21; Ps. 22:15), or the Christian burial service in which the officiant pronounces "dust you are and to dust you will return" (Gen. 3:19). While these references to death assert themselves to the thoughtful viewer, the scene's most gruesome elements are protectively veiled in a haze of biblical connotations and pictorial ash.

The centerfold, "Ghostly Remains," is the most artistically sophisticated image in the special issue. It shows the grey and silver skeletal remains of the Twin Towers silhouetted against a leaden sky and the ground covered in white-dusted debris. A few blood-red signs break the monochromatic scale. The scene looks artificially lit and as staged as a theater set. But this is no fictitious space. It is the remains of a vital commercial center and the burial ground of thousands of people. The panorama is haunting and incongruously beautiful. One letter to the editor commented: "The photos taken by James Nachtwey capture the aftermath of the dastardly act like no others I've seen. Many of his pictures conjure up the surreal. It is ironic that his mastery of light and his magnificent photographic eye have actually made such devastation look artistically beautiful" (Kaplan 2001, 10).

Jim Nachtwey, one of *Time*'s most venerable war photographers, happened to be on home leave and also happened to be in downtown New York on September 11. He "rushed to the World Trade Center to shoot photos for this issue" as soon as he knew what had transpired (Kelly 2001, np). His portraits depict the overwhelming material destruction. The human lives destroyed can be surmised, but the sculptural remains of the towers and the adjoining structures are what appear before the reader. The absence of all life is palpable. Not even a partial corpse indicates a trace of life. An eerie stillness prevails. The presence of death strikes the viewer in the stretch of dusty space and in the vacant ruins of twisted wrought steel; "sheared off buildings are almost as eloquent as bodies in the street" (Sontag 2003, 8). Death and loss carry connotations of a metaphysical power that is rarely present in an image of actual corpses. The emptiness articulates the idea of death as quintessential absence, as "negative materiality" (Ronald Schleifer 1990). Death hovers in the space surrounding the stillness of a few contorted steel beams. But damaged structures, however eloquent in their own way, can never speak vividly about the end of human life. The corpse is the link to the suffering body and is the ultimate site and evidence of death. That an image of death that lacks the bodily connection is easier for the imagination to endure is supported by the fact that *Time* received nothing but praise from the public for "Ghostly Remains."

"Ghostly Remains" may offer the viewer breathing room by allowing the attention to depart from the image's true content and focus on its formal qualities, but the picture also speaks emphatically of finality. As Susan Sontag has articulated through her primary protagonist in *The Volcano Lover* (1992), an artistic depiction is final and guarantees that while you are looking, things won't get worse. This aspect of the scene gave some viewers I interviewed an oddly comforting feeling, as if the picture said: "Something horrendous has taken place but now it's over. You, the viewer, are still here. You have to cope, but the destruction has stopped, at least for now."

Deflecting the Impact of Death by Focusing on Community

In its reporting on September 11, *Time* marginalized the dead for the benefit of the survivors, offering the living an array of coping mechanisms. An overarching strategy was to reinforce the idea of solid American communities, where friends, families, and neighbors support and nurture one another. To embrace the living community is not the same as denying death; it allows a positive alternative to simply looking away from the dead.

Not all communities have geographic proximity or even a physical space. Some are formed through common interests and experiences. The editors, reporters, and readers of a newspaper or magazine form a community, and the printed page is the place where they come together (Anderson 1991, chap. 2). To Nancy Gibbs (2002), the communal sphere in which *Time* is produced and read is "akin to a New England town hall meeting, where intelligent people share experiences, stories and ideas." If the pictures with their captions in the 9/11 issues are the voices of the community, some validate the fear and anger that many were feeling, while others help "the townsfolk" recognize themselves in their neighbors or confirm common, enduring values. With the exception of the brutal voice of "The Long Fall," all allow for and encourage the assembled community to keep the focus away from those who died.

The statement "Day of Infamy" is boldly printed over more than a quarter of an image of the burning towers a few pages into the issue. The words "Day of" are depicted in neutral white and "Infamy" in intense red. The words hover before the towers and cast a shadow over the smoking bulk. The large block letters, pasted like a label on the towers, condemn the act and endorse the reader's fury. Anger is a well-known defense against death. "Day of Infamy" directs attention to the heinous character of the act as well as pointing to the political shame of the nation, while de-emphasizing the loss of individual lives. Besides describing the current event, the words "Day of Infamy" invoke history and declare this assault comparable to the bombing of Pearl Harbor on December 7, 1941, and the entry into a major war. For older Americans, "Day of Infamy" may still primarily be associated with World War II, but for many younger Americans, the phrase may become the label for September 11, 2001, and the beginning of the "war on terrorism."

An image of a cloud of smoke and debris emerging between two office buildings and a church roof with a cross in the foreground carries the caption "Holy War." Among those I spoke with about this picture, several people interpreted this to mean that the terrorists, who are Muslim, are pitted against those who assemble under the cross. One woman, an ardent Christian, saw that in spite of the damage "the cross is still there." A young man who was vehemently against the idea of any military involvement by the United States in the Middle East noted that the cross is partially rusted, inferring that some long-held Western beliefs and practices are tainted. These divergent comments demonstrate how crucial personal, religious, and national contexts are to the meaning of these pictures and that what is suppressed or foregrounded is rooted in the individual.

Some of the images provided comfort by showing the readers that they were not alone in their experience of terror and grief; this was a communal American ordeal. September 11 struck at all Americans, and the reaction of ordinary Americans around the country to the events of the day was a key aspect of the story as the editors saw it. "Shock in the Heartland" shows three young people in Iowa staring at a television screen with expressions of sadness, terror, and concern. One college student I interviewed reacted to this image by saying, "this is exactly the way we all felt and looked throughout that day, as we followed the events on television. This picture could have been taken anywhere in America." The image validated the fear, confusion, and sadness that so many felt, and it offered support by showing that these feelings were shared by others.

During the day of September 11, many people shifted abruptly between determinedly carrying on with their daily tasks and sitting transfixed before the television. Torn between the horror of the imagery and a desire to know the story, they were alternatively repelled by and drawn to the images on the screen. "Reluctant Witnesses" catches two women, one staring in awe and the other covering her eyes. It reflects the common ambivalence in the minds of many readers and offers them companionship in their emotionally divided state.

Many of the pictures in the 9/11 issue featured values that much of America holds high and, with the accompanying texts, reinforced the aspects that unify a diverse nation. *Time*'s attention to spiritual values, compassion, courage, and patriotism encouraged the living to direct their gaze toward what mainstream America (*Time*'s audience) considered enduring and edifying qualities. It was, if not a denial of the dead, a deflection from the dead with a suggestion that for the moment, the mental and emotional health of the living mattered more.

"Lord Have Mercy" depicts a scene that many Americans recognized as they themselves gathered in their houses of worship to pray and comfort each other. The hand-holding congregants make visual what was heard repeatedly on television and from people on that catastrophic day: Americans are united in their opposition to terrorism and Americans are spiritually strong. Golon contacted the photographer Torsten Kjellstrand at an early stage in the production of the 9/11 issue. She knew of his ability to astutely capture the sentiments of the people in the American heartland. The photograph's angle from above gives a "celestial" perspective on the congregation and may suggest that a holy spirit is looking down on a faithful, humble, and united people.

Other images also promoted and reinforced the belief that there is goodness in the disaster, order in the chaos, and hope in the darkness. Americans practice their religion on a more regular basis than most other people in the Western world. Forty-four percent of Americans attend a place of worship in a given week compared with 27 percent of people in Great Britain, 21 percent in France, and 4 percent in Sweden (University of Michigan News and Information Services 1997). On September 11 and in its aftermath, worship attendance in the United States surged, and the name of God was routinely invoked in schools and government offices in spite of the Constitution's separation of church and state. *Time* magazine responded to the public need for spiritual sustenance without venturing into potentially divisive or controversial territory. Mosques were excluded for obvious reasons, but overt signs of worshippers' sectarian affiliation were also avoided. To convey the faith of the land, *Time* chose an image of a young girl lighting a candle in a devotional service. Keeping the focus on the living rather than the dead, the image was captioned "This Light of Mine." In many religions and sects, the candle symbolizes the light that brightens the darkness and the hope that can overcome despair. The caption allows this meaning to predominate, rather than the possibility that the girl is lighting a candle for a deceased person. The young girl embodies the reader's hope for the future and offers assurance that spiritual values will remain strong in America.

Americans pride themselves on being compassionate. They could see this trait reflected in *Time* in a picture of a room full of blood donors. The caption, "Laying Down Their Arms," contains a curious double entendre. Aside from referring to the bodily arms offered up for blood donations, the words suggest defeat and capitulation and evoke the idea of a cease-fire for the purpose of taking care of the wounded. Most of 9/11's casualties were fatalities. The injured were a relative small number, and American blood banks were briefly overstocked. This turn of events was not clear at the time when the special issue was produced, and the image gave the reader an opportunity to witness other ordinary Americans helping in the rescue effort. As one interviewee said, "it shows how we come together and support each other, when we are in need." The image speaks of a unity of purpose and of the common decency of the people on the sidelines—a message of comfort in a time of intense tragedy. The blurred quality of the background may be a consequence of an inability to identify all the persons portrayed and obtain releases from them. The effect, however, is one of a frenzy of activity in the service of life.

If the compassion of ordinary Americans was noted in the aftermath of the attack, it was the courage of the rescue workers—particularly of the firefighters, who lost more than 300 men from within their ranks—that captured the public's imagination. *Time* magazine recognized the developing cult and fed into it. "New York's Bravest" shows four dust-covered firefighters resolutely going about their work. The placement of this image between the "The Long Fall" and a photograph of a badly injured victim was psychologically wise. The reader needed a moment of respite while turning the pages from one horror to the next. Although the firefighters as a group sustained more casualties than any other group, it is the living, not the fallen among them, who are depicted. Golon explained that another picture, showing hundreds of firefighters swarming to the rescue of their colleagues trapped in a collapsed building, was included to demonstrate the scale of the rescue effort. The caption for that picture, "Fallen Comrades," suggests soldiers in a war and frontline fighting. Showing the number of fatalities would not have served the purpose of hero building.

Picturing rescuers in disaster situations is a tradition as old as the illustrated press (see Staudt 2001). The rescuers represent the positive in the negative, the proverbial silver lining. They balance the evil with good and offer solace in the face of catastrophe. The firefighters and policemen became the redeemers, the agents of good work and goodwill on September 11. The heroic firefighter as the male ideal for the new decade was born on this day. He would transition into the American soldier/protector after the beginning of the wars in Afghanistan and Iraq. (The male cultural success symbol of the 1990s, a bespectacled computer nerd who could earn millions through his brainpower, epitomized by Bill Gates, was tarnished with the bursting of the "tech bubble" and the steady downslide of the stock market during the previous 18 months.) Physical courage was perfectly exemplified in the strong firemen who bravely entered the burning towers when all others scrambled to get out. They became the designated heroes and secular martyrs in the war on terror. "The Long Fall" put death in the face of the reader, whereas pictures of the firefighters depicted those who were trained to conquer death by rescuing people from its grasp. The firefighters offer hope that imminent death can be defeated and allow the reader to evade the thought of those who are already dead. Heroes have an enduring appeal, and *Time*'s editors understood that the sight of them is uplifting and inspirational to many, although Becker (1973) would likely have seen the presence of these heroes in *Time*'s pages as a form of death denial through transference.

Showing the hero as human enhances his heroic status. Golon argued for the inclusion of a firefighter taking a break. It received the caption "Rare Respite." She calls it "the *Life* Magazine picture," referring to its human-interest quality. The picture shows that these brave men needed rest, food, and water; our heroes are not only brave and strong but also capable of overcoming their human limitations. They are like us, but they accomplish what we can only dream of accomplishing. This image gives the viewer an opportunity to reach out emotionally to those who performed brave acts and to connect with their humanity.

The depictions of rescue workers far outnumber the depictions of fatalities in *Time*'s 9/11 issue. Fatalities are implied in several images, but only one picture, "Evacuation," makes the corpse apparent, and even there the dead body is covered up and secondary to the medical personnel transporting it. Golon explained that there were plenty of pictures available of crushed corpses and torn body parts, but that while "we can do fatalities in the Middle East, we know we'll hear from the readers when we show the dead closer to home." Where American victims are involved, the reader demands a greater degree of decorum. At Ground Zero on September 11, the fatalities were too gruesome and too close, both emotionally and geographically, to depict. *Time*'s editors knew that they had to put the emphasis where the reader wanted and needed it.

In the company of the heroic rescuers, the president of the United States emerges as a tame and unimportant figure. In all, the special issue has three pictures of the president. They appear toward the end of the report, intermingled with Gibbs's story. The first picture of George Bush, "Clued In," shows how, in Golon's words, "he found out about the attack in the midst of an ordinary work day, the way the rest of the public did." It captures Chief of Staff Andrew Card whispering in the president's ear. Seven frames of the strike on the first tower are inserted at the top of the page as an illustration of what was communicated. The caption "clued in" could suggest to the reader that the president was previously "clueless." This caption in combination with a composed and serious president allows *Time* to appeal to both the critics and the supporters of the president. The second image, without a caption, is of the president's address to the nation from the Oval Office in the evening of September 11. As portrayed in *Time*, the president speaks to his country on the day of the disaster with pursed lips and furrowed brow. In my interviews, some supporters of the president saw him as calm but concerned; others viewed him as emotionally moved and sharing in the pain of the American people. His opponents gazed at a puzzled president with the "deer-in-the-headlights" look of someone who is not sure what to do or say. The third image, "Safe Haven," shows Mr. Bush on board Air Force One in consultation with Andrew Card. The caption "Safe Haven" may be interpreted as a criticism of the president for not returning immediately to Washington and for seemingly being more worried about his own safety than about his fellow Americans.

Time's editors claim political neutrality, but they did not attempt to present the president as a figure of authority that people turn to in their day of need. The three relatively small, uncompelling images of the nation's leader chosen for publication suggest that the *Time* staff did not perceive him as an important agent in bringing comfort to the people and in making sense of the events. He is presented as almost irrelevant and unrelated to the events of the day. The textual story has a vaguely critical tone, referring to the president as "unseasoned" and his address from the Oval Office as only "reasonably effective." The attack is described as being a "perfect mockery of the President's faith in missile defense." As if stating the obvious, Stephenson said that pictures of the president needed to be included but that he did not warrant a "spread" or full-page picture. This attitude was probably a reflection of the general population's attitude toward President Bush at the time of the disaster. According to CBSNews.com, January 18, 2004, his approval ratings in the polls were an unimpressive 50 percent in the weeks prior to September 11. The president was not a central figure in the immediate aftermath of the attack, which the American people perceived as an assault on the American way of life and its values. The symbol of the mythic concept "America" was not the president but the American flag. And it was under the "Star-Spangled Banner" that the country was brought together and patriotism surged in much of the country and in the pages of *Time*'s special issue.

A pledge of "allegiance to the flag and to the republic for which it stands" symbolically unites the heterogeneous population of the United States. The 9/11 attack on America inscribed in masses of its denizens a fervor for what they perceived as American values. John R. Gillis has proposed that identity is "inscriptive rather than descriptive" (1994, 20). Recent immigrants, who a week earlier would have identified themselves by their original homeland, hung the Stars and Stripes from their windows and referred to themselves as "we Americans." Flags decorated front porches, were displayed in offices, flew from cars and trucks, and quickly became a favorite among advertisers regardless of the product marketed. Flag waving became a way for

American Muslims (and others who feared they could be mistaken for Muslims) to signal their loyalty to America, genuinely or in fear of misdirected reprisals. The flag united the vengeful and the peaceable, the grieving and the wrathful—each person appropriating those aspects of the American Dream and the United States Constitution that suited his or her purposes. If individuals were not immortal, at least the values of the nation's symbol would endure. The patriotic fervor swelled quickly and *Time* tapped into this outpouring.

Golon claims there was no deliberate attempt to produce an issue of patriotic imagery. Pressed about the specific values she wanted to convey, she denied having selected images on that basis. She reiterated that she and the other editors knew their audience and instinctively picked images that appealed to it, and that if some of the images included flags, this was a reflection of the mood in the country. Even images that were not blatantly patriotic were interpreted as such by some of *Time*'s readers. "Survivor" captures a wounded woman attended by medical personnel. Surrounded by men in blue and white clothing and gloves, she is seen seated, wearing a red shirt, and with blood covering her face and arms. Several of those informally interviewed found the image striking, in part, because the color combination matched the American flag. One woman said it looked like "a wound in our national colors."

The last page of the special issue features an opinion piece by Lance Morrow (2001) entitled "Rage and Retribution." Morrow calls for "a unified, unifying, Pearl Harbor sort of purple American fury." His essay appears opposite a photograph without a caption on the inside cover by James Nachtwey. This image is similar to Nachtwey's ghostly centerfold photo with skeletal ruins bathed in eerie white light. The main difference is the conspicuous American flag in the right-hand corner of the image on the inside cover. Here the Ground Zero scene does not mainly suggest a generalized, abstract rendition of death-as-absence. Matched with Morrow's essay, this photo of the impact zone becomes a call to action under the American flag, and the pictured ruins become the justification for war. The dead, physically out of view, are symbolically wrapped in a mantle of red, white, and blue. As individuals they are invisible, but as a collective symbol of sacrifice for America they are serving the needs of the surviving population. The viewer is spared (denied) the gruesome aspects of their death and offered instead a battlefield claimed by the American flag.

The back-cover, summarizing image of September 11 shows the Statue of Liberty holding up her flame of freedom against a cloud of smoke, where the Twin Towers once dominated the skyline of southern Manhattan. The image declares with painfully obvious symbolism that although lives and material possessions have been lost, the terrorists are unable to destroy the true spirit of America. One person I spoke with found the image to be disturbingly "kitsch" but was still moved by it. The majority of those who commented to me on this photo felt that it captured the drama beautifully, like the writer of the letter to the editor who imagined "the Statue of Liberty looking at the New York skyline with a tear in one eye and steely resolve in the other" (Brooks 2001).

Senior Editor Nancy Gibbs, who supplied the single story for the special issue, denies any conscious attempt to minimize the focus on the dead or to promote certain values. For her, a key factor was that this was a common national experience for all of America, even though the physical targets were in specific locations. On the morning of September 11, she had begun her workday at home in a suburb 25 miles north of Ground Zero. She received a call from her managing editor, James Kelly, requesting her to stay where she was and prepare to receive e-mail and fax reports from *Time* correspondents around the country and to compile a story from them. Gibbs feels that her distance from the site of the tragedy and from the bustle of her office gave her the perspective to write a story that focused on the events in New York and Washington, D.C. yet was relevant to readers in the rest of the country.

Gibbs wanted to tell her readers what the attack felt like for people who were in the middle of it—the intensity, the horror, and the shock—but she also wanted to make a connection with all those who followed the events from a distance. She kept her tone conversational and was mindful not to appear cynical. She saw her article as a "tick-tock," *Time* magazine's shorthand for a straightforward, factual exposé. However, her account is not a dry dispatch but rather splendid storytelling in the tradition of one of several different formats for reporting on terrorism (for other conventional forms of terrorist reporting, see Picard 1993). The core of her narrative is constructed from dozens of anecdotes featuring specific people and selected from among the 950 e-mails she received that day.

Gibbs's text, running to 13 pages including illustrations, was important for weaving together the many anecdotes and facts that could not be included visually. The single narrative gave the readers a running chronicle of the day, much as they had experienced it themselves, and offered yet another opportunity to approach the events from a different perspective. Replete with symbolism and featuring heroes and villains, victims and perpetrators, Gibbs's narrative simultaneously simplifies and enriches a complex event by relating ordinary citizens' personal stories.

Gibbs developed her essay independently from the other editors and did not know which pictures would accompany it. Yet her story parallels the sequence and content of the pictures. She begins, as if commenting on the cover picture: "If you want to humble an empire it makes sense to maim its cathedrals. They are symbols of faith, and when they crumble and burn, it tells us we are not so powerful and we can't be safe." She writes about the people who jumped out of the towers and the streets slick with blood, about ordinary people coming to each others' assistance, about the firefighters' brave acts and the shock of being a fleeing participant. She describes how the country shuts down and what the president and the government were doing. She takes us to the private citizens who worshipped and gave blood. She offers specific details about time, place, and clothing but also describes emotions and mental states that supplement the pictorial information and stimulate the imagination.

Like the picture editors, Gibbs ends her exposé on a note of faith in the American spirit. In response to her own question, what we will do once the immediacy of the event is over, she answers: "What else but build new cathedrals, and if they are bombed, build some more. Because the faith is in the act of building, not the building itself, and no amount of terror can keep us from scraping the sky." She, too, chose not to dwell on the dead but instead to infuse Americans with a sense of pride in themselves and encourage them to go on with their lives.

CHOOSING TO "COVER UP" FOR THE SAKE OF THE READER

In the United States, no official government entity sets limits on the pictures that are permissible in the press. Based on reactions to previous issues, publishers and editors feel they know what resonates with their readers and sense when they risk overstepping the invisible boundary of what is considered "good taste" for a particular publication. In a reader's contemplation of pictures of horrific events, contradictory forces battle for emotional space. Fascination grows with the level of horror and excitement of a deadly scene, but outrage and sorrow also increase with the viewer's personal closeness to those depicted. At some point, the outrage or sorrow overwhelms the fascination and the viewer turns away. The image loses its attraction, becomes unacceptable and repulsive, and cannot be comfortably contemplated in the space where it is being presented. This threshold is personal, cultural, and variable from one geographic location to the next and from one space of dissemination to another. Each media outlet seeks content that suits its audience and maintains the loyalty of its readers and advertisers. The boundary is not directly articulated in the publication but can be surmised from apologies and comments by the editors in connection with reports and pictures that have crossed this hypothetical line and from irate letters to the editor (as was the case when *Time* published "The Long Fall" in its 9/11 issue).

In the 1980s and 1990s, the media and terrorist organizations were viewed by most analysts as having a symbiotic relationship. The dominant theme in the literature on terrorism and the media was that terrorists need the media to bring attention to their cause and that the media participates more or less wittingly, and frequently profitably, by reporting on events staged by terrorists (variations on this theme are offered by Alali and Eke 1991;

Bassiouni 1981; Farnen 1990; Livingston 1994; Nacos 1994; Paletz and Schmidt 1992; Schaffert 1992; Wardlaw 1982; and Weimann and Winn 1994). *Time*'s own commentator Charles Krauthammer argued after a previous attack that the media were irresponsible in their sensationalist coverage of terrorism and needed to introduce self-imposed limits on their reporting (Krauthammer 1985). Journalists' concern about playing into the hands of terrorists by featuring their actions seemed moot in the face of the atrocities of September 11. That attack was far more than a staged media event that "threatened use of violence against victims of symbolic importance in such a way as to gain psychological impact for the purpose of achieving political objectives" (Weimann and Winn 1994, 4, definition of the essence of terrorism).

On September 11, 2001, the terrorists did not just present a threat. They showed that they could inflict tangible injury in corporeal, psychological, and financial terms. Thousands of people were dead. The economic losses would be in the tens of billions of dollars. The colossal World Trade Center Twin Towers in New York had crumbled to the ground. The Pentagon had suffered a gaping hole in its side. A plane destined for a target in the nation's capital had gone down in Pennsylvania. The assault on these quintessential American symbols was a grievous insult to the United States and mocked its status as the world's economic and military superpower. For *Time*, how to report on this plethora of insults was a matter of serving its American readership, not a matter of concern about giving undue space to a terrorist act.

In light of the widespread psychological damage, *Time* could not place its primary focus on the dead and sufficiently resonate with the readers. *Time*'s editors kept the faces and bodies of the dead off the pages of the 9/11 special issue, motivated by a compulsion to produce a tasteful issue that communicated the tragedy in a manner that honored *Time*'s relationship with its readers. Also, they probably took into account the fact that the vast majority of *Time*'s audience did not have any personal connections to those who had died. For most Americans, the most disconcerting part of the attacks was that they themselves now had to live with uncertainty and with fear for their own lives. Thousands of families endured enormous personal losses, but the country as a whole suffered a serious and hurtful blow to its self-confidence and sense of invulnerability. The nation grieved collectively but vicariously, and the individuals who had died were not what most concerned the general public. Terrorism with its accompaniment of fear, uncertainty, and vulnerability was the central issue. As a consequence, on the day when the American public awoke to the undeniable reality of death in its midst, the unspoken aim of the *Time* editors became the creation of a product that avoided focusing on the unpleasant truth that death is unpredictable, an untimely death is always a possibility and eventual death a certainty.

The pictures were selected from among thousands that came across Golon's desk from the wire services, from *Time*'s own staff, and from independent photographers whom *Time* had swiftly contracted for this issue. The pictures that appeared most compelling to Golon were pinned on a wall for the other editors and art directors to review. (The art director, Arthur Hochstein, headed the layout team and the captions were a collaborative effort by several editors.) The mix and order changed as new material arrived. Golon saw several motifs as intuitively obvious to include: the planes striking the buildings, the reaction of the American people, the rescuers and the president. Discussions were continual about which pictures warranted a two-page spread and which were important but could not claim such extensive coverage; about which motifs needed to be included to tell the full story (as *Time* saw it) and which needed to be excluded so as not to offend the readership's sensibilities. Images of corpses and body parts that spoke viscerally of the dead were plentiful. The editors instinctively excluded them as candidates for publication.

Just as instinctively they addressed the readers' most pressing concerns. So as not to feel morally defeated, the country needed to draw on its mental, emotional, and spiritual resources. The nation needed to come together, to grieve and to celebrate its virtues. The extreme mental and emotional pain that America experienced called for representation to give form to the trauma. The survivors were looking to themselves and their communities, not only to honor the dead but also to address their own fears, incomprehension, and insecurities. Their grief for the dead was abstract and generalized, whereas their thirst for understanding and their terror were concrete and immediate.

It was (and is) one of *Time*'s principles not to publish images of corpses that may be identified by their readers, and for this issue the magazine chose not to publish photographs of body parts. Golon asserted that *Time*'s editors did not specifically refer to *Covering Violence: A Guide to Ethical Reporting about Victims and Trauma*, a book "premised on the conviction that news can tie the victim and the public together constructively through the rigor of thoughtful reporting practices" (Coté and Simpson 2000, 4). Nevertheless, the editorial board seems largely to follow the directives set out in the introduction to this work: "searching responsibly for the truth, keeping the public interest in mind, caring for the people in the story and others close to them, respecting the voices of people at the center of events, knowing that the storytellers also are at risk, and doing no harm." The editors heeded the guide's warning against "a penchant for voyeurism" and were aware that "the interviews, the stories and the photographs have potential either to add injury or help in the recovery" (4, 5).

A morbid depiction of the dead would have violated the covenant that *Time* has with its audience. In describing the process of picture selection, Golon repeated several times how important it was to share ordinary people's response to the attack. Ethical behavior turned out to be commensurate with what the editors intuitively understood on September 11: that the primary needs of the shaken reader were to find companionship and make sense of the turmoil. "Reporting on terrorism can clearly serve the goal of promoting public fear and disorientation," but there is also evidence "that the generation of fear by the reporting of violence can be reduced if coverage places specific acts of violence into perspective by helping audiences understand the origin of these acts and the potential risk to the public at large" (Picard 1993, 116). Presented with the suggestion that the magazine could alleviate fear, Golan responded that she did not deliberately think along those lines. To produce an effective pictorial news report was paramount in her mind. Although she believes she is sensitive to her audience, she stated that she is not in the business of giving psychological counseling. Nevertheless, the issue offered comforts akin to such therapy.

CONTAINING THE DEAD WHILE MEMORIALIZING THE DAY

Time's editors presumed that their readership would perceive the 9/11 issue as a historical document and memento. They felt a sense of mission, believing that the public relied on them to tell the story and to get it right. Early in the day on September 11, Kelly decided that their special issue would be a 48-page issue with no advertisements and only one story. None of the magazine's regular features would be included, and pictures would dominate the coverage. To indicate the tragedy of the event, a black border would frame the magazine on the front and back covers instead of the red border that has been *Time*'s trademark since 1927. In making this basic layout choice, Kelly made the first of several decisions to represent the dead symbolically.

The editors at *Time* believe that their readers look to the magazine to document important historical events, and they believed that *Time* had a responsibility to its readers to produce a special issue on September 11. They took this responsibility personally and seriously. When asked what purpose this issue might serve beyond documenting the event, Gibbs referred to the magazine as a space where people have an opportunity to see their own experiences validated. When Golon and Stephenson reflected on the question, seemingly for the first time, they said it was not something consciously articulated in the hectic days of producing the special issue. The editors had understood that a collection such as this can add insights by providing views and viewpoints that would perhaps not otherwise be available, and they sensed that people would want a tangible object dealing with the unique events, one that encapsulated and memorialized the terrifying and tragic day.

Objects and images have a history of participation in grief rituals and coping processes where death has struck. Photographs, memory books, and hair-locks, to name a few, are called upon to emotionally substitute for what has been lost. Although not originally designated as a memorial issue by *Time*, the special issue quickly became known as such by the public. Memorials, whether tombs or photographs or, as in this case, a collection of pictures, are objects before which those who have experienced a loss gather their thoughts and try to come to terms with what has occurred. They channel fear and grief. As is common with public memorials, the special issue speaks in both direct and symbolic language and reinforces cherished community values.

The magazine with its anecdotes and gripping imagery makes concrete people's ephemeral thoughts and feelings. It offers something different from television, the Internet, and radio, whose output is fleeting. It doesn't change while we reflect on it but allows for focused, lengthy contemplation; it literally provides "something to hang on to." Gillis has noted that "as the world implodes upon us, we feel an even greater pressure as individuals to record, preserve and collect" (1994, 14). With so much information to retain and with our concern not to lose it, we have become a nation of collectors. "What we can no longer keep in our heads we keep in storage" (1994, 15). The special issue is a token of the fatal day that readers can return to again and again. The collection of the imagery in a single issue communicates subtly that it is possible to confine and contain the deadly events. The paper issue turns the day into an artifact and makes the events seem graspable. We may not be able to control the attack or its consequences, but a tendency to transfer a sense of control from the artifact to the larger circumstance helps us gain a foothold, albeit an illusionary one. The reader can study the events in magazine format, edited and close up, and can chose to become engrossed in the content or bypass it. If an image is too disturbing, she can turn the page and remain in charge of the experience. Whether drawn to the issue by a thirst for information, morbid fascination, or a need for an object of contemplation, the reader's engagement with the momentous public event can remain private as she leafs through the pages within the confines of home.

While the magazine's collection of images draws the events close to the viewer by bringing them before his eyes, the representational form simultaneously distances them, the way that all representations declare themselves ontologically different from the original. The magazine format keeps the events literally at arm's length. Although the deadly catastrophe was photographed on location in New York and may have seemed shockingly close in some of the pictures, the physical size of the magazine reduces the event to a manageable and conveniently portable size. The disaster is comfortably locked into its medium, where it can be simultaneously acknowledged and hidden from view.

The report can be seen as substituting for—or complementing—family and communal rituals, which have largely been simplified or lost in modern times. In this way, *Time* contributes a healing service to the community. Experiencing the event within the representational form of the magazine, readers can follow the work of brave rescue workers and ordinary compassionate citizens. They can mentally reach out to the victims and empathize with them. Subsequently, they can share their impressions with others who have had similar, actual or virtual, experiences. A common body of pictures and knowledge enters the national discourse and produces a sense of community and shared lives. Friends, family, and strangers partake of the same imagery; individually and collectively the memory of September 11 takes form.

EXPLOITATION IN SPITE OF FORBEARANCE

Regardless of whether this issue of *Time* helped in the social recovery of the readers and regardless of how tastefully the disaster was presented, on some level the special issue may be interpreted as exploitive. In spite of the free copies sent to the subscribers and the ad-free pages, with or without *Time*'s financial cunning, a momentous tragedy takes the form of a commercial product for visual consumption, becomes a "spectacle" for sale. Viewed cynically, the *Time* issue is the commodification of a tragic national experience. The publication exploits not only the dead, the mourning, and the wounded city but also the readers' weakness for a titillating peek into the spectacle of death and destruction on a massive scale. *Time* can be seen as shamelessly mining a human frailty with the audience as a willing collaborator. The success of the special issue is not due simply to its function as grief and coping object and provider of comfort, but also to its ability to offer the thrill and pleasure humans find in facing their own fears and viewing the tragedy of others. To some extent, the special issue is a manifestation of a perverse yearning in the human soul to delve into the most horrendous nightmares in representational form, to virtually—and safely—play with death. (The theme of tragedy and fear as entertainment and pleasure is developed by Nuttall 1996, and by Kendrick 1991.)

Guided by the known needs of the subscribers and assisted by the invisible hand of the marketplace, the *Time* editors selected the right mix of information, solace, furor, spectacle, fright, and ideological value pronouncements to satisfy the readership. In doing this they also made a savvy business decision. While listing his goals for the magazine as "the best-reported, best-written, best-looking magazine," Kelly did not mention "best selling." This is understood. *Time* magazine is a commercial enterprise; in a market economy the profit motive is always present and the managing editor's presumed eye on the bottom line cannot be discounted in an analysis of the choices *Time* made for its September 11 issue. A company's first obligation is to its shareholders, and to be financially successful the magazine needs to continually attract advertisers and readers.

Time's decision to exclude advertisers from its September 11 issue—for the first time ever—was a gesture it could afford to make as part of a well-capitalized company. *Time*'s parent company is among America's largest corporate establishments.[3] Time Inc.'s Editor-in-Chief Norman Pearlstine asserted that it has editorial independence from the other divisions of AOL Time Warner, that "the financial success of Time Inc.'s magazines is inextricably linked to their credibility" (quoted in *Columbia Journalism Review* 2000). However, many issues of *Time* feature (albeit not always glowing) stories on media products produced by its sister divisions, which may give rise to skepticism over the claim of editorial independence.

Be this as it may, *Time* had substantial resources through its parent company, and there were several good reasons for not including advertisers in the 9/11 issue: First, it would have been very difficult to reach them and get approvals, given the short time schedule. Normally, advertisers are asked to participate several weeks in advance of a special issue. Second, if advertisers could have been found, both they and the magazine would have run the risk of seeming crass and insensitive for mixing tragedy with product promotion. In the days after the attack, many advertisers in the daily press withdrew their ads or revamped them to convey condolences or express patriotism. Finally, the issue would not have had the same impact aesthetically and emotionally if the story had been interrupted by advertisements. With its focused appearance, the issue assures that the reader's attention is never diverted from the topic at hand and this, in the final analysis, makes the special issue a better product. One letter to the editor confirms the feeling of many readers: "I was impressed not only by the amazing pictures but also by the fact that you let them speak for themselves—and did not allow ads to detract from the tragedy, giving people a sense of [the] seriousness of what occurred" (Jenkins 2001, 12).

Time took a financial risk by producing an extra issue without collecting any advertising revenue and by paying for the unbudgeted postage to its four million subscribers. The editorial staff briefly considered producing the special issue only for the newsstand, where the cost could be recovered through the sale of single copies, but they rejected this route, feeling a responsibility to the loyal subscribers. To encourage single copy sales, a special telephone number and a Web site were set up and listed in subsequent issues. Not to include advertisements was a reasonable risk based on the magazine's knowledge of its subscribers and the American public in general. Terrorist acts in the past had been good "box office" for the media. Peter Jennings, anchorman of ABC television, has commented: "What accounts for the extraordinary intensity of media coverage of hijackings and hostage-takings? Ratings? The answer is yes. We work for commercial enterprises. We all want to be number one. Number one means dollars and cents to our corporations and so ratings are certainly important" (quoted in Nacos 1974, 157–58.)

In the view of its readership, *Time* made the correct ethical and aesthetic decision in producing an ad-free issue. As it turned out, the enormous demand for single copies also made it the correct financial decision. The investment paid off with over three million single copies sold, and the industry honoring *Time* with the prestigious ASME award. When Golon, Gibbs, and the other *Time* employees learned about the attack, they did not go to work consciously focused on the company's bottom line. They set out to tell a story. However, as they kept in mind James Kelly's goal to produce "the best-reported, best-written, best-looking magazine," their objectives and the interests of the readers and the investors coincided. As it turned out, the space where these interests intersected had little room for the dead.

CONCLUSION

A point of turbulence where cultural values merge and emerge, death has a unique place in the study of human history. Anchored in an unknowable absolute, death provides a continuous point of reference in the studies of different cultures and historical periods. Although its meaning is culturally constructed and therefore perceived differently in every civilization, biological death is the one certain and immutable factor amidst the turmoil and uncertainty of life. "The history of death retains a specific and exemplary value....in the human adventure it stands as an ideal and essential constant. It is a constant which is quite relative, moreover, since people's relationships with death have changed, as has the way in which it strikes them. Nevertheless, the conclusion is always the same...death" (Vovelle 1990, 65).

The missing corpses in *Time* can be seen as the magazine's disinclination to take charge of the image of the dead for posterity, a modest acknowledgment of its marginal right to decide how the fatalities of 9/11 should be portrayed. The claim of authority over the representation of the dead would later become a gravely contested issue among the victims' families, city officials, real estate interests, and others. Corpses are the most powerful evidence and most concrete manifestation of death, and as such they hold rich and liminal meanings. They straddle two ways of being. They are venerated but act as poor substitutes for terminated lives. In the remains, the dead are both present as cadavers and absent as people. The dead—both here and elsewhere (or here and nowhere, depending on one's belief)—mediate between life and memory. To disseminate images of these powerful indices is to confront awesome metaphysical issues. The urge to cover them up is understandable.

In its special issue, *Time* gave form and definition to the events of September 11, 2001, in text and images that resonated deeply with its readers. It did not focus on the dead because, crass as it may seem, the fatalities were not what most concerned the readership. (In later issues the dead would occupy a proportionately larger part of the magazine.) Instead, *Time* addressed the readers' need to contend with and personally process an unprecedented and seemingly incomprehensible attack. This was done by presenting the horrific experience in psychologically manageable form as a tasteful product that encouraged contemplation. The issue was factually informative and spoke with authority about the comprehensible aspects of the events, while it reinforced a sense of community and featured comforting values. Spirituality, compassion, courage, and patriotism were important themes. By thus meeting the needs of a large segment of the American collective psyche, the issue became a bestseller. It was done by denying space to the dead and the dying, who by some measure could be conceived as the central part of the event but who were also its most frightening manifestation. Obscuring the dead proved to be an approach to covering this national tragedy that served both the readers and the magazine's bottom line.

"Death, in all its manifestations, is the best metaphoric guide to the problems of life" (Vovelle 1990, 80). The absence of corpses in the *Time* 9/11 special issue is explained by its editors as a matter of editorial policy and of the exercise of good taste. But policies change, and taste is a moveable target. The editors could have taken a different approach. A mounting tidal wave of death imagery in *Time* and other media outlets had been building since the late 1970s, and the American public might have been expected to be inured to images of death. The covering up of the dead is evidence that the editors knew that the American people, savagely awakened to the reality of death's ubiquity and unpredictability—on their until-then safe home turf—were not willing to be explicitly reminded of their mortality in gruesome ways. There may come a time when an American mainstream magazine finds cause to publish images that place its readers face-to-face with the mutilated bodies of their peers. But 2001 was not that time. Awakening and awareness are not synonymous with personal acceptance and acculturation. Death remained a territory that required, if not denial, carefully selected management tools, which were precisely what *Time* magazine provided.

NOTES

1. In the final account several months later, the number was adjusted to 2,795.
2. During the fall of 2001 and the winter/spring of 2002, I solicited anecdotal comments about the Time 9/11 issue from an arbitrarily selected collection of about two dozen men and women of different ages and backgrounds.
3. In 1989, Time Inc., with its several magazines, merged with the entertainment giant Warner Brothers. The combined unit merged with AOL in 2001.

REFERENCES

Alali, A. Odasuo, and Kenoye K. Eke, eds. (1991). *Media Coverage of Terrorism: Methods and Diffusion*. Newbury Park, Calif.: Sage.

Anderson, Benedict. (1991). *Imagined Communities—Reflections on the Origin and Spread of Nationalism*. 2nd ed. London: Verso.

Bassiouni, M. Cherif. (1981). "Terrorism, Law Enforcement, and the Mass Media: Perspectives, Problems, Proposals." *Journal of Criminal Law and Criminology*, 72, 1: 801–51.

Becker, Ernest. (1973). *The Denial of Death*. New York: Simon and Schuster.

Brooks, Louise L. (2001). "Day of Infamy." Letters. *Time*. 158, 15: 8 (October 1, 2001).

Beetham, Margaret. (1990). "Towards a Theory of the Periodical as a Publishing Genre." In *Investigating Victorian Journalism*, ed. Laurel Brake, Alex Jones, and Lionel Madden, 19–32. London: Macmillan.

Columbia Journalism Review. (2000). "At Time Inc., Editorial Independence in Writing (Excerpt)." Columbia University, Graduate School of Journalism. 39,1:46 (May 1, 2000).

Coté, William, and Roger Simpson, eds. (2000). *Covering Violence: A Guide to Ethical Reporting about Victims and Trauma*. New York: Columbia University Press.

Farnen, Russel F. (1990). "Terrorism and the Mass Media: A Systematic Analysis of a Symbiotic Process." *Terrorism*, 13, 2: 99–143.

Gibbs, Nancy. (2001). [Cover story. No title]. *Time—September 11, 2001*. Special issue. [No pagination. No publication date; arrived at newsstands September 14, 2001.]

Gibbs, Nancy. (2002). Personal interview with Ms. Gibbs at her home in Bronxville, N.Y., February 4.

Gillis, John R. (1994). "Memory and Identity: The History of a Relationship." In *Commemorations—The Politics of National Identity*, ed. John R. Gillis, 3–24.

Goldstein, Jeffrey H. (1998). "Why We Watch." In *Why We Watch—The Attractions of Violent Entertainment*, ed. Jeffrey H. Goldstein, 212–226. New York: Oxford University Press.

Golon, MaryAnne. (2002). Personal interview with Ms. Golon and her superior at *Time*, Director of Photography Michele Stephenson, in *Time* magazine's office, March 12.

Goodwin, Sarah Webster, and Elisabeth Bronfen, eds. (1993). *Death and Representation*. Baltimore: Johns Hopkins University Press.

Jenkins, Carrie. (2001). "Rapid Response Time." Letters. *Time*. 158, 15: 12 (October 1, 2001).

Kaplan, Warren. (2001). "A Surreal Beauty." Letters to the Editor. *Time*. 158, 13: 10 (September 24, 2001).

Kelly, James. (2001). "To Our Readers." *Time—September 11, 2001*. Special issue. [No pagination. No publication date; arrived at newsstands September 14, 2001.]

Kelly, James. (2002). "And the Envelopes, please..." *Time*. 160, 13:6 (April 1, 2002).

Kendrick, Walter. (1991). *The Thrill of Fear—250 Years of Scary Entertainment*. New York: Grove Weidenfeld.

Krauthammer, Charles. (1985). "Looking Evil Dead in the Eye." *Time*. July 15, 1985. http://www.time.com/time/magazine/article/0,9171,959641,00.html.

La Rochefoucauld, *Maximes 26, Oeuvres*. Paris: Pléiade, 1957.

Livingston, Steven. (1994). *The Terrorism Spectacle.* Boulder, Colo.: Westview Press.

Mediamark Research and Intelligence (MRI) (2002). *Survey of the American Consumer.* Fall 2002 issue. Syndicated research survey; unpaginated.

Monroe Mendelsohn Research. (2002). "Publication Audience Measurements, Average-Income Audience. *Mendelsohn Affluent Survey 2002—Household Income $75,000.*

Morrow, Lance. (2001). "The Case for Rage and Retribution." *Time—September 11, 2001.* Special issue. [No pagination. No publication date; arrived at newsstands September 14, 2001.]

Mott, Frank Luther. (1968). *A History of American Magazines* Vol. 5, 1905–1930. Cambridge, Mass.: Harvard University Press.

Nacos, Brigitte L. (1994). *Terrorism and the Media—From the Iran Hostage Crisis to the World Trade Center Bombing.* New York: Columbia University Press.

Nuttall, A. D. (1996). *Why Does Tragedy Give Pleasure?* Oxford: Clarendon Press.

Paletz, David L., and Alex P. Schmidt, eds. (1992). *Terrorism and the Media.* Newbury Park, Calif.: Sage.

Picard, Robert G. (1993). *Media Portrayals of Terrorism: Functions and Meaning of News Coverage.* Ames, Iowa: Iowa State University Press.

Schaffert, Richard W. (1992). *Media Coverage and Political Terrorism—A Quantitative Analysis.* Westport, Conn.: Praeger.

Schleifer, Ronald. (1990). *The Rhetoric of Death: The Language of Modernism and Post-modern Discourse Theory.* Urbana: University of Illinois Press.

Sinnema, Peter W. (1998). *Dynamics of the Pictured Page—Representing the Nation in the Illustrated London News.* Aldershot, England: Ashgate Publishing.

Sontag, Susan. (1992). *The Volcano Lover.* New York: Farrar, Straus and Giroux.

Sontag, Susan. (2003). *Regarding the Pain of Others.* New York: Farrar, Straus and Giroux.

Stamelman, Richard. (1990). *Lost beyond Telling: Representations of Death and Absence in Modern French Poetry.* Ithaca, N.Y.: Cornell University Press.

Staudt, Christina C. (2001). *Picturing the Dead and Dying in Nineteenth-Century L'Illustration.* PhD diss. Columbia University. Ann Arbor, MI: Bell & Howell.

Time, Inc. (2002/2007). "Issue Specific Performance." Mediakit.com, http://www.time.com/time/mediakit/1/us/timemagazine/audience/mri/issue_specific.html.

United States Census Bureau. (2000). *Income 2000.* "Table E. Income of Household by State Using 2- and 3-Year-Average Medians," http://www.census.gov/hhes/www/income/income00/statemhi.html.

University of Michigan News and Information Services. (1997). "Study of Worldwide Rates of Religiosity, Church Attendance," http://www.umich.edu/news/index.htm?Releases/1997/Dec97/chr121097a.

Vovelle, Michel. (1990). *Ideologies and Mentalities.* Chicago: University of Chicago Press.

Wardlaw, Grant. (1982). *Political Terrorism.* London: Cambridge University Press.

Watzlawick, Paul. (1976). *How Real Is Real.* New York: Random House.

Weimann, Gabriel, and Conrad Winn. (1994). *The Theater of Terror. Mass Media and International Terrorism.* New York: Longman.

Zillman, Dolf, and Jennings Bryant, eds. (1985). *Selective Exposure to Communication.* Hillsdale, N.J.: Lawrence Erlbaum.

PART II

From Awareness to Acceptance

CHAPTER 6

ACCEPTANCE OF MORTALITY: WHAT IS CONFIRMED, WHAT IS DENIED

Michael K. Bartalos

The Comte de St. Germain was a popular member of the court of Louis XV of France. He pretended to have lived for many centuries, entertained his audiences with tales of personal encounters with historical figures who had lived several hundred years earlier, and was very successful in selling an elixir that he claimed would arrest the progress of old age. He was believed by many, including Madame de Pompadour and the king himself (Mackay 1980). His popularity was largely explainable by the universal human aspiration for immortality or at least for a very long life, to which he was believed to possess the key. The human propensity to attempt to deny mortality made his audiences easy prey for the impostor.

THE TELL-TALE SIGNS OF DENIAL—OR ARE THEY?

In their treatment of what they call social thanatology, Leming and Dickinson (1990, 11–15) correctly emphasized the importance of *The American View of Death: Acceptance or Denial?* written by Richard Dumont and Dennis Foss (1972). In this book it is suggested that in the United States we simultaneously both deny and accept death. It is indeed possible to marshal evidence for this view by surveying our behavior. Among the assumed signs of denial of dying, Dumont and Foss listed several examples (35–43) of which Leming and Dickinson (1990, 11–15) choose the following, (a) our tendency to use euphemisms for death, (b) the taboo on death conversation, (c) the emergence of cryonics or body freezing, (d) the substitution of the concept of taking a long nap for dying, (e) the summoning of professionals in case of death in contrast to other cultures and to our earlier practices, and (f) our custom of not lowering the casket in the ground until the family and friends leave the cemetery, thus saving them from this traumatic experience.

If we agree that the above behaviors are abnormal, what are the behaviors we consider appropriate, or normal? Most likely it would be the opposite of the behaviors criticized above. Thus talking about death, preferably often and using its decidedly non-metaphoric five-letter designation; not fantasizing about the future feasibility of a high-tech resurrection of the body; not summoning the assistance of professional help with the handing of the dead body and with the fiscal and legal matters arising from the death of a family member; and lowering the casket into the ground in full view of those who followed the deceased to the cemetery would likely be the norm.

I for one would hesitate to advocate the replacement of the above criticized behaviors because outside of their novelty you can challenge every assertion they make. We could argue, for instance, that the use of euphemisms and the avoidance of the term death in conversations is simply a refinement of our social graces, which now include, besides money, politics, and religion, also age, race, sexual preference, health, and death as subjects to be avoided in polite conversations as too emotionally laden and thus potentially divisive. We likewise might argue that the emergence of cryonics and other techniques that offer experimentation ought to be tried even if the odds of success are small. After all, don't we hear—about Easter time—straight-faced discussions by educated men of the resurrection of long-decayed bodies? Cryonic preservation and reanimation appears to be a much safer—albeit still remote—bet for the money. Likewise, what is wrong with using available professional help with complicated and emotionally taxing situations? And while one might argue that it is traumatic for those who accompanied the body to the cemetery, and thus who were close to the diseased in life, to witness the lowering of the body into the ground, one might counter that such an experience might promote a more timely and less complicated closure.

Who is right? What are lamented by some as newfound signs of denial of death and dying merely represent practices that are new and strange but not necessarily the signs of a disease that is gripping our society. It is true that witnessing death is not part of most children's growing-up experience in today's industrialized societies. But this is not the result of a sinister conspiracy on the part of the elders or some evildoers in society to impoverish the children's emotional development. Dying and funerals moved out of the home with apartment living and with both parents employed, terminal care is often given in the hospital or hospice. Current practices are the outgrowth of societal changes, and it is our job to adapt to such changes.

In the rest of this chapter, I will undertake an analysis of the usage and implications of the term "denial of dying."

SOME FURTHER DILEMMAS WITH "DENIAL OF MORTALITY"

It is useful to recognize that denial is a rather unusual process and that it does not take place in a vacuum. It is not a phenomenon of nature, like wind or the sunset. It is a facet, albeit an important one, of human activity. More exactly it is a facet of human mental activity that gains expression either by vocal or written declarations or by the performance of certain acts. In the former case denial is explicit or overt, in the latter it is implicit or covert. In many respects the counterpart of denial is approval. In a final analysis all human activities boil down to an interplay of yes and no, to approval and denial of what we perceive through our senses or recognize as conscious thoughts.

What do we deny (or approve)? We can deny what we have seen, heard, smelled, tasted, or felt. We can also deny intentions (ours or others), we can deny the outcome of someone's reasoning process (negation in logic), we can deny the validity of someone's perception, we can deny the validity of someone's theoretical creation that lacks observational or mathematical foundation (such as immortality or the Trinity). Denials are usually interpreted as expression of disagreement regarding the existence, occurrence, validity, or legitimacy of what has been asserted.

Thus we have the act of denial, we have a person who is engaged in denial (that is he/she is in the act of denying something) and—crucially—we have other(s) who accuse some individuals of engaging in the denial of one thing or another. Denial can be viewed as a virtue or a vice, depending on one's perspective. We all are constantly involved in denial and approval of our impressions and thoughts. This is a dynamic process that is fed by the changing impressions we gather from our environment and we must be, at any time, in agreement with countless others and in disagreement with just as many different individuals. In fact, at any time we could find points of agreement and points of disagreement with any other individual involving many different perceptions and opinions. This recognition should be reason enough to stop the age-old folly of identifying and defining people based on their temporary approval or denial of certain mental constructs (such as different political or religious doctrines) and damn them for it.

COVERT DENIAL OF MORTALITY

Denial of death became a frequently heard distress call during the past half century. In the previously discussed scheme of denials it usually involved finger-pointing by one group toward another. In this case it was a blanket statement applied to all the so-called modern industrial societies—presumably exempting the accusers themselves.

This brings up the nature and fairness of accusing someone of a deed that the accused never stated and, in fact, never even consciously formulated.

There is also question about the evidence. Since in the above case the alleged "crime" (denial of death) was never explicitly admitted by the perpetrator (modern industrialized societies), the evidence must be gained by interpreting the accused behavior. How reliable are such observations? In order to get an impression of that let us examine some other examples involving the interpretation of observed behavior.

If an already successful individual, in late life, is still engaged in continued accumulation of wealth, power, or fame such person can be said to be in disregard of the finitude of his/her life, that is he is denying his mortality. Avoidance of the discussion of death or refusal to plan for the family in the event of the person's death are further signs to others that such individual is denying his/her mortality. Likewise we are quick to conclude that individuals who are terminally ill but refuse to acknowledge it are in denial of their mortality.

Correspondingly, numerous behaviors—some deplored, some not—have been labeled by observers as manifestations of a death wish or as outright suicidal acts. We are ready to assume that those who lead a life that involves the habitual use of narcotics, stimulants, alcohol, nicotine, and overeating, are wishing to die and are hastening their death. That is, they are performing suicide in slow motion. Because of the assumed motive and deleterious effect on health and the increased societal costs, these actions are deplored by society.

Daredevils, car and motorcycle speed racers, stunt performers, and extreme sport practitioners represent a contrasting subgroup. These are labeled as reckless. They are people who are performing potentially deadly acts that appear void of usefulness to others. While such individuals might be admired for their skill or daring, in general, they are on the fringes of society.

Individuals who save others by risking their own life, or those who volunteer for dangerous military missions, are considered to perform a potentially dangerous act in order to save others. Such acts are of benefit to society, are approved by society, and given society's highest accolade by being labeled as heroic.

Are Our Assumptions Correct?

It appears to me that our subconscious guides us to pinpoint what we consider a covert death wish is a behavior that we judge to be inappropriate. But what is "inappropriate" and what is "appropriate" behavior? In order to answer this question we need to make a brief detour to the philosophy I termed "contextual individualism" (Bartalos 1990, 575). I propose "an individualism, contextual individualism, whereby the individual is seen as a unique product of an evolutionary process, who is in constant interaction with the environment, who is constantly changing, whose inborn overriding aim is to maintain his structural and functional integrity,...who lives in an interconnected, interdependent, contextual relationship with the environment (which includes the physical environment, the mentality of the age and the company of others)" (575).

Part of contextuality is that our actions are interpreted within the framework where they take place. They are judged by taking into consideration the age, mental acuity, emotional stability, and intentions of the person and the appropriateness of the act to the environmental circumstances.

To be sure, in general this process of appraisal is taking place subconsciously and where the action appears to be inappropriate for the age of the person or to the circumstances, reprove ensues. When we hear uttered, "It is just not right," some person or some organization is not living up to our expectations, it is not acting appropriately, it is out of context as far as we are concerned.

Before you feel a tendency to dismiss such consideration I wish to remind you that the entire fields of psychiatry, the criminal justice system, and much activity of the legal profession is devoted to such instances.

Under superficial simplicity complexity resides. The examples reviewed previously appear inappropriate on first sight. However under the rubric of "unwarranted risk taking," diverse mechanisms are in operation. Such terms as death defiance or death negation are description of a phenomenon by a spectator who is projecting his/her feeling in the performance of the act. The villain or the hero of the act—depending on our point of view—is neither consciously defying death nor engaged in planned death negation; rather the person in question is enacting what his/her inborn genetic predispositions, personality traits, and past experiences, all in concern and in unique mix, nudges him/her on to do. (Konner 1990). Thus neither alcoholism, nor smoking, nor motorcycle racing, nor life-endangering altruism, nor lack of preplanning, not even suicidal ideation can be taken as sure-fire indicators of death denial. Yes, they might indicate a lowered preference for staying alive or an increased indifference of dying that, such attitudes in turn, can have diverse underlying causes or psychological mechanisms.

The propensity to what we consider unreasonable risk-taking is a phenomenon that has been observed not only in humans, but also in several other organisms. It is considered to represent a useful biological adaptive response that is maintained by natural selection and contributes to the survival of the species (Wilson and Clark 1996). Thus what we loosely label as a psychological denial of death is a symptom, a manifestation, that can have multiple causes. Therefore, in this volume, when we speak of apparent denial of death, explicit or implied, we assume the presence of an overt or covert psychological mechanism that, like other adaptive mechanisms, performs a physiological role. Finally, as is the case with other adaptive mechanisms, occasional glitches occur leading to over-responsiveness or under-responsiveness to environmental stimuli by the individual.

Our purpose is neither to extol, nor to deplore, unreasonable risk taking, we merely wish to acknowledge it and understand it better.

OVERT DENIAL OF MORTALITY

One of the definitions of denial by the *Merriam-Webster Online Dictionary* is "refusal to acknowledge a person or a thing." In the case of mortality denial, it occurs when we insist that we are immortal. Claiming immortality of our body represents an overt denial of human mortality.

Contrasting opinions are the mainspring of human verbal interactions. It is likely that no statement or opinion was ever uttered that remained unchallenged. It is well known that it has been proposed that there is a continuous existence after dying. Not surprisingly, this proposition, like many others, did not remain unchallenged. In this case the challenge is based on the allegation that the assumption of existence after death is not founded on reality or truth, and therefore it denies reality. Thus those who claim that there is life after dying, according to our present state of knowledge, are engaged in an overt, conscious, willful denial of reality.

Continued existence after death is part of the official teaching of most major religions and thus it is the professed belief of a number of individuals the world over. This we might consider an example of institutionalized denial of death, meaning that this belief is part of the institution's official doctrine and individuals, as long as they are members of the church, are expected to know this, accept it, and profess it.

I propose an exercise whereby we contrast the beliefs and the implications of the beliefs of those who openly support the concept of survival after dying with those who openly deny such proposition. By doing so we hope to further the clarification of issues such as: What is being asserted? What is being denied? Do these views really differ? In what respects? To what extent? With what consequences?

At this point a caveat is in order. Whenever we confirm or deny the validity of a concept, we automatically confirm or deny the existence of several related concepts. In the following section I will make reference to such related concepts because through such exercises we can better visualize the plausibility of our stance.

What Is Assumed when Dying Is Denied?

It is not the purpose of this communication to evaluate in detail the various religious teachings as they apply to survival after death, therefore let it suffice to remind the reader that survival after dying assumes that humans are composed of a material part or body and a non-material part referred to as soul or spirit (the so-called Cartesian duality in reference to the French philosopher Rene Descartes). Further it is proposed that dying is followed by either a resurrection with restoration of the ante-mortem bodily integrity and functions, or that the body disintegrates while a disembodied spirit survives. Some traditions hold that the disembodied spirits wander around while others preach that the spirits successively enter bodies, usually at or around the time of birth and usually continues to inhabit that body until its demise.

What Is Negated when Dying Is Denied?

Negated is the end to the continuity of our existence with the dying of our body. Also negated is a belief in scientific evidence and, by extension, negated are the values of scientific observations.

What Is Not Negated when Dying Is Denied?

Not negated is that human beings have a limited lifespan on earth as human beings. Not negated is the decline of physical and mental faculties of humans with age and not negated is that bodily adaptive responses of human beings to environmental challenges are getting less effective as one ages.

What Is Affirmed when Dying Is Denied?

When dying is denied you confirm your disregard for evidence perceived through your senses. You are willing to accept imaginary entities as building blocks for your private universe.

What Is Not Affirmed when Dying Is Denied?

When you deny dying and build a private universe from imagined entities, you do not change reality, you only change your perception of reality. Dying is still going on all around you whether you admit it or not. Your denial of a reality does not directly affect other's perception of it. Thus a reality that remains unrecognized by you does not loose its potential to be appreciated by others.

Possible Advantages of Denying Dying?

Reduction of fear from the unknown, reduced fear of dying.

Possible Disadvantages of Denying Dying?

For any assertions the human mind requires an explanation. In fact, we hold it necessary to ask "why?" The same is true when we are told that we will not die. Especially since we have seen people dying, being dead, buried, or cremated. In face of such experiences we are curious. What's more, we are incredulous.

Guessing can make an interesting game but when questions are answered by guesses that are claimed to stand for facts, according to the law of our land, fraud is perpetuated. If such statements emanate from a mind that is certified to be deluded, that could be a mitigating factor.

It is the nature of the game that the more we try to answer related questions about a nonexisting entity, the more guesses we have to make and the further we wander from reality. With every new assumption or invented answer our connection to reality diminishes in leaps. At one point, contact with reality becomes so miniscule that our only restriction in answering questions is the limit of our imagination. That is, we are simply guessing or imagining. When it comes to that, in the matter of the given, a high priest will not know facts any better than the average Mary and Joe do.

Now let us readjust our focus and consider the psychological dynamics of all this. Once we accept an unsubstantiated premise (such as we will not die), the premise requires and is given a set of collateral supporting statements. Why was that needed? Because our semi-scientific brain requires an explanation. I say semi-scientific because the human brain is evolved enough to ask: why? It demands and answer, but not necessarily proof. It appears that any answer will do if it is packaged adequately. While we demand an explanation, we do not demand that the explanation makes sense, we do not demand that the explanation correspond to our perceived reality. Thus our incompletely evolved brain is a liability. While it demands answers, it is willing to accept hubris if there is an internal coherence to the proposition. We are unsatisfied with the answer "I don't know," no matter how honest it might be. We rather prefer an explanation, even if it is not a factual one. To the human mind a mildly elaborated hypothetical answer is more satisfying and thus more acceptable than a sincere admission of ignorance.

The statement "you will die" is perceived as repulsive, horrid, and as such it immediately sends us on a search for an alternate explanation. It is likely an evolutionary feature that when we make a repulsive/dangerous finding that appears reasonably well-substantiated, we do not "waste" our time to look for collaborative evidence, rather we hastily embark on a search for alternatives.

Now contrast this with the statement "you will not die." We found this pronouncement much more palatable, even pleasing. We would like to believe it but it is too simple. We want assurances. Actually, we crave assurances. This underlying desire to find support for this rather sympathetic statement might serve to undermine our critical faculties and makes us susceptible to accept explanations that in other circumstances we would not find convincing. Please note, that when we are presented with a proposition that is to our liking, our immediate reaction is not to look for a contrasting statement, but for corroboration. In effect we are looking for a justification to accept something that we already like. It is no wonder that the selling is easy: we only need a reason. Under such circumstances almost any reason will do as long as there is an inner coherence to the story—that is, if we provide an explanation as to why we will not die, what will happen to us, how we will be rewarded or punished by the observance or transgression of rules, and so on. Correspondence to reality is not demanded, and hypothetical assertions can abound, and still most of us will buy the proposition if there is an inner structure, a structural logic to the assertion. Why? Because we *want* to believe it. It makes us feel good to believe in it, as it reduces our inner tension, and that is the final arbiter in the matters of our psyche. In this case tranquility equals the suspension of independent thinking. So if we insist on denying death we must accept an explanation that is fabricated by the human mind without a shred of evidence. There is simply no alternative. Thus the main disadvantage of denying dying is that it requires belief in unsubstantiated pronouncements.

What Is Assumed when Dying Is Accepted?

It is assumed that all human functions originate from and are performed by parts of the human body. That living represents myriads of adaptive responses by molecules, cells, organs, and other bodily parts performed in a coordinated fashion in response to changing environmental demands. In living organisms, humans included, such a feat is accomplished by the formation of hierarchically organized, interacting systems. These systems exhibit an innate stability (quasi-permanence) whereby they are able to interact with their environment (reactivity), exchange material and energy with the environment (openness), and maintain their structural and adaptive integrity within a certain range of environmental variations (equilibrium). This grand synthesis is referred to as the general system theory of von Bertalanffy (von Bertalanffy 1968). The degree of apparent stability of life is maintained by constant instability that is produced by negative feedback of metabolites to critical control points in the network of metabolic pathways (Goodwin 1963). It is the inherent property of negative feedback control processes to produce continuous oscillations in macromolecular concentrations (rhythmicity). The blueprint for the structure and inherent properties of open systems among living organisms is to be found in the chemical genetic code. The genetic code enables the individual to replace cells and cell constituents needed for adaptation of the individual (replication) as well as to reproduce entire organisms as needed for the survival of the species (reproduction) (Wilson 1978). In this context health is viewed as genetically conditioned harmonic interaction between the individual and the environment (Bugard 1964) and disease is seen as a gene—environment interaction gone awry (Bartalos 1968, 1988).

Death is seen as a process whereby bodily integrity and function is irreversibly altered to the extent that continued adaptation to the environment is made impossible. (when viewed as a phenomenon; death is defined as the permanent cessation of purposeful adaptive interaction of the organism with the environment (Bartalos 1989). The irreversible loss of the adaptive ability of the body is followed by disintegration of our organs and cells and their dissolution into molecules and atoms. It is in that form—as potential building blocks—that we rejoin the universe.

What Is Negated when Dying Is Accepted?

When dying is accepted, survival after dying in your present form is considered highly unlikely.

What Is Not Negated when Dying Is Accepted?

Gradual increase in human life span did occur over the past centuries. We do not know for certain—although it is likely—that there is a biological limit to the duration of life attainable by humans under the most ideal conditions and we do not know what that time limit might be.

What Is Affirmed when Dying Is Accepted?

When we accept dying we admit our material being, our complexity, our fragility, and our finitude. We admit that humanness and finitude are inseparable.

What Is Not Affirmed when Dying Is Accepted?

Neither is it affirmed nor negated that scientific advances might enable the postmortem preservation of some aspects of our personhood. The anticipated development of quantum computing might be able to preserve not only our genetic code and our intellectual output but such aspects of our consciousness that represents quantum phenomena (Zohar and Marshall, 1994). If that occurs, our current stance should not stand in the way to accept such evidence and to make appropriate changes in our outlook. For us adherence to scientific evidence is the supreme rule in formulating theories about ourselves and about our environment.

Possible Advantages of Accepting Dying?

You might raise your eyebrows at the seeming absurdity of this question, yet I maintain that advantages lurk within such a proposition. It is a sad commentary on our state of affairs that most individuals alive today are under the influence of a religion that has the negative effects of "bigotry, murderous fanaticism, oppression, cruelty, and enforced ignorance." (Dennett 2006, 56).

By accepting our finitude we declare our freedom from voluntary servitude to an ideology that lacks scientific credibility, that constricts our intellect and possibly renders us unwilling instruments for the political ambitions of others. That is, we are asserting our status as thinking, rational, and courageous specimens of the genus Homo sapiens.

Possible Disadvantages of Accepting Dying?

As one sheds the guidance of a controlling organization, there is an increased sense of isolation, and the realization that we alone are responsible for our decisions. There is no other person or organization to blame for our prejudice, hate, and murderousness, or for the consequences of many other antisocial acts.

But is that really a disadvantage?

I, for one, do not think so. Along with the increased sense of responsibility for individual choices comes an exhilaration as you recognize that you are able to run your life on *your* principles, that you don't need to listen to anyone when told that a person, or a group, or a party, or a religion is your enemy and how to relate to them. You know from life experience who your enemies are and who are your friends. Any reasonable person left to his/her devices will soon discover that help and hurt are not the privilege of any group of people, of any religion, or of any skin color, but are characteristics of individuals who can belong to any group of humans.

When you truly learn to live by your own devices you also learn not to judge anybody and anything by superficialities. You look deeper. When you see a clown don't get lost by fixating on the paint on the face and the funny outfit. Under all that catchy paraphernalia see the human being, hidden, who is trying to make an honest living, and respect him/her for that.

To sum up my answer to the above question: I really see no disadvantages in accepting dying.

WHAT CONSOLATION IS THERE IN ACCEPTING DYING?

Our eyes are not fixed on heaven, but focused on earth and on our fellow human beings. Their fate is our fate. While we do not set our hopes high for survival after dying, we strive for improving life for everyone on earth. Instead of yearning for postmortem bliss and inflicting or tolerating misery on earth, I propose that we accept responsibility for our shortcomings, cultivate tolerance toward our differences, make efforts to reduce misery, and encourage the development of human talents and potential for the benefit of all. In short, celebrate living on earth. After all, is it not this, our earthly existence, that is the only certainty that we know?

REFERENCES

Bartalos, M. (1968). Genetics and disease. In *Genetics in Medical Practice.* ed. M. Bartalos, 231–233. Philadelphia: J. B. Lippincott.

Bartalos, M. K. (1988). Disease and the role of the physician. In *The Responsible Physician: Standards of Excellence and the Critically Ill Patient,* ed. S. G. Wolf Jr., M. W. Hamolsky, A. H. Kutscher, and K. Muraszko, 95–101. New York: The Foundation of Thanatology.

Bartalos, M. K. (1989). Genetics and the ways we die. In *Genetic Disease: The Unwanted Inheritance. Loss, Grief and Care.* Vol. 3, Nos. 3–4, ed. J. D. Rainer, S. P. Rubin, M. K. Bartalos, J. E. Maidman, A. H. Kutscher, K. Anyane-Yeboa, P. Taterka, and J. Malin, 145–152.

Bartalos, M. K. (1990). Human survival from the viewpoint of contextual individualism: discussion paper. *Journal of the Royal Society of Medicine* 83: 573–575.

Bertalanffy, L. von. (1968). *General System Theory.* rev. ed. New York: George Braziller.

Bugard, P. (1964). *L'Etat de Maladie. Convergences Genetiques, Sociologiques et Psychosomatiques.* Paris: Masson et Cie.

Dennett, D. C. (2006). *Breaking the Spell: Religion as a Natural Phenomenon.* New York: Penguin Books, 56.

Dumont, R. G. and D. C. Foss. (1972) *The American View of Death: Acceptance or Denial?* Cambridge, MA: Schenkman.

Goodwin, B. C. (1963). *Temporal Organization in Cells. A Dynamic Theory of Cellular Control Processes.* New York: Academic Press.

Konner, M. (1990). *Why the Reckless Survive...and Other Secrets of Human Nature.* New York Viking, 125–139.

Leming, M. R. and G. E. Dickinson. (1990) *Understanding Dying, Death, and Bereavement.* 2nd ed. Fort Worth, TX: Holt, Rinehart and Winston, 11–15.

Mackay, Charles. (1980). *Extraordinary Popular Delusions and the Madness of Crowds.* New York: Harmony Books, 230–237.

Merriam-Webster Online. (2008). "Denial." Available at http://www.merriam-webster.com/dictionary/denial (Accessed August 19, 2008).

Wilson, D. S. and A. B. Clark. (1996). *The Shy and the Bold, Natural History.* New York: *Natural History* magazine, 26–28.

Wilson, E. O. (1978). *On Human Nature.* Cambridge, MA: Harvard University Press.

Zohar, D. and I. Marshall. (1994). *The Quantum Society. Mind, Physics, and a New Social Vision.* New York: William Morrow and Company.

CHAPTER 7

DEATH, TERROR, CULTURE, AND VIOLENCE: A PSYCHOANALYTIC PERSPECTIVE

Jerry S. Piven

I will tell you the greatest secret.... Mirrors are the doors through which Death comes and goes. Besides, look at yourself in the mirror throughout your life and you will see Death at work like bees in a glass hive.

—Cocteau, *Orphée*, 1950

Shall worms, inheritors of this excess,
Eat up thy charge? Is this thy body's end?

—Shakespeare, Sonnet 146

She was more beautiful than thy first love,
But now lies under boards.

—Yeats, *A Dream of Death*, 1893

The fear of death is among the most grave and constant in human sufferings. We dread old age, when the flesh may wither and sag from our bones. We despair the death of loved ones and lament despondent bleak decrepitude. We may mourn the transience of youth and beauty, regretting most painfully the ravaging of one we love by time and her transformation from breathtaking, breathing soul to ghastly, inert corpse.

In the flower of youth, however, and even until the autumn of our lives, most of us are not stricken by dread and horror, do not bewail the future of mortality, and do not bemoan our grotesque fate. We prefer to exist and persist by living presently, in blithe serenity, and think of death only in tragic moments of loss or accidental confrontation. We leave the contemplation of death to philosophers, poets, and melancholics, while immersing ourselves in pleasure, love, work, accumulation, rivalry, deeply significant minutiae, trivial phenomena of immense import, all our various schemes of pursuing happiness. We prefer our blitheness, though too many of us tranquilly or excitedly abide the contemplation or observation of the death of others.

Yet death is not merely an abstract concept pondered in moments of existential despair. Death also inspires blitheness and visions of resurrection, divinity, and salvation. We invent infinite stratagems for quelling the terror of death, and we succeed when we become oblivious to our struggles not to be aware. We may suffer from our avoidances, inflict them without realizing it, and our personality may itself consist of stratified reactions to terror, uniquely individual ploys for warding off and displacing death. As Langs (1997) writes, "death is a universal and inherently irresolvable adaptive issue, and conscious and unconscious forms of death anxiety are ever-present. As a result, these grave concerns are significant factors in the development of virtually every type of emotional dysfunction" (p. 30).

THE ETIOLOGY OF DEATH ANXIETY

> Why shouldn't children be afraid of being killed?...Is there anyone more "killable"? To be born tiny and defenseless in a world where even a mouse has the advantage of mobility is surely to find oneself at the mercy of every living being.
> —Bloch, *"So the Witch Won't Eat Me,"* 1978, p. 3

The fear of death begins in infancy and owes its origins to the prematurity of human birth, the phenomenon known as neoteny or infantilization (Becker, 1971; La Barre, 1970, 1980, 1991).[1] We emerge from the womb in a state of incompleteness, physiologically underdeveloped because our crania are too massive to emerge from the maternal body without killing her, if the skull were fully formed. This renders the infant both physically and emotionally vulnerable to the world. It has been proposed that the child is terrified in its vulnerability and traumatized by the amorphous fear of disintegration, though these anxieties are preconceptual. The child is overwhelmed by terror and need not understand why (cf. Bloch, 1978; Klein, 1946; Kohut, 1971; Ogden, 1989; Piven, 2004a, 2005; Soldz, 2006; Yalom, 2008).

It may take years before a child comprehends death or even accepts that dead people or animals remain dead and do not return to life. The child clings to the mother as the source of comfort and protection. Her body is warmth, nourishment, solace, the magical enveloping refuge from frailty and exposure, from precategorical dread and death itself. The child experiences the threat of loss or abandonment as a most excruciating terror.

Thus the child must feel secure and protected in his or her experience of the world, must feel a secure "holding environment," supportive attachments, and "conditions of safety" if he or she is to begin venturing away from the mother.[2] At the same time, the awakening sense of one's environment exposes the child to a panegyric of exciting and fascinating objects and images. But emergence is replete with terrifying dangers. The child can increase the radius of his or her wandering from the mother only with firm support, and cannot tolerate frustration or fear for some time.[3] The child is in the midst of experiences that will gradually determine dispositions in the emerging ego structure of trust or mistrust, autonomy versus shame or self-doubt, confidence or inferiority, identity or insecurity, intimacy or isolation (Erikson, 1950).[4]

Fears of annihilation coincide with destructive and persecutory fantasies, followed by attempts at reparation and immanent fantasies of abandonment.[5] The child will also displace frustration and anger toward the mother, splitting her into distinct positive and negative visages, repressing the negative impressions in order to cope with fears and hostilities and retain the image of a perfect and nurturing mother.[6]

The child will always run back to the mother for protection and security when life is frightening or painful, and it is only with the incremental development of the capacity to endure frustration that the child will expand her or his radius. Consequently, the child comes to conceive of the mother both as a supporting nurturer and as a controlling, punishing reminder of dependence and weakness. In other words, both separation *and* individuation threaten the child with death. The child both desires independence and fears it, and must inevitably make the transition from dependence to autonomy, but dreads it terribly.

Throughout adulthood, the individual will always be drawn to the desire to return to the mother's protection when life is too frightening or painful. Such wishes will often be displaced into symbolic substitutes for the mother, whether they be mate, home, church, ideology, or religion, any cozening bromide that recreates bygone feelings of shelter, bliss, nurturance, and sanctuary (cf. Chasseguet-Smirgel, 1975; Freud, 1917; Fromm, 1941, 1955, 1964, 1966; Jones, 1924, 1928; Stein, 1994).

DEATH ANXIETY, SEPARATION, AND INDIVIDUATION

> They always stay where they were born, so that the individual compelled by
> reality to eternal wanderings...has never left his mother.
> —Roheim, *The Eternal Ones of the Dream*, 1945, p. 239

Understood historically, one might recognize the longing for an afterlife or salvation, the erection of a church, burial mound, omphalos,[7] or pyramid, as symbolic fantasies of reunion with the mother of infancy. Separation from the mother is freedom but it is also a traumatic alienation, and we can always find fantasies of surrogate wombs, protecting and sheltering architecture, substitutes for the lost body of the mother. Freud interpreted God as the projection of a divine paternal substitute onto the cosmos, a way of hallucinating a protective father (1907, 1913, 1927, 1930, 1939). Religion is not simply the projection of an Oedipal god or obsessive ritual into the social structure, however. The very establishment and sacredness of the father god may be seen as a reaction to separation-individuation anxieties and the need for a father who enables the transition from infancy and dependence to autonomy. Faber eloquently describes the enduring cadences of separation and the fear of death:

> Death is always and forever mixed up integrally with the problem of separation; that is, we can't even apprehend death, let alone comprehend it, apart from our conscious and unconscious preoccupation with separation from others. At the root of this separation issue, or perhaps obsession, is the first, primal separation from the parental figures, or as Erikson would put it, from the maternal matrix. For humans, death does not mean nothingness but separation, aloneness, isolation, the end of vital contact with nurturing, salvational others, and it is always felt this way or experienced this way in the core of the self. Hence the great religious promise of eternal life boils down to the promise of no separation, no truncation of the ties that bind. God takes the parent's place, and God is always there, forever. The anxious human animal is thus soothed and reassured when it comes to his primal fear of separation. (personal communication, January 28, 2004)

The question, for both boys and girls instilled with the terror of separation and individuation, is to what degree the fear of death is inculcated, and which particular choices the developing children make with regard to enduring the reality of separation, or searching for sources of security and means of denying death. Those choices involve emotional investments, relationships, identifications, and gender roles that help them feel secure, confident, and protected against vulnerability, shame, hatred, weakness, and death. They also involve cognitive, emotional, and behavioral choices that range from perceptual distortions, psychic retreats from love and independence, and a virtually infinite number of symptoms of the inability to cope with death (examples may include obsessive ritual, compulsive sexual seductiveness or predatory behavior, gender rejection, even political ambition), to connections and relationships that nurture confidence in the face of anxiety and despair.[8] (This does *not* mean that everything can be explained in terms of death anxiety, but that many of our choices and lifestyles are designed to escape terror and despair, whether we are aware of such motives or not.)

Any number of controlling, stifling, invasive, neglectful, or physically abusive modes of parenting can inculcate varieties of what Rheingold (1967) terms the "catastrophic death complex." In this sense, pathological personality styles are both injurious consequences and defensive measures to avoid disintegration, annihilation, weakness, vulnerability, and death (cf. Pearce & Newton, 1963; Wolman, 1973).

"Death anxiety is related to degree of individuation and self-actualizati on....death anxiety increases as people relinquish defenses, refuse to conform to familial and societal standards, reach new levels of differentiation of self, or expand their lives" (Firestone, 1994, pp. 236–237). Consequently, individuals engage in flights from life and self, limiting their emotions and sexuality, sabotaging themselves and succumbing to psychic deadness, if not more physically dangerous activities (cf. Bollas, 1987; Eigen, 1996; Salomon, 2008; Yalom, 2008). As Firestone (1994) maintains, ordinary individuals often commit acts of "microsuicide" and self-destruction "to achieve mastery over death" (p. 234). I would even suggest that actual attempts at suicide can represent attempts to kill off the noisome decaying body and often involve fantasies of rebirth shorn of shame, guilt, impurity, decay, and death, in reunion with the fantasied symbiotic object (cf. Maltsberger & Buie, 1980; Wahl, 1957, 1958). One murders oneself in the agony of separation and death.

If children have erotic wishes (consciously or unconsciously), may this not also be a means of attaining security? Cannot even adult sexuality be *psychologically* symbolic of the need for emotional security, intimacy, love, and pleasure against the terror of alienation, abandonment, helplessness, and death? Amid psychosexual tribulation, the terror of violent injury, abandonment, and disintegration saturates the emotional life of the child and leads to defensive responses and derangements. The substratum of psychopathology is the dread of annihilation and death, whether these terms imply a conceptual understanding of death or inchoate and even precategorical images or feelings of being killed. The anxiety impelling defense and pathology is ultimately an overwhelming terror, a threat that scares the human organism into fearing for its life, whether it knows death as a concept or not.

We can posit a continuum from ubiquitous and evolutionarily adaptive (pre-)Oedipal attachment to ordinary yet neurotic symptoms of the inability to tolerate death, from the belief in an afterlife to the morbid extremes of murder and necrophilia, which represent a drastic inability to tolerate separateness and death. Within the matrix of conflict and illusion, the terror of death always holds sway as the impulsion for erotic, religious, individual, social, and political fantasies, and the psychological investigation of history must contend with the horrific facts of human frailty, transience, and putrefaction.

SYMBOLIC AND DELUSIONAL IMMORTALITY

> And death shall have no dominion.
> Dead men naked they shall be one
> With the man in the wind and the west moon;
> When their bones are picked clean and the clean bones gone,
> They shall have stars at elbow and foot;
> Though they go mad they shall be sane,
> Though they sink through the sea they shall rise again;
> Though lovers be lost love shall not;
> And death shall have no dominion.
> —Dylan Thomas, "And Death Shall Have No Dominion," 1936

How can the awareness of the salience of mortality deepen our under-standing of psychodynamics, of human motivation, of fantasy and history? The book of Job reads as follows: "Man born of woman is short-lived and full of disquiet. He blossoms like a flower and then he withers; he slips away like a shadow and does not stay.... His flesh upon him becomes black, and his life-blood dries up within him" (14:1–3, 22). Tolstoy (1879) asked in despair: "Is there any meaning in my life that will not be destroyed by my inevitably approaching death?" (p. 35). Nishitani (1982) declares that "when one comes face to face with death and the existence of self—one's 'self-existence'—stands out clearly in relief against the backdrop of nihility. Questions crowd in upon one: Why have I been alive? Where did I come from and where am I going? A void appears here that nothing in the world can fill; a gaping abyss opens up at the very ground on which one stands. In the face of this abyss, not one of all the things that had made up the stuff of life until then is of any use" (p. 3). How do we cope with death, loss, and decay, the ineluctable modality of the visible?

To philosophize is to learn how to die, Montaigne (sixteenth century C.E.) said. Sagacious wisdom can be found in so many cultures. Sufi poet and mys-tic Jalal ud-Din Rumi (thirteenth century C.E.) advises us to avoid loss, widen our vision, realize the trivial, and cease fleeing from death. Such counsel is echoed by Zen master Dogen (thirteenth century C.E.), who also instructs us neither to despise nor to desire death. Epicurus (fourth century B.C.E.) advises us to accustom ourselves to the belief that death is nothing, and thus unworthy of fear or trepidation. Ecclesiastes advises us to enjoy ourselves, since all is emptiness and wind chasing, and "dead flies make the perfumer's sweet ointment turn rancid" (10:1). Philosophy is but one means of approach-ing death, and is often an intellectual endeavor that may itself be defensive, a retreat into unemotional intellect, words that masque and deceive one about one's actual terror and dread. Philosophy may enlighten or rationalize, and a philosophy that genuinely confronts death is not mere advice on how one should think or feel (no matter how wise such advice may be).

A psychology of death must reach beneath the intellect and analyze the defenses, fantasies, and delusions that acclimate the soul to dread, despair, and disgust. To understand the human relation to death, we must consider not merely the surface of what people have believed about death but what such ideas mean, what they conceal, exclude, symbolize, and eradicate. Belief is already fantasy and symptom, and rarely unconflicted reason. So we seek again to find out how the soul acclimates to death, and inquire of its myriad apotheoses, epiphanies, realizations, and revelations and also of its ceaseless contortions, figments, deliria, and hallucinations.

Lifton (1973, 1979) posits the phenomenon of "symbolic immortality" to elucidate the attempt to derive meaning from life and death by investing oneself in practices and values that provide palpable feelings of continuity, connection, and transcendence of death. Symbolic immortality can take a variety of forms, all of which are reflected in the sacred and transcendent, whether ideological, revolutionary, religious, or even secular and occupational.

It should be understood that each mode of symbolic immortality spans a continuum from healthy to deeply pathological investment and derangement.[9] For instance, the first form of symbolic immortality is through one's progeny, as parents feel a part of them will survive into future generations through their genes, their faces, and their ideas and teachings. Though many parents are comforted by the idea that they will survive through their children, however, many parents also fulfill their own pathological needs by manipulating and violating their children. The children become extensions of the parents' egos, satisfy the parents' unrequited need for love, gratify their frustrated pathways to admiration or success, and derogation the way the parents might have when they were young (Donaldson-Pressman & Pressman, 1994; Eigen, 1999). Innumerable parents have little empathy for their children, see them as a nuisance, disdain their children's individuality, or even experience their children as the threat of their own waning and death, as intimated previously.

This form of symbolic immortality mitigates death anxiety through the idea of continuing progeny but is also applicable to immortality through attachment to a religion, ideology, group, organization, nation, or one's own species. One may experience a sense of survival through others identified with oneself in some way, and the extension of oneself into a group or ideology may inflict the same pathology as that allotted to children as elucidated above. This brings the discourse to the psychodynamics of neurosis and transference on a *social scale*. The group becomes the target and container of intrapsychic fears, defenses, and conflicts, the repository for communal fears of death, a means of evacuating terror within the group, ritually displacing communal dread, surviving through the group, sharing fantasies of death denial and symbolic (or even literal) immortality. Shared fantasies may avert the fear of death, while specific victims are chosen to contain terror and pathology, and unite the group in rituals of celebration, elimination of evil, and salvation (Girard, 1972; Jaques, 1955). The dynamics of symbolic immortality unite the psychopathology of individuals and developmental complexities with group semiotics and the sacred.[10] In other words, varieties of social and religious experience can be correlated with modes of development or mental illness, the variant inculcations and deflections of death anxiety.

This is a framework in which cultural development and change can be viewed as transference dynamics, regression, restitution, and the projection of defense mechanisms and compromise formations into new modes of belief and practice that satiate dreams of immortality. Lifton (1970) states aptly that "the shifting and recombining of modes of immortality mark the great turning points in history" (p. 38).[11] Or as Becker (1975) avers, "The unfolding of history is precisely the saga of the succession of new and different ideologies of organismic self-perpetuation" (p. 25). And again, he writes: "History...can be understood as the succession of ideologies that console for death" (p. 64).

Lifton's other modes of symbolic immortality also span a similar spectrum of healthy and pathological dimensions. The second form of immortality is attained through belief in an afterlife or higher plane of existence. This often connotes the transcendence of death through spiritual achievements (1973, p. 276).[12] One may experience the numinous (a sense of connection with God), grace, enlightenment, harmony, ubiquitous intergalactic oneness, or synchronistic awareness. One may of course also believe literally in Heaven, the Happy Hunting Grounds, and the Pure Land, in angels, spirits, or *jizos*, an infinite array of theological entities that believers might be loath to conceive of as mere metaphors. Consequently, such belief and faith are more concerned with hallucinating soothing substitutes for reality than with transforming the psyche through wisdom or spiritual discipline, and they describe the more defensive means of avoiding death.

A third mode of attaining immortality is through one's achievements and works, the influence and permanence of sculpture, architecture, poetry, literature, science, philosophy, and political, social, or environmental accomplishments. Civilization itself may be seen as the dire need to erect enduring symbols of immortality. As with the previous modes, the emotional investment can vary from creative engagement to obsessive and destructive cravings for immortality. One can experience the sense of immortality by leaving behind something people will read, ponder, or enjoy, or one can engage in far more narcissistic, grandiose, compulsive, or fanatical behavior, even acts that will traumatize and decimate the world in revenge against survivors, future progeny, and death itself. One can raise a statue to immortalize someone, or one can raze jungles to eradicate the threat of nature and declare the superiority of humankind.[13] Or one can seek to fulfill the wishes of one's god by purifying the world of infidels and restoring it to its sanctimonious utopian origins (cf. Piven, 2004a, 2006, 2007a, 2008a, b; Stein 2008; Wirth, 2008a).

Lifton's fourth mode of symbolic immortality is survival through the en-durance of nature, as seen in Japanese Shintoism, the European Romantic movement, and the Anglo-Saxon cult of the great outdoors. Survivors of the atomic bomb in Japan found consolation in the perdurance of nature, quot-ing an ancient Chinese proverb, "the state may collapse, but the rivers and mountains remain" (1979, p. 22). Today many people feel that this sense of immortality is threatened, as it becomes increasingly convincing that we are in danger of destroying our environment irrevocably even without nuclear explosions. Symbolic immortality through nourishing nature can unite com-munities and provide fulfilling feelings of enhancing life.

There are also numerous extremes here, for instance, cases where people punish themselves for accidentally squishing an ant. Sometimes the preser-vation of nature can be reparation for feelings of being bad, enabling the per-son to save weak, helpless things, which represent the self. One wonders if the ancient Jain phobia about killing the tiniest insect, combined with ascetic and punitive self-denial, is not some manifestation of these conflicts. Those who see the carnivorous nature of nature itself as a disgusting evil, which must be purified through peaceful coexistence where the lion lies down with the lamb, are reviling death and decay. Digestion, death, and putrescence are so horrific that one needs to redesign nature and eliminate its disgusting or horrific reality.

A more severe case is the preservation of nature in opposition to human life. I am not referring here to people who wish to protect nature, or even to those who see nature as more important than individuals. Environmental groups may sometimes displace the wish for a nurturing mother and guilt over separation into the fantasy of saving nature. But extremist groups such as Earth First, who are willing to extinguish human life for their goals, seem to be revenging themselves against those perceived to be poisoning the planet, who are the source of all evil.

Among such extremists, nature becomes a reparative idealizing fantasy, while the enemy displaces far more conflicted object relations. This can even approximate terrorist activity, and the immortality of nature here represents the preservation of fantasies that prevent conflicts and toxic influences from overwhelming and annihilating the psyche. Nature becomes the delusional path to goodness, purity, eradication of evil, absolution, ablution, and salvation.

Lifton's fifth mode of attaining symbolic immortality is through experi-ential transcendence, "a state so intense that in it time and death disappear" (1973, p. 277). This recalls the rapture of religious conversions or festivals, the "oceanic feeling" described by Freud (1930) in *Civilization and Its Discontents*, though at times attaining a more intense, Dionysian ecstasy. Thus such feel-ings can also be achieved during dances, concerts, sports events, drug-induced states, love, sex, childbirth, and even violence. The intensity, transcendence, and joy experienced during moments of artistic or intellectual creation, love, and orgasm may indeed involve the temporary and rapturous dissolution of ego boundaries—experiences that can signify the ability to love and feel deeply, whereas many people are too ensconced in their defenses to love or feel passionately about art, music, or other human beings. Sadly, they may be immune to feelings of joy or rapture, awe, the *mysterium tremendum*, so to speak, whether in Chartres Cathedral, atop the Acropolis, before the 1001 gleaming statues of Kannon in Sanjusangendo Temple, beneath Niagara Falls, or with a wonderful human being.

Group experiences, especially violent ones, induce a somewhat different rapture and involve different emotions. One is tempted to wonder if euphoria or transcendence may not sometimes be defensive experiences, escape from the self, one's feelings, needs, desires, ideas, loneliness, isolation, and depression through ecstasy (lit., to be external to oneself), or the response of catatonia to extreme stress, and even the will to world denial when sought addictively or religiously.

Sex can be oblivion, manic obliteration of time, and alienation. One can even merge with God in erotic rapture, reenacting the need to fuse with a parent in symbiotic, deindividualized, infantile precognitive bliss. One may seethe with sensual joy when eradicating the boundaries between self and God, abolishing one's own ego as well, masochistically punishing the despised self and sinful body while imagining the love of an absolving parent.

Ecstasy, religion, hallucinosis, and regressive fusion are often deeply coalesced. Schumaker (1995) catalogues a plethora of religious and ritual practices designed to induce dissociative trance states, and La Barre (1980) details the ecstatic and visionary use of hallucinatory chemicals in numerous religions. Not only drug use, for example, but certain ways of practicing Zen Buddhism, and religious faith, provide horror-easing ecstasy and escape from misery and despair.[14] The crowds attending Hitler's speeches were often roused to ecstatic fury, sometimes thrilled with visions of German supremacy, often deluged by violent anti-Semitism, sometimes even excited into wanton sexual acts (Kline, 1984). Violence can feel transcendent and orgasmic, a penetrating laceration, an effulgent explosion liquidating evil (on which more anon). Hence the attainment of symbolic immortality as described by Lifton also implies the possibility of defensive death denial, serious pathological states, and withdrawal from reality (cf. Becker, 1971; Davis, 2006; Freud, 1930; La Barre, 1970; Lasch, 1978).

CHARACTER AND CULTURE AS DEFENSE AND DELUSION

> the danger of death appears to be the most fundamental and universal source of adaptive and defensive structures.
>
> —Langs, *Death Anxiety and Clinical Practice*, 1997, p. 4

If we are to fathom the depths and fundaments of how people have coped with death, we must elucidate exactly what utterly sustains the emotional life or a person or group against terror and dread. We must ask what belief or practice dispels anxiety and allows one to proceed with a sense of meaning and purpose while armored against thoughts and anxieties of mortality and annihilation. Tillich's (1951) concept of "ultimate concern" captures this well but may not articulate the pathology sufficiently—the degree to which reality is distorted and the emotional and cognitive structures altered in the avoidance of death anxiety.

Symbolic immortality remolds the world in accordance with the wish for meaning and transcendence, while simultaneously isolating and compartmentalizing perception and cognition, such that these illusions are believable and one's anxieties are unconscious. This involves not only denial and repression but myriad defenses, evasions not only of the outer but of the inner world as well. If certain fantasies bring ecstasy, other stratagems may again deaden our inner emotions to enable us to escape the terrors of life and death (Becker, 1975, pp. 147–148; Eigen, 1996; Yalom, 2008).[15]

This is in agreement with Lifton's concept of "psychic numbing," the process of dissociating dystonic feelings or ideas defensively. Lifton (1973) writes: "Psychic numbing is a form of desensitization; it refers to an incapacity to feel or confront certain kinds of experience, due to the blocking or absence of inner forms of imagery that can connect with such experience" (p. 273). Restitution of safety is also attained through fantasy, but here the psychological apparatus for apprehending the world is calibrated for precise misperception. Lifton continues: "The 'psycho-formative' perspective would stress that a human being can never simply *receive* a bit of information nakedly. The process of perception is vitally bound up with the process of inner re-creation, in which one utilizes whatever forms are available in individual psychic existence" (1973, p. 273).

The shifting modes of immortality deconstruct the emotional lives of individuals and cultures in history. How they imagine death becomes a key for discerning the patterns of their emotional lives—one does not merely claim they need an afterlife to deny death. The imagination of death is far more intricate, and our oblivion more shrewd and deceptive. Ariès's prominent treatise, *Western Attitudes toward Death* (1974), explains the difference between the blasé medieval acceptance of death and the Romantic poets' erotic longing for death. Ariès reads little, however, into the psychodynamics of why these differences might occur. Is blasé acceptance truly acceptance, or is it repression of affect and soothing via fantasy? Is the romantic longing truly the love of death, or a repetition of the infantile wish to regress to symbiotic merger commingled with the idealized (non–maternally engulfing or violent) feminine? Do these fantasies differ in terms of how developmental vicissitudes engender desires and anxieties relating to which gender can soothe the soul against the fear of death? In one case, the departed unites, disembodied, with the idealized benign father in Heaven, while in the other, one is reunited nec-rophilically via suffering and diseased consumption with the mother in the grave-womb. How does the sight and smell of decay arouse a man?

The relationship between sexuality and the terror of death is not to be underestimated. As Brown (1959) writes, "One effect of the incapacity to ac-cept separation, individuation, and death is to eroticize death" (p. 115). This means not only wishing to die and romanticizing death, but sensualizing it. Eroticizing death is a morbid means of transforming terror and despair into soothing sensual release and fantasies of emotional and sexual intercourse.

Your carcass has its delights! (Baudelaire, "Le monstre," 1866)

Young soul, put off your flesh and come
With me into the quiet tomb,
Our bed is lovely, dark, and sweet. (Beddoes, "The Phantom Wooer,"1837,
   in Binion, 1993, pp. 12–13)[16]

The disparate means of coping with mortality are ripe for dissection. Why did the Gnostics seek transcendence of the body while early Christians dreamed of the reintegration of the resurrected body and soul? Why did a priestly, monotheistic Judaism spurn the cult of the dead, and why did that cult persist occultly (cf. Abe, 1997; Hallote, 2001; Keck, 1992; Mendenhall, 1992)? Why does one group invest itself in nature and another in violent conquest? Such perplexities embody the very axes of the terror of annihila-tion, that which inculcates or absorbs it, and the repetition and restitution that are being enacted through these phenomena.

The human organism subsists on sacred illusions to palliate fear and solidify our projected importance and divine justification in the cosmos. *Homo sapiens* is the animal whose magnificent capacity for thought and imagination is the very frailty constricting the perception of reality, molding, twisting, and sanitizing it from the terrors of which consciousness enables one to conceive. We become animals too anxious to endure ourselves, and too sickened by consciousness to confront reality without distorting or destroying it. We create ourselves, our identity, meaning, society, and cosmos as the projection of an illusion over an "abyss," as Kristeva (1987) terms our expansive ignorance of reality (p. 42).

One might ask if illusions are absolutely necessary. Becker (1973) asserts that we are frightened of our weakness, our helplessness, and anything that re-minds us of it, whether tangible danger or symbolic threat, and that we create "character armor," psychological defenses that veil the truth, and we repress ideas that are too fearsome, that threaten to fracture the understandable, predictable, livable world we have made for ourselves.[17] The mind employs defense mechanisms that prevent consciousness from accepting that which threatens it, and this means either effacing the threat through repressing, denying, or dissociating the idea completely, so that one is either completely unaware of the threat, or creating compensating ideas that attempt to convince the consciousness that the feared threat is something entirely different. Human beings are thus *fetishists*, for we constrict meaning and experience by evading the apprehension of terrifying truths and threats, while our fantasies define the horizon of perception, truth, and action. We could not endure existence without such distortion.[18] Ostensibly simple things can become symbols of one's own weakness or worthlessness, even impersonal ideas, while distortions and fantasies are believed so that the world may become understandable, and hence less threatening and overwhelming.[19]

This creation of "character armor" and the means people employ to obscure their death anxieties constitute the very phenomenon of neurosis. People need myths, coherent worldviews, compartmentalized, defined systems of signification, and assurances of immortality to survive. Ideologies, whether social or individual, are "sick" because they are needed for emotional survival, and they erase some part of the world in order to make the world acceptable and endurable. We are left with a view of the human psyche that considers "healthy adjustment" a defensive adaptation, a sickness defining *Homo sapiens* as the animal that cannot live without projecting into the external world its wishes for a reality distinct from what is actually real. And so we can say with Becker that "neurosis for man is unavoidable" (1971, p. 174); indeed, we might even assert that "normalcy *is* neurosis" (Becker, 1971, pp. 151, 181; Becker, 1973, p. 269).[20]

But how could "adaptation" mean the willful creation of illusion or even delusion? How would *Homo sapiens* survive in a real and dangerous world if they ignored danger because it was frightening? For the human organism to function, one cannot efface the tangible immediacy of the real world, for one could not feed or defend oneself. As Segal (1985) notes, fantasies "provide protection against undesirable and contradictory information from the point of view of the phantasy....from an outsider's view they may seem to be perversely limiting or crippling" (p. 33).

We thus have defensive, or "coping" mechanisms that *partialize* reality by both projecting fantasies onto the world and denying what causes terror: "the essence of normality is the *refusal of reality*" (Becker, 1973, p. 178); consequently, it is a "vital lie" (pp. 47–66). In this way, one's individual defensive molding of perception and action constitutes the uniqueness of one's character. Character itself is character armor. Rather than claiming that *Homo sapiens* could not survive by avoiding reality, I am asserting with Becker that we could not survive psychologically by being fully aware of reality, because it is so horrific.

The establishment of culture is more than repressed animal aggression or sexual drives, neurotic guilt or sublimation; it is the fear of our own vulnerability, helplessness, and mortality, our inevitable putrescence and nonbeing. We are governed by an immense reaction-formation process that causes us to flee desperately from death into symbols of immortality.[21] As Freud (1927) writes in *The Future of an Illusion,* our frailty and insignificance before nature is an injury to our narcissism. A central component of this self-delusion that protects us from the anxiety of death is thus the narcissistic fiction of personal significance and importance. Narcissism is fundamentally the evolutionary expression of self-preservation and expansion—not merely the vain overconcern with oneself that we see as a superficial, unpleasant characteristic, but the vital concern with self-esteem, the sense of self-worth, security from helplessness and powerlessness (cf. Libby, 2007; Perrulli, 2005; Wirth, 2008b).

Against the narcissistic injury of nature and death, human beings inflate their own importance, attaching themselves to objects and projects that make them seem significant, unforgettable, invulnerable to the ravages and forgetfulness of time. Status systems, wealth and fame, artistic and cultural achievements, the grandest temples and edifices stand for the desperate need to deny evanescence, temporality, weakness, and inevitable dissolution.[22] As Brown (1959) reminds us, "life remains a war against death—civilized man, no more than archaic man, is not strong enough to die—and death is overcome by accumulating time-defying monuments" (p. 286).[23] It seems as though the denial of reality (and thus mortality) is a requirement for enduring life.

VIOLENCE, TRANSFERENCE, AND SEARCH FOR SALVATION

War is beautiful because it establishes man's dominion over the subjugated machinery by means of gas masks, terrifying megaphones, flame throwers, and small tanks. War is beautiful because it initiates the dreamt-of metalization of the human body. War is beautiful because it enriches a flowering meadow with the fiery orchids of machine guns. War is beautiful because it combines the gunfire, the cannonades, the cease-fire, the scents, and the stench of putrefaction into a symphony.

—Filippo Tommaso Marinetti, c. 1932

And we? We glow as One,
A new creature invigorated by death

—Rilke, *Fünf Gesänge.* August 1914

Smile in the face of death, young man for you are on your way to everlasting paradise!

—Letter left behind by hijackers, September 11, 2001

Our frenetic need to escape is both the genesis of character and culture and the genesis of all those destructive displacements and "murderous enactments" that, Brown (1959) and Langs (1997) remind us, reveal our fundamental discomfort with the reality of our nascent death and decay (see Langs, 1997, pp. 84, 96–97). Attempts to control others, to gain power, to achieve invulnerability through conquest, are destined to tragic failure, as we are left with merely our insignificance, evanescence, frailty, and mortality. Violence emerges as a reaction to the horror of human weakness, mortality, and inevitable putrefaction. The terror of death and dissipation engender a disgust with life and the body. Intense loathing catalyzes the wish to trample the guts of others to overcome both humanity and one's own impotence against inevitable consumption.[24]

As Brown (1959) and Becker (1973) put it, this is also the essence of anality: it is the denial of our "creatureliness," our decay, the stinking creation of the body and its excretions. As Beauvoir (1949) writes, men are disgusted by mortality, and disgusted by women because the fetid odors of uterine shreds and blood, of their vaginae, too much resemble the soft viscosity of carrion. This mortal disgust compels Augustine to claim contemptuously that man is born between urine and feces. Thus Róheim (1943) writes: "We can now attempt to show how the profession of the primitive medicine man, this nucleus of all primitive societies, originates. It is evolved on the basis of the infantile body destruction phantasies, by means of a series of defense mechanisms. The first formula is abreaction in phantasy (my inside has already been destroyed) followed by reaction-formation (my body is not something corruptible and full of feces, but incorruptible, full of quartz-crystals" (p. 65). Disgust and the awareness that the body putresces engender fantasies of invulnerability and immortality. We recall Hamlet's ironic words on our human genius:

> What a piece of work is man! how noble in reason! how infinite in faculty! in form and moving how express and admirable! in action how like an angel! in apprehension how like a god! the beauty of the world! the paragon of animals! And yet, to me, what is this quintessence of dust? (act 2, scene 2, 332–33)

I have been arguing that the fear of death originally derives from our earliest feelings of aloneness, when we started separating from our parents and learned the terrifying anxiety of helplessness and independence. Though I have suggested that parenting can allay or exacerbate separation-individuation trauma and inculcate a "catastrophic death complex," depending on the toxicity or nourishment of the child's internalizations, it is critical to understand how the denial of death derives from *inherent* childhood conflicts—not just suffering inflicted abusively. No child is exempt from the struggle, from what Brown (1959) has termed the "Oedipal project" (p. 118ff) of mastering one's own body and its frailties, weaknesses, and limitations. We all traverse experiences of helplessness, of a body that can be injured, that may sicken or leak;

a thing with its own refractory processes and coarse defects, a body that defecates and infuriates one with the equation of helpless, excreting body with self and identity. We attempt to control the body, its impulses, puniness, and vulnerability (cf Becker, 1973; Ogden, 1989).

Many of us learn to live with frustration, and much shame and disgust is repressed, deflected, and even absorbed by love, independence, and joy in the body and its pleasures. Freud (1905) and Brown (1959) already see pleasure and even orgasm as truncated, diminished, distorted, and repressed remnants of a formerly healthy, polymorphously perverse sexuality. The degree to which terror, disgust, shame, and humiliation are exacerbated and envenomed reflects how much rage will be directed toward the hapless and fallible body, sexuality, and desire. As Brown (1959) writes, "To rise above the body is to equate the body with excrement" (p. 295), or a tomb, or even a living cadaver. This malicious derogation makes its appearance in both Eastern and Western philosophy, in the *Phaedo* and *Gorgias* of Plato, the Upanishads, and the Pali canon in Buddhism (Faure, 2003; Piven, 2003, 2007a). *Nikaya Samyutta's Sakkasamyutta* reads as follows:

> The humans stuck in a putrid body,
>   Those submerged inside a corpse...(Bodhi, 2000, p. 336.20.932–933)[25]

This aspersion spans Platonic philosophy, Gnosticism, Neoplatonism, Christianity, Cartesian philosophy, and the continuance of the mind/soul-body splits that devalue and disparage the erotic.[26] As suggested, its extreme is the persecution of the flesh, not only in masochistic punishment but in the sanctimonious murder of the wickedly sexual body as direst evil.

> Western civilization is the negation of biological reality; and unavoidably, since life and death are inextricable, the denial of death comes finally to be a denial of life. At its worst it results in overt hostility to life. (Des Pres, 1976, p. 206)

Even the more contemptuous of sex and decay do not merely destroy wantonly, however. Human vulnerability generates the need for power, to disparage and dominate that which threatens one's weakness and dissolution (cf. Bamyeh, 2007). To varying degrees we proceed through life seeking a secure base, parental surrogates who secure meaning, order, and protection, and projecting these fantastic needs into ideological, material, and religious attachments. Anything that denies death for us is of ultimate concern since emotional survival depends on it—and thus the sacred must be seen as that which denies death (Becker, 1975, p. 73). Hence all power is functionally sacred (p. 81). Even when we are adults, our physicality also reminds us of our frailty, our lack of control over ourselves, over our desires, over nature. The more insignificant and helpless we feel, the more we are conflicted, seeking resolutions to the source of discontent.

One attempt at resolution, consequently, is to find parental surrogates in whom we can invest our need for protection and self-esteem. We require transitional objects and phenomena, emotional security blankets (Winnicott, 1953). As Freud (1917) wrote of the mourning process, we can invest ourselves in ideas, fantasies, ideologies, which all become substitutes for parental protection. Fromm (1955) describes ideologies as "libidinal fixations to mother" (p. 38ff). Or as Chasseguet-Smirgel (1975) argues, immersion in a group can be experienced as a safe and nurturing womb, as alluded to previously. More than mere submersion in a cozening womb, however, one may attempt to control fate through transference, engaging in regressively dependent relationships to empower oneself through merging with the powerful other, whether that other is a lover, mentor, ideology, group, or leader (Becker, 1973, p. 166).[27] One transcends weakness and death through transference. This is why we are "so *eager* to be mystified, so *willing* to be bound in chains" (Becker, 1975, p. 50). Human beings need transference in order to endure life (p. 148; cf. Firestone, 1994, p. 231; Liechty, 1995, 2008a, b; Yalom, 1980, pp. 195–196).[28]

Transference absorbs the invulnerability of the other. It can be the submersion of one's own ego in the leader or group, but it also draws vampirically on the vast power of the other as well, amplifying the self through fusion as one flows with the vital blood of the idealized and divinized target of that transference. Ensconcement in the leader denies death, and it is the sated fantasy of protection and love that falsifies and hallucinates leaders, effects our inability to perceive who they are, as we so often invest them with our own idealizing wishes and endow them with benevolent, loving intentions and sublime perfection (cf. Bion, 1955; Lipman-Blumen, 2006; Mazlish, 1990).

It is this euphoric, soothing, enlightening amphimixis with the sublime other, the subjective oceanic experience of merging with a god, the fantasy of being embraced by divine love, and the yearning to receive divine love that also inspires such joy in the delirious idea of murdering lovingly for one's god. We expect slaughter to resound with cadences of seething rage and malice. The language of sanctimonious murder, including recent acts of terrorism, can also include words of joy and divine rapture when inflicting death (Davis, 2006; Kressel, 2007; Stein, 2008).[29]

Death and its transcendence can be enacted through murder, torture, sacrifice, and warfare—passionately and morally, when the ruling leader, king, or hierophany sanctifies its cause and removes the inhibition of the lustful, violent gratification of our immortality strivings. As intimated above, violence can be pleasurable, especially if it extinguishes evil (cf. Piven, 2006, 2007a, b, 2008a, b). We tend to view "savage" or mythic sacrifice as a practice confining itself to the particular area of cultural belief and practice known as (atavistic) religion. But even when violence is secularized or sublimated into games and competition, it is still a matter of denying one's impotence and decay through violent mastery. If we sanction violence in the name of God, state, necessity, or justice, we may in fact be rationalizing our motives in order to make them acceptable and thereby pursue atrocity lustfully and righteously. As Becker (1975) and Loy (1996, 2008) write, all wars are holy wars because they are fundamentally intended to eradicate competing immortality ideologies that threaten the eternal truth of one's beliefs and vital lies (Becker, 1975, p. 115). They are sacred because conquest obliterates evil, provides immense relief, and gives rise to feelings of transcendence. Or as Hillman (2004) writes, "war is a religious experience. It summons gods of war and death, unfathomable possession, winds, dins. The death, ravagement, and apocalypse are Aries striding the battlefield, maddening men, through a swamp of putrescent corpses" (p. 178ff).

Aggressive impulses and a paranoid potential will always be lurking in the human organism, to varying degrees depending on one's psychological makeup and cultural conditions, but regardless of one's *conscious* valuation of violence (Davis, 2006; Robins & Post, 1997; Volkan, 1988). Subsequently, these impulses can erupt with such passion that an observer might not wonder if the person is a practicing sadist. We all harbor some sadistic feelings, if only they remain for the most part suppressed, repressed, or deflected. Becker (1973, 1975) and Fromm (1964, 1973) explain sadism as the fetishization of immortality striving, the efflorescence of violent energy as a reaction to the fear of death that seeks to vanquish it by torturing or murdering others. In this sense, sadistic impulses are *normal*, since we all need to deny our own creatureliness and weakness. Even in submission to a leader or group, we find power over others a particularly satisfying and tempting solution, though we may not acknowledge or act upon such wishes.

Massive amounts of bloodshed and slaughter have been inflicted in the name of righteous gods, sanctified through ritual and the immense feelings of empowerment, community, and release that such social events generate. As Becker (1973) says, "it is no longer murder: it is holy aggression" (p. 136). People do indeed use their leaders and gods as excuses. As Fenichel (1944) argues, we long to be hypnotized to feel that magical sense of awe and protection (p. 260). Thus the transference mechanisms that deify leaders and focus the community have this unfortunate propensity to isolate difference, seek scapegoats, and invent enemies, for *this is the only means by which the group can survive*. As Volkan (1988, 1997) argues persuasively, we have a need for enemies and allies. Volkan believes that warfare is a means of inflicting internal conflicts on externally fabricated enemies. I would add that in the reenactment of conflicts and the attempt to evacuate pain and hostility on surrogates, the immense terror of death is overcome by inventing and vanquishing foes as loci of evil and danger (cf. Davis, 2006).

It is the very ecstasy of defeating one's mortality and helplessness that perpetuates the search for violence. It is the *erotic* joy in violently eradicating an enemy that enables virtually anybody to become sadistic under conditions where threat is overwhelming and violence is liberated from prohibition.[30] What this means is not only that sociopathic or overcompensating neurotics can be seduced by cruelty but also that almost all of us, under drastic conditions, can be liberated from inhibition and *"kill lavishly out of the sublime joy of heroic triumph over evil"* (Becker, 1975, p. 141). An abyss of insignificance, non-being, vulnerability, and incipient decay is decimated by ecstatically crushing and slaughtering an enemy.

> when a band of warriors passes before me with flowing banners... I feel the indestructible life, the eternal spirit, and the eternal God. (Fichte, quoted in Kohn, 1967, p. 261)

Not everyone succumbs to the ecstatic joy of killing. One can never ignore those who refuse, the soldiers who imposed themselves protectively between ecstatic soldiers and their victims at My Lai (Glover, 1999), or those who would not commit violent acts no matter how banal or sanctioned by authority, ideology, or theology (Arendt, 1963; Milgram, 1974). Individuals diverge vastly in the loving or neglectful cradle of emotional development, in the internalization of loving or malicious parental influences, the efflorescence of trust, industry, and autonomy versus shame, doubt, and inferiority. Individuals are suffused and possessed by vastly different benign or toxic introjects, strata of ego development and defense, flourishing of love, rage, or metastasization of paranoid and persecutory terror and ideation, sadistic or supportive superegos, and autonomously thoughtful or externally dependent consciences (Fromm, 1966). People are terrified to different degrees by separation, independence, and parental punishment or threat, have been nurtured, cherished, traumatized, injured, or psychologically annihilated in infinite ways, make the transition to adulthood with varying degrees of success, and diverge in their joy of individuality or yearning to hurl themselves back into infancy, dependence, obedience, protection, oblivion, and stupefaction. We do not all dread death equally; nor do we crave the same void of soothing illusions, delusions, and deceptions of self and world with theological ornament.[31]

However, it would be naïve to believe that we are simply the happy few who live without the dread of death. Most of us have been molded by some variance of dread, terror, love, and rage, and have some inevitable self-deception that quiets consciousness. Illusions do not necessarily abolish our unconscious dread or our continual predilection to displace terror into myriad unacknowledged cruelties. If we are irrational and possessed by some aspect of madness, if we avoid aspects of reality, deceive ourselves, and have adopted countless stratagems to raze dread from consciousness, how do we ever know for sure whether we are not fooling ourselves? One cannot blithely assume accurate perception, self-awareness, assessment of good and evil, or sanctimonious action. Given the sanguinary nightmare of history, we must seriously consider how disturbingly ubiquitous bloodshed, conquest, violation, and vengeance are perpetrated *enthusiastically*. Thus, this essay maintains that the threat of death too often impels the eroticization of violence and murderous means of transforming helplessness and vulnerability into invulnerable satiation.

CONCLUSIONS

Death is never death plain and simple. As I have attempted to explain, the manifest imagery of death is intricate and overdetermined, elusive, stratified, displaced, and repressed. Thus, the complex nature of death anxiety may be incorporated into further researches by capable scholars, who can determine the specifics of how the imagery and conceptuality of death were formulated, nurtured, and inculcated in a particular culture or individual, how that culture symbolized death, and how it defended itself against the terror of annihilation and decay. In what manner did a people experience trauma, strife, catastrophe, bliss, or conquest such that they would conceive of death in their own way? With what imagery did they deny death and proclaim their eternity, immortality, or aplomb in the face of impending disintegration and putrescence? What was conscious and unconscious about death?

The purpose of this writing was to introduce a set of salient propositions into the extant corpus of psychoanalytic theory. I have argued that the complex fear of death pervades the psychic life of the human organism and is inextricably bound with the matrix of psychopathology, fantasy, and illusion. If indeed we evade and deny death anxiety, even resist awareness of its significance in human motivation, then incorporating this awareness will not only complicate the subject matter of psychoanalysis, anthropology, and history when we analyze a culture or historical phenomenon. It will also complicate the manner in which inquiry is conducted in the first place, if we are excluding death from *our own* cognitive processes. I hope that this essay will influence scholars to incorporate these ideas into their work, as it seems essential to the history of the psyche that death has always lingered as an immanent source of terror and despair.

As for a therapy for coping with death, this essay has attempted to demonstrate the intricate stratagems deployed to avoid awareness of death. There are no techniques that simply eradicate or transcend the fear of death.[32] There are innumerable palliative fantasies that soothe us, deceive us, lie about ourselves or the cosmos, or create a metaphysical alternative to reality where some divine order cares for us and will guide us into paradise after the death of the body. There are any manner of facile solutions that offer meditative bliss, enlightenment, or altered states of consciousness. The problem here is that such solutions do not quell the underlying dread and horror. Some exacerbate pathology by inflating narcissism and escaping the self and its fictions, its ways of acting out, manipulating, and suffering. The terror of being killed, abandoned, consumed, of rotting, of transience, insignificance, and nonexistence may be blotted out by illusions, and that may be the most some people desire. Unfortunately, there are psychological consequences when one opts for soothing lies. The dread reemerges, insinuates itself into one's theology or social relations, inhabits one's relationships, is displaced onto and inflicted on others.

The repressed can return to haunt one, or worse, to terrorize another while the deceived self remains oblivious. It resembles an infection that one tries to ignore and that metastasizes whether or not one ever acknowledges it. This is why Lifton's symbolic immortality is wonderful when it really works but has such potential for destructiveness for so many. It is why even Zen master Dogen's advice not to despise or desire death does not absorb unconscious tremors, and why Becker's solution that we all find the most humane transference illusions also evades the depths of our psychological relation to death. Reinscribing illusions only invites unconsciousness of oneself, one's propensity to succumb to fantasy, and the very infantilism and regression that occlude thought and potentiate violence. It is why easy solutions are only soothing potions, elixirs, or sedatives, why there are no simple answers, instructions, medications, or cures, and why any genuine remedy requires the agonizing struggles of confronting terror, working tortuously through one's attachments, releasing one's metaphysical or theological wishes, or even dispensing with aspects of the defensive ego that seem to obscure the pain and provide solace.

NOTES

This paper recapitulates and expands considerably on materials from *Death and Delusion: A Freudian Analysis of Mortal Terror* (Information Age Publishing, 2004) and my introduction to *The Psychology of Death in Fantasy and History* (Praeger, 2004).

Following many contemporary psychoanalytic authors, I have included in my list of references the initial date of publication in parentheses following the name of the author, while the date of the edition cited in this document appears at the end of the publication details. When I cite book chapters, I have sometimes included two dates at the end. These indicate the original date of publication of the book containing the chapter, followed by the date of the edition cited in the text. Where no date appears at the end, the original edition has been cited.

1. Rank (1924) emphasized the trauma of birth as the primal matrix of the fear of life and death. Debating Rank, Freud (1926) writes of birth as the prototypical experience of anxiety, and numerous researchers today still believe that the trauma of birth affects the emotional life of the individual, even influencing dreams, the

imagination, and the structure of the psyche itself with images and recollections of painful emergence from imprisonment, suffocating engulfment, extrusion, and alienation. There are even those who believe that perinatal experience is recalled in emotional experience and in visions of placental imagery such as mandalas, trees of life, and so forth, which can even make their way into art and film, in the form of images of engulfing pink blobs, gelatinous monsters (Boyd, 2001). For the purposes of this chapter, it is experiences after birth that engender the matrix of terror or aplomb in life.

2. Cf. Buckley (1986, p. 150), Eagle (1984, pp. 27, 45, 68–69, 97, 126–130), and Winnicott (1958).

3. Cf. the differentiation and practicing subphases of individuation in Mahler (1967, 1968, 1979).

4. To paraphrase some of the critical issues outlined by Erikson (1950), especially pp. 48–97 and 247–275.

5. Cf. the oral and anal sadistic stages described by Abraham (1924), or the paranoid-schizoid and depressive positions of Kleinian theory (Klein, 1961, 1975), and the rapprochement subphase of individuation in Mahler's (1979) schema.

6. For more on the processes of splitting object representations and the vicissitudes of infancy, see Eagle (1984, pp. 80–83, 131), Fairbairn (1941, pp. 28–9, 35–6), Freud (1938), Mahler (1968, p. 100), Mitchell & Black (1995, pp. 68, 117–120, 125–129, 135, 174).

7. *Omphalos* literally means "navel" in Greek. It is a white stone ovoid, hemisphere, or pillar that is thought to be a navel, womb, or egg (occasionally a clitoris has been suggested), representing a symbolic world center from which life emanates.

8. Cf. brief references to the relationship between seductive behavior and death in Langs (1997), pp. 5, 59, 133.

9. I provisionally define the emotional investment as "pathological" in terms of how much it derives from psychic wounds, and how conflicted, defensive, fanatical, obsessive, sadistic, annihilating, and/or delusional it is. This is developed with considerably more detail in Piven (2008b).

10. Semiotics is the study of signs, that is, the study of significations of meaning, how language refers to phenomena by attributing meaning.

11. See also Lifton (1973), p. 277.

12. Lifton may be in error when he states that the Japanese word *kami* and the Polynesian term *mana* also express this "spiritual state." *Kami* most often refers to an actual being or state of godhood, not a state of spirituality, while *mana* most often describes the magical and often dangerous power inhering to an object. I believe these concepts are distinct and ought not to be conflated. A spiritual experience and a belief about the workings of the universe are drastically different.

13. cf. Bamyeh (2007) and Wirth (2008b) for discourse on the ways in creativity, culture, and civilization are catalyzed and impelled by death. I cannot help but recall the words of the antagonist in the film *Seven*, who haughtily asserts that his murderous deeds will be pondered and puzzled over by future generations.

14. Claiming that Zen Buddhism is an escape from reality will no doubt arouse the ire of many readers, and for good reason. Zen can be viewed as the realistic recognition that life is suffering and the attempt to transcend attachment and desire. Zen is also far too complicated to be explicated responsibly in this chapter. The point raised in the text, however, is that what is sometimes viewed as a stoic acceptance of reality can sometimes be a rejection accompanied by a regression and return to symbolic symbiosis.

15. I previously referred to "psychic deadness" when describing the deadening of self in response to fears of individuation. Here the deadening is also a defense against innumerable other terrifying aspects of the inner and outer world.

16. See Binion (1993) for a truly disturbing record of such verse, and Davis (2006) for adumbration of the eroticization of death in violence.

17. The term derives from Wilhelm Reich (1933): "on the one hand, it serves as a protection against the stimuli from the outer world, on the other hand against the inner libidinous strivings. The character armor can perform this task because libidinous and sadistic energies are consumed in the neurotic reaction formations, compensations and other neurotic attitudes. In the processes which form and maintain this armor, anxiety is constantly being bound up, in the same way as it is, according to Freud's description, in, say, compulsive symptoms" (p. 44).

18. See especially Becker (1969), pp. 14, 17, 19, 85–87, and Becker (1973), pp. 223, 234–244, as well as Liechty (2008a, b).

19. Becker (1971) describes how one's attachments become pseudopods of the ego more integral to the self-image than one's own body. Thus, one's social status is guarded and coveted with sacred reverence, and a dent in one's Ferrari becomes a paralyzing event threatening emotional breakdown (pp. 33–34). For more on fetishism, and its relation to sadism and masochism, see Becker (1968), pp. 179, 184–185.

20. Or, as Fromm (1955) has termed it, the "pathology of normalcy" (pp. 12–21; Becker, 1971, p. 149, and Becker, 1969, pp. 1–38). See also Gruen (1987) on the "insanity of normality."

21. Cf. Bamyeh (2007), Becker (1973, 1975), Brown (1959), and Roheim, (1943). Reaction-formation usually refers to an attitude unconsciously taken in opposition to the original desire, wish, or impulse. In this case, though, I am using the term to describe attitudes that oppose the original emotion or idea, as Róheim (1943) does below.

22. This is opposed to the traditional psychoanalytic view, which views them as sublimations of libidinal drives. See also Becker (1971): "Modern man is denying his finitude with the same dedication as the ancient Egyptian pharaohs" (p. 149).

23. Though Lifton (1979) sees civilization and monument in terms of continuity, I again make the case that the celebration of life and symbolic immortality differ from massive fanatical attempts to deny death, decay, and insignificance, for which structures such as the Egyptian pyramids were explicitly designed. There is some difference between soothing gratification in a monument and infatuated erection against the humiliation and terror of disappearance.

24. This implies a paradox: though I have just stated that the conscious awareness of death motivates a disgust for that which dies and decays, I have also argued that the terror of death is molded by the tribulations of infancy. Disgust is the result of repression and reaction formations against arousal by things the parents consider forbidden and dirty. The child comes to despise his own weakness and the bodily products his parents tell him are messy. His vulnerability, his inability to protect himself, the humiliating experiences of enuresis, and the anxiety of encopresis and incontinence all motivate fantasies of overcoming the body, messiness, and vulnerability. The body may to some degree be a source of shame, a contemptible thing that must be mastered and transcended. Hence, disgust for the body may engender a disgust for death even *before* the disgust for death in adulthood engenders a disgust for the body.

25. Submersion in a corpse does not merely refer to the sense that one's own body is putrescent but also alludes to immersion in the mother during the fetal stage, the stage in which one is "submerged for 10 months in a corpse, namely, in the mother's womb" (p. 499).

26. For disparate examples of how these splits occur in the history of religion and philosophy, see also Barrett (1958), Beit-Hallahmi (2008), Clack (2008), Liechty (2008b), Phillips (1996), Piven (2004c, 2005, 2006), and Salomon (2008).

27. Becker (1973) points out that people cannot possibly satisfy the need for the dependent to have a pure and perfect transference object, thus they turn to a god, who is beyond immediate fallibility and is therefore beyond reproach. We shall examine the consequences of this below.

28. See Liechty's (2004) thorough adumbration of the relationship between transference, attraction to leaders, and violence.

29. Here the transference recreates not the actual joy but again the hallucinating idealized parent split from all the wickedness he really had, and it is the rage toward the real hostile father that is displaced into the murder of enemies in his name.

30. Violence against others is often accompanied by sexual excitation. Soldiers in Vietnam repeatedly described attaining erections during firefights, so exhilarating was the experience of dominating one's enemies and expiating fear.

31. Consider the ways in which protracted trauma can wreak havoc on the psyche, inculcating a sense of "death in life" that may span psychic deadness, abjection, and even paranoia. As Nadhmi (2006) and Soldz (2006) delineate when describing the ubiquity of death in Iraq, these trauma and disruptions may become part of the psychic architecture itself, ravaging the soul, and destroying its ability to live and love. El Saadawi (1980) writes poignantly of the ways mothers become emotionally deadened as well, as women are brutalized from infancy.

32. For the therapeutic implications regarding the excruciating existential struggle to work through the fear of death (as opposed to resorting to fictive palliatives), see Eigen (1996, 1999), Hurvich (2006), Langs (1997, 2007) and Yalom (1980, 2008).

REFERENCES

Abe, M. (1997). *Zen and comparative studies* (S. Heine, Ed.). Honolulu: University of Hawaii Press.

Abraham, K. (1924). *On character and libido development.* New York: Norton, 1966.

Arendt, H. (1963). *Eichmann in Jerusalem: A report on the banality of evil.* New York: Penguin, 1994.

Ariès, P. (1974). *Western attitudes toward death: From the Middle Ages to the present* (P. M. Ranum, Trans.). Baltimore: Johns Hopkins University Press, 1983.

Bamyeh, M. A. (2007). *Of death and dominion: The existential foundations of governance.* Evanston, Ill: Northwestern.

Barrett, W. (1958). *Irrational man: A study in existentialist philosophy.* New York: Anchor, 1990.

Beauvoir, S. de. (1949). *The second sex* (H. M. Parshley, Trans.). New York: Vintage, 1989.

Becker, E. (1968). *The structure of evil.* New York: Free Press, 1976.

Becker, E. (1969). *Angel in armor.* New York: Free Press, 1975.

Becker, E. (1971). *The birth and death of meaning.* 2nd edition. New York: Free Press.

Becker, E. (1973). *The denial of death.* New York: Free Press, 1975.

Becker, E. (1975). *Escape from evil.* New York: Free Press, 1976.

Beit-Hallahmi, B. (2008, in press). Through signs and wonders: Religious discourse and miracle narratives. In J. H. Ellens (Ed.), *Miracles: God, Science, and Psychology in the Paranormal.* Westport, CT: Praeger.

Binion, R. (1993). *Love beyond death: The anatomy of a myth in the arts.* New York: New York University Press.

Binion, R. (2004). Europe's culture of death. In J. S. Piven (Ed.), *The psychology of death in fantasy and history* (pp. 119–136). Westport, Conn.: Praeger.

Bion, W. (1955). Group dynamics: A re-view. In M. Klein, P. Heimann, & R. E. Money-Kyrle (Eds.), *New directions in psycho-analysis* (pp. 440–477). London: Maresfield, 1977.

Bloch, D. (1978). *"So the witch won't eat me": Fantasy and the child's fear of infanticide.* Boston: Houghton Mifflin.

Bodhi, B. (Trans.) (2000). *The connected discourses of the Buddha: A translation of the Samyutta Nikaya.* Somersville, MA: Wisdom Publications.

Bollas, C. (1987). *The shadow of the object: Psychoanalysis of the unthought known.* New York: Columbia University Press.

Boyd, C. (2001). Uncovering perinatal fantasies in Hollywood films. In J. S. Piven & H. W. Lawton (Eds.), *Psychological undercurrents of history* (pp. 271–288). New York: iUniverse.

Brown, N. O. (1959). *Life against death.* Middletown, Conn.: Wesleyan University Press, 1985.

Buckley, P. (1986). Object relations and the development of the child. In P. Buckley (Ed.), *Essential papers on object relations* (pp. 147–152). New York: New York University Press.

Chasseguet-Smirgel, J. (1975). *The ego ideal: A psychoanalytic essay on the malady of the ideal* (p. Barrows, Trans.). New York: Norton, 1984.

Clack, B. (2008). After Freud: Phantasy and imagination in the philosophy of religion. *Philosophy Compass, 3*(1), 203–221.

Davis, W. A. (2006). *Death's dream kingdom: The American psyche since 9–11.* Ann Arbor, MI: Pluto.

DesPres, T. (1976). *The Survivor.* New York: Oxford.

Dogen (d. 1253). *Shobogenzo* (T. Cleary, Trans.). Honolulu: University of Hawaii Press, 1991.

Donaldson-Pressman, S., & Pressman, R. M. (1994). *The narcissistic family: Diagnosis and treatment.* San Francisco: Jossey-Bass.

Eagle, M. N. (1984). *Recent developments in psychoanalysis.* Cambridge, Mass.: Harvard University Press, 1987.

Eigen, M. (1986). *The psychotic core.* Northvale, N.J.: Jason Aronson, 1993.

Eigen, M. (1996). *Psychic deadness.* Northvale, N.J.: Jason Aronson.

Eigen, M. (1999). *Toxic nourishment.* London: Karnac Books.

El Saadawi, N. (1980). *The hidden face of Eve: Women in the Arab world.* London: Zed Books.

Erikson, E. H. (1950). *Childhood and society.* New York: Norton, 1993.

Fairbairn, W.R.D. (1941). A revised psychopathology of the psychoses and psycho-neuroses. In *Psychoanalytic studies of the personality* (pp. 28–58). New York: Routledge, 1952/1992.

Faure, B. (2003). *The power of denial: Buddhism, purity, and gender.* Princeton, N.J.: Princeton University Press.

Fenichel, O. (1944). Psychoanalytic remarks on Fromm's book *Escape from freedom.* In *The collected papers of Otto Fenichel.* Second Series (pp. 260–277). New York: Norton.

Firestone, R. W. (1994). Psychological defenses against death anxiety. In A. Neimeyer (Ed.), *The death anxiety handbook* (pp. 217–242). Washington, D.C.: Taylor & Francis.

Freud, S. (1886–1939). *The standard edition of the complete works of Sigmund Freud* (J. Strachey, Trans.). London: Hogarth, 1953. Hereafter given as *SE*.

Freud, S. (1905). *Three essays on the theory of sexuality. SE* 7 (pp. 123–243).

Freud, S. (1907). Obsessive acts and religious practices. *SE* 9 (pp. 115–128).

Freud, S. (1912/1913). *Totem and taboo. SE* 13 (pp. 1–161).

Freud, S. (1917). Mourning and melancholia. *SE* 14 (pp. 243–258).

Freud, S. (1926). Inhibitions, symptoms, and anxiety. SE 20 (pp. 77–172).

Freud, S. (1927). *The future of an illusion. SE* 21 (pp. 5–56).

Freud, S. (1930). *Civilization and its discontents. SE* 21 (pp. 64–145).

Freud, S. (1939). *Moses and monotheism. SE* 23 (pp. 7–137).

Fromm, E. (1941). *Escape from freedom.* New York: Rinehart & Company, 1960.

Fromm, E. (1955). *The sane society.* New York: Rinehart & Company.

Fromm, E. (1964). *The heart of man.* New York: Harper & Row, 1980.

Fromm, E. (1966). *You shall be as gods: A radical interpretation of the Old Testament and its tradition.* New York: H. Holt, 1991.

Fromm, E. (1973). *The anatomy of human destructiveness.* New York: Holt, Rinehart and Winston.

Girard, R. (1972). *Violence and the sacred* (p. Gregory, Trans.). Baltimore: Johns Hopkins University Press, 1989.

Glover, J. (1999). *Humanity: A moral history of the twentieth century.* New York: Random House, 2001.

Gruen, A. (1987). *The insanity of normality: Realism as sickness: Toward understanding human destructiveness* (H. & H. Hannum, Trans.). New York: Grove Weidenfeld.

Hallote, R. S. (2001). *Death, burial, and afterlife in the biblical world.* Chicago: Ivan R. Dee.

Hillman, J. (2004). *A terrible love of war.* New York: Penguin.

Hurvich, M. (2006). Psychic trauma, annihilation anxieties and psychodynamic treatment. Retrieved from http://division39.org/sec_com_pdfs/HurvichPSYCHIC TRAUMA.pdf.

Jaques, E. (1955). Social systems as a defense against persecutory and depressive anxiety. In M. Klein, P. Heimann, & R. E. Money-Kyrle (Eds.), *New directions in psycho-analysis* (pp. 478–498). London: Maresfield, 1977.

Jones, E. (1924). Psycho-analysis and anthropology. In *Psycho-myth, psycho-history* (Vol. 2, pp. 114–144). New York: Hillstone, 1974.

Jones, E. (1928). Psycho-analysis and folklore. In *Psycho-myth, psycho-history* (Vol. 2, pp. 1–21). New York: Hillstone, 1974.

Keck, L. E. (1992). Death and afterlife in the New Testament. In H. Obayashi (Ed.), *Death and afterlife: Perspectives of world religions* (pp. 83–96). Westport, Conn.: Praeger.

Klein, M. (1946). Notes on some schizoid mechanisms. In *The writings of Melanie Klein volume III: Envy and gratitude and other works 1946–1963* (pp. 1–24). New York: Free Press, 1975.

Klein, M. (1961). *Narrative of a child analysis: The conduct of the psycho-analysis of children as seen in the treatment of a ten-year-old boy.* Delacorte Press, 1975.

Klein, M. (1975). *The writings of Melanie Klein volume III: Envy and gratitude and other works 1946–1963.* New York: Free Press.

Kline, P. (1984). *Psychology and Freudian theory.* New York: Methuen.

Kohn, H. (1967). *Prelude to nation states: The French and German experience, 1789–1815.* Princeton, N.J.: Nostrand.

Kohut, H. (1971). *The analysis of the self: A systematic approach to the psychoanalytic treatment of narcissistic personality disorders.* New York: International Universities Press.

Kressel, N. J. (2007). *Bad faith: The danger of religious extremism.* Amherst, NY: Prometheus.

Kristeva, J. (1987). *Black sun: Depression and melancholia* (L. S. Roudiez, Trans.). New York: Columbia University Press.

La Barre, W. (1970). *The ghost dance: Origins of religion.* New York: Dell, 1972.

La Barre, W. (1980). *Culture in context.* 2nd edition. New York: Psyche Press, 1994.

La Barre, W. (1991). *Shadow of childhood: Neoteny and the biology of religion.* Norman: University of Oklahoma Press.

Langs, R. (1997). *Death anxiety and clinical practice.* London: Karnac Books.

Langs, R. (2007). *Beyond Jesus and Yahweh: Bringing death's wisdom to faith, spirituality and psychoanalysis.* Northvale, NJ: Jason Aronson.

Lasch, C. (1978). *The culture of narcissism.* New York: Norton, 1979.

Lederer, W. (1968). *The fear of women.* New York: Harcourt.

Leifer, R. (1997). *The happiness project.* Ithaca, NY: Snow Lion.

Libbey, M. (2007). On narcissistic mortification. Paper presented at the Shame Symposium, March 2006, sponsored by the C3PO, the Committee of Psychoanalytic and Psychotherapeutic Publications and Organizations. Retrieved from: http://internationalpsychoanalysis.net/wp-content/uploads/2007/07/libbey paper.pdf.

Liechty, D. (1995). *Transference and transcendence: Ernest Becker's contribution to psychotherapy.* Northvale, N.J.: Jason Aronson.

Liechty, D. (2008a, in press). Terror and transference. In J. S. Piven, C. Boyd, & H. W. Lawton (Eds.), *Terrorism, jihad, and sacred vengeance.* 2nd edition. Giessen, Germany, GER: Psychosozial-Verlag.

Liechty, D. (2008b, forthcoming). Mortality, denial and truth: Diffusing the rancor in conflicting cultural worldviews. In J. Piven (Ed.), *Death, religion, and evil.* Giessen, GER: Psychosozial-Verlag.

Lifton, R. J. (1970). On psychohistory. In R. J. Lifton (Ed.), *Explorations in psychohistory* (pp. 21–41). New York: Simon & Schuster, 1974.

Lifton, R. J. (1973). The sense of immortality. On death and the continuity of life. In R. J. Lifton (Ed.), *Explorations in psychohistory* (pp. 271–287). New York: Simon & Schuster, 1974.

Lifton, R. J. (1979). *The broken connection.* Washington, D.C.: American Psychiatric Press, 1996.

Lipman-Blumen, J. (2006). *The allure of toxic leaders: Why we follow destructive bosses and corrupt politicians—and how we can survive them.* New York: Oxford.

Loy, D. R. (1996). *Lack and transcendence: The problem of death and life in psychotherapy, existentialism, and Buddhism.* Atlantic Highlands, N.J.: Humanities Press.

Loy, D. R. (2008, in press). On the nonduality of good and evil: Buddhist reflections on the new Holy War. In J. S. Piven, C. Boyd, & H. W. Lawton (Eds.), *Terrorism, jihad, and sacred vengeance.* 2nd edition. Giessen: Psychosozial-Verlag.

Mahler, M. (1967). On human symbiosis and the vicissitudes of individuation. In *Separation-individuation* (pp. 77–98). Northvale, N.J.: Jason Aronson, 1979/1994.

Mahler, M. (1968). Observations on adaptation and defense *in statu nascendi*. In *Separation-individuation* (pp. 99–118). Northvale, N.J.: Jason Aronson, 1979/1994.

Mahler, M. (1979). *Separation-individuation*. Northvale, N.J.: Jason Aronson, 1994.

Maltsberger, J. T. & Buie, D. H. Jr. (1980). The devices of suicide: Revenge, riddance, and rebirth. In J. T. Maltsberger & M. J. Goldblatt (Eds.), *Essential papers on suicide* (pp. 397–417). New York: New York University Press.

Mazlish, B. (1990). *The leader, the led, and the psyche*. Hanover, N.H.: Wesleyan University Press.

Mendenhall, G. E. (1992). From witchcraft to justice: Death and afterlife in the Old Testament. In H. Obayashi (Ed.), *Death and afterlife: Perspectives of world religions* (pp. 67–82). Westport, Conn.: Praeger.

Milgram, S. (1974). *Obedience to authority*. New York: Harper Colophon, 1975.

Mitchell, S. A., & Black, M. J. (1995). *Freud and beyond: A history of modern psychoanalytic thought*. New York: Basic Books.

Montaigne, M. E. de. (1580–1595). *Essays* (Vols. 1–3) (G. B. Ives, Trans.). New York: Heritage, 1946.

Nadhmi, F.K.O. (2006). University professors in Iraq and death anxiety. Retrieved from: http://www.brusselstribunal.org/DeathAnxiety.htm.

Nishitani, K. (1982). *Religion and nothingness* (J. Van Bragt, Trans.). Berkeley: University of California Press, 1983.

Ogden, T. H. (1989). *The primitive edge of experience*. Northvale, N.J.: Jason Aronson, 1992.

Pearce, J., & Newton, S. (1963). *The conditions of human growth*. Secaucus, N.J. Citadel Press, 1980.

Perrulli, R. (2005). The fear of death and narcissism. *Graduate Philosophy Bulletin, 3*(1), 43–77. Also appears in J. Piven (Ed.), *Death, religion, and evil*. Giessen, GER: Psychosozial-Verlag, forthcoming.

Phillips, A. (1996). *Terrors and experts*. Cambridge, Mass.: Harvard University Press.

Piven, J. S. (2003). Buddhism, death, and the feminine. *Psychoanalytic Review, 90*(4), 498–536.

Piven, J. S. (2004a). *Death and delusion: A Freudian analysis of mortal terror*. Greenwich, CT: Information Age Publishing.

Piven, J. S. (2004b). *The madness and perversion of Yukio Mishima*. Westport, CT: Praeger.

Piven, J. S. (Ed.). (2004c). *The psychology of death in fantasy and history*. Westport, CT: Praeger.

Piven, J. S. (2005). Birth, death, dread, and religion, *Psychoanalysis and Contemporary Thought, 26*(3), 387–412.

Piven, J. S. (2006). Narcissism, sexuality, and psyche in terrorist theology. *The Psychoanalytic Review, 93*(2), 231–265.

Piven, J. S. (2007a). Aum shinrikyo, arukushikabane, seijoutoiukoto (Aum Shinrikyo, the walking dead, and normality). In J. S. Piven and Yuko Katsuta, Nihon no kyoki (Japanese madness) (pp. 77–126). Tokyo: Nihon Hyoronsha.

Piven, J. S. (2007b). Terror, sexual arousal, and torture: The question of obedience or ecstasy among perpetrators. *The Discourse of Sociological Practice, 8*(1), 1–22.

Piven, J. S. (2008a, in press). Terrorist theology and hallucination. In J. S. Piven, C. Boyd, & H. W. Lawton (Eds.), *Terrorism, jihad, and sacred vengeance.* 2nd edition. Giessen: Psychosozial-Verlag.

Piven, J. S. (2008b). Psychological, theological, and thanatological aspects of suicidal terrorism. *Case Western Reserve University Journal of International Law, 39*(3), 731–758.

Plato (c. 360 B.C.E.). *Phaedo* (R. Hackforth, Trans.). New York: Cambridge University Press, 1972.

Plato (,. 380 B.C.E.). *Gorgias* (R. Waterfield, Trans.). Cambridge, Mass.: Oxford University Press, 1998.

Rank, O. (1909) The myth of the birth of the hero. In O. Rank, Baron Raglan, & A. Dundes, *In quest of the hero* (pp. 3–86). Princeton, N.J.: Princeton University Press, 1990.

Rank, O. (1924). *The trauma of birth.* New York: Dover, 1929/1993.

Reich, W. (1933). *Character analysis* (T. P. Wolfe, Trans.). London: Vision, 1976.

Rheingold, J. C. (1967). *The mother, anxiety, and death.* Boston: Little, Brown and Company.

Ricoeur, P. (1970). *Freud and philosophy* (D. Savage, Trans.). New Haven, Conn.: Yale University Press.

Robins, R. S., & Post, J. M. (1997). *Political paranoia: The psychopolitics of hatred.* New Haven, Conn.: Yale University Press.

Róheim, G. (1943). *The origin and function of culture.* New York: Anchor, 1971.

Róheim, G. (1945). *The eternal ones of the dream.* New York: International Universities Press, 1971.

Salomon, E. (2008, forthcoming). The splintered self: The illusory nature of reality. In J. Piven (Ed.), *Death, religion, and evil.* Giessen, GER: Psychosozial-Verlag.

Schumaker, J. F. (1995). *The corruption of reality.* Amherst, N.Y.: Prometheus.

Segal, J. (1985). *Phantasy in everyday life: A psychoanalytical approach to understanding ourselves.* Northvale, N.J.: Jason Aronson, 1995.

Shafer, R. (1968). *Aspects of internalization.* Madison, Conn.: International Universities Press, 1990.

Shakespeare, W. (1601). *Hamlet.* New York: Cambridge University Press, 1990.

Soldz, S. (2006). Death in life in Iraq. Retrieved from: http://www.brusselstribunal.org/DeathAnxiety.htm.

Stein, H. F. (1994). *The dream of culture.* New York: Psyche Press.

Stein, R. (2008, in press). Evil as love and as liberation: The mind of a suicidal religious terrorist. In J. S. Piven, C. Boyd, & H. W. Lawton (Eds.), *Terrorism, jihad, and sacred vengeance.* 2nd edition. Giessen: Psychosozial-Verlag.

Tillich, P. (1951). *Systematic theology* (Vol. 1). Chicago: University of Chicago Press.

Tolstoy, L. (1879). *Confession* (D. Patterson, Trans.). New York: Norton, 1884/1993.

Volkan, V. D. (1988). *The need to have enemies and allies.* Northvale, N.J.: Jason Aronson.

Volkan, V. D. (1997). *Blood lines: From ethnic pride to ethnic terrorism.* New York: Farrar, Straus & Giroux.

Wahl, C. W. (1957). Suicide as a magical act. *Bulletin of the Menninger Clinic, 21,* 91–98.

Wahl, C. W. (1958). The fear of death. In H. Feifel (Ed.), *The Meaning of death* (pp. 16–29). New York: McGraw-Hill, 1959/1965.

Winnicott, D. W. (1953). Transitional objects and transitional phenomena. In *Playing and reality* (pp. 1–25). New York: Routledge, 1971/1994.

Winnicott, D. W. (1958). *Through paediatrics to psycho-analysis.* New York: Basic Books, 1975.

Wirth, H.-J. (2008a, in press). Thoughts for the times on terrorism, war, and death. In J. S. Piven, C. Boyd, & H. W. Lawton (Eds.), *Terrorism, jihad, and sacred vengeance.* 2nd edition. Giessen: Psychosozial-Verlag.

Wirth, H.-J. (2008b, forthcoming). Creativity and death in psychoanalysis. In J. Piven (Ed.), *Death, religion, and evil.* Giessen, GER: Psychosozial-Verlag.

Wolman, B. B. (1973). *Call no man normal.* New York: International Universities Press.

Yalom, I. D. (1980). *Existential psychotherapy.* New York: Basic Books.

Yalom, I. D. (2008). *Staring at the sun: Overcoming the fear of death.* San Francisco: Jossey-Bass.

Zilboorg, G. (1943). The fear of death. *Psychoanalytic Quarterly, 12,* 465–474.

CHAPTER 8

When the Time Is Ripe for Acceptance: Dying, with a Small "d"

Thomas A. Caffrey

"We're going to have to tell people [I'm dying], you know."
"There's no appropriate etiquette for this."
—Michael Keaton and Nicole Kidman in *My Life*

Yearly anniversaries celebrate birth. Bar mitzvahs, sweet-16 parties, driver's licenses, and high school graduations celebrate budding maturity. Marriages, wedding receptions, and wedding anniversaries document and celebrate mature love and the birth of family units. Retirement marks the completion of a life's work or career. And funerals, in their diverse ways, recognize death.

But what trumpet call, or marker, alerts us to the beginning of our end? How do we celebrate the start of the two weeks, or five years, that lead up to our momentary demise? What universally recognized markers do we have, if any, to signal our entrance into the final phase of our lives? Signing a DNR (do not resuscitate) order, entering a hospice, or formally and publicly putting our affairs in order constitute such markers. Few of us take these steps, however, and, as discussed later, when we do, it is so late in our dying process that we leave little or no ground for the process to bear its natural fruit.

At first glance, disregarding the beginning of our end makes supreme sense. We prefer life to death. We therefore prefer to spend as little of our lives as possible consciously heading toward death. But this depiction of the dying process does not reflect a full view. It depicts a view born of fear and denial. Fearful of death as we tend to be, we do all we can to deny its relevance to ourselves. We think fleetingly about it, rather than squarely and soberly. By avoiding thinking and talking about death, we invest it, and every-thing related to it, with a greater power and emotional salience than these realities in fact possess.

For instance, we immediately frame the dying process as an event *about death*. That is, because of our avoidance of thoughts about death, death springs up as the salient backdrop to our thoughts about the dying process. However, as documented 40 years ago in Kübler-Ross's basic study (1969), when the dying subjects of her seminars became engaged in conscious, dialogic thinking about their dying, it was their *lives*—and the "unfinished business" thereof—that they spoke about. The physicians working with Kübler-Ross were repeatedly surprised to find how little the patients spoke about death in their reflections about their dying, and how much they spoke about their lives. As these patients' reflections and dialogues exemplified, thinking about and talking about dying changes the salience of death and life. Life rises in salience, and the dying pro-cess, rather than being locked in a definition dominated by death, comes to be seen and felt as a crucial phase of one's life. Thus even during the 1960s, while the subject of death was still "tabooed territory" (Feifel, 1959), when squarely encountered and sufficiently reflected upon, the topic helped individuals weave their closing days into the fabric of their entire lives.

THE RECENT STATE OF DYING IN THE UNITED STATES

But in spite of the worldwide popularity of Kübler-Ross's work, for the 25 years that followed, and in spite of the AIDS epidemic, spikes in violent crime, and the assisted suicide movement, most of us continued to be reluc-tant to think and talk about dying—or anything else that suggested death. As a result, we compressed the dying phase of life so severely that we effec-tively squeezed it out of existence. In the early 1990s, well after Kübler-Ross's world-shaking effort to heighten our appreciation of the dying process, our contraction of that process persisted. This elision of dying was revealed (un-intentionally) in the course of the most ambitious and expensive study ever conducted of the way we Americans die. The study—of thousands of dying hospital patients—was funded by the Robert Wood Johnson Foundation, and was called SUPPORT.

> The [4,301] SUPPORT patients [of Phase I] were all seriously ill, and their dying proved to be predictable, yet discussions and decisions sub-stantially in advance of death were uncommon. (SUPPORT Principal Investigators, 1995)

This handful of words summarized the findings of Phase I of SUPPORT ("The Study to Understand Prognoses and Preferences for Outcomes and

Risks of Treatments"). Disappointingly, the same words came to characterize the findings of Phase II as well, the study's intervention phase. As such,
the words probably came closer to describing the level of consciousness that
accompanied death in the United States 15 years ago than any other observation or speculation. That is, in general, "Discussions and decisions substantially in advance of death [were] uncommon" for us in this country, even
when we were seriously ill and when our dying was predictable.

In their $30 million study of a total of 9,105 hospitalized adults in the
advanced stages of life-threatening diseases, the SUPPORT investigators
initially learned that in spite of the relevant life-and-death information the
project made available, discussions about life and death were uncommon, and
decisions that affected the final period of life were seldom made. Moreover,
in the project's second phase—its sophisticated effort to improve this state
of affairs—the investigators learned that even a carefully planned and executed multimillion-dollar intervention could not significantly change the
prevailing level of life-and-death consciousness (or other targeted conditions
of death) for the patients involved in the study. The intervention group of
2,652 patients—just like the control group of 2,152, and the whole Phase I
group of 4,301—continued to die with DNRs written two days before death,
after eight days in an intensive care unit (ICU), and often in significant pain.
That is, the costly and professionally implemented procedures that were designed to make changes in these circumstances resulted in no measurable
improvements.

Thus, our way of dying in America proved more intractable, or "established," than the investigators initially expected or hoped—and surely more
intractable than Kübler-Ross enthusiasts of the mid-1970s would have predicted. Moreover, the SUPPORT study also revealed that the bulk of the control as well as experimental patients in its intervention phase (68% and 69%
respectively) rated their medical care as excellent or very good. "Business as
usual" never sounded so sure. People were content as things were. In spite of
the common belief that the sharing of relevant information, increased communication with one's physician about end-of-life wishes, and relevant decision
making by patient as well as physician will lead to an improved quality of life in
the final months of life, the SUPPORT study showed that providing these
purported benefits to large numbers of patients did little or nothing to change
the targeted circumstances of their final days. This result threw into question
the belief that making available life-and-death information and doctor-patient
communication improves the dying person's final days.

COMMENTARIES

Many essays and studies followed the SUPPORT project. They elucidated ways in which the project's findings can be used. They questioned the

assumptions that led to the project. They sought further details about the project's intervention. And they suggested alternate emphases for future projects aimed at ameliorating the lives of dying persons. Lynn, a member of the project's steering committee, focused on the apparent widespread passivity among the project's patients (1997). For instance, of the patients who did not speak with their physicians about resuscitation, 58% would prefer not to, even if given the opportunity. Further, almost all the patients preferred that family and doctors make resuscitation decisions in their stead. Lynn found that patients and family members often claimed they needed to know what to do at a given time. She came to conclude that in their confusion and reluctance to make wrong decisions, such persons were not seeking a better way to proceed so much as to learn how most people would act under their circumstances. If this is true, she said, our illusion that we are making decisions, and thus are to some extent controlling our actions, becomes no more than a ritual by which we move through acceptable procedures.

Callahan (1995) criticized the project's underlying belief that people are clear in advance about what they want, or that clear yes/no decisions present themselves to them. He goes on to say that the results of the SUPPORT project indicate that improving the dying process will be complicated and difficult. Nodding to the enthusiastic 1970s, he asserts that after a quarter century we have finally got the point. He concludes with a call for total change.

In a further reflection, Lynn (1997) highlighted the widespread denial that dying makes up an important part of patients' lives. This denial occurs at the institutional level, as well as at that of the individual patient. Lynn noted that hospitals and other institutions can follow their own routine procedures, without consulting the patient, even when the patient's wishes have been formally declared.

This recent observation is consistent with earlier findings that a hospital's mission and culture are incompatible with the dying patients in its care. Kübler-Ross noted that "Hospitals are institutions committed to the healing process, and dying patients are a threat to that defined role" (1975, 7). In a more prescriptive vein, Mauksch (1975) asserted:

> Our hospitals and our health professions have built super highways of medical technology in which the patients' diseases and their organs loom large and where we focus with efficient specificity upon the disease process which we seek to cure. Patient care, however, writes its own script and the dying patient is but one extreme example of the time when the professional challenge demands that we abandon the comfortable road of predictable mileage and dare to venture into the narrow byways which adapt themselves to the individuality of the real world—in this case to the specific needs and human processes of the patient who has entrusted himself to the care of people who could most effectively use themselves as the instruments of help and of hope. (23–24)

For her part, Lynn (1997) advocated for institutional policy changes that would incorporate thoroughgoing anticipatory planning, planning that would include steps to be taken when complications occur that are serious but predictable. She found that institutions now lack such planning—in spite of the complications occurring predictably and daily.

At the level of *individual* denial, Lynn noted that the problem was not so much that physicians did not always hear their patients' requests. It was that no one—administrators, physicians, other staff, family, and patients themselves—was talking about these matters. This includes whether a cure is possible, what it means if a cure is not possible, what measures should be taken in the event of imminent serious complications, whether a DNR should be signed, and whether the ICU should be used. In a recent work, Wanzer and Glenmullen (2007) argue for focusing intently on the very subjects the SUPPORT staff, family, and patients did not talk about: the extent to which a cure is possible; the severity of the interventions still available to attempt the cure; the alternative(s) to making the intervention(s); the patient's and family's wishes; and the promulgation of those wishes, in detail, to professional staff. They also provide repeated instances of Wanzer himself, as physician, investing the time and energy needed to help patients and their loved ones clarify the reality of their medical circumstances to such a point that they can accept that reality and make decisions consistent with it. By contrast, Lynn noted, staff and others typically engage in an all-out effort, with all medical equipment and personnel at the ready, until it becomes 100% certain that the patient not only cannot be cured but has entered upon a definitively downward course.

Lo (*End of Life*, 1995) offers a graphic example of one such full-court press. A 56-year-old smoker with chronic obstructive pulmonary disease developed pneumonia and respiratory failure and was placed on mechanical ventilation. He died two weeks later, after a stormy ICU course complicated by gastrointestinal bleeding and septic shock. The next morning, the ICU team questioned how such a series of events occurred. Although each intervention could be justified as a response to a treatable complication, did the team truly consider the patient's overall prognosis or determine whether he really wanted such aggressive care?

In a separate reflection, Lo (*Improving Care*, 1995) suggested that the SUPPORT project did not go far enough in providing such patients with prognostic information and with input from their physicians about the nature of life-sustaining care, aggressive or otherwise. He noted that when enough energy and time are invested, physicians and patients, or their families, invariably come to an agreement over the appropriateness of life-sustaining measures. But, he pointed out, these discussions can take hours per day, over a period of weeks. Sounding much like Kübler-Ross's physicians' extensive contacts with the dying subjects of her seminars, such time commitments, foreign as they are to hospitals' currently defined objectives, would strain the institutions' resources, as they would those of modern medical practices of all kinds. To use Callahan's (1995) terminology, only a revolution in medical and hospital practice could fold the ingredient of adequate discussion of end of-life issues into the routine procedures of medical treatment. Thus, when the required time, energy, and institutional support are provided, as in the Kübler-Ross project and in Wanzer's practice, the conscious encounter with death bears fruit. Where these supports are compromised, as suggested by Lynn's and Lo's comments about the SUPPORT project's shortcomings, the intervention yields ambiguous results.

A NEW STAGE OF LIFE

When the choice is presented as between being "among the living" or "about to die," those who, like Lo's example, suffer serious, incurable, and eventually fatal illnesses surface as straddling some middle ground. Though these persons are not about to die, they are not among the living, either, in the same way as a healthy 25-year-old is. They inhabit a mysteriously transitional stage of life, where a heightened awareness of (future) death necessarily thrusts itself upon them, and where the whole (past) stretch of their lives also presents itself. Thus there is an advanced stage of our lives that bristles with an ambiguity that we have never named and that most of us will go through for differing lengths of time. To ease the either-or trap marked by comments like "I'll beat this thing" (that is, I'm going to stay among the living) on the one hand, and "Why, I was just talking to her yesterday!" (she suddenly and inexplicably died) on the other, we need to acknowledge, or better, define, "carve out," and name the stage of living-and-dying that precedes the about-to-die stage of our life. This pre-final stage of life might be called "dying, with a small 'd,'" or, for short, "small-d-dying."

It may be true that such a phase of life can be detected. It may also be true that we all ought to become more aware of this phase, even talk and think about it, and eventually integrate it into our lives. It may even be true that our lives are significantly poorer for our obstinate contraction of this phase of our lives into a sliver of its proper self. All this may be supremely true. True as it may be, Americans' dying behavior during the 25 years following Kübler-Ross's purportedly influential work, as documented in the SUPPORT project, remained deeply impervious to her calls for heightened consciousness of the finiteness of our lives. It appears, therefore, that this truth has remained confined to articles, books, classrooms, words, ideas, and theories. Though emerging in these venues and, more practically, in the lives of patients fortunate enough to receive adequate end-of-life care, the truth has somehow failed to find its way into the mainstream of our everyday thinking and practices. It is not yet a phase of life we plan on entering one day, much less look forward to entering upon. It is not something we allude to in our conversations with seriously ill family or friends. In short, the revolution remains mostly at the theoretical stage.

ART AND MEDICAL LEADERSHIP: A CHANGE IN THINKING

The worlds of literature, theater, dance, film, and music—happily divorced as they are from our worlds of life and death—offer models for the kind of life we can envision during this small-d-dying stage. The denouement, or "outcome" (*Merriam Webster Collegiate Dictionary*, 1995), of a novel, play, or film embodies infinitely more than the word "End" found on a work's last page or frame. The neutral word "outcome" suggests a richness of findings—of good, of bad, and of pleasant surprises. The more literal "unraveling" suggests relaxation, clarification, and again, surprise. Denouement, outcome, unraveling—each connotes promising possibilities for our much-avoided small-d-dying process. Other expressions, like "finishing up," "taking care of business," "wrapping up," "catching one's breath," "slowing down," "taking a breather," "pausing," "resting," "looking around," "taking stock," "settling accounts," and "winding down," also carry individually distinctive meanings and suggestions that add to the richness of this phase of life.

Taking a cue from the beginning, middle, and *end* that make up plays, films, and novels, medical leaders could immediately initiate a practice of reviewing patients' overall conditions with an eye toward unifying treatment, or modulating the splintering of treatment caused by the specialists' focus on individual systems. The means to achieve such a counterbalance to excessive specialization are already in place: patients are assigned to a specific physician when admitted to a hospital; primary care physicians tend to coordinate outpatient treatment; a single chart reflects diverse caretakers' observations. But how often does a treatment unification agent advocate for reduced physical treatment on all fronts because of a patient's overall, unsalvageable, dying condition? It does happen. But the SUPPORT data indicate that it happens far too infrequently.

What rewards are there to encourage a medical overseer to step in and direct colleagues to refrain from further intervention? What segment of the public is asking medical professionals to assume this role? Medical leaders could initiate this kind of practice. It could probably be initiated without much delay in settings that house an active ethics committee, in which the committee includes medical personnel with high standing in the hospital, and in which these medical personnel would be willing to assume, or train others to assume, this kind of role. Some institutions may have already implemented this practice. In others, such an end-of-life ombudsperson would serve as an immediate constraint on the kind of treatment excesses that reduce the end of a person's life to physiological struggles.

But the question of rewards, and public demand, for this kind of intervention remains. What might it take, for instance, for such an initiative to be moved from a hospital's ethics committee to the office of the institution's medical director? The latter office could then integrate into hospital-wide staff development an alertness to patients' *overall* condition, to conditions for reducing physiological interventions, and to conditions for increasing family, counseling, chaplain's, or other social interventions. But for this kind of routine practice to find itself at the center of our medical practices and institutions, a thoroughgoing rehabilitation of our thinking about life and death will be necessary. Only then will we call upon our medical leaders to help us detect that juncture in our lives when we and our families might reasonably agree that further physiological intervention would constitute an excess, and that we could more profitably—without the distraction of physiological efforts—turn toward the matter of "taking stock," "catching our breath," or "finishing up."

WHY YIELD?

But why should we change our thinking? Why should we yield to the reality of impending death and reject excessive treatment? We should not do this primarily to emulate artistic productions. We should do it, I feel, because others have done it before us and by doing so have benefited inestimably. Imara (1975) described how an embittered, hardened, and ruthless businesswoman of 68 was extremely difficult to deal with while being treated for a terminal disease. After meeting regularly with Imara, the hospital's chaplain, and serving as a subject in Kübler-Ross's seminar on death, this woman changed into a person with a "quiet voice" who spoke "thoughtfully" about pain and about regrets from her past. In the presence of the seminar, she stated:

> I have lived more in the past three months [of the meetings] than I have during my whole life. I wish I knew forty years ago what I do now about living. I have friends. Thank you.

Caffrey (2000) described how a patient, a provocative and verbally aggressive, HIV-positive ex-prisoner, suffered from a seriously weakened heart, drug addiction, and periodic heart attacks that left him too weak even to undergo heart valve replacement. Like his mother before him, the patient heard within himself the "whisper of death," knew he would be dying before long, and used his psychotherapy to speak of this and of matters he wanted to attend to. Subsequent weeks, and the discovery in his psychotherapy of the roots of the posttraumatic stress disorder that caused his drug addiction, led to a softening in his relationships with family and friends, the cessation of his drug use, a return to an active spiritual life, and refraining from murdering his sister (something he would have done when he learned she stole his Social Security check). These changes occurred after the patient learned he was HIV-positive and would die soon from his weakened heart.

Richman (1993) described the improvement in a suicidal member of his ground-breaking group for depressed and suicidal elderly persons. The 78-year-old man had multiple medical problems and had been walking around with a suicide note in his breast pocket. Once in the group, he was "sometimes drunk, usually difficult, and persistently suicidal." Yet he had a sense of humor, and he invited one group member who argued with her brother to argue with him so that he could "get into a big temper and feel better." After eloquently presenting the reasons why another suicidal member should live, he added, "This does not apply to me." Eventually, after telling Richman he had opened a window and almost jumped, he burst into convulsive sobs. He began to improve, and became "significantly less suicidal, more socially active, less depressed" (143).

Consciously integrating our death's proximity into our lives can give our lives, past as well as present, greater definition and clarity than they ever had before. Such lucidity admits of otherwise impossible actions. No one questions the role that the impending death of the *New Testament's* good thief played in the man's conversion from crime to righteousness. Could Tom Dooley's Vietnam clinics ever have been founded without his cancer diagnosis? Even the Pope has a body, and, by suffering in it, he can show us how to live in a new way. Neuhaus (2002) described Pope John XXIII's final sufferings—which he dedicated to a separate intention each day (prisoners, the unborn, the hungry)—as efficiently productive, as the work of a craftsman making use of everything at his disposal.

THE FUTURE

What markers might emerge to signal the start of the important final phase of each of our lives? Significant *pre*-markers are already in place: the widespread acceptance of hospice care; geriatric medicine's systematically restrained treatment; the growth of gerontological psychology; and, as noted earlier, the acceptance among diverse academicians of the need for improved end-of-life practices. But in addition to hospice admission, publicly putting our affairs in order—as Carl Jung reportedly did a year before his death (Keleman, 1974)—or signing a DNR, what kind of clarion call might each of us sound to announce the beginning of the final segment of our lives? "Each of us," because a culturally supported practice of this kind—still widely resisted at the time of the SUPPORT study—will develop gradually, and largely as a result of our individual, diverse expressions to one another of our awareness and acceptance of the reality of our own impending deaths. Countless influences, some less obvious than others, stand at the ready to assist us in this enterprise: works of art, scientific findings, religious convictions, the family, the inspiration of others, and sensitive professionals. Living among these influences and within the unique course of our individual lives, each of us will arrive at the threshold of our life's last stretch. At that juncture, as we acknowledge, yield to, and accept the future, we can in some fashion—perhaps with a sigh, perhaps with an e-mail message—proclaim the start of the final phase of our life. As with the squeal of the newborn, our proclamation, whatever form it takes, will signal that something noteworthy is getting underway.

REFERENCES

Caffrey, Thomas. "The Whisper of Death: Psychotherapy with a Dying Vietnam Veteran." *American Journal of Psychotherapy*, 54, no. 4 (Fall 2000): 519–530.

Callahan, Daniel. "Once Again, Reality: The Lessons of the SUPPORT Study." Special Supplement, *Hastings Center Report* 25, no. 6 (1995): S33–36.

Feifel, Herman (Ed.). *The Meaning of Death*. New York: McGraw Hill, 1959.

Imara, Mwalimu. "Dying as the Last Stage of Growth." In Elisabeth Kübler-Ross, *Death: The Final Stage of Growth*. Englewood Cliffs, N.J.: Prentice-Hall, 1975, pp. 147–163.

Keleman, Stanley. *Living Your Dying*. Berkeley, Calif.: Center Press, 1974.

Kübler-Ross, Elisabeth. *On Death and Dying*. New York: Touchstone, 1969.

Kübler-Ross, Elisabeth. *Death: The Final Stage of Growth*. Englewood Cliffs, N.J.: Prentice-Hall, 1975.

Lo, Bernard. "End of Life Care after Termination of SUPPORT." Special Supplement, *Hastings Center Report* 25, no. 6 (1995): S6–S8.

Lo, Bernard, "Improving Care near the End of Life. Why Is It So Hard?" *Journal of the American Medical Association*, 274, no. 20 (1995): 1634–1636.

Lynn, Joanne. "Program on the Care of Chronically Ill Hospitalized Adults (SUPPORT)." Chapter 8 in Robert Wood Johnson Foundations, *Anthology*. San Francisco: Jossey-Bass, 1997.

Mauksch, Hans, "The Organizational Context of Dying." In Elisabeth Kübler-Ross, *Death: The Final Stage of Growth*. Englewood Cliffs, N.J.: Prentice-Hall, 1975, pp. 23–24.

Merriam Webster Collegiate Dictionary Tenth Edition. Springfield, Mass.: Merriam-Webster, 1995.

Neuhaus, Richard. *As I Lay Dying*. New York: Basic Books, 2002.

Richman, Joseph. *Preventing Elderly Suicide*. New York: Springer, 1993.

SUPPORT Principal Investigators, "A Controlled Trial to Improve Care for Seriously Ill Hospitalized Patients." *Journal of the American Medical Association*, 274, no. 20 (1995): 1591–1598.

Wanzer, Sidney, and Glenmullen, Joseph. *To Die Well*. Philadelphia: Da Capo Press, 2007.

CHAPTER 9

ALIVE AND CONTENT: THE ART OF LIVING WITH MORTALITY AWARENESS

Michael K. Bartalos

There is no death in mortal things and no end in ruinous death. There is only mingling and interchange of parts, and it is this we call "Nature."
—Empedocles

Dying is "ubiquitous and ultimately inescapable" wrote Richard G. Dumond and Dennis C. Foss in the introduction to their slim but intellectually weighty volume *The American View of Death: Acceptance or Denial* (1972, p.1). At around the same time appeared the late Ernest Becker's book, *The Denial of Death* (1973, 1997), that, along with his subsequent writings justly gained many adherents. His earnestness struck sympathetic chords in many as they reflected the "blind alley" outlook of late twentieth century Western intellectuals. In the twentieth century, Ernest Becker and his contemporaries witnessed with incredulous desperation the manifestation of power-lust and indifference to human suffering played out on a gigantic scale by their statesmen, who had easy access to the latest advances in technology for their ill-conceived deeds. Thus it is not surprising that Becker accepts the gloomy view of human existence held by the twentieth century's most acclaimed philosophers. He accepts the view that human existence is full with sorrows and sufferings, and that "Creation is a nightmare spectacular taking place on a planet that has been soaked for hundreds of millions of years in the blood of all its creatures" (283); that human beings must die too and when they do, they go "the way of the grasshopper," that is, becoming fodder for worms (26). Becker shares the existential philosophers' tenet that man's life is tragic, and he sides with those who maintain that human beings' consciousness of their eventual dying and their knowledge that everything they do and create is—presumably—devoid of lasting value are the most important sources of human anguish and despair.

Becker's acceptance of the basic stance of the existentialists, however, does not prevent him from differing on subordinate issues. While the existentialists, in general, recommend the cultivation of a deliberate, intense, and persistent surface consciousness of our mortality, Becker's efforts are directed toward accepting mortality and then eliminating or blunting its noxious influence by transference. Becker recommends submission, a form of transference, to a higher mysterious power, "to project one's problem onto a god-figure, to be healed by an all-embracing and all-justifying beyond" (1997, 285), to adapt a childlike trust and hope for the human condition and leave open the realm of mystery (204). In his view, to retain sanity, "man must reach out for support to a dream, a metaphysic of hope that sustains him and makes his life worthwhile" (275). He feels that the *ideal* of Christianity, while not necessarily its current practice, most closely approximates such a requirement (159–60, 204).

THEORETICAL CONSIDERATIONS

The Cause of our Discontent with Twentieth-Century Philosophy

We expect human endeavors, all human endeavor, to improve the quality of our existence. Labor is believed to do this, commerce is believed to do this, art and entertainment are believed to contribute to this, and science is accepted by most to do this, so why is twentieth-century philosophy an exception? In our utilitarian society, a discipline that fails to provide assistance in our daily struggles, that fails to provide reason, fails to promote human understanding, fails to give hope, fails to give direction, fails to contribute to physical comfort, and fails to produce economic benefits is disappointing, and at the same time, the reason for its existence is called into question. Philosophy, once dubbed the queen of human endeavors, has an urgent need to prove its relevance to twenty-first-century human beings. We need a coherent, nontechnical view of ourselves in today's world, a view that is nonsectarian, positive, all-inclusive, and conducive to cooperation and survival.

As the foregoing suggests, I deplore our general reliance on a philosophy that fails to point the way out of our nihilism and fails to facilitate beneficial interaction between people. Indeed, I believe that we need to couple the tenet of conscious mortality with a forward-looking, positive philosophy.

One might ask: do we need a philosophy? I am of the opinion that we do need a total view of what we are, how we should live, and how we should die. We need a sense of place, a sense of purpose, and a sense of what is right and what is wrong. For such reasons, our actions need to conform to selected principles and need to reflect a cohesive view. To die is the fate of the living. Because dying is part of living, our eventual demise cannot be exempted from the rules that apply to our living. We need, therefore, a cohesive view of ourselves that takes full cognizance of both our living and our dying.

I am also of the opinion that for many of us, today, a return to blind faith in the mystic realm is not an acceptable way to deal with our most pressing problem. I wish to make it clear that my quarrel is not with organizing our philosophy around the tenet of conscious mortality. In fact, I share the view that this is the central issue of existence for *Homo sapiens*. Thus, a truly humane philosophy should be cognizant of this tenet and should revolve around it. My disagreement is with Becker's choice of philosophy for this purpose. Thus, I recognize the necessity of the union; I merely object to the persona of the marriage partner.

That being said, the reader can rightly ask if I have an "alternative proposal"? How would I proceed? By way of a confession,I wish to state that I too join those who lament the shortness of our life span. However—as the only prudent alternative—I urge us to accept our world and our predicament and spend our allotted time on earth wisely. And yes, in the proposal that follows, I strive to speak to all, religious or secular.

Alternative Rationale Proposed

My proposed alternative will require a brief discussion of some aspects of a philosophical stance I like to call contextual individualism (Bartalos 1988, 1989, 1990 ["Psychosocial Aspects" and "Human Survival"], 1992 [Phenomenon of Death" and "Tensates"], 1995, 1999, 2000). As some aspects of contextual individualism figure prominently in my argument, a discussion of them is necessary here. I have singled out adaptive psychology in particular, due to its relevance to our purpose, namely, how to spend our time while alive and how to face our dying.

As the first step I would recognize human beings as breathing, breeding, feeling, thinking, and mortal animals who are engaged in a permanent struggle to satisfy their biologically conditioned needs and to survive. Further, as animals, they are subject to the laws of biology; and as conscious and thinking individuals—despite their limited understanding of the world around them—they are engaged in the conscious transformation of that environment. The rest of my proposal flows from these observations.

The preeminent philosophy of the twentieth century was characterized by gloom. It rejected the timeworn views that saw the "common man" as one who in life seeks pleasure, wealth, and approval. In the view of the new philosophers, the attainment of such goals failed to provide human beings with more than short-lived relief from their all-pervading anxiety. In contrast, the philosophers of the last century saw anguish wherever they looked (Olson

1962). Their primary disagreement with each other was over what kind of anguish is of the greatest importance in determining human actions. They variously spoke of the anguish of choice, anguish of freedom, anguish of life, anguish of being, anguish of human particularity, anguish of death, and so forth. They agreed that human existence is inherently tragic and that we experience anguish in making the choices that living demands, that dying demands and that the postmortem disposition of our physical and intangible remains requires. And for our efforts, what do we get? Anguish, aloneness, mortality, and nothingness (Shibles 1974).

Who were right, the old philosophers or the more recent ones? In my view, they were both right and they were both wrong. They were right in ascribing importance to the vegetative drives that make us seek food, shelter, and a copulating partner, and they were right in discovering humanity's universal and all-permeating anxiety. Where they were wrong was in their attempt to claim exclusivity for any one factor or for a combination of certain factors in explaining the essence of the individual human's existence. For instance, Becker along with Otto Rank considered humans to be primarily terrified, death-denying, death-avoiding animals while for Freud, they were mainly sexual pleasure seekers. In fact, humans are all that these claims describe them as, and at the same time, they are also much more.

Reformulation of the Nature and Significance of Anxiety or "Anguish" in Humans—The Theory of Tensates-Emsates

The order of things, as they appear to us, consists of change, a change that is brought about by the interaction of the entities making up our world. In our world, everything at all times is in the midst of interaction. Everything interacts with objects found in its surroundings. The principles of interaction and change apply both to the inanimate and to the animate world, humans included. The more complex the organism the more complex is the mechanism of interaction and the resulting change. In the case of human beings, a change in the environment is followed by a human adaptive response. For example, when there is a change in the outside temperature, our bodies initiate a variety of reactions to prevent a cooling or warming of our bodies, as the case might be. This is a form of adaptive responsiveness.

Existence, for living organisms, means active interaction with the environment; it means constant sensing and reacting to environmental changes and the maintenance of organisms' ability to enrich themselves from the environment. We are born with a response-readiness to selected environmental challenges.

In the case of a living organism, it is customary to speak of a sensory system, that is, a group of organs that acts as a reconnaissance unit, a data-gathering system that registers changes in the environment and forwards such information to the brain. Our eyes, ears, taste buds, and tactile nerve endings in our fingertips are part of this system. Our responses to perceived changes are executed by another functional group termed the motor (that is, action-imparting) system, by which we generally mean the muscles and the nerves that carry messages to the muscles from the brain. Between the system that carries encoded information about the environment to the brain and the system that conducts the likewise encoded message to the muscles from the brain, specifying the kind, strength, duration, direction, and speed of the response, is a less well-understood "black box," in which the received impulses are evaluated and appropriate responses formulated.

Every human being is a composite of millions of individual cells. Each of these cells is capable of independent existence, under certain conditions. Millions of interactive cells tightly bound and organized within a human body produce a supersensitive organism in which hubs of cells are organized into organs, like the skin, heart, lungs, and brain, all of them performing some specialized function. I envision the "black box" in the brain as an organ in which the basic hum of millions of interacting cells creates a state of tension, a state of reactivity, a state of readiness to respond to a large number and variety of stimuli. Within the central nervous system, this background state of tension can be perceived as the ebb and flow of reactivity, of acuity, of response readiness. In analogy with the sensory and the motor systems, I will refer to this intercalated functional unit as the tensory system, the tensorium,

Changes in the environment act as stimuli, as triggers for reaction by the organism. Such stimuli cause a burst of reactivity, a challenge-specific response, a localized temporary spike in the ocean of energy flow within the tensory system, causing a defined increase in our tension state, or "tensate." Our underlying, basic state of tension is the hallmark of our reactivity to the environment; it is the hallmark of being alive.

In addition to our basic "tensamatic" activity, we are able to generate a large number of challenge-specific tensates, that is, tensates that possess a specificity in terms of eliciting factors and in terms of their relief mechanisms. Such tensates serve as instruments of adaptation to selected changes in our environment. (The theory of tension states or tensates and the concept of a "tensory organ" in living organisms, form the foundation of what I term adaptive psychology. This view of human mental functioning in turn is part of the philosophical system of contextual individualism.)

In human beings, we find all levels of tensates functioning side by side in a coordinated fashion. The macrophages as they engulf and digest bacteria exhibit the characteristic responsiveness of unicellular organisms; deep tendon reflexes require two cells for their execution and thus represent a higher complexity; an unconditioned reflex such as the constriction of the pupil in response to bright light represents a more complex reaction pattern;

the development of a conditioned reflex requires a still higher complexity; while the dogged pursuit of a chosen goal over one's lifetime is probably the expression of the most complex of tensates known to us, one that, in fact, engages the entire body over a prolonged period of time.

While this is not the place for a comprehensive discussion of tensates and related concepts, the consideration of human reactivity to environmental influences does require a brief mention of the concept of "emsates" or emotional states. Reactions to environmental stimuli by our central nervous system involve a dual system of reactivity: that of the generation of tension and that of the generation of an accompanying emotion. Thus we can classify each interaction not only according to its intensity and duration, that is, according to its tensamatic characteristics, but also according to whether the interaction was perceived as good—bad—indifferent, positive—negative—neutral, attractive—repulsive—inconsequential, or pleasurable—painful—immaterial. Such emotional states or emsates serve as amplifiers and refiners of our perceptions of the environment that we are required to interact with, and they enrich our quantitative perception, as provided by the tensates, with a qualitative attribute.

Our basic tension state is the reason for our eventual dissatisfaction with everything. No matter what we do, no matter how long our bliss lasts, our state of tension eventually will recur, will impel us to move on. It is part of being human. We cannot eradicate it, short of taking our life with it. Being alive means possessing tension states. If we could live as long as we pleased, we would find other reasons for dissatisfaction, for the desire to make changes. Without this urge we would not have created anything. It was and is the guarantee of our continued development. We cannot afford to get rid of it even if we could. Our only choice is to come to terms with it, learn to live with it, and harness its power for our benefit. [The interested reader can find a more extended, albeit dense, explanation of my views on tensates in the appendix following the main text of this chapter.]

Living and Dying, Health and Disease Reinterpreted

If we accept the premises (a) that tensates produce discomfort, (b) that we seek relief from such discomfort, and (c) that our preferences are indicative of a tension state that is relieved or at least diminished by a certain defined activity, than we can conclude that a common characteristic of the animal world, termed by Sir Peter B. Medawar (quoted in Medawar 1990, 10, 167) as the "very decided preference for remaining alive," must be a reflection of a tension state.

We can ask the question: what is this state of primary preference and do we always and under all circumstances prefer to remain alive? Many individuals have felt at various points in their earthly existence that suicide

is preferable to remaining alive. Many individuals in advanced age are likewise ready to die. Still others, whose illnesses are associated with much suffering, are looking forward to leaving this existence. Thus, the preference
for remaining alive is present in all living organisms at some time, yet it is
not an immutable characteristic. It is reasonable to postulate that there is a
tensate that imparts a preference for remaining alive, a tensate that makes us
ready to respond to the challenges of our environment, a tensate that, at the
conscious level, anticipates a change for the better. Such expressions as *vis vi-
talis, élan vital, will to live,* and so forth, used by other thinkers, seem to reflect
speculations along similar lines. The Latin saying "dum spiro, spero" (while
I breathe, I hope) suggests that such speculation is indeed ancient. While
conceding the presence of such an inner impulse, we need to recognize that
its intensity is not constant. Advancing age, physical and mental suffering,
emotions, and conscious thoughts all seem to affect its intensity.

I consider the inborn state of elevated reactivity and readiness to explore
our environment to be a biological phenomenon that is "wired" in our genes,
a product of an evolutionary selective process. We share these characteristics
with other animals. Like other animals, we exhibit a preference for staying
alive not out of any philosophical or religious conviction but reflexively. In
general, we formulate justifications for (or criticisms of) our life-preferring
actions long after we start practicing them. In humans, in contrast to other
animals, such natural reactive patterns can be overcome by conscious mental
processes, as seen, for instance, in suicide bombers.

It is proposed that activities that further living are promoted by the next
layer in this hierarchy of consciously perceived tensates. Such tensates are
operational in living organisms; they represent functions that animals possess from birth or hatching or emerging from a pupa, functions that most
likely are the product of an evolutionary selective process.

In my view, the evolutionarily earliest tensates, which we share with all
animals, are those that (a) impel us to keep our physical structure functioning, (b) impel us to reproduce, and (c) impel us to persevere in these activities, that is to survive, to remain alive (I equate this last-mentioned function
with Medawar's earlier mentioned "decided preference for remaining alive").
Animals are not aware of these impulses, which nevertheless govern their
existence. For humans, sentient beings as we are, these constitute our basic
states of sentience. While we could refer to these functional states, or states
of sentience, by selecting letters of the alphabet or numbers, I am of the view
that in nonmathematical discourse, descriptive designations are preferable.
Accordingly I propose to name these basic tension states as *uncertainty, isolation,* and *hopefulness.* It is worth noting that one does not need to be aware of
tensates in order to be influenced by them. The tensates are assumed to be
present in all living organisms. However, humankind is most likely the only
organism that is consciously aware of them.

Adhering to our view of living organisms as actively interacting bodies, we can define the activity of *living* as a series of purposeful reactions in response to the environment by way of generating appropriate tensates. Conversely, during the process of dying, the physical structure of the body is irreparably damaged and thus loses the ability to generate tensates. Accordingly, dying represents the cessation of purposeful interaction with the environment caused by the irreversible failure of the generation of tensates appropriate to changes in the environment.

The tensate concept likewise allows us to redefine some health-related concepts. Using such terminology, the *healthy* state refers to a living organism that interacts effortlessly with its environment by adequate tensamatic and emsamatic responsiveness.

Chronic stress represents a state of adaptive strain between the organism and the environment, in which adequate tensamatic and emsamatic responses are maintained only with difficulty.

Ailment, illness, or *sickness* represents the inadequacy of the organism in responding to an environmental challenge, due to the failure to generate adequate tensamatic and/or emsamatic responses. In such cases, either the organism eventually regains adequate responsiveness or its functional integrity becomes irreversibly compromised, in irreversible tensamatic failure.

In my view, the basic, spontaneous, undulating state of potential reactivity, the all-underlying tension state or tensate, is the source, in fact the equivalent, of the all-permeating anxiety or angst that became the focus of attention of so many of the twentieth century's intellectuals. Yes, I am in agreement with the view that there is an ever-present state of tension in human beings. I, however, consider this a by-product, in fact, an indication of the living state; not an aberration, not an anguish that makes living worthless, but a necessary part of being alive. It is a kind of background noise generated by our engine of adaptation, and while at times it might need tempering, we literally cannot live without it.

A Sprinkle of Common Sense or "… to Know the Difference"

The theological disputant and philosopher Fausto Sozzini (*De Jesu Christo Servatore,* 1578) and Thomas Reid (*Inquiry into the Human Mind on the Principles of Common Sense,* 1764) are the best-known early exponents of the view that knowledge should be built upon principles that are self-evident. Such common-sense knowledge is seen in an oft cited prayer that has been reprinted with minor variations many times and stems from the pen of an unknown author. It goes something like this: "Let me have the courage to change what can be changed, the serenity to accept what cannot be changed, and the wisdom to know the difference." That the insight reflected in the prayer is not new is indicated by a German saying of unknown attribution: "Was man nicht kann meiden, muss man willig leiden" (What cannot be avoided must be endured).

General obsolescence, including the mortality of living creatures, cannot be changed, only modified. The same applies to our anatomical structure, as its characteristics are encoded in our genes. While one day it may become technologically feasible to create human beings from fertilization to birth in a laboratory vessel, still, for most, to be given birth to by a female member of our species, to mature, to age, and to die will remain the sole possibility for a long time. Thus we have no choice but to come to terms with it.

The Human Propensity to "Zero In" or the Power of Cognitive Focusing

The ability to "zero in" is an important adaptive tool that has not received the scientific attention it deserves. There is no doubt that it is genetically conditioned, congenital, and shaped by evolution. Only that way could a device that is helpful to animals in their ability to rapidly shift their full attention and efforts to a suddenly appearing threat be retained by evolution and become in humans a partially controllable device. Humankind appears to be the only living organism that is able to select the object of concentration at will. By conscious effort, humankind is able to concentrate on one entity or on a part or aspect of an entity at the expense of the rest. The power of cognitive focusing is evident in the training of people for suicide missions, in which their inborn preference for remaining alive is overridden by the brainwashing to which they are subjected.

While the ability to engage in "cognitive focusing" is helpful when one has to identify a quick escape route for, it can be counterproductive when we elect the wrong subject or the wrong aspects of a subject for our special attention and contemplation. I am of the opinion that this is what happened to philosophy in the twentieth century. It is unfortunate yet understandable that Becker's eyes, too, remained fixed on the negative aspect of human nature and existence, and that considerable efforts were spent on the unproductive endeavor of coupling conscious human mortality to existential philosophy. But again it only proves—and this applies to us too—that we cannot avoid bearing the stamp of our time, being a reflection of our zeitgeist.

The Mortality of Humankind—Or Pragmatism As an Aspect of Evolution

At times the world of physics might be viewed as opportunist, a world where processes occur in the direction of least resistance. Is biology different? Biological organisms respond as effectively as their ability allows to every change in the environment. A drastic alteration in the environment might wipe out all of them, or there might be some who happen to have the right build and chemistry and thus survive the new challenge. Among the offspring of such surviving individuals, those who are born with the structure and function of their parents will also survive and will eventually repopulate the area with their similarly endowed descendants. Such descendants, while preserving and perpetuating the special genetic endowment stemming from their parents, will display genetic diversity, increasing with every generation, due to random mutations and gene mixing via sexual reproduction. This process will continue until a new catastrophic event occurs and a new major adaptive shift is called for. Once again survival will depend on the presence of the right genetic constitution, that is the right combination of genes that allows adaptation and thus survival for some under the changed conditions. In this process, the death of the old and the birth of the *different* new are key events. Where the old cannot adapt and thus survive, some of the new might be different enough to survive and reproduce and thus ensure the continuation of the species. Among living organism, where survival is everything, diversity is the most precious characteristic to have.

Death and birth are key events in assuring survival of the species. Through the death of the individual the larger community survives. The old have to yield their place to the new and different. Please note that this process is fully automatic. The technical terms "natural selection" and "evolution through sexual reproduction" in essence refer to such processes and are now coupled with the name of Charles Darwin. Let us now pull back and take a bird's-eye view of the process. We realize the similarity between the realm of physics and that of biology. In both instances, the outcome of an interaction is determined by the best response the organism is able to marshal at the time of the challenge (in biology, this is called selective pressure). To my mind, this is built-in opportunism, or pragmatism if that term suits you better when speaking of humans. Terminology aside, without birth, without death, and without sexual reproduction that allows the reshuffling of the genes of two individuals to create new genetic combinations in their offspring, evolution as we know it, would stop.

The Latin saying, "hora incerta, mors certa" has survived to this day. Indeed while the time of our death is uncertain, its occurrence is not. The fact that our existence on earth is limited, and that we are aware of this fate, does not need to be considered a curse. We have a given time, a limit, a life span, for the development of our potential, whether destructive or constructive. While we have a limited period in which to cause misery to others, our time to do good is also limited. The limit on potential harm is thus achieved only with a corresponding limit on the time for the performance of benevolent acts. If we are interested in furthering human survival and evolution, then the choice is obvious: we should spend our allotted time in furthering universal human aspirations. Rebelling against the rules that prevail in nature would only make us like Don Quixote or an immature child in the midst of a temper tantrum.

Besides, if living is full of misery, why would we want to extend it? Furthermore, just as we are never satisfied with the amount of wealth we possess, we would likewise never be satisfied with the time allotted to us on earth. We would continuously strive for more and more and, eventually, clamor for "eternity" (even though we do not know what that word entails).

There Are Times When Choice Is Not a Given

As to statements that we come to this world "between urine and feces" and that when we die "we go the way of the grasshopper," that is, "became fodder for worms," my reaction is that I find nothing degrading about any part of human anatomy and bodily function or about any creature of the earth. While it is possible that my stance is conditioned by my medical training, I do not see why other individuals should have difficulty in adopting this view. Every part of the body is performing a needed function; all of these functions are and need to be considered normal; all of them ought to be accepted by us, just as we accept so many other products of evolution.

In all earnest, if so many of the earth's creatures are good as food and serve us in other ways, why can we not return to the earth some of the nutrients we took from it while building and maintaining our bodies? Through our decomposing body, we are simply taking part in the process of recycling earth's resources. Our taking part in this process is logical, fair, in fact obligatory, and therefore should in no way be regarded as demeaning.

Insight and Acceptance

I do not want to subscribe to a gloomy view of human existence. This would be counteradaptive as well as counterproductive. Our basic state of tension or anxiety is a necessity for reactivity and thus for survival. It is our constant companion, one that is meant to be appeased again and again.

Evolution is continuous adaptation to the environment at the species level. It is an ongoing process. Evolution by natural selection requires sexual reproduction, it requires that the old generation be succeeded by a new one and the new one by a still newer one, and so on. The old generation, including its old genes and old social arrangements, has to yield to the new one, to one that is more suitable to the continuously changing environment. Uncompromising mortality is nature's way to ensure this process.

The evolutionary importance of "zeroing in" (that is, cognitive focusing) by humans is little appreciated. While its presence in other animals is evident and the value of this tensate-based or tensamatic reaction in case of sudden danger is obvious, its conscious priming for long-term projects in humans is overlooked. The mechanism allows us to select long-term goals and to program ourselves to reach them. It is a tool that we have left unused by allowing nearly unbridled anarchy in the ordering of our social affairs. An important tool in assisting natural selection thus left neglected in favor of a *laissez faire* approach in the mistaken belief that the process of natural selection will automatically lead to a resolution of such problems as overpopulation, the unfair distribution of wealth, epidemics, and human beings' cruelty to other human beings, just to mention a few. It will, indeed, but at the price of untold human suffering.

THE LOGIC OF CONTEXTUAL THANATOLOGY

In the foregoing discussion, with the exception of the tensate-emsate system, there is little that has not been said by others before me. In the field of intellectual knowledge, I have picked certain flowers, at times elaborated on them, and combined them into a bouquet suiting my predilections. Fellow Columbia University seminarian Dr. Thomas A. Caffrey suggested the utility of providing an enumeration of the givens, deductions, and inductions employed in the composition of this bouquet. This indeed will not only indicate my indebtedness to the many people who uncovered these now generally accepted facts—and whom it would be impossible to give credit to individually here—but might also fulfill the function of a summary.

The nature of my effort is the construction of a theory by starting with a small selection of generally agreed upon facts (that is, generally observable entities), considering these as "givens," offering from them a selection of deductive thoughts, and finally, based on these processes, arrive by induction at proposals for action.

> What are the requirements? Agreement with commonsense observations.
> What are our expectations? To arrive at a simple, unifying concept of ourselves and of our relationship with the environment.
> What are the possible long-term benefits? The reformulation of our moral principles and ethical deportment.

Givens

(about human beings and their place in the universe)

About the Universe

A constant interaction is taking place between the various constituents of our universe at all levels of existence, resulting in constant change.

About Living Organisms in General

1. Humans are living organisms and are thereby subject to the laws of biology;
2. The form of interaction found in living organisms is adaptive response;
3. Adaptation means the preservation of the structural and functional integrity of an organism during changing environmental conditions;
4. Living organisms have the ability and tendency to maintain their physical and functional integrity for prolonged periods of time.
5. Successful adaptive response by a living organism means survival by the organism;
6. Living organisms reveal an underlying tension state—"tensate"—that is affected by changes in the environment and conditions reactivity to it;
7. Due to such tension states (tensates), living organisms exhibit purposeful responses to environmental stimuli;
8. Permanent cessation of purposeful reactivity to environmental changes is one definition of a dead organism.

About the Sphere of Human Endeavor

1. We are members of the larger human family that includes all of humanity;
2. Our abilities are limited: there are certain things we can do and there are entities that resist being changed by us;
3. Human existence is relatively short and finite;
4. Human existence is based on interconnectedness and interdependence;
5. Our actions have an effect on others;
6. Some human efforts are more effective in promoting our survival than are others; thus, selective actions are preferable to random ones;
7. Humans differ from other living organisms in their capacity to *consciously* register their experiences, remember them, compare them, and use them when planning ahead; thus, humans are capable of making *deliberate* choices based on anticipated outcomes;
8. Humans can willfully select entities to be subjected to intense concentration (that is, cognitive focusing) and maintain such concentration for prolonged periods of time.

Deductions

(about human interactions)

1. As members of the human family we benefit from all the knowledge, art, and technical know-how that human intelligence produced;
2. As members of the human family we suffer from the effects of the many forms of wickedness that human drives and intelligence have produced;
3. Our interactions can be enabling or hindering for the survival of others;
4. Our existence has a different meaning for different individuals;
5. The meaning of our existence for others is defined by the way our actions affect them;

6. Our actions are dependent on our capabilities, on consideration of their anticipated consequences, and (often regrettably) on our prevailing emotional state;

While we are able to extend the duration of our existence on earth to a limited extent, our body cannot be made immortal in its present form and function: that is, we are mortal and will remain so for the foreseeable future.

Inductions

(actions that are conducive to personal contentment and promote humanity's survival)

We have the power, by virtue of our attributes of remembering, planning ahead, and cognitive focusing, not to leave our interactions with the environment entirely to chance but to choose them and modify them to our advantage, that is, to further our survival. The quality of our living is far more amenable to change than is its length. Since we cannot eliminate our dying, let us concentrate on improving our living. For the most part it is up to us to decide how we want to spend our brief existence on earth and what kind of person we want to be. This is possible because these depend in large measure on our attitude toward others, on our attitude toward work, and on our attitude toward our environment.

1. We need to recognize the benefits we receive from others by virtue of belonging to the human family and to recognize that we have the obligation to be responsible, reciprocating members of this family;
2. We need to be cognizant of how our deeds affect the existence of others, as this will define the meaning of our existence to them and, consequently, will influence their attitudes toward us;
3. We need to take charge of our existence and direct our efforts to places where results are most likely;
4. Our attitudes are capable of being changed by conscious self-effort and can be influenced through public education and by examples set by respected others;

It is up to us to look for goodness and beauty instead of cruelty and ugliness. Since both beauty and ugliness are found in abundance, we will find what we seek with relative ease and surround ourselves with it.

In our interaction with our contemporaries we receive messages from others and we send out messages to others. We are also receivers of messages left by the people who lived before us, and we are transmitting messages to those who will follow us. Thus each of us constantly receives messages, filters messages, and selects messages for transmission to others. We need to make this process a conscious one and refrain from transmitting messages that could promote discord, destruction, or human suffering.

It is up to us to find meaning in what we do. It is up to us to make ourselves useful and thus be important for others. It is also up to us, when the time comes to die, to feel that our existence was not in vain, that our time on earth was spent wisely, and that we helped to make our planet a better place to inhabit than we found it. We have the power to influence our living, because we can determine how we relate to others. The key to contentment is in *our* hands.

PRACTICAL CONSIDERATIONS—CONFIDINGS OF A MORTAL

Let us follow the forgoing, largely theoretical, considerations with more practically oriented thoughts. The expected benefit of such an exercise is the assertion of our individuality and nondestructive independence in facing the challenges we encounter during our conscious existence on earth. This means feeling that we have managed to remain in charge of our affairs. The ancient Greeks and Romans spoke of virtuous living and virtuous dying. Socrates comes readily to mind as an example. The ancients' virtue—as I perceive it—presupposed that they were in control of the way they lived and died and that they exercised this freedom in such a manner as to gain the approval of their peers.

What Does It Mean to Be Born a Mortal Human Being?

The world over, practically from the moment of birth, diverse interest groups begin to claim proprietorship over every child. At birth every child becomes a member of a population group or state and often soon thereafter a member of a religion. Our world is a collection of population groups speaking diverse languages, having different cultures, adhering to different worldviews and religions, possessing differing physical features, and so forth, and all instilling in their children that their customs and their religion are the only correct ones. Everything that is different is an aberration at best or an abomination marked for elimination at worst. Today we cannot avoid being born into allegiance to a culture and/or a religious group, and once we grow up under such an influence it is extremely difficult for us to objectively evaluate the beliefs that have been implanted in our developing, uncritical mind. Additionally, we all were taught not to dare question the teachings of our elders. Such indoctrination notwithstanding, in fact because of it, it is highly desirable that we subject to critical examination the precepts by which we were brought up, even if this means that some of our cherished views might turn out to be invalid and some of our respected teachers might appear, in hindsight, to have been misinformed, or bigots, or worst, cynical liars.

[*Challenge to all:* What will it take to raise children who are both proud members of their cultural group and enlightened citizens of humanity at large?]

Make Your Consciousness Your Ally

Consciousness makes us aware of the present and allows us to imagine the future. Some of our imaginings are wishes, others are possibilities, and still others, a precious few, are certainties. Consciousness has provided us with ample examples in all of these realms. The most unsettling of all is the certainty that eventually we will die. We don't know when, we don't know how, but the assumption that at some time we will die can not be disputed.

Our conscious intelligence, the faculty that warns us of our finitude, can also serve as our compass guiding us to live our life and live our dying as upright members of the human family. To my understanding, a dignified farewell means dying in a manner I choose. It is a death that is not hastened, assisted, or shaped by an outside agent or agency in order to derive an advantage from how I lived or when and how I die. Here I have in mind nondemocratic political entities but also organized religions that might want to select the time, the place, and/or the manner in which I die. Why would anyone want to do such things? Because they might not like what I have said or written; because they might want to sell my body parts; because they might want me to function as a human guided missile; or because the treatment of my illness is too expensive; and so on. The reasons for exploiting us while we are alive and exploiting us when we are dying are manifold and can come from many directions.

It is my contention that feelings of uncertainty and isolation are our constant companions in life and are the spur of our actions, including our search for companionship. These twin engines of life that are so successful in keeping us striving through the vicissitudes of living become a hindrance when we are facing our demise. In order to achieve a dignified death, in order to face our finitude as self-relying independent human beings, we are required to use our conscious faculties to keep in check our feelings of uncertainty and isolation.

I propose the use of the following measures, in combination, to enable us to face our finitude without reliance on an outside agency that, while seeking profit, will rob us of our independence.

Dignified Dying Means Facing Up
to Your Mortality Readily and Often

The conscious realization of our mortality is a traumatic experience. While all living organisms are mortal, we humans are the only creatures who are aware of their mortality. Probably we have all made causal remarks like "everybody will die someday" but moved on with our daily chores, attacking our minor problems with zeal while the big question, the why of all of our efforts, remains unexplored. We might feel that nothing is accomplished by thinking about mortality, *our* mortality. It is like entering a dead-end street; we cannot change it, and therefore we should not waste precious time on it. And so it goes until someone close to us dies, or we get sick, depressed, or older. These are the times when our ephemeral nature forces itself into our consciousness. When this happens, I suggest that you gather up your courage and face up to your finitude. There is no way to be rendered immortal, but there are benefits to be obtained by facing up to our mortality, Thus, admit to yourself that one day you are going to die! Admit it, understand it, and let this understanding sink deep into your mental labyrinths. Like a computer that is updated with new information, your outlook, your attitude, and your value system also suddenly undergo an update, a rearrangement. A poorly understood, unarticulated inner tension begins to dissipate, as quiet serenity lends the word "wisdom" a new meaning. From the outside nothing has changed, but for you, because you have changed, everything has changed. You have become wiser.

Thus, dare to think about dying, dare to read about it, dare to write about it, and dare to talk about it. Familiarize yourself with something that is certain in your future and yet very difficult to articulate. Yes, it hurts, because it makes you feel sorry to contemplate the eventual demise of such a splendid human being as you are. But such observations help to remind you of your membership in humanity, regardless of how privileged you are or of the outstanding achievements that are associated with your name. They help to put things in perspective, help you to realize that you need to look ahead and accept the fact that you too are a human being, that—despite your present station in life—you face the same future as every other human being. The recognition of your finitude demands that you discard your arrogance. When you manage to do that, you will realize your brotherhood with all, including the most downtrodden, and thus renew your membership in the larger community of human beings.

[*Digression:* It makes one wonder, would the world be different if, before sending millions to their death, Stalin, or Hitler, or Mao Tse-tung had arrived at the conscious realization that there was very little difference between them and those whose suffering and slaughter they so causally ordered for some perceived momentary political expediency. Both they and their victims were feeling and thinking human beings with ambitions and limited time on earth, main difference being that one had managed to gain temporary power over the others to rob them of the opportunity to live out their dreams, their ambitions, and their talents and—unfathomably—chose to exercise this power.]

Logic of Living

Use logic to understand that dying is the counterpart of birth: one signifies the beginning of human existence, the other marks its end. They are both parts of human existence. There is no existence without birth and there is no existence that does not end with dying. There is no human existence that lasts forever. Dying is a necessity. Living, dying, and being born are part of human existence and we need to recognize that.

Our limited tenure on earth calls for selectivity and economy in choosing our goals and activities and must take into account our capabilities and the anticipated effect on society of what we intend to do.

[*Digression:* Logic also suggests that we arrange our affairs in such a way that the talents and constructive ambitions of every human being are allowed to develop for the common benefit. This requires healthy bodies (with adequate nutrition and health care), recognition and encouragement of the development of talents (with access to good educational facilities), and a supportive instead of an exploitive social system. We are wasting much of our natural resources, and not the least among them is unrealized human potential.]

Establish Dedicated Connections between Yourself and Your Environment

You might find it useful to populate your inner (i.e. psychological, imaginary) space by creating imaginary assistants and assigning them different functions. For instance, in your virtual inner space, you can "appoint" one to remind you to take your medication, or to wake you up at a certain time, or to remind you to go to sleep at another time, and so forth. It is one way of quasi-programming your brain for certain tasks.

You can also select items in your environment, such as animals, statues, or figures on paintings or even things like the whistle of a passing train, to remind you of something. You might "appoint" one as your protector, another as the one who cheers you up, still another who fills you with energy, and so on. Such imagined "auxiliaries" help to reduce your isolation by serving as targets for the projection of your thoughts, sorrows, and concerns. In the absence of such objects, a paper on which to write, a canvas on which to paint, a musical instrument on which you can play, or a pet for which you care can serve as substitutes. I read somewhere that Sigmund Freud had a number of small figures on his desk from various cultures and of diverse epochs and at times addressed them loudly. Before we hasten to the conclusion that this is insane, we should remember how often we talk to babies who are not expected to answer us, and how many pet owners talk to their charges. Talking, for humans, before it assumed the role of a medium of information exchange, was a means of exploring the environment and connecting with it. Voice production is another form of reaching out and touching, and in that endeavor literally more far-reaching than our hands are. Singing, speaking, or even shouting—whether in the wilderness or in a prison cell in solitary confinement—helps to confirm our existence, helps to confirm our presence in the universe, helps to integrate us into the order of things around us. I suspect that Freud by greeting those figures in the morning acknowledged that at some level they and he were connected, that they were the same in that that they were both constituents of the cosmos. That is, speaking to someone or something is an act of integration into the same environment, and an act of acknowledging our common ties. After touching, it is speaking—whether screaming or singing or cursing—that appears to be the next best way to express this sentiment.

There is still another aspect to lifeless companions that is worth mentioning. Probably it was due to the utterly harsh conditions under which I grew up, as an orphan protected and nurtured by a widow, while in succession Nazism and Communism shattered human rights and human lives all around us. I learned early on that human beings come in two varieties, the benevolent ones and the brutes, those who would hurt you for no reason and those who would be kind to you; and that any attempt to tell them apart by obvious, superficial criteria was doomed to failure. No body build, no gender, no nationality, no ethnicity, no religion, no education or intelligence, not even the wearing of a uniform or gun helped me to a quick understanding of who belonged in which category. This problem, which became an existential issue for me as a child, made me interested in psychology and has remained with me into old age. I scrutinized people who were genuinely helpful and nurturing and people who insensitively manipulated and exploited others. My observations were not supported by research grants and no statistical data were collected.

Thus, here I am talking about impressions, not data. What I noticed was that the "exploiter" was not part of his environment; that s/he controlled but did not interact in a reciprocal fashion; and that there was no considerate giving and taking relationship with others. In fact, in such individuals the prevailing relationship was based on insecurity, suspicion, and hostility. Money and power only made such persons more controlling, more suspicious, and apparently more insecure and more alienated from the rest of the world. If such people have pets, whether animals or diamonds, they do not integrate them into their environment and enjoy them for their decorative value but display them as emblems of power or new items in their arsenal. In contrast, a genuinely pro-human individual is able to cherish commercially worthless "junk" items as prized possessions because of the memories associated with them, and when she/he displays them, it is like showing a new baby or introducing a new friend. Thus, to me, the quality of one's connectedness with items in one's environment is of prognostic importance, because it reveals how well one is integrated, how well one is embedded in the environment, how well one is coping with reality. As for me, as a child, during those turbulent times in Central Europe, beside my stepmother our dog Vandor was my most trusted companion. I knew she would never hurt me and would never betray me.

When we talk of loneliness, we often think of an elderly person living alone. It is useful to realize that you can be a child, or a young adult or a middle aged person, and be lonely. You can be lonely not only in the wilderness but living in a metropolis surrounded by thousands or millions of individuals.

The mere sight of people does not automatically relieve your feeling of isolation. In fact, through its threatening aspect, they might increase it. If there is a shortage of human beings who are suitable (i.e. trusted) companions to whom you can relate, use recorded music, movies, poems, novels, lectures, videos, theatrical performances, and so on. Use the Internet. These should be objects that cheer you, relax you, and fill you with tender feelings, such as photographs of certain individuals, art objects from different time periods and different parts of the world, books, paintings, objects received as presents from favorite acquaintances, research into the history of your family or find other hobbies. Playing and listening to music can be very beneficial for its calming and mood-elevating effect. Activities that involve the creation of something that grows, be it a plant, a corporation, a school, a hospital, or an idea that helps millions to live better, are like investments whose steady flow of dividends come to you in the form of emotional benefits.

The ways whereby you can make yourself feel connected is literarily unlimited. But just being open to such endeavor is often not enough, you need to take the initiative.

Cultivate an Inner Peace via Periodic Self-Appraisals

Now being anchored to the environment and to your inner self, review your life.

> How did I fare as a human being?
> How did I fare as a family member?
> How did I fare as a productive member of society?

If you were not idle, if you treated others with respect and goodwill, if you spent your life in furthering the survival and orderly functioning of society by making a living from honest work, and if you had children and raised them to be responsible, considerate, and productive members of society, you lived up to your responsibilities as a member of the human species. If you failed to do these, try to make amends while it is still possible.

Work on Your Image of How You Want to Be Remembered

By embarking on this project, you are hammering home the message to yourself that you are rather prudently looking ahead, that you are dealing with your mortality, and that you are coming to terms with it. Our importance to others is determined by the way our actions affect their existence. It is really a measure of the degree of dependency and the graciousness with which the dependency status is maintained. In some cases, one is dependent on psychological support, in others the needed support is material, and in still others it is both.

How long are we remembered? Generally not too long. The late Dr. Arthur Linksz, a wise and kind ophthalmologist in New York City whom I had the good fortune to know, wrote a book entitled *Fighting the Third Death* (1986, 1–5). He said that we suffer our first death when our body dies. We undergo a second death when those who remember us as living individuals die too. Thus, this is the death of the memories of us. Our third and final death occurs when everything that we did is forgotten, when there is no more evidence that we ever existed on this earth. In writing the above-mentioned book, and presumably his previous books too, Dr. Linksz was aiming to postpone his own third death.

Transcend Your Individual Existence

Attempts to transcend one's death are considered normal activities and have, in fact, been credited with extraordinary achievements. The pyramids in Egypt spring immediately to mind. But books, art pieces, organizations, corporations, universities, and so forth have preserved the names of their creators or benefactors long after everybody who knew them has died. One's progeny, too, can be considered as an instrument with which to transcend individual finitude. Mythical beliefs, of course, represent a large number of such endeavors. Ideas about an afterlife are varied: Valhalla, the Champs Elysées, Hades, Paradise, Hell, reincarnation, and others. While these concepts were and some still are influential in the hands of organized groups bent on controlling others, there is not a shred of evidence to support their existence. In our more enlightened, evidence-based existence, seeking transcendence in an imagined entity cannot be recommended. We need something factual and long-lasting for that purpose, something that involves us, something in which our individual interest is involved and interwoven. Do we have such a candidate? We do indeed. It is humanity itself.

Until quite recently cosmologists and physicists assumed that our universe must have had a beginning and thus must have an end. The scale that scientists were using for such assumptions was truly "astronomical": they were talking in trillions of years. Of course, our immediate concern for humanity is to survive this decade and this century before we feel warranted to look farther. But it makes sense to hope that somehow a global enlightenment will allow us to work together to solve our common problems and survive this dangerous period in human development and then to take a glimpse at the distant future. In fact such vistas are evolving.

During the last few years, scientists have worked out a possible scenario, whereby in compliance with the known rules of physics and by using the trajectories of current research in informatics and energy resources, a way might be found to transfer essential information from our dying universe into another universe for future use (Kaku, 2005). Thus, science comes close to pointing the way to the indefinite survival of the human creative spirit, if not the human body itself. But for that to happen, humankind has to create a physical and psychological environment that furthers its survival (see the final chapter in this book for the logic and for the assumed processes involved in the possible survival of humanity or its achievements in another universe after our own becomes uninhabitable).

I feel that humanity is a suitable and worthy object through which to transcend our sojourn on earth. It is already a marvelous monument to the efforts of those who preceded us, and if we manage our affairs well it might develop into a self-perpetuating entity as durable as anything in our universe.

[*Remark:* No religion can seriously make similar claims.]

Don't Dwell on Past Mistakes

If you failed in any respect attempt, fill in the gaps while it is still an option for you. Remember that errors cannot be undone; they can only pale in comparison to beneficent deeds. Thus, compensate for your mistakes or missed opportunities by benevolent gestures and deeds.

[*Digression:* Here is a trap lying in wait for you; if you endear yourself too much to those around you, you increase the pain they will feel upon your death. Conversely, if you want to minimize their sorrow when you die, you need to be cruel in your life. It is a no-win situation, because you will be causing pain either way. Perhaps the best course is to live as a caring human being all your life, and when the end comes near, attempt to fade out gradually from the life of those who care for you.]

Prepare Written Directives

Prepare a will and state in it how do you want to dispose of your body and of your belongings. Also have a health care proxy and a living will/medical directive completed to ensure that, when you are no longer able to make informed decisions, your pre- and peri-mortal medical management will approximate your wishes.

Chose a Location in Which to Die—If Possible

No doubt you want a place where no bill collectors, unwanted clergy, executioner, former spouse(s), or anyone else you don't want to see can gain unauthorized access to you.

Whether we have been able to conduct our affairs in life as we saw it fit— probably none of us has been able to achieve this on a continuous basis—it is still possible to achieve a peaceable, dignified death. By accepting our finitude, we declare our freedom from voluntary servitude to ideologies that lack scientific credibility, that attempt to constrict our intellect, that might want to make us instruments of the political ambitions of others. That is, we are asserting our status as thinking, rational, and courageous specimens of the *Homo sapiens.*

APPENDIX: COMPENDIUM OF ADAPTIVE PSYCHOLOGY

The Concept of Tensates

The sudden encounter with a potentially dangerous situation, and an increase in anger, hunger, and sexual arousal are examples of a subjective experience that we can come closest to identifying as involving "tension." These and similar sensations caused by a variety of events can be regarded as representing tension states, or tensates. Most tensates arise in response to changes. Tensates can cause a sense of urgency and impel action that achieves rapid relief through a well-defined act on the part of the organism. Tensate generation and the act of relieving it form the basis of the general mechanism of organismic reactivity.

For a living organism, such as a human being, survival means sensing the environment, detecting potentially deleterious changes, and responding to such changes in a way that will preserve the organism's structural and functional integrity. Survival, in this sense, is equates to the adaptation of the individual to changes in the environment.

Adaptive efforts require the smooth functioning of three interconnected yet functionally distinct components of the human body. These are the sensory system, the response or "motor" system, and the "tensor" system. Changes in the environment are detected by the sensory systems (the organs of vision, smell, etc.) and this information is transmitted to the brain. The response to the detected changes is formulated in the brain by what I call the "tensor" system, and the order is executed by the "motor" or response system. In its most elementary form, the response consist of a movement either from away or toward the detected environmental challenge.

It is proposed here that the responsiveness of a living organism to changes in the environment is based on the ability to generate challenge-specific tension states or tensates and the ability to perform a specific act that leads to the relief of such tensates.

Characteristics of Tensates

A brief enumeration of several of the characteristics of tensates is attempted below:

1. Every bodily action is the result of some "inner stirring" due to either externally induced stimuli or internally produced chemical changes. Under

certain conditions, such a chemical imbalance triggers in certain other chemical pathways a readiness, or rather an inclination, to proceed. A tension state or tensate thus arises.

2. Tensates are expressions of underlying physico-chemical processes.
3. Tensates represent mechanisms of coping, mechanisms of adaptation to rapid changes in the environment.
4. Tensates are the product of evolutionary processes.
5. The capacity to form tensates is inborn. The capacity to respond to certain tensate-reducing stimuli is inborn (i.e., a calming response to stroking), while for other stimuli it may be acquired (i.e., a preference for alcoholic beverages). The generally observed inborn preference for sweets and aversion to bitter tastes and the inborn preferences for certain structural, color, harmonic, and olfactory stimuli might have their basis in an inborn tendency to respond to such stimuli with a reduction of tensates. Conversely, an inborn tendency to respond to certain stimuli with a buildup of tensates might explain what has been called startle reflex, the prompt response to a sudden shriek or our intense aversion to events that make us jittery, such as the sound produced by scratching a chalkboard with our nails, or our urge to join others in such "herd actions" as fleeing, marching, or singing or our propensity to yawn in response to seeing others yawning.
6. Genetic influences are likely involved in the characterization of both "spontaneous" and "reactive" tensates.
7. The actions impelled by tensates can be as simple as the constriction of the pupil in response to bright light and as complex as the composition of a symphonic work.
8. Not all tensates are consciously perceived by us. Among those that we perceive consciously, we gave names to some while many remained nameless. Unnamed tensates can be found in literary works, especially in poetry, and we encounter them in artistic creations as varied as paintings, musical compositions, and body movement compositions. Some examples of consciously perceived tensates are pain, hunger, sexual arousal, anger, restlessness, the so-called creative impulse, cravings, longings, wants, desires, and expectations. Urges such as the urge to steal, to kill, or to start a fire and the states of being curious, tense, and so on also represent tension states. The acts of blinking, swallowing, breathing, sweating, defecating, and urinating are activities that are preceded by a tensate buildup in response to specific stimuli. The acts of sighing, yawning, weeping, and attacking and the collection of response patterns named as miserly, arrogant, or pious, among others, appear to represent collections of specific tension states. Unconscious mechanisms with characteristics of tensate generation and relief include conditioned as well as unconditioned reflexes, habits, obsessions, phobias, and paraphylias.
9. An increase in tensates, when consciously perceived, leads to a subjective sensation of unease or discomfort.
10. A release of consciously perceived tensates results in a reduction of discomfort.

11. Tensates that usually are not consciously perceived can become conscious when challenged above and beyond their usual limits. Extremes of temperature or hindrances to the passage of intestinal or urethral contents can call attention to themselves as burns, frost bite, and intestinal and urinary colics, respectively.

12. Items and activities that we choose to perform, among the multitude of those available, are preferred because they reduce a tensate. Anything that pleases us reduces tensates. Thus our preferences are clues to our tensates.

13. Some tensates, apparently generated by a process of internal chemical change, are present continuously and exhibit periodic "ebb and flow"–like changes. Examples are mood swings, changes in perceived energy levels, and changes in states of irritability. We might find it useful to differentiate between such "spontaneous tensates" and the more easily observable "reactive tensates."

14. Some reactive tensates are generated by external stimuli (e.g., pupillary constriction in response to light), others by internal stimuli (e.g., the urge to urinate in response to a distended bladder), while still others are generated by both (e.g., the sensation of pain).

15. All of our sense organs are able to perceive discomforting, that is, tensate-promoting stimuli. All of our sense organs are able to perceive soothing, that is, tensate-reducing, stimuli.

16. It seems reasonable to assume that among the many tensates each of us is able to generate, a majority of them are shared by most of us. In contrast to such "public" tensates, we possess "private" tensates that are shared only by a small number of individuals, and it is likely that we also have a few "exclusive" tensates that are unique to us.

17. In humans, tensates can be generated not only through sensory organ perception but also by thought content. Tensate-enhancing thoughts can be produced at will by thinking about tensate-producing events (e.g., certain foods, erotic acts). They can also arise spontaneously or in response to some subconscious cue (as in hypochondriasis) or be induced by externally administered agents (such as certain psychoactive substances). Inflammatory speeches, the so-called art of propaganda, and the advertisement industry can all thus be regarded as examples of deliberate, self-serving, externally induced thought-content modifications with the purpose of inducing or modifying certain tensates in others.

18. Many tensates, when not relieved in a timely fashion, have a tendency to abate with time (e.g., hunger, anger, and sexual arousal).

19. Currently, at least some tensates can be subjected to scientific analysis. Many tensates that are perceived consciously can be identified, characterized, reproduced, and measured via various psychological tests. Some testable assumptions about tensates are the following:

   a. Under identical conditions, the various characteristics of tensates remain relatively constant, and thus reproducible, over short periods of time.
   b. Within the same individual, different tensates vary in strength, in duration, in ease of inducibility, and in speed of buildup and relief.

c. Within the same organism, a given tensate undergoes changes with the passage of time: changes in intensity, duration, and ease and speed of formation and relief.

d. Identical tensates, when compared in different individuals of identical age, sex, ethnic background, and environmental conditions will exhibit varying degrees of variation in their parameters. Such differences might be due to both genetic differences and past environmental exposures.

20. On occasion, tensates can arise not only in response to specific stimuli but also in response to nonspecific stimuli (i.e., the general adaptation syndrome of Hans Selye (1964, 53–54).

21. Tensates can be reduced by specific as well as nonspecific relievers. Examples of the latter in humans are tranquillizer drugs, alcohol, and sexual-union.

22. Tensates are subject to emotional influences or coloration. It is the emotional component that differentiates anger from rage and pleasure from ecstasy. Thus, one differentiation between tensates might be based on the amount and kind of emotional coloration present.

23. Tension states that are of survival benefit in a given environment can be regarded as adaptive, or physiological, in contrast to tensates that hinder adaptation and thus are disadaptive, or pathological. Such a distinction between tensates is environment-specific, since a tensate that is disadaptive in one environment might prove to be survival-promoting in a different environment.

24. A further subdivision between tensates can be made on the basis of their mode of relief: The relief of some tensates can be brought about simply by the production of changes within the organism. An example of such an autologuous tensate relief is the widening of the pupil in response to darkness. In contrast, a heterologuous tensate relief engages the help of the environment; it forces us to interact with the environment in a defined fashion. Examples are the act of locating a tree and rubbing against it, locating edible material and ingesting it, and locating a mating partner and copulating with him/her. These complex acts and the urges, or tensates, that induce them in order to obtain relief are present in humans as well as in primitive animal organisms. The difference is that humans are conscious of these tensates and thus have given them names such as itching, hunger, and libido.

25. The relationship between different tensates might be studied in terms of their evolutionary appearance (phylogenic hierarchy), in terms of their chronological appearance during a person's life span (ontogenic hierarchy), and in terms of their functional relationship (functional hierarchy).

26. If we accept the premises that (a) tensates produce discomfort, (b) we seek relief from such discomfort, and (c) our preferences are indicative of a tension state that is relieved or at least diminished by the preferred activity, then we can conclude that a common characteristic of the animal world, which Sir Peter B. Medawar (J. Medawar 1990, pp. 10, 167) called the "very decided preference for remaining alive," must be a reflection of a

tension state. For the identification of this tensate, the term "hope" might be an adequate choice.

27. It is helpful to distinguish different levels of functional organization in a living organism. The highest level represents spheres of actions, or operational categories. These include the maintenance of bodily structure and function, reproduction, and the will to survive. The next lower level of organization represents bodily functions needed to accomplish the above listed three operational goals. These are functions that will be needed in a coordinated fashion. Examples are visual perception, locomotion, respiration, memory storage and retrieval, and so on. The next lower level of organization consists of the myriad of tensamatic reactions taking place at the cellular and subcellular level. Coordination of action is assured by communication channels that run through the nerves and the blood vessels. In the case of the former, messages are carried in the form of electric impulses, and in the latter by chemical molecules traveling via the bloodstream and acting as messengers. The hormones are the best known examples of the latter.

Tensates, of course, do not come with names. When we observe a hitherto unrecognized phenomenon it is our role to describe it and name it. How do we go about naming the tensates that are behind our inherent want to survive, to feed, and to reproduce? My approach is to search our vocabulary for words that characterize the subjective feelings that are provoked by these tensates. Consequently I propose that the driving sensation associated with search for food and shelter be identified by the word uncertainty, the driving sentient associated with reproduction as isolation, and the sentient associated with the preference for remaining alive as hope. They constitute our most basic tensates and are also the ones we can readily get in touch with because they are operational at all times, though at varying intensities. Whenever we are hungry, are in the mood for intimacy, or are contemplating a career change we are experiencing these tensates. On final analysis they make us search, communicate, copulate and persevere.

Evolutionarily these tensates are the most ancient ones we possess and due to their ancient origin they are also the most widespread in the animal kingdom. Every living organism that searches for food, looks for a mating partner, and attempt to escape when cornered possesses these tensates.

28. Adhering to our view of living organisms as actively interacting bodies, we can define the state of being alive as a series of purposeful reactions in response to environmental stimuli. Dying, on the other hand, is characterized by the cessation of purposeful interaction with the environment.

It is stressed that the three more-or-less basic tensates of uncertainty, isolation, and hope are assumed to be present in all living organisms. Most likely the human being is the only organism who is consciously aware of the presence of these states and has attempted to define and name them. However, one does not need to be aware of tensates in order to be influenced by them.

Summary of Adaptive (Tensate) Psychology

As we are part of a larger whole, it is important that we understand ourselves and the world around us in an integral, contextual way. As part of a larger conceptual model, referred to as contextual individualism, it is proposed here that we look at our interaction with the environment in terms of tension states or tensates.

Tensates are measures of the reactivity of living organisms. Functionally, tensate generation is a sign of organismic reactivity. Tensates are a sign of being alive. Tensates are of inestimable survival value to the organism; they are instruments of adaptation to rapid environmental change. We have the inborn, probably genetically encoded, ability to generate a variety of tensates. The various tensates, in general, possess a specificity in terms of their eliciting factors and in terms of their relief mechanisms. We function through tensates. Tensates, which are defined here in terms of functional characteristics and subjective experiences, are the expression of physico-chemical processes in the body. The chemical reactions underlying the responsiveness of a unicellular organism are different from those operating at the level of a multicellular organism, yet the reaction of both is based on the generation of an internal tension state in response to environmental stimuli that are relieved by a specific, genetically "prewired" response. In humans, we find all levels of tensates functioning side by side in a coordinated fashion: the macrophages exhibit the characteristic responsiveness of unicellular organisms; deep tendon reflexes require two cells for their execution and thus represent a higher complexity; an unconditioned reflex such as the increased secretion of gastric acid in response to food intake represents a more complex reaction pattern; the development of a conditioned reflex requires a still higher complexity; and the dogged pursuit of a chosen goal over one's lifetime is probably the expression of the most complex of tensates known to us.

After some reflection the thoughtful observer will notice that the syncretic concept of tensates bridges the gap between the animate and inanimate, connects molecular processes with subjective experiences, penetrates the apparent barrier between the subconscious and the conscious, eliminates the perceived incompatibility between the objective and the subjective, and reveals a unity between the arts and the sciences. That is, it might serve as arbiter between C. P. Snow's "Two Cultures" (1969).

NOTE

I wish to express my gratitude to Thomas A. Caffrey, Ph.D., for his insightful comments.

REFERENCES

Bartalos, M. K. Diversity and Interaction: Foundations of a Contextual Individualism. University Seminar on Death, Ferris Booth Hall, Columbia University, New York, December 13, 1988.

Bartalos, M. K. Notices of Death and Freedom of the Press: Public Communication from the Viewpoint of Contextual Individualism. Symposium: Death, the Media, and the Public—Needs of the Bereaved. Columbia–Presbyterian Medical Center, New York, February 14–16, 1989.

Bartalos, M. K. Human Survival from the Viewpoint of Contextual Individualism: Discussion Paper. *Journal of the Royal Society of Medicine* (London), 83 (1990): 573–75.

Bartalos, M. K. Psychosocial Aspects of Visual Loss from the Viewpoint of Contextual Individualism. National Symposium on Vision Impairment: Psychosocial Well-Being and Positive Approaches to Rehabilitation in Patients with a Limited Life Span. The Lighthouse, 111 East 59th Street, New York, February 8, 1990.

Bartalos, M. K. The Phenomenon of Death and Contextual Individualism. University Seminar on Death, Faculty House, Columbia University, New York, October 14, 1992.

Bartalos, M. K. Tensates, Emsates and a Theory of Drug Abuse. *Symposium Abstracts of the American Institute of Life-Threatening Illness and Loss* (New York), 19, no. 3, Abstract no. 1 (1992).

Bartalos, M. K. Why Not Immortality—A Physician's Perspective on Living and Dying. Society of Fellows in the Humanities, Heyman Center for the Humanities, Symposium, Columbia University, New York, November 9, 1995.

Bartalos, M. K. Zetetics: A Personal Spin on Life and Death. University Seminar on Death, Kellogg Center, Columbia University, New York, October 13, 1999.

Bartalos, M. K. *Zetetics: Zealous Search for Answers.* College Station, Tex.: Virtual Bookworm.com, 2000.

Becker, Ernest. *The Denial of Death.* New York: Simon and Schuster, 1973; reprinted as a Free Press paperback, 1997.

Dumond, Richard G. and Dennis. C. Foss. *The American View of Death: Acceptance or Denial?* Cambridge, MA: Schenkman, 1972.

Kaku, Michio. *Parallel Worlds. A Journey through Creation, Higher Dimensions, and the Future of the Cosmos.* New York: Anchor Books, 2005.

Linksz, Arthur. *Fighting the Third Death.* New York: n.p., 1986 (pages 1–5).

Medawar, Jean. *A Very Decided Preference—Life with Peter Medawar.* New York: W. W. Norton, 1990 (pages 10, 167).

Olson, R. G. *An Introduction to Existentialism.* New York: Dover Publications, 1962.

Selye, Hans. *From Dream to Discovery. On Being a Scientist.* New York: McGraw-Hill, 1964 (pages 53–54).

Shibles, W. *Death, An Interdisciplinary Analysis.* Whitewater, WI: The Language Press, 1974.

Snow, C. P. *The Two Cultures and a Second Look: An Expanded Version of the Two Cultures and the Scientific Revolution.* Cambridge: Cambridge University Press, 1969.

PART III

Societal Aspects of the Acceptance of Dying

CHAPTER 10

Coping with Mortality: A Societal Perspective

Michael K. Bartalos

Audacter et sincere.

—Unattributed

On September 11, 2001, the Twin Towers of the World Trade Center were destroyed by political terrorists motivated by Islamic religious beliefs. The terrorists took control of two commercial airliners and caused them to crash, with their human cargo, into the two New York City skyscrapers. We know from their utterances and from materials left behind that the terrorists overcame their fear of death by believing in a higher authority that would reward them for their act after they died. In a display of extreme selfishness, they went on a mission that to outsiders appeared to be an act of self-destruction but to them was a guarantee of direct entry into Paradise. It was a callous act because for their own perceived benefit they were willing to kill all who were traveling in those airliners and the thousands more who were in the buildings at the time of the attack.

To the present writer, the outstanding features of this almost incomprehensible drama were the intense desire of the terrorists to ensure their existence after dying, their willingness to embrace a man-made theory of an afterlife for which there is not a shred of evidence, and their willingness to kill uncounted others for their own perceived benefit. It is not unreasonable to assume that this action of the terrorists was—paradoxically—motivated by their intense love of earthly existence, an existence that they valued so much that they wanted to ensure its continuity for "eternity," because this is what their religious teachers promised to them in return for their action. Their love of earthly living and their extreme insecurity regarding their postmortem fate could have made them embrace a teaching that, ironically, induced them to cut short their life on earth. One cannot help but feel pity for these young men who were duped into exchanging solid earthly existence for empty promises. They were manipulated into entering into a transaction in which the deal was based not on the merit of the merchandise but on the believed credibility of the salesman. How can something like this happen?

ON THE FEAR OF DYING

We are the product of evolutionary changes. Consequently, our perceptive abilities and our modes of reaction to various stimuli are the outcome of an evolutionary process as well. These perceptions and reasoning abilities tell us that we will die one day. Indeed, we were born as perishable objects and perish we will. As this realization has nothing cheerful about it, understandably we have invoked multiple ways of dealing with the discomfort triggered by it. There are those among us who dream of a greatly expanded or even limitless life span, while some want to believe that mortality is only the lot of others. In the eighteenth century, the followers of the socioreligious reformer Johannes Kelpius in Pennsylvania believed that their leader would live forever (Holloway 1966, 42). Still others today earnestly explore possible modes of survival after our body dies (Toynbee and Koestler 1976).

The realization of our mortality is a perceived threat that triggers a response on our part that cannot be characterized as pleasant. In the terminology of the "adaptive psychology" that I advocate (the reader is referred to chapter 9 in this volume, "Alive and Content," for further details), the realization of our mortality is a powerful stimulus based upon and enhancing our innate tensate of uncertainty.

METHODS OF COPING WITH THE
KNOWLEDGE OF OUR MORTALITY

Our responses to the conscious realization of our own mortality are not uniform. The method we select for our response is determined by social factors, such as the value society places on individual human beings, and by the belief systems into which the individual and those around him/her have been indoctrinated. It appears to me, although others might differ, that the methods invented by humanity to deal with the recognition of human finitude—that is, the ways invented to reduce the tensate generated by the conscious recognition of mortality—can be classified into the categories of *avoidance* of the offending thought (for example, the Stoics, including Marcus Aurelius); *desensitization* to the offending thought through repetition (the existentialists, the *Tibetan Book of the Dead* [Evans-Wentz 1960]); *displacement* of the offending thought through activities that outlast the individual's life span (transcending death by such deeds as erecting buildings, writing books, establishing institutions, and siring/giving birth to children); *transference* of our concerns to a purported "higher authority" (urged by proponents of the Abrahamic faiths, including Ernest Becker, 1973, 1997); and—the most desirable, the most sensible, and also the most difficult to achieve—*acceptance* (the "logical monism" of Spinoza [1677]; the secular or agnostic humanism of Bertrand Russel (1957), and currently Richard Dawkins (2006), Daniel E. Dennett (2006), Sam Harris (2007), Christopher Hitchens (2007), David Sloan Wilson (2002), the present writer, and others).

Although my intention here is not to provide an exhaustive treatment of coping methods and mechanisms, a warning is in order. Classifications such as this do not provide a true description of human experience. This is because humans at any time employ a cluster of coping and defense mechanisms, with the often-changing predominance of one or the other. Nevertheless such a classification can be useful as a heuristic devise and as a tool for consciously striving for or intentionally avoiding certain recognized mechanisms.

Today, in the world of the post–9/11 World Trade Center attack, transference assumes the greatest importance among these coping maneuvers. From the point of view of humanity's future, transference as widely practiced today proves to be the most divisive, the most capricious, the most far-reaching, and potentially the most perilous method of coping. Having said that, I am obliged to elaborate.

Imperfections of the Spoken (and Written) Word

I wish begin with a reminder to the reader that our language and probably all languages represent an amalgam of words and expressions with meanings of variable precision. This realization is important, because language is "not merely a vehicle which carries ideas. It is, itself, a shaper of ideas" (Spender 1980). "Hunger," "wetness," and "windy" are words with a meaning that is relatively clear to us. Contrast these with the words "spirit," "mind," or "infinity." According to famed American philosopher John Dewey (see Rattner 1939), the meaning of a word is in its consequences. The meaning and thus the consequences of the last-mentioned three words are far from uniform. In the interest of clear communications, we should strive to use the words that are most likely to be interpreted identically or nearly identically by most persons to whom they are addressed.

Perhaps because of my special training in the life sciences, it occurred to me that those expressions that refer to experiences detectable through our senses of vision, hearing, taste, smell, touch, and position sense are the least ambiguous. Through these senses and their extension by such devices as microscopes, telescopes, stethoscopes, ultrasound detection devices, remote sensor devices, and the like, we can detect the presence or absence of objects, along with such characteristics as shape, color, and surface qualities; we can detect changes in their location, form, and other qualities; and we can detect sounds and such attributes as pitch, loudness, duration, and rhythm, as well as quantitative and qualitative differences in smell, and so on. Such objects, attributes, and the like are detected in our environment by our sense organs, they are perceived as to exist in a three dimensional space, and they are seen to evolve in time. This is the nature of our perceived reality. These are perceptions that we generally share and thus understand when we hear references to them (Bartalos 2000, 73–75).

References to the fourth or higher dimensions (Kaku 1994, Pickover 1999), to infinity, and to the superego are met with far less uniform understanding, as these are the products of our intellect, and not of our direct and shared sensory experiences.

Applying the above conclusions to humans, we can say that from observation of physical attributes and the changes they undergo, we could also reach conclusions regarding their *state*, that is, whether they are alive or dead. More prolonged observations would provide us with information on changes in the attributes of the individual who is being observed; thus we could gain also a sense of the *direction* of the changes that are taking place—deducing whether the observed individual is—for instance—in the process of dying, living, improving, or deteriorating.

Application to End-of-Life Issues

Let us now apply this newly won insight to end-of-life issues. As has just been said, we can detect the activities of living and dying and the states of being alive and dead. How about the often used words "life" and "death"? We can quickly see that there is nothing in our sensed environment that corresponds to such words. There is nothing that can be seen or felt or heard or tasted or smelled that the words "life" or "death" refer to. These words appear to be inventions of the human mind, perhaps as shorthand notations for the "the processes of living" and the "state of being dead," respectively. They are abstractions. For our purposes, I consider as abstractions words that refer to concepts that we cannot verify by our sensory organs or by such extensions of our sensory organs as telescopes, microscopes, remote sensing devices, infra- and ultrasound recording devices, and the like. They do not correspond to a detectable entity in our environment. Such primary abstractions can and perhaps are bound to undergo changes, whereby they become secondary and even tertiary abstractions in our usage of words. As this happens, during transformation processes, however, they lose *all* connection with reality. Let us take a look at this process.

The words "life" and "death" are abstractions. By this, I mean that they do not denote an object, or subject, or quality, or quantity, or process that is definable by physico-chemical means. That is, abstractions are not part of our sensed world.

When we talk of giving or taking life, we treat these abstractions as objects, and thus we perform an objectification on our abstraction. Such objectification can be followed by further abstraction, such as personification. The expression "life left him" endows our initial speculative abstraction, "life," with characteristics suggestive of independent, animated, existence. Not only does it exist, but it is able to come, stay, and leave. It is now, in our language, a mobile subject with a will of its own.

When we direct our attention to the word "death" we can make parallel observations. This word too is the product of the mind without any corresponding observable entity in our sensed world.

This abstraction, too, has been objectified: we speak of death as a form of penalty. The concept of death becomes personified when it is depicted as a shrouded entity resembling a human skeleton holding a scythe and finally as an animated entity that can take you away.

You might ask what is the problem with such abstractions? There are many problems. As soon as we leave the realm of perceived reality, we are not bound by commonly verifiable experiences, that is, we are not guided by physical experiences that are anchored in reality. When our bond to sensory experiences is severed, our imagination is free to roam. While nobody ever saw an entity called death, once the word came into existence in everyday language it became an object and then a subject. Objects and subjects have characteristics. If the objects and the subjects are imaginary, the characteristics we endow them with must likewise be a product of our imagination. This is an example of how language can become a shaper of ideas, a modifier of our thought process. Boundless elaboration on abstractions seems to be the rule, rather than the exception. How else could it be when reality ceases to be our guide? When we are operating in a realm remote from human experience, any object can be chosen to stand for an imaginary entity. Jerry Piven has pointed out the innumerable associations that different cultures made with death, ranging from beautiful perfumed flowers to dung beetles, to a sphinx that throttles its victims, to seductive femininity (Piven 2004). In medieval Europe the skeleton was the choice to signify the imagined entity named death, perhaps because after dying the corpse become denuded of flesh and/or because, I suspect, it was judged best suited for crowd control purposes by the church.

The Emergence of Anthropoid Gods

In the realm of ideas, as with genetic mutations, the one with the greatest survival value for the group that adopts it will eventually prevail (Layng 2003). During human history, the worship of objects and animals (such as the sun or fire or the jaguar) were superseded by anthropoid characters endowed with superior power, as well as human weaknesses. The gods of the Greek pantheon and the African spirit gods, (Gonzalez-Wippler 1994; Raboteau 1980;

Rigaud 1969), had a greater staying power until they too became supplanted by the most recently invented, human-like, solitary figure, who is aggressively promoted by both Christian and Islamic missionaries and is endowed with many of the characteristics we humans have and some we only desire, namely omnipotence and permanence.

I approach religion from the point of view of naturalism. It appears to me that once the idea of a greater power, a transcendent entity, was conceived, this primary abstraction become objectified as the sun or fire, then became personalized in the various henotheistic and pantheistic conceptions before becoming an imaginary emperor-like character. According to the Old Testament, this god is said to have chosen Abram, known by Muslims as Ibrahim and—since making his covenant with god—as Abraham by the Jews, and sent him out to become the Father to a multitude of nations. Today the three dominant faiths, all monotheistic, Judaism, Christianity, and Islam, claim Abraham as their patriarch. How did it happen that these sister religions become adversarial toward each other? How did this kind of anthropomorphic monotheism arrive at its present crisis point?

On Some Types of Psychological Pollutants

Emile Durkheim (1912) and his followers called attention to the power of society to mold the minds of its members. They considered the gods to be imaginary beings fabricated unconsciously by society as instruments of control. I find myself in sympathy with this view. I can visualize a process whereby once the concept of an unknowable and all-mighty god was invented, it was up to us to invest her/him with views, power, demands, and modes of retaliation for nonadherence to the rules attributed to him. Someone must have realized that the clamoring of uncertainty-stricken people for higher authority and the complete freedom to design an imaginary supreme ruler— under whose approval the earthly rulers could claim to rule—provided a unique opportunity for crowd control. Indeed, we can see god represented as a superior commander, with the rulers—*Dei gratia*—ruling as his earthly representatives. Since the survival of the ruling group—usually an entwined political and clerical system—depended on the survival of the entire population, the group designed policies that promoted the group's interest and the status quo. Since they were operating in the realm of fantasy, any views proposed were fair play. Once the general policy was established, the details were tailored by the desires and credulity of the flock and the charisma and at times the brutality of the proponents of the idea.

As I see it, the individuals whose responsibility it was to nurture the three aforementioned religions, in the absence of reality-based restrictions, used their imagination to modify the doctrines to the needs and circumstances of their respective flocks. There is no doubt that the assurance of the survival of their people, which included the perpetuation of their power, was of overriding importance in the subsequent manipulation of the doctrines. Due to their diverse needs and diverse coping strategies, it is of little wonder that by today the similarities between the three religions are less apparent than are their differences. I say this despite the often-heard argument that all religions were created to relieve suffering, promote goodwill, encourage charity, and so forth. While such acts are indeed included in the written programs of most, if not all, religions, in practice a religion's beneficence cannot cross its own boundaries as long as that religious group considers itself the exclusive bearer of truth. Such a stance automatically causes all people of other religions to be seen as people in need of conversion. Under those conditions, a charitable act toward another group is suspected of ulterior motives, that is, subversion or ingratiation with the eventual aim converting the people being helped to their own belief system. Thus, compassion and love, which some religious teachings loudly proclaim, remain most of the time reserved for individuals of the same religion.

In the past, the three major religions in question all had capable leaders and they were all forward looking: that is, they were geared toward optimizing their group's adaptive ability, to promoting their group's survival as well as its future prosperity. We might say that, by necessity, they all were possessed of an imperialistic outlook.

The Clash of Belief Systems

The interests of the population group and those of its leader require the fighting of wars. As time progressed, the groups got larger, the stakes got bigger, and the wars were fought by increasingly destructive means. In their process of survival and expansion—the latter in the interest of future survival—today, the three sister religions find themselves in conflict. Currently there are many millions of people on our planet who are manipulated into fighting others and sacrificing themselves, ostensibly on behalf of one view or another; in reality, however, they are soldiers in a power struggle conducted for the survival of their group. Through the multiple changes that the official views of Judaism, Christianity, and Islam have undergone during history, we have arrived at a point where the children of Abraham, at times, appear to be set on each other's extermination. All in the name of god and for perceived self-preservation. That is what appears to be demanded. It is ironic that in support of their hostile actions they invoke, as their authority, the very same god whose command Abraham once supposedly followed when he set out to spread that god's glory, and the very same god to whom they all still claim allegiance and offer their prayers.

It is striking and instructive to see how divergent and distant the religions have become in the details of their adaptation to their given environment since the time of Abraham. This recognition struck me with particular force recently, as I was perusing an English version of an Islamic text printed in India and entitled *The Spectacle of Death Including Glimpses of Life beyond the Grave* (Khawaja Muhammad Islam 1994). Regarding the afterlife, in this book there are promises of a pleasant climate (242), boy servants (243), and silver utensils (242), and the promise that "each man shall have two wives"(246) but according to some teachings as many as "seventy-two wives from among the Houris and another seventy-two from among worldly women" (262). It self-assuredly provides such further details as "Each wife shall be wrapped in seventy gowns" and "They will not fall ill: They will not urinate or defecate; nor will they spit; neither will they need to clear their noses" (253). It is promised that you will "eternally remain young and never grow old" (254).

Under the heading "A Fighter in the Way of Allah, a Guardian of the Frontier of an Islamic State and a Martyr," we read about the rewards for those who die in the service of Islam. "God Almighty gives the following six rewards to a martyr: (1) As soon as the first drop of his blood trickles down, he is forgiven and his abode in paradise is shown to him; (2) He is kept safe from the torments of the grave; (3) He will be free from that great anxiety which the people will feel at the time when the trumpet will be blown; (4) A crown of honour will be put on his head. Each gem of the crown will be more valuable than the world and all that it contains; (5) He will have seventy-two celestial brides, having big eyes; (6) His recommendations in favour of seventy relatives will be accepted" (129). Later, as if for reassurance, it is stated that "the Heavenly man would be endowed with such virility that he would be able to cope with seventy-two women" (248). Clearly, dying in the service of Islam is encouraged, even promoted, by the magnitude of the promised rewards.

To me all this appears to be like a film script based on a very simple marketing principle: identify what people greatly desire, then say that they will receive it if they only follow your prescripts. If you do it well, people will believe you, will never ask how can you make such promises or what guarantees you have. They will follow your directive and will even be ready to kill themselves at your command.

Religious doctrines could not have survived had they not offered survival advantages to their adherents at some time. The molders of the doctrines themselves, while supporting the needs of the group, looked out for their own survival as well. As one aspect of that consideration, the teachings of all three large monotheistic religions assign great importance to group loyalty, that is, loyalty to their respective religion. Further, "any ground for believing a particular religion to be true must operate as a ground for believing every other religion to be false" (Hick 1983, 108). Thus, whenever the different religions interfaced, much suffering resulted from their mutual efforts to convert each other's adherents to their worldview, to the "only correct" worldview. Through the wide divergence of the various religious teachings, and because of the demands of each of them for the unconditional acceptance of their teaching by their members, it is unavoidable, if not outright necessary, that in being a good Christian or a good Jew or a good Muslim, one must also subscribe to such undesirable, antisocial, and human progress–denying characteristics as the suspension of critical thinking, blind obedience to authority, belief in the superiority of one's own faith, intolerance of contrasting views, relating to people as "us versus them," and, not infrequently, being prejudicial, hateful, and having a tendency to justify questionable means for "desirable" ends.

This is where I see a problem in recommending transference to a religious body or concept or doctrine as the solution to our death anxiety.

WHY IS TRANSFERENCE TO AN ECCLESIASTICAL AUTHORITY FRAUGHT WITH DANGER?

The effectiveness of the transference of one's anxiety stemming from the conscious realization of one's mortality, that is, the reduction of anxiety caused by the knowledge of the self's finitude, is directly proportional to the person's acceptance of the religious belief system to be embraced. In other words, if you become a dutiful believer of any of the three above-mentioned monotheistic faiths, the demands placed on you will prevent you from fully identifying with humanity as a whole. It appears, in contradiction to superficial belief and religious pronouncements to the contrary, that as you become a better member of your own group, in direct proportion, you become a less valuable member of humanity as a whole. By the transference of your fear of dying to a religious authority, you obtain your peace of mind at the price of giving up part of your humanity. As witness on September 11, 2001, in New York City and continue to witness in Israel, Iraq, and other places, complete acceptance of a religious teaching can turn you into a remote-controlled, self-destructing killing instrument. Dealing this way with our apprehension about dying is clearly not in humanity's or in our individual best interests.

Death, Dying, and Tarnished Self-Image

Are we really engaged in a denial of death? As was pointed out earlier, "death" is nonexistent. Death is a nonentity. It exists only in our imagination. Can we believe in something that does not exist? Are we so irrational as to invent a concept and believe in its existence so earnestly that we begin to fear it? No, we cannot and do not fear "death," since an entity called "death" does not exist.

Then perhaps we are afraid to face our eventual nonexistence? The evidence for the eventual cessation of the functioning of a living organism, of all living organisms, is so overwhelming that its denial would call into question the sanity of the person who denies it. No, we cannot deny the fact of dying and be considered rational or objective.

As explained in chapter 6 of this book, what is commonly understood as "denial" is a psychological reaction. In my view, such a reaction stems from our abhorrence of the prospect of nonexistence, of annihilation, of leaving our exalted status as the most evolved creature in the known universe, and disintegrating and dissolving into molecules and atoms and rejoining this universe in that lowly form. That prospect appears humiliating; it does not mesh well with our perceived self-importance. The prospect is so painful to face that we have invented elaborate schemes to erase it from our conscious thoughts.

PROPOSAL FOR THE REORIENTATION OF OUR ATTITUDE TOWARD OTHER HUMAN BEINGS

We human beings constitute a special, probably unique, sentient creature in our galaxy, perhaps even in our universe. The recognition of our singularity obliges us to do everything within our power to ensure the survival of this precious conglomeration of atoms and molecules called humanity. We have a dictate to act toward each other as helping sisters and brothers and not as enemies bent on each other's extermination.

Character Traits to Be Encouraged

The recognition that we as a species are unique and the further recognition that every single human being is genetically, chemically, and adaptively unique, unlikely to have had in the past or to have in the future an exact copy, dictates that we welcome and cherish our differences and encourage the development of our individual talents to the fullest extent for the benefit of humanity at large. Thus, the furtherance of healthy bodies and minds and the nurturance of constructive talents should be the hallmarks of our public policy.

Further, our attitude should reflect a willingness to participate in the creation of a just social system, characterized by tolerance of individual differences, benevolence, beneficence, and nonmaleficence, consideration of the effect of our contemplated action not only on us but also on the larger community, a belief in social justice, a belief in just rewards for work, a belief in mutual aid, a belief in equality before the law, and freedom from economic, political, monetary, physical, or emotional exploitation by individuals and by legal, commercial, religious, administrative, political, and other entities.

HUMANKIND AS TRANSCENDENT ENTITY

I cannot do better than others. I too feel the need to look for a transcendent entity. For that role, I propose humanity itself. Humanity is real, it is tangible, it is our past, it is our present, it is our future. We don't need to go to heaven for it and we don't need to invent it. It exists. It is on earth. It is here. It is ourselves and its future depends on us. I propose that we consider the welfare, current and future, of humanity as our raison d'être. We came into existence because there was a human community that enabled our birth and nurtured us, and there will continue to be a human community to perform similar deeds if we perform our civic duties in a responsible manner. We are a link in the chain that stretches back millions of years in the past, and it is our duty to ensure that this chain is not interrupted. We do not need to know whether there is a purpose to the evolutionary process that gave rise to us. The fact that we were born into humanity and benefited from its collective nurturing is enough to obligate us to help other human beings to thrive and to develop their talents for the benefit of all. To be born into and to labor on behalf of a group of sentient human beings who are peerless in the universe, who—if they conduct their affairs wisely—can help humankind to ascend to now unimaginable intellectual and spiritual heights, is, in my opinion, as noble an effort as there can be for a human being.

PROPOSED PRINCIPLES OF ETHICS

If we accept the welfare and future survival of humanity as our ultimate goal and responsibility, then our principles of ethics become easy to define. A good ethics for humanity is an ethics that promotes humanity's survival. Let me quote now from my book *Zetetics* (2000, 157):

> The resolution of ethical issues requires the acceptance of a *First Principle of Morals* to which all parties could make an appeal in cases of disagreements. As our most important task is the assurance of the survival of our species, our overriding ethical principle must reflect that goal. Accordingly, I propose, as the First Principle of Morals, that an action be considered right if it promotes adaptation by our species. I propose further, that the nature of good is an act which promotes the adaptation, and thus survival, of our species. Finally, I propose, that the ultimate source of morality should be the knowledge we posses about the requirements for our species to survive. Conversely, an act is to be considered wrong if it hinders adaptation by our species; and the nature of evil is an act which impedes the adaptation of our species as a whole.

CONCLUSIONS

Different belief systems, most based on unfounded speculations, were adopted by groups of people as instruments of survival. These systems invariably included a scheme for the avoidance of facing individual finitude. However, the uncritical acceptance of some ecclesiastical system's teachings could mean today, as it did in the past, that you trade your death anxiety for martyrdom, that you exchange your death anxiety for being molded into a living guided missile, to be put in service for the advancement of a political goal.

For reasons outlined in another chapter nine of this book, I prefer perceived reality to fantasy. I believe in the power of reasoned thought. I believe in reflection, in self-censure, and in self-correction. I favor an active and constructive way of living. I urge daring in our daily endeavors, magnanimity and understanding toward others, and courage in facing the finitude of our earthly existence. I urge all of us to strive for the acceptance of our impermanence through unceremonious acknowledgment of our mortality. Now you might care to query me on my view on the coping mode of *avoidance*. I do not reject avoidance out of hand. I can well imagine that there are individuals for whom this might serve as a viable alternative. As in medicine, if it works without serious side effects, it might legitimately be the choice of medication for some. And for *transference?* I liken transference to a medication that has a "narrow therapeutic range," being helpful in doses that fall within narrow, defined limits but becoming rapidly toxic with increasing doses. Such medications require great caution in their use.

I find *displacement* comparatively nontoxic. I recommend that humanity as a whole should serve as the subject of transcendence for us. I recommend that we identify with humanity as a whole: with our ancestors, with our contemporaries, and with our anticipated descendants. I recommend that we look at our fate as a derivative of their fate. I recommend that we look at humanity as the only possible vehicle for the survival and fruition of the aspirations that motivated us and gave meaning to our efforts and existence. Humanity and ourselves are one and the same.

As for the new millennium, we need to stop the exploitation of humanity's inherent uncertainty for political purposes; we need to stop the dehumanizing practice of manipulating others. We need to unveil the merchants of death as they promise eternal life to the unsuspecting in exchange for self-sacrifice; we need to spot and de-fang those words in the language that cause one to sidestep reasoning and facilitate the process of being molded into an easily manipulated puppet.

Why is it so easy for us to accept the murder of others yet so difficult to face our own mortality? True humanness is inconceivable without honest attempts at objective self-appraisal and without sincere attempts at understanding and accommodating others.

It is high time to accept our finitude, it is high time to accept the human-ness of others, and it is high time to put an end to human exploitation and killings. Indeed, it is high time for humaneness to become the earmark of humanity.

REFERENCES

Bartalos, M. K. Zetetics—Zealous Search for Answers. College Station, Tex.: Virtual Bookworm.com, 2000.

Becker, Ernest. *The Denial of Death.* New York: Free Press, 1973 and 1997 (pages 159–60, 204).

Dawkins, Richard. *The God Delusion.* Boston: Houghton-Mifflin, 2006.

Dennett, Daniel C. *Breaking the Spell: Religion as a Natural Phenomenon.* New York. Penguin Books, 2006.

Durkheim, Emile. *The Elementary Forms of the Religious Life.* London: George Allen & Unwin, 1912.

Evans-Wentz, W. Y. *The Tibetan Book of the Dead.* New York: Oxford University Press, 1960.

Gonzalez-Wippler, Migene. *Santeria: The Religion. Faith, Rites, Magic.* St. Paul, Minn.: Llewellyn Publications, 1994.

Harris, Sam. *The End of Faith. Religion, Terror and the Future of Reason.* New York: W. W. Norton, 2005.

Hick, John H. *Philosophy of Religion.* Third edition. Englewood Cliffs, N.J.: Prentice-Hall, 1983.

Hitchens, Christopher. *God Is Not Great: How Religion Poisons Everything.* New York, Twelve, 2007.

Holloway, Mark. *Heavens on Earth. Utopian Communities in America 1680–1880.* Second edition. New York: Dover Publications, 1966.

Kaku, Michio. *Hyperspace. A Scientific Odyssey through Parallel Universes, Time Warps, and the Tenth Dimension.* New York: Anchor Books, 1994.

Khawaja Muhammad Islam. *The Spectacle of Death Including Glimpses of Life beyond the Grave.* Revised edition. New Delhi, India: Alfa Publisher and Distributors, 1994.

Layng, A. Supernatural Power and Cultural Evolution. In P. Kurtz (ed.), *Science and Religion—Are They Compatible?* (pp. 291–297). Amherst, N.Y.: Prometheus Books, 2003.

Liechty, Daniel, Personal communication, 2004.

Marcus Aurelius. *The Meditations.* Written almost 2000 years ago. Several English-language editions are available.

Pickover, Clifford A. *Surfing Through Hyperspace. Understanding Higher Universes in Six Easy Lessons.* New York: Oxford University Press, 1999.

Piven, J. S. Personal communication, 2004.

Raboteau, A. L. *Slave Religion. The "Invisible Institution" in the Antebellum South.* Oxford: Oxford University Press, 1980.

Rattner, Joseph (ed.). *Intelligence in the Modern World—John Dewey's Philosophy.* New York: Random House, 1939. See "The Development of Meanings," 857ff.

Rigaud, M. *Secrets of Woodoo.* San Francisco: City Lights Books, 1969.

Russel, Bertrand. *Why I Am Not a Christian and Other Essays on Religion and Related Subjects.* New York. Touchstone Book, Simon and Schuster, 1957.

Spender, D. *Man-Made Language.* Boston: Routledge & Kegan Paul, 1980.

Spinoza, Baruch. *Ethics, Demonstrated in the Manner of Geometry.* Originally published 1677. Several English-language editions are available.

Toynbee, Arnold, and Arthur Koestler (eds.). *Life after Death.* New York: McGraw-Hill, 1976.

Wilson, David Sloan. *Darwin's Cathedral: Evolution, Religion, and the Nature of Society.* Chicago: University of Chicago Press, 2002.

CHAPTER 11

QUEST FOR PERMANENCE: SCIENTIFIC VISIONS OF SURVIVING THE EVENTUAL DEMISE OF OUR UNIVERSE

Michael K. Bartalos

Recognition of a boundary seems to beget the desire to transcend it. Did not humans want to swim, to fly, and to live forever? Forever? Yes, forever. But where? The world is not going to last forever. It does not matter, humanity wants to live forever. If not here, somewhere else. Somewhere else? Where? In heaven. What is that? Let's imagine that there is a place where humans can live forever, and let's call that place heaven. The ancient dialogue must have gone like that. Farfetched, but many believed in it. People felt better for believing in eternal life, if not on earth, then somewhere else, no matter how implausible such a dream was.

Now we are doing better. Some cosmologists came up with startling new ideas. In fact it is good that they did, because their self-defined professional interest is "the study of the origin and evolution of the entire cosmos" (Greene 2005, 14), and their working assumption is that the universe had a beginning and will have an end. Pretty gloomy. It means that not only are individual human beings mortal, but humanity and its achievements too are destined for eventual oblivion. Concern or perhaps sorrow over the ultimate demise of humanity led some cosmologists to speculate about possible ways of saving humanity, or at least its intelligence and knowledge base. And along the way they came up with some intriguing propositions. To me, such propositions appear as ideas competing with the age-old dreams of heaven and eternal life. And while the new ideas are somewhat more complicated than the old ones, they have a ring of greater plausibility to them, simply because they are compatible with known laws of physics.

Cosmologists are not talking about events anticipated in the near future and are not discussing the fate of individual human beings. Their discussions are based on the optimistic assumption that humanity survives its growing pains of mismanagement of the earth's resources, gross maldistribution of its wealth, degradation of its environment, overpopulation, epidemics, and the resulting political, ideological and sectarian strife. Cosmologists are looking far into the future. They are concerned about our 14-billion-year-old universe, which is expanding, and cooling slowly. They are anticipating the "big freeze," "when the universe is plunged into darkness and cold, and all intelligent life dies out" (Kaku 2005, xvi). They are asking, can an advanced civilization save itself in the face of such an event? (Kaku 2005, 306).

Can we put the brakes on unfolding celestial events? Can we stop the universe from expanding or the suns from depleting their nuclear fuel? Of course not. The known laws of physics would not allow us. How about running away? Is there a place to go? Are there other universes beside ours? To this last question, many physicists would give a cautious nod. The existence of multiple universes has been entertained by serious physicists, and the subject of information transfer between parallel universes has received attention. Such considerations, of course, must anticipate future technological developments while remaining cognizant of the known laws of physics.

Since this chapter is intended for a general readership, various technical terms and concepts will require an explanation in order to make the scientists' arguments and propositions intelligible. Let us start, therefore, with the basics.

OUR VIRTUAL REALITY

The *observable* universe—the universe as we know it—is constituted of matter and energy. The word "observable" deserves special emphasis here. Our power of observation is limited by the construction of our sense organs. Our impressions are limited to what we perceive through our optical (visual), auditory (hearing), olfactory (smell), gustatory (taste), tactile (touch), propriore-ceptive (position), and pain-sensing systems. All the rest is conjuring. With our eyes we can sense electromagnetic radiations of between about 400 to 750 nanometers (we refer to this width of electromagnetic radiation as light); with our ears we perceive sound waves propagated through the air or other media if their frequency lies between 20 and 20,000 vibrations per second.

Please note that electromagnetic radiations below 400 and above 750 nanometers are outside our sense of perception, as are sound waves with frequencies below 20 and above 20,000 vibrations per second. Thus, only part of reality is directly accessible to us through our sense organs. We can only wonder what our perception of the world would be if we could smell with the acuity of a dog, see in the ultraviolet and infrared range, or perceive sounds

in the infrasound range (as elephants do) or in ultrasound range (as por-
poises and bats do). Or just try to imagine the world of the pigeon: it senses
the world in terms of air pressure changes, infrasonic sounds, polarized light
patterns, ultraviolet light, subtle vibrations, naturally fluctuating magnetic
fields, and perhaps other yet-to-be-discovered cues (Walcott 1989).

It is useful to keep in mind that we, human beings, recognize our environment on the basis of a rather incomplete virtual reality rendering from the
data supplied by our sense organs and interpret them on the basis of inborn
and acquired theories (i.e., programs), and yet—almost miraculously—we
have survived by formulating response patterns on the basis of such very partial information (Deutsch 1997, 120–21). While humans' scientific exploits
led to the creation of various instruments that have allowed us to explore our
world far beyond the resolution of our sense organs, we still remain ignorant
of many aspects of our universe.

THE WORLD WE PERCEIVE

It is important for us to understand how we perceive reality and how
we evaluate, interpret what we perceive. It is likewise desirable for us to be
aware of what it is that we *fail* to perceive from our environment.

Currently, a single theory for perceived reality is emerging from the integration of four fields of endeavor: quantum physics, the (Darwin-Dawkins)
theory of evolution, the Popperian (after Karl Popper) epistemology, and the
Turing (after Alan Turing) theory of universal computation (Deutsch 1997,
28). Through the unified application of the insight derived from studies conducted within these areas, we have the opportunity to explain such emergent phenomena—that is, high-level simplicity emerging from low-level
complexity—"as life, thought or computation" (Deutsch 1997, 20, 30). (For
reasons elaborated in chapter ten of this volume I would prefer a more cum-
bersome but more accurate—and perhaps more productive—terms: having
the ability to be alive, to think, and to compute; or to be engaged in the processes of living, thinking, and computing; or having the attributes of being
alive, being discerning, and being computational.)

Matter

All phenomena perceived by us as objective are composed of matter and
energy. This visible matter (plants, animals, other humans, mountains, plan-
ets, stars, and galaxies), however, constitutes only about 4–5 percent of the
total amount of matter and energy calculated to be present in our universe!
What is the remaining 95 percent of the universe made of? What are its
functions? What is it doing to us? We will later attempt to provide an admit-
tedly meager answer to this.

Most of what we know about our universe is restricted to ordinary matter and energy, that is, to that portion of the universe that we perceive through our senses and interpret through our conscious thoughts. We know that the matter we perceive is made up of submicroscopic particles that we have decided to call molecules. Molecules, in turn, are composed of atoms, and atoms can be subdivided further into subcomponents ("subatomic particles") named electrons, protons, and neutrons. Of these, the protons and neutrons can be still further subdivided into particles named quarks. As mentioned, this knowledge applies only to one-twentieth of the known universe. We are embarrassingly ignorant of the remaining 95 percent of what is around us.

Diverse observations and calculations suggest to us that a large part of our universe is made up a substance we call "dark matter." It is totally invisible to us but has weight and makes up about 23–25 percent of the universe. The remaining 70 percent of the universe is believed to be made up of a rather mysterious form of energy, the nature of which is almost totally unknown, and which is dubbed—rather appropriately—"dark energy."

Living Matter

It is noteworthy that the visible matter—a small (constituting only about 4–5 percent of the universe) but for us very important constituent of the universe is made up largely of the light elements of hydrogen and helium. It is also noteworthy that animals and humans—these are understandably of prime importance to us—are composed principally of heavy elements. These elements, which are so abundant in our bodies, comprise only 0.03 percent of the total matter/energy content of the universe (Kaku 2005, 347). Because of our rarity in the cosmos, we are tempted to conclude that living matter must indeed be an extremely rare and thus precious component of our universe.

Self-Reflecting Matter

Living matter, while vanishingly minuscule in mass in comparison to other constituents of our universe, exhibits an astonishing range of variations. We are aware of approximately 1.4 million animal species inhabiting the earth (Wilson 1992). Humanity, the self-reflecting living matter, is one of the 1.4 million animal species found on planet earth. Among all the species comprising the realm of living organisms, only individual human beings—scientifically designated as *Homo sapiens*—have the distinction of being material units with the ability to feel, self-reflect, communicate, and consciously anticipate. The impact of humans on planet earth and on the rest of our co-inhabitants has been overwhelming. Our disproportionate biomass and even more disproportionate impact on other inhabitants of earth through our technology have given us unparalleled importance and unparalleled re-sponsibilities. Our self-view is ripe for a reappraisal. Our uniqueness, the realization of our impact on others, and our hitherto anomalous behavior demand honest self-examination.

Energy

The great forces of nature, as deduced from observations within our "vis-ible matter" universe, are as follows: (a) *gravity* (responsible for anchoring us and everything around us to the surface of the earth); (b) *electromagnetic force* (responsible for magnetic attraction, electricity, light, microwaves, ultra-sound, radar, lasers, electronic computers, etc.): "it helped us to tame nature," as Kaku stated (1994, 100); (c) the *weak nuclear force* (responsible for radioac-tive decay, and thereby contributing to the heat that drives volcanoes); and (d) the *strong nuclear force* (providing the energy that fuels the stars, such as our sun, and is also unleashed in a hydrogen bomb) (Kaku 1994, 14).

It is generally believed that under certain conditions energy and matter are interchangeable, as proposed by Einstein in his relativity theory (Greene 2005, 354; Kaku, 2005, 33).

THE UNIVERSE WE PERCEIVE

We are part of a universe that had a beginning and will have an end. The most recent calculations suggest that our universe is about 14 billion years old (Greene 2005, 226).

This universe is composed of galaxies surrounded by blackness. Galax-ies are large aggregates of gas, dust, and billions of stars. Their constituent parts are held together by gravitational attraction, and rotational movement prevents them from collapsing on themselves. The typical spiral galaxy is shaped like a giant flat disk.

The space between celestial bodies, which appears black to us, is not empty. It is filled with faint microwave radiation that is believed to be a remnant of the big bang (Kaku 2005, 8–9). A further constituent of interstellar space is the likewise nonluminous "dark matter" (Greene 2005, 294–86). The amount of dark matter is estimated to be about five times greater than the mass of our visible universe. It is invisible, has an uneven, clumpy structure, and exerts a gravitational pull. It is believed to represent a "scaffold" for the celestial bodies. "It is the infrastructure of the cosmos, literally holding the universe together" (Massey, Christensen, and Frankel 2007).

A still further proposed constituent of our universe is the "Higgs ocean," a relic of the big bang. We are immersed in an "ocean of Higgs particles" that interact with quarks and electrons. It is said that we have to overcome the resistance produced by the Higgs ocean every time we exert force to change the velocity of an object. According to Greene, "We believe that, today, the Higgs ocean fills all of space, so there is no way to remove particles from its influence" (2005, 262). Up till now, the existence of the Higgs particles have been only inferred but never physically demonstrated. Thus we really know precious little about them.

By far the largest portion of our universe is made up by a form of energy that appears to be the driving force in the entire universe: this we have named "dark energy." As stated previously, this "dark energy" constitutes up to a whopping 70–73 per cent of the universe (Greene 2005, 432; Kaku 2005, 11–12). Despite its overweening presence, we have very limited knowledge about this mysterious force too.

Our planet earth is located in a galaxy to which we have given the name Milky Way. The Milky Way galaxy is about 150,000 light years in diameter and 10,000 light years thick, and it contains about 100 billion stars.

When astronomers tell us that there are more than 100 billion galaxies similar to ours in our universe (Greene 2005, 168), we sense that this is a very, very large number, indeed, "astronomical" in every sense of the word. But even after writing the number down with all the requisite zeroes, while the immensity of the number becomes clearer, comprehension of its true magnitude still escapes us.

Within this immense universe we know of only one place, only one location where a peculiar group of creatures are found, made of some rare heavy elements (mainly carbon atoms) and very unusual in some other ways, perhaps even unique—they possess intelligence: that is, they are able to reflect on themselves and on their environment. In the English language they are called "humans." The home of these creatures is the third planet (called earth) of a minor star (called the sun) in the minor spiral arm of a minor galaxy (called the Milky Way) that is found in a minor group of galaxies near the Virgo supercluster (Kaku 1994, 333).

A rather inconspicuous address in the universe.

The Laws of Our Universe

The laws discovered by humanity that describe the nature and functioning of our universe and everything within it fall into three large groups. The name of Isaac Newton (1642–1727) is connected most prominently with the scientific descriptions of what is sometimes termed classical reality or classical physics. With the help of a few equations, Newton was able to describe what was known about motion on earth and about the motion of heavenly bodies. The theory of general relativity, formulated by Albert Einstein (1879–1955) around 1916, described rules that apply to the macro world, to stars, galaxies, quasars, black holes, the big bang, and the cosmos. The third group of physical laws, termed quantum mechanics and based on an equation discovered in 1926 by Erwin Schrodinger (1887–1961), applies to the micro world, that is to the molecules, atoms, and subatomic particles, where instead of certainty, probability prevails.

It is noteworthy that there is a conflict between general relativity and quantum physics. According to some, this discrepancy might be due in part to our ignorance about what happened at the beginning of the formation of our universe (Greene 2005, 338). Also, as was pointed out by Kaku (2005, 186), the two theories are based on different mathematics, different assumptions, different physical principles, and different domains. It is important to remember, however, that these laws are valid when applied to their respective subject areas. It is only that they cannot be combined into an all-embracing super law by our conventional mathematical methods, which is rather frustrating to our theoretical physicist friends.

In recent years, however, a single theory—a theory of everything, or grand unification theory—began to emerge with the promise of unifying these three disparate groups of laws. This is called *superstring theory*, or *string field theory*.

Quest for a Theory of Everything: Superstring Theory

The unification of the laws of classical physics, general relativity, and quantum mechanics appeared to be made possible by introducing calculations in dimensions higher than the three spatial dimensions in which we are accustomed to act and think. While we are unable to visualize those higher spatial dimensions, their existence cannot be outright denied. Scientific interest in these higher spatial divisions, referred to collectively as hyperspace (Kaku 1994), has been ignited by the discovery that calculations performed in the ninth and tenth spatial or space-time dimensions appeared to eliminate the contradictions between our three main theories. This was the first time that a theory in physics said "anything at all about the number of spatial dimensions in the universe" (Greene 2005, 367).

According to superstring theory, the fundamental ingredients in our universe are elongated, string-like, subatomic structures; these structures are in a state of vibration and "the different vibrational patterns in string theory correspond to different kinds of [subatomic] particles" (Greene 2005, 346). Professor Michio Kaku is quoted as having described it in this way: "a string is concentrated energy from which everything else is made. A string is so tiny that it can't be seen with any of our instruments. But if we could see it, it would look like a tiny rubber band. If you twang it at a certain frequency, it becomes a subatomic particle called a quark. Twang it at another frequency and it becomes an electron, and so on. By twanging enough strings … you get all the subatomic particles in the universe" (Kaku 2006, 29).

It has been conjectured that the Higgs ocean—a mysterious constituent of the universe—is made up of strings and that the drag force they exert may be approached as an interaction between the strings of the Higgs ocean and the strings that make up other matter, and therefore it might be calculable (Greene 2005, 374).

Membranes (Branes, M Theory, Matrix Theory)

Subsequent study of superstring theory and its implications resulted in the discovery that beside one-dimensional strings, basic reality also includes two-dimensional structures, named *membranes*. Because of their two-dimensional character, these membranes are also called *twobranes* or—for brevity's sake—*branes*. It is believed that the one-dimensional strings are attached to such two-dimensional membranes.

A reformulated version of the string theory was proposed by Tom Banks, Willy Fischler, Leonard Susskind, and Stephen Shenker and became known as the M theory. Still another version of the string theory that incorporated aspects of the M theory carries the name of *matrix theory*. The matrix theory led to the concept of *zero-branes* as fundamental ingredients that can be combined to generate strings and higher-dimensional membranes. According to Greene, this discovery "might mean that everything—strings, branes, and perhaps even space and time themselves—is composed of appropriate aggregates of zero-branes" (Greene 2005, 489).

Higher Spatial Dimensions

Today many scientists, including Brian Greene and Michio Kaku, seriously entertain the possibility of the existence of higher space-time dimensions (Kaku 1994). In Greene's latest book (2005, 391–94), we find a discussion of the possibility that our life in our four-dimensional space-time is nothing but a three-brane existence through time. That is, our three spatial dimensions correspond to three branes that circumscribe and limit our experiences. Further, the possibility was left open that this three-brane existence might be embedded in a still higher spatial dimension.

THE MULTIVERSE CONCEPT

The most recent findings, especially what we have learned from the distribution of microwave radiation in the universe, are compatible with the assumption that our universe was experiencing an expansion from the moment of its beginning in the primordial explosion that is referred to as the big bang. The existence of universes other than ours is seriously considered. One mechanism that could conceivably produce multiple universes harks back to the big bang. It is argued that when our universe was produced in the mayhem of the gargantuan explosion, the explosion likely produced several other universes, each with distinct properties. Thus according to this proposition, the big bang gave rise, largely simultaneously, to many very dissimilar universes. This proposition is referred to as the [Alan] Guth theory.

Another proposition envisions not parallel but rather sequential production of universes. According to this theory, new universes can arise from an existing universe. This is assumed to occur as new universes "sprout" from older ones. This theory is associated with Andrei Linde's name (see Greene 2005, 321; Kaku 2005, 14).

Stages in the Existence of a Universe

Universes, not unlike human beings, go through stages of existence. Fred Adams and Greg Laughlin (1999), based on available scientific information, proposed the following five "developmental stages" for a universe (see Kaku 2005, 292–99):

1. Primordial Era—rapid expansion, cooling, breaking up of the "superforce" into the four forces of today, fusion of primordial hydrogen into helium creating the combustible mixture that is the current stellar fuel. (Our sun is a hydrogen burning star with a lifespan of several billion years.)
2. Stelliferous Era—this is the stage we live in today. Conditions are right for creation of DNA and life. Intelligent life faces a number of hurdles—not a few of its own making—such as nuclear weapons, man-made infectious agents, environmental pollution, and global warming. Others are daunting natural disasters, such as recurrent ice ages and meteor, comet, and asteroid impacts. According to the laws of physics, in an accelerating and thus cooling universe such as ours—eventually all intelligent life is doomed to perish.
3. Degenerate Era—the process of burning hydrogen and thereafter helium comes to an end. Red dwarf stars will continue to emit energy the longest, but eventually—like other stars—they too will turn cold and black.
4. Black Hole Era—In this stage the only source of energy will be the black hole. Black holes radiate a faint amount of energy that is referred to as "evaporation."
5. Dark Era—all heat sources are exhausted; the temperature approaches absolute zero. This is the end of the universe. Is the stage set for a new beginning?

Stages in the Existence of Our World

I am keenly aware that the announced goal of this chapter is to review possible routes and means of escape from our universe when its long-projected doom appears imminent. At this point the reader might correctly surmise that in such cases the likely destination would be another universe. However, we are still not ready to enter headlong into a discussion of that subject, as such scenarios must be built on anticipated conditions and anticipated technological developments. Thus, next we need to review what informed thinking has helped us to deduce about the future of our planet.

As was pointed out by Kaku (2005, 306), the feasibility of an eventual escape from our universe has an engineering aspect, namely, whether will we have sufficient resources to build a machine that can perform such a difficult feat; and it has an aspect for the physicists to solve, namely, whether the laws of physics, in the first place, allow the existence of such machines. Some physicists contend that a sufficiently advanced technology would make an escape into another universe possible. What are the prerequisites and what are the conditions for that to happen? The deciding factors appear to be energy and information.

CLASSIFICATION OF CIVILIZATIONS
BASED ON THEIR ENERGY USAGE

The Russian astrophysicist Nikolai S. Kardashev in the 1960s proposed a classification of civilizations depending on the amount of energy used for communication purpose:.

> Type I—a civilization that is able to muster the equivalent of the entire present power output of the planet earth for communications purposes. This is estimated to be around 10^{16} watts. This amount of energy makes it possible to control the weather, change the paths of hurricanes, and accomplish such feats as building cities on the ocean. As noted by Kaku (2005, 307), "Such civilizations are truly masters of their planet and have created a planetary civilization."
>
> Type II—a civilization that has exhausted the power of its planet and learned to harness the entire energy output of its star (in our case the sun). Total energy generated is 10^{26} watts.
>
> Type III—a civilization that has exhausted the power of a single solar system, has colonized large portions of its galaxy, and is able to utilize the energy from 10 billion stars. Total energy generated is 10^{36} watts.
>
> Type IV—we are told by Kaku (2005, 317) that the laws of physics allow us to speculate that an advanced civilization, which has exhausted the power of the stars, can develop methods to tap into by far the largest energy source in the universe, the dark energy. In this case the total energy generated would be around 10^{46} watts.

Please note that in this scale each civilization differs from the next lower type by a factor of 10 billion (watts).

On this scale, in terms of energy production for communication purposes, our present civilization is 0.7, that is, still about a thousand times smaller than a type I, but not impossibly far from that goal. The transition from a type 0 to a type I civilization is considered to be the most perilous, "because we still demonstrate the savagery that typified our rise from the forest... [and] the forces of entropy (the greenhouse effect, pollution, nuclear war, fundamentalism, disease) may yet tear us apart" (Kaku 2005, 310).

CLASSIFICATION OF CIVILIZATIONS BASED ON THEIR INFORMATION CONTENT (AFTER CARL SAGAN)

The American astronomer Carl Sagan (2000, 234–38) suggested a finer gradation of civilizations according to the amount of information a civilization stores. He proposed the use of letters to describe a civilization's information storage. "There are twenty-six letters in the English alphabet. If each corresponds to a factor of ten in the number of bits, there is the possibility of characterizing with the English alphabet a range of information content over a factor of 10^{26}—a very large range, which seems adequate for our purposes" (237). In this system, each letter "corresponds to a factor of ten in the number of bits." The type A civilization with an information content of 10^6 bits would correspond to a primitive civilization with a spoken but no written language. In contrast, our society's current information content is estimated to be about 10^{14} bits. If we define civilization B as one with an information content of 10^{15} bits, civilization C as one with an information content of 10^{16}, and so on, then our civilization, characterized by Sagan as having 10^{14} bits of information, would be a type I civilization. Thus by considering both our energy output—as discussed above—and our information content, using these joint criteria, our civilization can be designated as a type 0.7I (in Sagan 2000, 238,—the designation 0.7H appears to be a misprint).

TASKS TO ACCOMPLISH BEFORE A SUCCESSFUL ESCAPE ATTEMPT

We cannot leave this world and expect to survive in another universe unless we undergo major changes in our physical and mental structure and capabilities. Yet that alone is not enough. There are also technical prerequisites for such an undertaking.

Let us first consider the changes that us humans will need to undergo. Until now, in living organisms, adaptive changes have been produced by evolutionary processes. In the undertaking we are considering, evolution cannot be relied upon. First, evolution by natural selection occurs in response to changes that have taken place in the environment. Adaptation and evolution—the latter in effect constituting a collective adaptive response, a response that takes place at the population level—are moves in reaction to the changing environment. In contrast, in our present example we need to act in advance of expected changes, not to react to them. Thus we need to be proactive in our moves.

A further consideration is that evolution as we know it involves the recombination of genes by sexual reproduction. It is doubtful that our descendents millions of years from now would still be using such an unpredictable, inconvenient, wasteful, and difficult to control mechanism as sexual reproduction to propagate their kind. The magnitude of the changes that are called for and their conformance to exact specifications also argue for mechanisms that allow detailed planning, careful monitoring, and precise execution with the least possible energy usage. In the distant future, direct manipulation of the human organism appears to be the only practical way of shaping human beings to handle the challenges that the traversing of the barrier separating universes would present.

It is possible to engage in an informed guessing game as to the path or paths that might lead us to decide to shed our DNA-based genetic code. This will be when we find it to our advantage to encode our genetic information in a different—perhaps more compact or more stable—form, to embed it in a novel medium, and to entrust it to a carrier that no longer bears any resemblance to today's humans.

Cyborg Technology

One noteworthy recent development is the physical coupling of computers with human beings, with the purpose of extending human capabilities. We do not mean here the replacement of lost functions by computer-assisted bodily parts, but rather the amplification of normal human potential by computers. We mean connecting the computer to the nervous system of a human being and thus establishing a direct connection, via the nerves, between the brain of the individual and the computer. Under such conditions the computer is under the direct control of the brain, but due to a two way communication between the brain and the computer, information can be fed to the brain from the computer using the nerve in the arm that, in this case, functions as a connecting wire between the computer and the brain. It turns out that our central nervous system is uniquely qualified for such feats (Clark 2003). In this regard, an epoch-making announcement was made in 2002 by British professor Kevin Warwick, who demonstrated the feasibility of creating a man-computer hybrid by using himself and, to a lesser extent, his wife Irena as experimental subjects (see Warwick 2004). The term cyborg is used to designate such human-computer hybrids.

Tissue Engineering

Another field that is rapidly gaining prominence is called tissue engineering technology, while its medical application is known as regenerative medicine. It is the approaching realization of the science fiction dream of growing new organs from one's own cells to replace damaged body parts. According to the U.S. Health and Human Services publication *2020—A New Vision: A Future for Regenerative Medicine*, produced by an interagency federal working group, the "revolutionary technology" of regenerative medicine "offers the opportunity to create a tremendous new global industry." The publication estimated that the projected U.S. market for regenerative medicine stands at $100 billion in worth and the current world market stands at $350 billion. According to this publication, approximately $4 billion has already been spent by the U.S. private sector on regenerative medicine and the establishment of a federal initiative for regenerative medicine is proposed.

I hold it likely that by the combined use of cyborg and tissue engineering technology, the redesigning of living organisms, including humans, will become reality well within this century.

Artificial Adaptive Reactions by Means of Robotics

One can foresee the use of robotics technology in recreating and, perhaps, improving upon the adaptive response patterns seen in the animal world.

Let us recapitulate schematically what is happening when we detect a change in our environment. The change is detected by one or more of our sensory organs.

From these organs, information is channeled through appropriate nerves to the brain, informing it about the nature of the detected environmental change. Its size, color, and movement, if any, are perceived and reported by the eye; its smell or lack of it by the olfactory apparatus; if it is accompanied by any noise, the auditory organ within the ear will report it, and so forth. The brain integrates these messages into a coherent unit, appraises the emergent picture to assess whether immediate action is needed, and if yes, decides what the nature of the action should be. The choice is between approach or retreat. If approach is chosen, is the confrontation going to be hostile (i.e., an attack) or friendly (i.e., an embrace or handshake), how intense should it be, and how long should it last. Such information, along with the emotional content of the encounter (e.g., was it pleasing, was it unpleasant, was it threatening, etc.), is saved in a memory bank and will be ready for subsequent retrieval. Such retrieval might be called for when a similar environmental challenge is encountered or when, during planning, foresight suggests a potential encounter with the same threat.

Every new encounter is believed to produce this chain of events. Subsequent encounters with the same or similar object or subject, however, will trigger a modified response. This is so because every time the encounter is experienced, its memory trace will undergo modification. Thus, the detection of changes in our environment consists of and leads to the activation of the sense organs(s) and the transmittal of sensed impression(s) to the brain. In the brain, the integration and appraisal of the finding, the formulation and execution of a response, and connotative (that is, ordered according to certain features) storage of the experience will take place. In addition, the brain can render the stored information, along with pertinent newer information (appended retrieval), for review when needed.

If I were a robotic expert and wished to imitate a fairly differentiated organism, I would plan to install the following basic output or reaction patterns I would install an on/off switch—the on switch puts the machine in a "reactive" or "tensimatic" mode (see my discussion on tensates in chapter nine of this volume). In the on mode, the reaction parameters would be approach/retreat. In the case of approach, there would be two parameters, hostile/amicable (to and fro). Both of these alternatives would have parameters for speed (ranging from very rapid to very slow), intensity (from hard to very gentle), and duration (from brief to prolonged).

Robots that mimic well the adaptive reaction seen in the animal world can find many uses. Not the least of their virtues are their sturdiness, the relative ease with which damaged parts can be replaced, and the almost limitless forms and sizes in which they can or might be constructed.

It is taken for granted that eventually, perhaps billions of years from now, as the universe is cooling, our fragile bodies will not be able to withstand the harshness of the environment, and the functions performed by human brains will require relocation into carriers where greater protection is afforded from the vagaries of the environment than the skull can provide. Robot-like creatures just might prove to be the right candidates for such a purpose.

And one day our descendants might wake up to the realization that human brains are not the ultimate evaluators of environmental changes, are not the ultimate planners of response strategies. Human beings, at that point, might be replaced in their entirety by sturdier, higher-functioning, robotic organisms who will learn with pitiful sympathy about their humble beginnings as fragile, timid, gullible, erratic, and overly emotional Homo "sapiens."

Technical Feats to Be Accomplished before Leaving the Universe

Kaku in his book *Parallel Worlds* enumerates some of the technical feats that humanity would likely need to accomplish before a visit/escape to another universe can take place. Kaku's list contains the following items (2005, 321–42):

Step 1: Create and test a theory of everything. Such a theory is needed to perform quantum calculations on celestial phenomena that have been formulated in terms of general relativity. This needed process is also referred to as "quantum corrections to Einstein's equations" (321);

Step 2: Find naturally occurring wormholes (passageways between two universes) and white holes (the end of black holes from which objects are ejected);

Step 3: Send probes through a black hole to determine the amount of radiation present inside the black hole and to determine its stability;

Step 4: Construct a black hole in slow motion in order to learn to manipulate the properties of a black hole;

Step 5: If black holes prove to be too unstable or their radiation too intense, the alternative might be the creation of a baby universe. In theory this might become possible by concentrating a few ounces of matter into enormous densities and energies;

Step 6: Create huge atom smashers as sources of very high energy; and/or create implosion mechanisms as sources of very high energy; and/or create negative energy from squeezed states for use in opening and stabilizing wormholes;

Step 7: Build an Alcubierre warp drive machine. This is a mechanism proposed by the physicist Miguel Alcubierre for space travel. This warp drive machine would transport you to different time zones by shrinking the space in front of you and expanding it behind you;

Step 8: Wait for spontaneous quantum transitions (although this might be impractical and too unpredictable).

THE DEMISE OF OUR UNIVERSE

Over the billennia, as the temperature drops in the universe, human adaptation will be called for. Once adjustment to the outside environment is no longer practical or feasible, intelligent beings might be forced to assume a robotic existence (Kaku 2005, 300). Thus, one by one, our physical functions are likely to be replaced by robotic body parts. Artificial extremities, mechanical hearts, and kidney dialysis machines are already part of our medical armament, while the restoration by mechanical means of lost hearing and sight are at an experimental stage. We have to pause, however, when it comes to the brain. Our central nervous system, more precisely the brain, is a command center, a coordinator of activities, a memory storage site, the creator of a composite virtual reality, and a self-aware plotter of strategies by taking into account past experiences and foreseen consequences. In addition, it generates diverse mood states and reflects on its own experiences, thoughts, and emotions. Thus it reflects an awareness of the self and of others. The question arises: Can these functions be replicated by a man-made device?

The Turing principle says, as cited by David Deutsch (1997, 140), that it is possible to build a universal virtual-reality generator. The implication is that—in theory at least—much of what the brain does may be imitated eventually by a computer.

PROPOSED ESCAPE ROUTES FROM OUR DOOMED UNIVERSE

Let us assume that billions of years from now it will be possible to encode all information from the brain onto a compact storage device, make it resistant to physical damage, and use it to reprogram other robotic/humanoid entities. Likewise, let us assume that all the knowledge that has been accumulated during humanity's existence, including the knowledge from which one can recreate a civilization, can be recorded and saved by quantum computing methods on a small storage device. Theoretically such a "cosmic egg" could be transported through a wormhole or a black hole into another universe and, once there, cause the recreation of our civilization from the transported information (Kaku 2005, 341–42).

EPILOGUE

Thus the scientific promise is that the end of our universe does not have to mean the annihilation of human intelligence and all it has produced. But in order to survive to the times when our universe has depleted its energy sources, we need to learn to live in harmony on this earth or on some other planet in our universe, maintain a supportive environment, and continue our scientific and technological explorations. In this way, billions of years from now—when cold and darkness is about to envelop our universe—our descendants might be able to transfer their intellectual heritage into another universe and live there—hopefully—happily ever after (or until that universe, too, approaches its doom).

Is the process outlined above assured of coming about? No, not by any means.
Is it compatible with the known laws of physics? Yes.
Is it based on technological developments foreseen to take place in the future? Yes.

I am struck by the parallel between the scientific promise presented above and the Biblical pronouncements on faith, ethical living, apparent death, resurrection, and (for the elect) the promise of eternal life in heaven. However,

I find the scientific projection far more credible than the biblical one. The fact that astronomers/physicists/cosmologists are able to visualize an indefinite survival of human knowledge past a universe's demise should serve as an antidote to a nihilism that regards all human efforts as ultimately useless.

REFERENCES

Adams, Fred, and Greg Laughlin. *The Five Ages of the Universe—Inside the Physics of Eternity.* New York: Free Press, 1999.

Clark, Andy. *Natural-Born Cyborgs—Minds, Technologies, and the Future of Human Intelligence.* Oxford: Oxford University Press, 2003.

Deutsch, David. *The Fabric of Reality—The Science of Parallel Universes, and Its Implications.* Penguin Books, London, 1997.

Greene, Brian. *The Fabric of the Cosmos—Space, Time, and the Texture of Reality.* New York: Vintage Books, 2005.

Kaku, Michio. *Hyperspace—A Scientific Odyssey through Parallel Universes, Time Warps, and the 10th Dimension.* New York: Anchor Books, 1994.

Kaku, Michio. *Parallel Worlds—A Journey through Creation, Higher Dimensions, and the Future of the Cosmos.* New York: Anchor Books, 2005.

Kaku, Michio. "In Tune with 'Strings.'" *TIAA-CREF Magazine,* Winter (March) 2006, 29–30.

Massey, Richard J., Lars L. Christensen, and Felice Frankel. "Dark Matter Comes to Light." *American Scientist,* May–June 2007, 257–59.

Sagan, Carl. *Carl Sagan's Cosmic Connection—An Extraterrestrial Perspective.* Updated edition. New York: Cambridge University Press, 2000.

U.S. Department of Health and Human Services. *2020—A New Vision: A Future for Regenerative Medicine.* Report prepared by the Interagency Federal Working Group on Regenerative Medicine, Chair: Howard Zucker. Year of publication not given, but was 2006 or 2007. Retrieved from www.hhs.gov/reference/newfuture.shtml.

Walcott, C. "Show Me the Way to Go Home." *Natural History,* November 1989, 40–46.

Warwick, Kevin. *I, Cyborg.* Urbana: University of Illinois Press, 2004.

Wilson, Edward O. *The Diversity of Life.* New York: W. W. Norton, 1992.

SERIES AFTERWORD

The interface between psychology, religion, and spirituality has been of great interest to scholars for a century. In the last three decades, a broad popular appetite has developed for books that make practical sense out of the complicated research on these three subjects. Freud had a negative outlook on the relationship between psychology, religion, and spirituality, and thought the interaction between them was destructive. Jung, on the other hand, was quite sure these three aspects of the human spirit were constructively linked and one could not be separated from the others. Anton Boisen and Seward Hiltner derived much insight from both Freud and Jung, as well as from Adler and Reik, and fashioned a useful framework for understanding the interface between psychology, religion, spirituality, and human social development.[1] We are in their debt.

This series of general interest books, so wisely urged by Praeger Publishers, and particularly by its acquisitions editors, Debbie Carvalko and Suzanne Staszak-Silva, aims to define the terms and explore the interface between psychology, religion, and spirituality at the operational level of daily human experience. Each volume in the series identifies, analyzes, describes, and evaluates issues of both popular and professional interest that deal with the psycho-spiritual factors at play (1) in the way religion takes shape and is expressed, (2) in the way spirituality functions within human persons and shapes both religious formation and religious expression, and (3) in the ways in which spirituality is shaped and expressed by religion and in secular modes.

The books in this series are written for the general reader, the local library, and the undergraduate university student. They are also of significant

interest to informed professional persons, particularly in fields related to religion, spirituality, and social psychology. They have great value for clinical
settings and ethical values as well. These matters of the interface between
psychology, religion, spirituality, and secular cultural values are of the highest
urgency in human affairs today, when religious motivation seems to be playing an increasing role, constructively and destructively, in the areas of social
ethics, national politics, and world affairs.

The primary interest in this present volume, edited by Michael Bartalos,
is in how human beings are handling the issue of death and dying today.
Denial of death in Western culture has been the focus of much scholarly
concern for the last three-quarters of a century. The authors of this volume
give evidence, in their individual contributions and in the unity of thought
their chapters form together, that they have the objectivity to affirm in ring-
ing terms the heroic strength, insight, honesty, and courage to see through
the counterproductive stereotypes in our models of death and dying. They
have set forth analytically and with vigor what needs to be done and how to
do it. Facing death constructively is one of the most crucial achievements in
quality living. Their fine book is an enormous help to our culture and society,
at the individual and global level. Living well requires a thoughtful psychological and philosophical model that comfortably incorporates death as an
inherent component of a full life.

J. Harold Ellens
Series Editor, Psychology, Religion, and Spirituality

NOTE

1. L. Aden and J. H. Ellens, *Turning Points in Pastoral Care: The Legacy of Anton
Boisen and Seward Hiltner* (Grand Rapids, Mich.: Baker, 1990). Anton Boisen was at
the University of Chicago for decades and developed models for understanding the
relationship between psychology and religion as well as between mental illnesses,
particularly psychoses, and the forms of meaningful spiritual or religious experience. Seward Hiltner was one of a large number of students of Boisen who carried
his work forward by developing theological and psychotherapeutic structures and
modes that gave operational application to Boisen's ideas. Hiltner was on the faculty
of Princeton Theological Seminary, occupying the chair of pastoral theology and
pastoral psychology for most of his illustrious career. While Boisen wrote relatively
little, Hiltner published profusely and his works became notable contributions to
church and society.

INDEX

AARP. *See* American Association of
  Retired Persons
ABC television, 178
ABMS. *See* American Board of Medical
  Specialties
Abraham, 271, 274–76
Abram, 274
"Abstractions" as defined by Bartalos:
  primary (objectification of a concept),
  272, 274; secondary (animation
  of false object), 272; tertiary
  (anthropomorphisms of false
  animated object), 272
Acceptance of dying: advantages of,
  194–95; consolation in, 195–96;
  disadvantages of, 195
Accreditation Council for Graduate
  Medical Education (ACGME), 18
ACGME. *See* Accreditation Council for
  Graduate Medical Education
Acquired Immune Deficiency Syndrome
  (AIDS), 10–11, 228
ACT. *See* Advanced Cell Technology
Adaptation, 193–94, 209, 241, 244,
  246–47, 249, 259–60, 262, 264, 275,
  279, 293, 297
Adaptive psychology (of Bartalos), 239,
  241, 259, 270

Adaptive response, 189, 191, 193, 240,
  249, 294–95
Adolescents, 68, 81
Advanced Cell Technology (ACT), 105
Afterlife, 78–79, 81–83, 85–98
Age, 105–6, 109–11, 114, 119–22,
  124–25, 127, 132, 137, 143, 156,
  186–87, 189, 191, 197, 243, 245, 255,
  262, 291
Age retardation, 109, 136
Aging: prevention of, 105;
  unproductive, 122
AIDS. *See* Acquired Immune Deficiency
  Syndrome
Ailment, 104; as redefined by
  Bartalos, 244
Alali, A. Odasuo, 172
Alexander, D., 48
Allen, Woody, 102
Alternative medicine, 107
Alzheimer's disease, 127
America Online (AOL), 97
American Academy of Anti-Aging
  Medicine, 109
American Academy of Hospice and
  Palliative Medicine (AAHPM), 18
American Association of Retired Persons
  (AARP), 30, 33

About the Editor and Contributors

EDITOR

Michael K. Bartalos, M.D., is a practicing physician. He has been chair or co-chair of the University Seminar on Death at Columbia University in New York for the past 15 years. His works include *Medical Cytogenetics* (with T. A. Baramki, 1967), *Genetics in Medical Practice* (ed., 1968), and *Zetetics* (2000).

CONTRIBUTORS

Robert Belknap, Ph.D., is professor emeritus of Russian and director of the University Seminars at Columbia University in New York. He writes about literary theory, higher education, Dostoevsky's works, and other Russian and European prose.

Thomas A. Caffrey, Ph.D., a clinical psychologist, has been practicing in New York City for 34 years. He specializes in evaluating and conducting psychotherapy with federal offenders, in conducting evaluations for family court, and in working with suicidal individuals. One of his research projects reduced suicidal and assaultive behavior in prison by 50 percent.

Kevin T. Keith, M.A., has a background in philosophy, with a concentration in bioethics, and is finishing a Ph.D. in that subject. He has taught bio-ethics at the medical-school and undergraduate levels and served on clinical ethics and research-safety Institutional Review Board (IRB) committees.

He specializes in patient autonomy and the theoretical grounding of health care ethics.

Jerry S. Piven, Ph.D., teaches philosophy at Case Western Reserve University. His publications include *The Psychology of Death in Fantasy and History* (ed., 2004), *Terrorism, Jihad, and Sacred Vengeance* (ed., 2004), *Death and Delusion* (2004), *The Madness and Perversion of Yukio Mishima* (2004), and *Nihon No Kyoki* (*Japanese Madness*, 2007).

Sherry R. Schachter, Ph.D., is director, Bereavement Services, Calvary Hospital, Bronx, N.Y., and has worked with dying patients for over 27 years. She is a recipient of the Lane Adams Award for Excellence in Cancer Nursing from the American Cancer Society and past president of the Association for Death Education and Counseling (ADEC).

Alan F. Segal, Ph.D., is professor of religion and Ingeborg Rennert Professor of Jewish Studies at Barnard College, Columbia University, in New York City. He is the author of *Two Powers in Heaven: Rabbinic Reports about Christianity and Gnosticism, Teaching "Arabs and Jews," Rebecca's Children: Judaism and Christianity in the Roman World, Paul the Convert: The Apostolate and Apostasy of Saul of Tarsus, Life After Death: A History of the Afterlife in Western Religion,* and *A Concise History of World Religions.*

Christina Staudt, Ph.D., an independent art historian (her Columbia University Ph.D. dissertation is titled "Picturing the Dead and Dying in Nineteenth-Century 'L'Illustration'"), co-chair of the Columbia University Seminar on Death, president of the Westchester End-of-Life Coalition, and a hospice volunteer. She has worked on death-related matters for over 20 years and frequently addresses both professional and lay audiences.

About the Series Editor and Advisers

EDITOR

J. Harold Ellens is a research scholar at the University of Michigan, Department of Near Eastern Studies. He is a retired Presbyterian theologian and ordained minister, a retired U.S. Army colonel, and a retired professor of philosophy, theology, and psychology. He has authored, coauthored, or edited 165 books and 167 professional journal articles. He served 15 years as executive director of the Christian Association for Psychological Studies and as founding editor and editor-in-chief of the *Journal of Psychology and Christianity*. He holds a PhD from Wayne State University in the Psychology of Human Communication, a PhD from the University of Michigan in Biblical and Near Eastern Studies, and master's degrees from Calvin Theological Seminary, Princeton Theological Seminary, and the University of Michigan. He was born in Michigan, grew up in a Dutch-German immigrant community, and determined at age seven to enter the Christian Ministry as a means to help his people with the great amount of suffering he perceived all around him. His life's work has focused on the interface of psychology and religion.

ADVISERS

LeRoy H. Aden is professor emeritus of Pastoral Theology at the Lutheran Theological Seminary in Philadelphia, Pennsylvania. He taught full-time at the seminary from 1967 to 1994 and part-time from 1994 to 2001. He served as visiting lecturer at Princeton Theological Seminary, Princeton, New Jersey, on a regular basis. In 2002, he coauthored *Preaching God's Compassion: Comforting Those Who Suffer* with Robert G. Hughes. Previously, he edited four books in a Psychology and Christianity series with J. Harold Ellens and David G. Benner. He served on the board of directors of the Christian Association for Psychological Studies for six years.

Alfred John Eppens was born and raised in Michigan. He attended Western Michigan University, studying history under Ernst A. Breisach, and received a BA (summa cum laude) and an MA. He continued his studies at the University of Michigan, where he was awarded a JD in 1981. He is an adjunct professor at Oakland University and at Oakland Community College, as well as an active church musician and director. He is a director and officer of the Michigan Center for Early Christian Studies, as well as a founding member of the New American Lyceum.

Edmund S. Meltzer was born in Brooklyn, New York. He attended the University of Chicago, where he received his BA in Near Eastern Languages and Civilizations. He pursued graduate studies at the University of Toronto, earning his MA and PhD in Near Eastern Studies. He worked in Egypt as a member of the Akhenaten Temple Project/East Karnak Excavation and as a Fellow of the American Research Center. Returning to the United States, he taught at the University of North Carolina–Chapel Hill and at The Claremont Graduate School (now University), where he served as associate chair of the Department of Religion. Meltzer taught at Northeast Normal University in Changchun from 1990 to 1996. He has been teaching German and Spanish in the Wisconsin public school system and English as a Second Language in summer programs of the University of Wisconsin. He has lectured extensively, published numerous articles and reviews in scholarly journals, and has contributed to and edited a number of books.

Jack Miles is the author of the 1996 Pulitzer Prize winner, *God: A Biography*. After publishing *Christ: A Crisis in the Life of God* in 2001, Miles was named a MacArthur Fellow in 2002. Now Senior Advisor to the President at J. Paul Getty Trust, he earned a PhD in Near Eastern languages from Harvard University in 1971 and has been a regents lecturer at the University of California, director of the Humanities Center at Claremont Graduate University, and visiting professor of humanities at the California Institute of Technology. He has authored articles that have appeared in numerous national publications, including the *Atlantic Monthly*, the *New York Times*, the *Boston Globe*, the *Washington Post*, and the *Los Angeles Times*, where he served for 10 years as literary editor and as a member of the newspaper's editorial board.

Wayne G. Rollins is professor emeritus of Biblical Studies at Assumption College, Worcester, Massachusetts, and adjunct professor of Scripture at Hartford Seminary, Hartford, Connecticut. His writings include *The Gospels: Portraits of Christ* (1964), *Jung and the Bible* (1983), and *Soul and Psyche: The Bible in Psychological Perspective* (1999). He received his PhD in New Testament Studies from Yale University and is the founder and chairman (1990–2000) of the Society of Biblical Literature Section on Psychology and Biblical Studies.

Grant R. Shafer was educated at Wayne State University, Harvard University, and the University of Michigan, where he received his doctorate in Early Christianity. A summary of his dissertation, "St. Stephen and the Samaritans," was published in the proceedings of the 1996 meeting of the Société d'Etudes Samaritaines. He has taught at Washtenaw Community College, Siena Heights University, and Eastern Michigan University. He is presently a visiting scholar at the University of Michigan.